# THE DREAM BOOK

*Writing American Women*
Carol A. Kolmerten, *Series Editor*

# T · H · E
# DREAM
# B · O · O · K

## An Anthology of Writings by Italian American Women

Revised Edition

*Edited with an Introduction by*
## HELEN BAROLINI

SYRACUSE UNIVERSITY PRESS

First Syracuse University Press Edition 2000

08   09   10   11   12   13        7   6   5   4   3   2

Originally published in 1985 by Schocken Books

The paper used in this publication meets the minimum requirements of American National Standard for Information Sciences—Permanence of Paper for Printed Library Materials, ANSI Z39.48-1984.∞™

**Library of Congress Cataloging-in-Publication Data**

The dream book : an anthology of writings by Italian American women / edited with an introduction by Helen Barolini.—revised ed.
p. cm.—(Writing American women)
Includes bibliographical references and index.
ISBN 0-8156-0662-1 (pbk. : alk. paper)
    1. American literature—Italian American authors.  2. Italian American women—Literary collections.  3. Italian Americans—Literary collections.  4. American literature—Women authors.  5. American literature—
20th century.  I. Barolini, Helen, 1925– II. Series.

PS508.I73 D7 2000
810.8'09287'08951—dc21        00-056298

*Manufactured in the United States of America*

*This book is dedicated to*
*Teodolinda, Susanna, and Nicoletta,*
*my daughters*

# Contents

FICTION

DRAMA

POETRY

# Preface to the Revised Edition

Paths are made by walking. Books are made by questioning.

My questions—long dormant—surfaced in the early 1980s when I was invited to address a conference for Italian American women. I was asked to speak about the women of their background who were, and are, writers.

Who are they? I wondered then. To be able to call up the few names I knew was not sufficient to wipe out the prevailing notion that there are no Italian American women writers as there are, so notably, Black women writers, Jewish, Asiatic, Hispanic. In histories, sociological tracts, bibliographies, and learned conferences the names mentioned as Italian American writers were exclusively those of male authors; it was a totality of male presence that effectively undercut the importance and witness of women in the Italian American experience. And as I wondered about the unnamed women, there echoed in my mind what a reader of my novel *Umbertina,* had written me: "When I first saw your book I was drawn to your name, a novel by a woman with an Italian surname is rare."

I knew she was right, but why? Who were the others? Why had I never heard of their work? Why was it that though we Italian American women existed as writers, we were not perceived? Before I had many answers, I addressed the conference with a talk called "Breaking the Silence," more a statement of hope than of fact. But I had started on a path. The rest came to fruition with the searching that led to *The Dream Book: an Anthology of Writings by Italian American Women.*

When the Before Columbus Foundation gave my collection an American Book Award in 1986 it was cited as a ground-breaking work for my Introduction had placed Italian American women authors for the first time in a historical-social context and presented their work in various literary genres as a cohesive voice.

*The Dream Book* was intended not as an act of separatism, of setting a specific ethnic group apart from the main body of American literature. That it spoke to women of all backgrounds was made clear by Alice Walker's generous endorsement of the work and Amy Ling's statement in *Feminisms: An Anthology of Literary Theory and Criticism* of how *The Dream Book* helped her understand her own predicament as an Asian American woman writer. Nor did I intend to set Italian American women writers apart from their male counterparts, but rather as an act of inclusion and completion, to restore to the body of the national literature the names of women authors who had been overlooked even as men were being documented as the only examples of Italian American writing.

For when the record is not recognized, it is in effect denied. This was the case for Italian American women writers.

The question had always been, why were Italian American women silent? It might well have been, instead, why were they not heard?

Does the Italian American woman writer exist? Yes she exists, and her experience is registered in an honorable literary record; if her voice remained silent to the larger culture, it is because no established critic or reviewer amplified it. If the writers seemed women of the shadows, it was because the spotlight of attention never reached them.

Women, particularly, were long overlooked not only by the established majority, but also by feminist critics engaged in the recovery of women writers, and certainly by an inimical publishing world. That does not, however, excise Italian American women writers from existence, precarious as that existence may be. They are the true "lost women writers," still to be recovered as their Black sisters so notably have been.

Although in the course of preparing *The Dream Book* I met many Italian American women writers—in person, in correspondance, in their work— others remained unknown to me, deceased, or "lost" or still unpublished. Exceptionally (an exception that proves the rule), it was in Andrew Rolle's *The Immigrant Upraised* that notice was given of Antonia Pola, an author who was silenced before she was formed. Her work, as far as is known, remains one book only, the 1957 novel *Who Can Buy the Stars?*, so tentative, unpolished, and yet so forceful in a woman's voice crying out for notice long before the women's movement opened a way. There are women writers even more lost than Pola, for she left a book while others remained unpublished, unknown.

I wanted to "name the names" as much as I was able and to put on record a part of our national literature that had been overlooked or thought unworthy of attention. The collection, which dramatist Karen Malpede wrote me "feels like coming home," never claimed to be exhaustive. It was a start.

I got a great deal of personal enrichment from my contact with many of the contributors. They enlarged my thinking, moved me by their stories, and broke, by their presence, the confinement of isolation and oddness in which we singly struggled. They brought the warmth and sharing of personal revelation to my work, the joy of their enthusiasm, and the answer to the question, Where are the women?

Several writers were very generous in bringing to my attention others of whom I was unaware. Novelist Dorothy Bryant told me of Alma Rattini Vanek, a then seventy-eight-year-old former student of Bryant's creative writing course. I went to see Alma on the heights of Berkeley where she and her husband lived with orange trees in the front yard and rear window views out to the Bay. Alma's Italianness was re-awakened by my search, and it came in an outpouring of memories which she shared with me.

She told of being born in a mining camp at Telluride, Colorado, where her parents had immigrated from the Trentino-Alto Adige region of Italy, on the border with Austria, at the beginning of this century. She then put into my hands an old, yellowed, oil-cloth covered manual she called the dream book. I opened the ragged-edge, loose-paged book. On a front page, in awkward, uphill handwriting was the notation in Italian of one Angela Zecchini who, with many misspellings and an incorrect date for the inception of World War I, recorded this terse account of her life: "I was born in 1884 in the commune of Folgaria, district of Rovereto. Departed the old places the day of May 7th. Arrived in Telluride June 12th and on July 20th [sic], in Europe, there erupted a powerful war of the European powers. Written October 7, 1914."

That handwriting was the first I had ever seen of an immigrant Italian woman; and the book itself was the first piece of immigrant "literature" I had ever encountered. It was, Alma told me, a book the Italian women of Telluride used constantly, the Baedecker of their dreams. Through it any dream could be interpreted by consulting meanings in the alphabetized subject entries; looking up dreams gave them explication for the strangeness around them and a clue to their *destino*.

I tried it, too, for that very morning my daughter Linda had told me her dream of my holding a baby in my arms. I myself had dreamt of stacks and stacks of white paper. In the Italian language dream book I looked under *"bambino"* and *"carta"*. The reading was of an auspicious beginning for a creative venture. I took it for the sign of the anthology I was beginning, and from that original dream book came the title and meaning for mine.

The old tattered and much fingered Italian dream book had been the companion of those displaced women in Colorado, giving them hope or warning, speaking to them of their hidden longings and fears. It had been their counsel and guide, as, in another immigrant society, the Bible was for the English pilgrims.

Alma related how those isolated women in Colorado shared any popular Italian novel that might find its way to them. Her mother, and the others, craved those stories that embodied their other lives in the language of their birth. A *romanzo* would circulate among all of them until it fell apart from sheer reading and re-reading, satisfying in part their need to transcend their lives. But having a novel to read was the rare occasion.

For everyday, they had their dream book. Their men, the rough miners, might ridicule and scorn them, but the women knew the power of dreams. They charted their ways through the unknown with the help of divinations from the little book. It had to serve until the day came when their daughters and granddaughters would be mistresses of the new language, able to lay out lives and signs in their own words in order to make sense of them, and understand the past.

The neglected literary record of Italian American women's experience *as narrated by themselves* is a great lacuna in the national literature. To present a people from only one viewpoint—the male—is to falsify their total creativity.

Thus, being Italian American, being female, and being a writer was being thrice an outsider, and why this was so is partly in the history and social background of the immigrant women who came to this country, partly in the literary mold of the country itself. The loneliness of seeming marginal is something well understood by an Italian American woman with literary aspirations who seems to stand alone, unconnected to any body of literature or group of writers—an anomaly, a freak occurrence, a frequent non-repeater, ephemeral.

After probing why Italian American women writers were isolated and few, a more difficult question was, if grouped, do they form a cohesive identity and have a specific resonance to their writing? I believe it to be so. The superabundant tradition from which we derive has given us a powerful identity, has bequeathed specific strengths and weaknesses, and has presented common problems as well as passions. The writing reveals the commonality. For no matter how oblique the themes or broad the views, overtones of who we are and how we feel, as formed by our values and history, show up in the work.

A common base for Italian American women writers was the prior realization, as readers, that it was all but impossible to find writing in which to recognize the transcultural and transgenerational complexities of who we are, where we've come from, and what the journey has been.

Sandra M. Gilbert (née Mortola), who is well known under her non-identifying married name as a literary theorist, feminist critic, and editor, but perhaps less known as a poet of passionate Italian American identity, stated the problem in a letter to me very precisely: "I am always struck by how few people have written about what it meant to be *us!*"

At the same time that there is a longing to validate one's identity, there are qualms about being too narrowly defined. Barbara Grizzuti Harrison remarked in a panel discussion that she did not think of herself as an Italian American woman writer, but as an author who is all of that and more. That's agreed. It is not the qualifiers that are important, it is the writing. But it would be disingenuous to deny the influence of the ethnic factor, and the outsider position it has put us in. It was the aim of *The Dream Book* not only to create a record of literary achievement, but also to help Italian American women find strength in solidarity, and a means to greater visibility and voice. From the outpouring of commendatory reviews, readers' letters of self-discovery, teachers' use of the book in courses, and continual citations in scholarly works, that goal seems to have been attained.

Still, in the end, each writer must transcend ethnic-gender qualifiers through the work itself. There is a great range among the Italian American women writers—of age, education, geographical provenance, occupation, as well as in their work and experience as writers and in their literary reputation. Some have a remote Italian connection, others were born in Italy. The degree of generational distance from Italy, or even the part of Italy one's people came from can influence a writer. There are perceptible differences in style—from the older, wry, humorously cast family stories of Marie Chay or Rose Grieco to the more hidden allusions in the younger generation of writers like Agnes Rossi or Mary Caponegro. From the vivid realism of novelists Julia Savarese or Marion Benasutti to the intense, linguistic control or esoteric surrealism of poets Ree Dragonette and Leslie Scalapino, great distances and changes are denoted. It indicates angles and complexity denied to the popular image of the Italian American woman.

The grandparent is a rich mine of the Italian American imagination— mythical, real, imagined, idealized, venerated, or feared. The grandparent embodies the tribe, the whole heritage, for that, in overwhelmingly the most cases, is as far as a present-day Italian American can trace his or her descent. Often, uncannily often, what the women write of, where they start, is with a grandmother—those old women, sometimes illiterate or very little schooled, who had only their dreams, premonitions, and feelings to read for guidance. Going back beyond the Americanized generation of their parents, the writers feel an intense connection with older generations and revere their icono-

clasm, peculiarity, unconventionality, and strength. Some of this wild oddness of the elders (before homogenization into standard American), was recalled by Beverly Donofrio in her piece "My Grandma Irene" which
appeared in *The Village Voice*, August 18, 1987.

After the immigrant grandparent, or, at most, great grandparent, there are
only faceless hordes stretching back into the past—unknown, unvisualized,
unnamed. Most Italian Americans embody the paradox of coming from very
ancient roots of an ancient civilization but knowing their past only as far back
as a grandparent. Most often there are no written records beyond the grandparent to tell us more of our ancestry; there are no Victorian photo albums in
velvet covers. In our grandparents is incorporated all of the past, all of tradition and custom, and, we imagine, some archetypal wisdom and native intelligence. We start from the people who came here.

Rosemarie Caruso's vision of her grandmother walking down to her from
the moon came in a dream—a benevolent vision where the harsh reality
never enters—and which inspired Caruso's interesting exploration of tradition between mothers and daughters in a play called *Shadows of the Morning
Moon*.

How often the grandmother figure turns up in dreams! From *The Dream
Book,* Sandra Gilbert's poem "The Grandmother Dream" evokes the "Sicilian grandmother, whom I've never met/ . . . . sitting on the edge of my
bed . . ." Diane di Prima's moving re-dedication of herself to the ideals of her
grandfather is given stirring voice in her poem "April Fool Birthday Poem for
Grandpa."

Carole Maso's stunning first novel, *Ghost Dance,* included unforgettable
images of two Italian grandparents, one turned to the old ways of the past, the
other looking toward the future. Tina DeRosa explored strong ties with
grandparents in her novel *Paper Fish*. My own novel *Umbertina* developed
from the imagined strong grandmother who inspires her descendants.

The veneration, the awe, the wish for the strength of the ancestor is an enduring topos, ineluctable and omnipresent, a reference for almost every Italian American writer even when not specifically a grandparent but some older
relative as in Mary Gordon's essay on her great-aunt, "Zi'Marietta." Mary
Gordon an Italian American? it might be asked. It was Gordon herself, at the
beginning of her writing career, who presented herself as Italian American
when she entered the UNICO national literary contest for young Italian
American writers. To be noted is that while the 1976 winner of the UNICO
contest was a young man who has not been heard of since, the three young
women who got honorable mention were Camille Paglia, Teodolinda
Barolini, and Mary Gordon, all of whom went on to publish notable work.

In "Zi Marietta" Gordon recalls the old woman's silverbacked brush and
comb and her admonition: "Brush your hair five hundred strokes a day and

put olive oil on your hair after you wash it. American girls kill their hair. Your hair is alive; it is your glory as a woman." Left to her at her great-aunt's death, Gordon writes, "Now I have begun to use them, not often, but at those times when I most need to feel like a beautiful woman who has come from a line of beautiful women. When I most need that weight, Zi'Marietta's heavy silver comb and brush are there for me. . . . The silver comb and brush lie on the top of my dresser, heavy, archaic, ornate as history, singular as heritage." And, it may be added, symbolic of Italian stylishness and the aesthetic and sensual sense of self that is part of Gordon's heritage. To all Italian American writers, it seems, the archetypal presence of an ancestor ("ornate as history, singular as heritage") is present.

In their writing Italian American women expose the signs and symbols, the auguries and directions of lives which were—and are—subject to great ambivalence, to dual pulls from opposing cultural influences, to dual vision. They assign meanings through their poetry, novels, stories, essays, and plays. In the written word, now finally *their* written word, can interpretation and direction for lives and futures be found. Their writings interpret the experiences of a collective past and bring into view what had been inexplicable, painful, dubious, conflicting. By writing their stories and reading each other, Italian American women have come to know themselves.

Almost two decades have passed since *The Dream Book: An Anthology of Writings by Italian American Women* broke new ground in American literary studies by presenting a group of American writers who, individually, had seldom been represented in the national literature, and as a group not at all. This collection has stood the test of time and I am grateful to Syracuse University Press for this new edition, and again to the National Italian American Foundation for their continued support of a collection that has been affirming to so many readers.

Hastings-on-Hudson, New York                                    Helen Barolini
July 2000

# THE DREAM BOOK

# Introduction

## The Historical and Social Context of Silence

A question to ask rather than why Italian American women were silent so long, is what were the conditions that impeded the act of writing? What were their lives as they were transplanted from one culture to another?

The words of a cultural representative from Italy to New York in the early 1980s seem emblematic of a past engrained attitude towards Italian Americans. A reference to Italian American women writers had been met with words of impatience and even a certain derision: "Who *are* they? "Why aren't they stronger? . . . more important? Who has heard of them or ever seen their books on racks at an airline terminal? How many people would any of them draw to a lecture?"

Significantly, at the same time, in 1980, the Agnelli Foundation issued a monograph, *The Italian Americans*, stating it was time for the mother country "to revivify relations with the descendants of emigrants from our shores . . . that there be a rapprochement between the Italian American world and contemporary public opinion in Italy."

In a time of hype when the prevailing standard is whether or not one has been interviewed on television for fifteen minutes of celebritydom, the Italian representative's statement was a dispiriting display of lack of critical judgment and historical understanding, and of a popularity chart mentality which lingers in the mother culture and asks impatiently of its descendants abroad (the runaways from home), why aren't you better than you are?

The why is in their history.

And it is not negative history, a litany of ineptness or missed opportunities. Quite the contrary: given the adverse factors of extreme deprivation and provenance from areas that provided them with no practical preparation of language, civil or political skills, schooling or even basic literacy, the Southern Italians who made up the bulk of the late nineteenth century or early twentieth century exodus did, in large part, translate their innate strengths and canniness into successful American terms. They did secure an economic foothold in their new environment and started the educational process that has led their children to professions, to politics, to managerial positions.

At the same time they also secured a sense of double alienation. The Italian immigration to the United States was preponderantly by people who were not wanted or valued in their land of origin, then found they were not wanted or valued in their new home country when they aspired to more than their exploitation as raw labor. Some of this discrimination still sticks in the Italian American memory, regardless of social advance. Senator Robert Torricelli has told of a childhood experience when he raised his hand in school after a teacher told his class that he was the only one whose ancestors were not from Europe. "Excuse me," he said, "Italy is in Europe." To which the teacher replied, "Only technically."

That the literary arts lagged behind pragmatic ones in development is not hard to understand. A people without a written language and a literature (for Italian was as foreign to the great mass of dialect-speaking immigrants as was English) had first to acquire not only the words and concepts of their new world but the very *notion* of words as vehicles of something beyond practical usage. In contrast, the ease and style of African American writers attests to the centuries of their exposure to and absorption of English. For Italian Americans, a realistic people for whom hard work and modest economic gains took precedence, that literary writing does not immediately—or even usually!—produce financial rewards meant it had to wait.

Italian Americans cannot be conveniently generalized. They are differentiated by a multitude of variables, including class, political activism, occupation, religion, education, the region of Italy from which their ancestors came and where they settled here, and to which generation in the United States they belong.

But, by and large, the women have a commonality.

They are women who with rare exceptions had never before been authorized either by their external world nor by their internal one to be authors of themselves or of the word. A woman like Bella Visono Dodd (1904–1969), born in south Italy and brought to this country as a child, managed to have an education and become a college professor, later acquiring a law degree. She was known as a labor activist and public speaker on the rise in the Communist party. But glory was transitory and at high personal cost as she relates in her ominously titled but curiously unrevealing autobiography, *School of Darkness* (1954). She defied the old ways for the sake of her successful career and for marriage to Mr. Dodd. She remained childless only to lose her marriage, her closeness to her family of origin and their ways, and then find herself cast out of the party to which she had given so many years of her life. Her story ends with a desperate sense of loneliness and a return to the religious beliefs of her childhood. It is a stark and foreboding morality tale of the over-achieving woman, one that could give little comfort to any mid-century Italian American woman looking for someone to emulate. Her story remains a testament of how even a super-educated Italian American woman was unable to transcend her background to write deeply of relationships and to evoke in vivid personal terms the depths of her internal turmoil.

The very thought of making one's life available to others through publication was alien to earlier Italian American women and even Dodd, quite extraordinary at the time in writing an autobiography, was not forthcoming concerning many areas of her life. She seems to have approached her story more as an act of contrition for past sins than as an illumination of the choices she made.

Italian American women did not come from a tradition that considered it valuable for them to narrate their lives as documents of instruction for future generations. They were not given to introspection and the writing of thoughts in diaries. They came from a male-dominant world where their ancillary role was rigidly, immutably restricted to home and family. They came as helpmates to their men, as mothers of their children, as bearers and tenders of the old culture. The creativity went elsewhere: into managing the homes, growing the gardens, making the bread, elegant needlework. Though they brought native strengths—sharp wits, tenaciousness, family loyalty, patience and courage, which are skills for survival—they did not acquire until generations later the nascent writer's tools of education, confidence of language, the leisure to read, and the privacy for reflection.

When you don't read, you don't write. When your frame of reference is a deep distrust of education because it is an attribute of the very classes who have exploited you and your kind for as long as memory carries, then you do not encourage a reverence for books among your children. You teach them the practical arts not the abstract ones.

Italians attach little value to exact meaning and the literalness of words. *Parole femmine,* they say in Italian: words are feminine, words are for women, frivolous and volatile, a pastime in the marketplace. *Fatti maschi:* deeds are masculine; men engage in action which is concrete, real. This is unlike the Jews, people of the Book, for whom the survival of race identity was closely tied to a constant reading and analysis of the Bible, and unlike Fundamentalist Christians, believers in the Word, who implicitly trust words and honor them as revealed truth.

It is useless for disgruntled self-appointed critics to ask why there are no Norman Mailers or Eudora Weltys among Italian American writers, as if our writing could or *should be* homogenized into a Wasp, or a Jewish, or any other framework. What has been written authentically from the unique experience of being of Italian background in America may yet prove to be more valuable in the long run than writing that conformed to prevailing majority notions.

The long history of the Italian people has made them skeptical. It is as if, numbed by the rhetoric which continually whirls about them, inured to the conventional formulae of empty *complimenti,* they tend to lose all notion of words as conveyers of anything "real." What is real is life in the *piazza,* church ceremonies from birth to death, the family at the table.

Words themselves are meant for fanciful approximations, polite artifice. They are relative and circumstantial, illusory and masking, but not for relying on. Even more distrustful of words, then, are those who cannot read or write them; thus the distancing from that most abstract act with words, the writing of them into imaginative literature. It would take time before the habit of literature was widely rooted among Italian Americans.

The first survey of their literary activities was a bibliography compiled by Olga Peragallo and published in 1949. She listed fifty-nine authors (with an amiable inclusiveness that welcomed Nicola Sacco and Bartolomeo Vanzetti), eleven of whom were women and of those only two whose names are known today: Frances Winwar and Mari Tomasi. In a preface to that work, the late Italian critic, author, and professor emeritus at Columbia University, Giuseppe Prezzolini, lent his keen and acerbic observations. He noted that at the time of Peragallo's compilation, there were, by census count, 4,574,780 Italian Americans in the United States of whom 3,766,820 still declared their mother tongue to be Italian. "This leaves," he wrote, "only 827,960 who spoke English at home; that is a very small minority from which one could expect writers to come forth . . ." He also noted of the fifty-nine writers that "the amount and value of their literary output would certainly be greater if the members of the first generation had come to America endowed with a culture of their own and if they had been able to absorb also the culture of the United States. They found two barriers: the language and the social background. . . . Since these families were driven from Italy by poverty, the ghost of poverty followed them throughout their lives and influenced the education of their children."[1]

Those children, including any hypothetical aspiring authors, were but one or two generations into the use of the English language in any way, let alone as a literary vehicle; they had yet to acquire the skill of becoming book readers. It was their American schooling which provided the beginnings of relating to literature, a literature not of their own world nor of their own experiences, but of Anglo-American models that would, in turn, feed their sense of alienation.

And though, by the early years of this century, some men of Italian American background had begun to write and publish books, for the women it was to be a much longer, harder, and later development. Again, there are exceptions. Two notable women stand out as beacons rendering even deeper the dark void around them.

Sister Blandina Segale (1850–1941), a teaching nun of the Sisters of Charity, whose letters describing her mission to the far west from 1872 until 1893 were published in book form as *At the End of the Santa Fe Trail* (1948), is the earliest known author among Italian American women. She was of Northern Italian stock and arrived in this country in 1854 at a time when Italians were so few and far between that there was no developed prejudice against them as would later be the case. She was educated, bilingual, and her letters show a cultivated person who delighted in arranging a Mozart Mass for Christmas in a mining town, who made knowing allusions to Dante's *Commedia,* and who taught a quartermaster's daughter Italian by reading Alessandro Manzoni's novel *I promessi sposi* with her in the Santa Fe outpost where they were stationed. Sister Blandina became a civic influence in the Western territories, and a social activist who was instrumental in ending lynch law.

She wrote, as she says, in scraps of time, on scraps of paper, throwing the pieces into her desk drawer for a moment of leisure when she could enter them into her journal as a faithful record of the mission life and work of the nuns in Santa Fe under the authority of Bishop Lamy. In Sister Blandina's case, there is a tantalizing non-crossing of paths with another recorder of mission life, the author Willa Cather who was to immortalize Lamy and other French-born Jesuits in her novel *Death Comes for the Archbishop.* Regretfully, Cather omitted not only the work of the Italian Jesuits in the West but certainly the achievements of the female religious in the Western territories.

Willa Cather's oversight is rather symbolic of the displacement and neglect of Italian American women writers. From Sister Blandina on, these writers have been omitted from the record.

Sister Blandina was far more autonomous than other women of her day, and many generations ahead of the later-arriving Southern Italian immigrants among whom she would return to work in Cincinnati for the rest of her long life. Her memoirs leave no doubt of her enterprise, her adaptiveness, her self-reliance, and her deep satisfaction in her work. She is justifiably impatient with those who wonder how she could give up "everything" to be a nun.

Despite Sister Blandina's having all the resourceful and adaptive qualities of the celebrated Anglo-American pioneer women, her story has been omitted from collections celebrating women in the West. Her singular voice is unique in written records of immmigrant Italian women in the form of diaries, memoirs, or letters.

In 1961, a novel by Marie Chay called *Pilgrim's Pride*, pieced together from individual stories based on family lore and first appearing in a number of noteworthy journals including *The Saturday Review*, documented the experience of her Northern Italian immigrant grandparents in the same mining territory that Sister Blandina had worked in. Chay's novel is humorously written; it had to be to be publishable, for a skewed and stereotypical vision of Italian Americans made them acceptable on the margins of the national literature as easy to take, humorous ethnic types rather than as substantial invidiuals fraught with the full range of human problems and emotions. Chay's dedication page carries an interesting disclaimer which indicates that there was more depth and darkness to her characters than was allowed into the book: "Thanks to the imagination and memory, the people are no longer what they once were, and the harsh, sad and tragic events they often went through are now something that even they might laugh about."

Sharing the stereotype of Italians as sunny, easy-going types is Camille Paglia who flaunts as her trademark, "That's Italian!," whenever an explanation for some of her extravagant notions is required. She routinely overstates, as in this passage from her UNICO essay "Reflections on Being Italian in America": "The vivacity of our responses to the realm of the five senses makes it nearly impossible for us to suffer from that alienation which is the modern dilemma; the sense of absurdity and meaninglessness is a northern-European invention. Gothic gloom has never made much of an impact upon the sunniness of the Mediterranean temperament." Already a Ph.D. from Yale and in her fourth year of teaching literature at Bennington when she wrote that, Paglia seems not to have heard of Pirandello who invented the theater of the absurd, nor does she seem to know the despairing and powerful novels of Verga, the sombre poetry of Montale, or to know anything of the unsunniness of actual Italian American life. She has certainly no inkling of Andrew Rolle's psycho-history of Italian Americans, *Troubled Roots* (1980).

Preceding Paglia, Rose Basile Green, in her comprehensive study, *The Italian American Novel* (1974), offered a similar notion of sunniness in the thesis that the basic optimism of Italian American writing will eventually win it success and a place in the American showcase of literature. Yet beneath the cliches of optimism and sunny temperament, there are other, shadowy, complicated layers in the Italian American character manifest in the literature. A way to dismiss a people is to see them in simple terms, as the critics have, and not give recognition to the reality of their yearning, defensiveness, humiliation, and anguish as reflected in their plays, novels, and poetry.

The second notable exception, after Sister Blandina, to the late appearance of Italian American women in writing, is Frances Winwar, born Francesca Vinciguerra in Taormina, Sicily in 1908. She came to this country at a young age and was fortunate in having educated parents and a father who gave a great deal of attention and encouragement to her. Going through American schools with precocious ease in acquiring English, she started writing poetry and her first publications were poems in Max Eastman's *The Masses* when she was only eighteen. As was the case with later writer Mari Tomasi, Winwar had the inestimable good fortune to find a mentor in the then WASP publishing world: Lawrence Stallings, the literary editor of the *New York World*, hired Winwar as a book reviewer. She went on to become a successful, prolific writer, not unaided by the anglicization of her name which, she has related, was a condition to the publication of her first book, *The Ardent Flame* (1927).[2] Astutely, it now seems, she had destroyed her first manuscript, an autobiographical novel, and thereafter was able to turn away from herself in order to concentrate on historical novels or the biographies of literary figures. This distancing from herself and her origins must be taken into account as part of the price paid for getting on in a publishing world not interested in Italian American material, regardless of the quality of writing. In Winwar's case the writing was distinguished enough to win her the esteemed and lucrative first Atlantic Monthly non-fiction award in 1933.

Winwar's non-identification as an Italian American (paralleled these days by the very successful Evan Hunter who also writes as Ed McBain but was born Salvatore Lombino, or by women whose married names camouflage their origin) was reflected in the remarks of a curator of a large collection of books and manuscripts by American women. Asked if any Italian American women were represented, she said, "No, this collection represents *la crème de la crème*. For instance, if Christina Rossetti were American, not English, she'd be here." Then, asked about Frances Winwar, she said, "Oh, yes, of course she's included, but I never thought of her as Italian."

The historical and social context of literary silence and the clues to the missing women writers can also be understood in Italian family mores. It is a story of conflicting cultures, alienation, unschooled parents' fear of the American school which they sensed, rightly, was taking their children from their authority, the growing resentment of American children toward their Italian parents, the resulting split in loyalties and personalities, the passing of the old ways, and the painful rites of passage into the new.

Italian women who came to this country did so as part of a family—as daughter, wife, sister—or "on consignment," chosen, sometimes by picture or sometimes by hearsay from an immigrant's hometown to be his wife. But always in context of a family situation. There was no pattern of the independent Italian woman emigrating alone to better her lot as there is, for instance, of Irish women who, advantaged by having the language, came over in droves to be hired as maid-servants, many then living out their lives unmarried and alone. But an uneducated Italian woman could not exist, economically or socially, outside the family institution which defined her life and gave it its whole meaning. She came bonded to her traditional role. The oral history of Rosa Cassettari, first published in 1970 as *Rosa: The Life of an Italian Immi-*

*grant,* is that of a young girl given by her guardian to an immigrant man in Arkansas who had requested her. Rosa's story was recorded by Marie Hall Ets, a social worker at Hull House in Chicago and reflects the lives of many other immigrant women who never had the chance to tell their stories.[3]

The Italian woman had little choice but to put herself under the protection of a man. Women outside the family structure were scorned as deviants from the established order; they were either wicked or pitiful, but always beyond the norm. Unmarried or widowed women, who were thought, in their single-ness, to be consumed with envy and full of spite toward women partnered with men, were thus commonly held to be the chief casters of the evil eye. In Grazia Deledda's novel *The Mother,* filled with the intensity and supersti-tions of the harsh Sardinian world of a century past, a mother watches her son, a priest, fall under the spell of a woman who, being "rich, independent, alone, too much alone" was outside normality and thus a threat to all around her. In a patriarchal society, any female (save nuns) whose life was not de-fined by a man's would be suspect.

Rosemary Clement (a name truncated from Clemente during immigration processing) has Lena, a character in her play *Her Mother's Daughter* boast: "I'm a thinker—I thought myself right out of getting married." But eventually Lena's place in society is legitimized when she becomes a mother to her young orphaned niece and nephew, thus redeeming her womanhood and re-moving suspicion of egocentricity from her life. In Clement's *October Bloom,* the psychological warfare between the old family and the new woman is still being fought as a young girl's desire to go away to college is opposed by her mother. Beverly Donofrio's vivid memoir, *Riding in Cars with Boys: Confes-sions of a Bad Girl Who Makes Good* (1990), also recounts her own desire for education being thwarted and how her reaction was played out in a wildness that could have left her life a permanent ruin.

As with Caruso and Clement, the Italian American playwrights Donna De Matteo and Michele Linfante have written works with deep connections to the mother-daughter bond—a connection heightened in a culture that still worships the ancient goddess as madonna—and to the wider world of women. A model of the Old World Italian woman who was resourceful, strong, and able to live by her wits and hard labor when it was demanded of her (as it often was when her husband preceded her to America and often was gone for years at a time without any word) appears in Lucinda LaBella Mays' 1979 novel *The Other Shore.* In Mays' book, the mother must pit herself against the elements, poverty, outside hostility in order to survive. She keeps herself and her child alive by her unremitting sacrifice and strength until the long-awaited ticket to America arrives. The child, Gabriella, will find for herself that the long-dreamt-of street of gold is actually the American public school. She will sepa-rate her life from her mother's through education and self-direction, thereby providing an elevating but historically uncommon ending.

For this much is certainly true of Italian women: they have resources of strength which is denied in the stereotype of them as submissive and servile creatures to their men. At the beginning of the twentieth century, Jacob Riis, who photographed and wrote of the immigrants in their tenement life on the Lower East Side of New York noted, "There is that about the Italian woman which suggests the capacity for better things." Did he mean her tenaciousness, her endurance, her grace under pressure, her faith? Those are the qualities her granddaughters, in particular, cherish and have reintegrated into their lives, adjusted for new uses.

There are certain mindsets, however, brought over with the immigrants, which take longer to reshape. Self-denial was the psychological preparation among peasants for survival in regions where *la miseria* was the norm of life and there was no chance of a better one: denial of aspirations, denial of any possibility of change, denial of education to children as being futile, denial of interest in anything beyond one's home walls, denial of goals as being unreachable and therefore an emotional drain and psychological impairment. Strength, psychic and physical, was conserved just for sheer life support. If they could not better themselves in the old country, what they could do, however, and did, was to leave. It was an act of enormous courage and faith, but inevitably there clung to them remnants of the old *miseria* mentality, for survival had once more to be secured, and this time in alien land.

The ingrained suspicion of education used to be expressed in the saying, *Fesso è chi fa il figlio meglio di lui*—it's a stupid man who makes his son better than he is. American schools were not always regarded as the road to a better future. Often they were seen as a threat to the family because they stressed assimilation into American ways and gave children a language their parents did not have. Reading was ridiculed as too private, too unproductive, too exclusive an enjoyment. Free time should be spent with the family group, not on one's own. What the family wanted was cohesion and no threat of change. Learning gave children ideas, made them different; writing produced nothing. These were the criteria of a people involved completely in economic survival. And for their time and place, they were right. Reading and writing are the rewards of a well-established class.

Studies show that Italian American students in the main still demonstrate a predilection for pragmatic and vocational studies over the liberal arts, and are relatively disinterested in cultural activies, do not get involved in extracurricular activites, and in general feel alienated from faculty and other students at their colleges. A 1986–8 study of Italian American college students at the City University of New York yielded the disquieting finding that "Italian American young people still have difficulty in establishing personal independence from their close, and in many cases, 'enmeshed' families." The profile of the female student of Italian American background is of someone extremely anxious and suffering from low self esteem, often depressed, and with an "irrational anxiety about appearance and other issues of self-worth."

At best women are getting a mixed message: yes, better yourself through education, but don't get beyond your family. Learn the wherewithal to gain economically, but not how to develop an independent mind and spirit which might take you away from us. Still present is the concept of education as a practical tool to help one earn more money, not as the door to autonomy and lifelong self-development.

The 1970 film, *Lovers and Other Strangers*, reiterated the theme of not growing beyond the old style of doing things as the father in an Italian American family confronts a son who is contemplating divorce: "What do you mean you're not compatible? What do you mean divorce? What are you, better than me? Look at me, do I have to be happy to be married! What makes you think *you* got to be happy? Why do you think we keep families together? For happiness? Nah! It's for *family!*"

Thus is the dialectic set up: there is resistance to change, but change is inevitable. In the very title of Louise DeSalvo's incisive essay, "A Portrait of the *Puttana* as a Middle-Aged Woolf Scholar," is the recognition that an educated woman was (is) looked upon with deep suspicion: an emancipated mind puts her outside familial control, beyond male authority, and that has to mean intolerable anarchy. The psychological warfare of former generations is perhaps only now abating.

Italian American writing is full of the dilemma of the individual on the road to selfhood who is caught in the anguish of what seems betrayal to family. Yet breaking out of the family, or the neighborhood, is a step in the search for one's autonomy.

The very solidity of the Italian American family, which is its success, makes it hard to break away from. And to be a writer means breaking away and taking distance from where one came in order to see it better, more truly. This puts the Italian American woman writer in a precarious position. That is, do you keep close to family, enjoying its emotional warmth and protectiveness, and lose your individualism, or do you opt for personal independence? Do you go against the grain of your culture to embrace the American concept of rugged individualism? Do you choose loneliness over denial of self for the family good?

The working out of independence/dependence factors is critical in the development of both men and women and for people of all backgrounds. But some cultures, in effect, demand too enormous a ransom to release the individual from benevolent captivity.

Strangely, the ways of the past have hung on with Italian Americans even as Italy has radically changed from what it was just fifty years ago. An industrialized and transformed Italian society makes an Italian American community like Marianna De Marco Torgovnick's Bensonhurst in Brooklyn, which tenaciously holds onto the old isolation, seem a remote backwater by comparison. Now a scholar, author, and professor of English at Duke University, she wrote of her early background in *Crossing Ocean Parkway*, noting the sea-change she underwent.

There is an irony here, for the Italian thrust and talent as a people was always towards individualism. The Renaissance was created of giant personalities. But none of that high culture touched the masses of people who would form the major immigrant population and who, in arriving in America, would find their rebirth here.

Sounding like an analyst pointing the way to group maturity, Jacob Burckhardt wrote of the Italian people in *The Civilization of the Renaissance in Italy:* "This it is which separates them from the other western people. . . . This keen eye for individuality belongs only to those who have emerged from the half-conscious life of the race and become themselves individuals."

The immigrants who left Italy took the first step towards lifting themselves from that "half-conscious life of the race" in the very act of taking passage to America. That act linked them and their descendants to the American ideal of the self-made person. And the paradox is that by becoming self-made in America, Italian Americans may finally be more authentically Italian than they ever could have been remaining submerged in the old way in Italy.

In a sense Italians transplanted to America were asked to mature immediately from a state of child-like dependence (on family or Church or landlord), to a state of self-reliance in order to be what America said they should be. It went against the grain of their very being and most deeply held convictions about life.

Mario Puzo, touching in *The Godfather Papers* on the enormous exodus of the poor from the south of Italy, says: "They fled from sunny Italy, these peasants, as children in fairy tales flee into the dark forest from cruel step-parents."[4] Interesting that he casts it that way. It seems a very apt simile. If they came as children, they had either very quickly to grow or to remain as vulnerable as children, dependent on family and familiar surroundings, their impetus halted.

The Italian American woman comes out of a family-oriented, patriarchal view of the world in which women stayed at home or, at most, worked alongside her immediate male kin, but was always dependent upon a male—her father, brother, husband, and, eventually, if widowed, her sons. Family was the focal point of the Italian woman's duty and concern and, by the same token, the source of her strength and power, the means by which she measured her worth and was in turn measured, the reason for her being. Historically, the woman's role as central to family life was crucial because of the importance of the family over any other institution. It was the only unit that protected its members from the abuses of others and helped them recover from natural disasters.

Within Italian culture, reinforcement of the woman's role and definition in the family was gained through the strong Italian cult of the Madonna—the Holy Mother—who prefigured all other mothers and symbolized them, the quintessential *mamma mia*. But as Andrew Rolle, who has made a unique contribution to the psychological understanding of Italian Americans, has observed, "The Madonna had been a mother but scarcely a wife."[5] And so too, the Italian woman reduced her sexual role as her husband's lover to take on that of *mater dolorosa*.

This acute observation helps explain the often vexed sexuality of the Italian American woman and how, in contrast to other couples, she was in the past so little a companion and friend to her husband. What she was mainly was Mother, the continuum of life to whom her children will be bound forever by the stringent strings of respect, weekly visits, confidences, and obedience. Such restrictiveness may explain the performer Madonna's obsession with publicly acting out sex when she sang "Papa, don't preach." She was vehemently cutting loose from the childhood bonds of Catholic education and strict patriarchal family mores.

Becoming ourselves is why some of us write, the being is part of the writing. Pietro Di Donato who died in 1992, described *The Gospels,* his work in progress, as his revenge, his answer to all the past constraints: "I am writing [*The Gospels*] because I was . . . a true believer, and I outgrew that and have to replace it with Gods of my own creation."[6] Or, as Marguerite in *Umbertina* puts it, "What world is there that's not beached first in ourselves?"

The caustic of the American experience changed the old role to a new one at the cost of an enduring psychological split and a tension which has, in Italian American women writers, become the material of much of their work.

The women who are second and third generation Italian Americans know and honor their special background, but they also question it and are aware of deeply ambivalent feelings about family and about those bonds, both healing and constricting, that are suffered as the heavy cost of preserving tradition. Barbara Grizzuti Harrison in her essay, "Godfather II: Of Families and Families," has stated the dilemma: "I think of the strength of Italian women, of strength perverted and strength preserved. And I am painfully confused. I want all of these people to love me, to comprehend me; I want none of them to constrain or confine me. And I know that what I want is impossible."

In a harsh environment, a woman was recognized as life sustaining by being the central pivot of the family in a way every bit as concrete as the Navajo's traditional hogan, which is built on four poles named after female deities, so that the support of the home literally rested upon the female principle.

Richard Gambino's *Blood of My Blood* (1975) examined the background of the Italian American experience and its past dynamics. He has described well the positive qualities expected of the female who was to become wife and mother: she was socialized at an early age to be serious, active, sharp, and practical. In the chapter Gambino devotes to women, *"La Serietà*—The Ideal of Womanliness," his espousal of those qualities is, however, too idealized a male vision of woman's place. True, she was the center of life of the whole ethnic group. True, it was she who expressed the emotions of the men; true she must be useful to her family, for her value is based on practical usefulness, but women view it as less acceptable than do men like Gambino that this ideal of *serietà* should be the end-all and be-all of a woman's life. Gambino finds women's traditional role pleasingly full of the dignity and gravity that would honor an ancient Roman matron. Contemporary women stuck with the role are less gratified with it than Gambino has ventured to imagine.

"I have it like heaven now," says the widowed Rosa Cassettari towards the end of her life. "No man to scold me and make me do this and stop me to do that. I have it like heaven—I'm my own boss. The peace I've got now, it pays me for all the trouble I had in my life."[7] Even unlearned and unlettered women like Rosa, once they got to America, gained a sense of there being potentially something more to their lives than family service.

Why, if the *donna seria* is such a paragon of sturdy virtues, has the Italian American male (including Richard Gambino), as he evolves educationally, professionally, and socially, fled her company so completely? As one member of Dr. Aileen Riotto Sirey's ethnotherapy group admitted, "I never wanted to marry an Italian girl, I wanted to marry a WASP, someone who was educated and could help me to get ahead."

The most verifiable phenomenon of educated Italian American males is that they marry outside their ethnic group. Fleeing the traditional woman and her feudal role, Italian American men find social mobility and better company in educated Jewish or Irish wives. Still, they want their mothers and sisters to keep the traditional ways to which they return on festive occasions, filled with nostalgia and sentiment for old ways that can safely be left behind when it's time to go.

That flight was given recognition in a popular film of some years ago, *Saturday Night Fever,* in which the woman protagonist, named Stephanie MacDonald, becomes the symbol for the Italian American hero, Tony Manero, of what is better, achieving, and upward in life. Tony, played by John Travolta, leaves his Italian American Brooklyn neighborhood (and the Italian girl who pines for him) to follow Ms. MacDonald by crossing the bridge into her realm, Manhattan, thus signifying his willingness to grow beyond his ethnic group.

The one thing, according to the men, that an Italian American woman must not do was change. Since everyone leaned on her for support, she must be permanently accessible and permanently unchanging, a lynch-pin of traditional values. She could not exist as an individual with her own needs and wishes for that would have toppled the whole patriarchal order and under-

mined the common good of the family. That is a heavy price to pay for the
pedestal and a Holy Mother image.

A very contemporary use of the self-nullifying theme in the Italian
woman's life is the metaphor of Rosemarie Caruso's play, *The Suffering
Heart Salon* where the ritualization of women's sacrificial lives is played out
in a New Jersey beauty salon and embodied in the line, "You don't like it?—
do it anyway!" Caruso parallels women to the sanctified host of the sacrificial
Mass, who exist to be consumed by the officiating priesthood of men. In their
sacrifice is their blessedness and specialness. Thus they are revered by those
who consume them and they, themselves, made to feel consecrated by their
role. In contrast, their daughters assert a need for self-identity and want to
free themselves from the past patterns; in their self-actualization they *must*
react against their mothers, but in denying the value of the mother's role by
their rebellion against it, they lay upon themselves a terrible dilemma.

As early as the 1943 publication of Michael DeCapite's novel *Maria,* a different kind of Italian woman from the submissive women portrayed in Di
Donato's *Three Circles of Light* or popularized as Mafia women in *The Godfather* and elsewhere, was presented—one far beyond the stereotypes they
had already become in the larger culture. *Maria* is a penetrating study of a
woman in conflict with the role she is expected to fulfill while she yearns for
something else.

First depicted as a young girl, Maria submits to the marriage her father
arranges with a harsh, silent, and ultimately stupid man. She experiences divorce and abortion when both were not only unusual in American life, but
matters of extreme gravity in an Italian enclave. She befriends a Jewish
woman; she expresses sexual interest in a man not her husband; she finds intense satisfaction in her comradeship with women at work. She knows the reality of life and achieves a sense of belonging in her city environment and at
work. Only in her final action when she rejects her second husband through
feelings of guilt toward her eldest son, does something contrived enter the
novel. It's as if Maria, by accepting the maternal role as more important, is
acting as the male author thinks she should. Still, it is a choice, not something
forced upon an unformed person, as her first marriage was. In the difficulty
of the choice lies the seeming nobility of her self-sacrifice. Despite ending on
the traditional note of a mother's sacrifice, one feels the truth and depth of
feeling of the character. Maria is beautifully realized and is resonant with an
inner turmoil not normally accorded Italian American women who seem to
act only as automatons of their tradition.

But such female characters have not fared well with critics who are more
comfortable with predictable stock figures, having certain assumptions about
Italian Americans that they find hard to relinquish. Thus, Julia Savarese's
novel *The Weak and the Strong* (1952) got a very harsh reception. Critics
called her strong descriptions of poverty and the depression era "Bleak,"

"tough," "unrelenting," and—the ultimate pejorative!—"humorless." Of course, for an established male writer like Di Donato, or women writers like Jean Rhys, or Flannery O'Connor, that kind of unsentimentality would be *verismo* of the highest order.

Antonia Pola's fictional character, Marietta, in *Who Can Buy the Stars?*, impatient with a weak husband, had the stamina to become a bootlegger as she tried in vain to buy happiness for her family and herself. Mari Tomasi also created women who acted independently of the notions of how they should act and suffered reviewers who misread her work as "quaint . . . unpretentious . . . pastoral."

The women's voices, whether in literature or in the recorded interviews of Professor Valentine Rossilli Winsey, in their poignant resignation or in anger, strongly contradict the image of Gambino's ideal stoic matron, *la donna seria*. A chorus of female voices speak of unhappy marriages, no choices for their lives, and a kind of bewildered regret for what life had been. All that sustained them was that they did what was expected of them.

The Italian immigrant woman met her duties and responsabilities and showed again and again her strength, her resilience, and her time-worn patience. Indeed, her success in keeping the family together has earned her recognition and tributes from sociologists and other scholars. But no barricade around the family unit is large enough or strong enough to keep out the winds of freedom wafted on the new world air. The minute their children set foot in the American school and imbibed the notions that in this land all is possible and each person has the right to be self-fulfilled and seek personal happiness, something happens to the old bonds. They do not disappear, but they loosen. They allow for new thoughts, new arrangements.

It became apparent that in Anglo-American life (for that was the dominant ethnic pattern and became the standard by which American society judged all other ethnicities as up to par or not), the family had less importance than political or economic institutions, or even the school system. It was soon perceived that "Americans" rated self-sufficiency over family ties. Individual success and achievement was what counted, not sacrificing oneself for the family. As a result, the value of the Italian woman was diminished in the new land; she became old-fashioned, backward. She became the focus of well-meaning social workers who wanted to "save her" from what they viewed as a undemocratic patriarchal system without recognizing that in that very system she had found validation and had nothing, immediately, with which to replace it.

The psychological battering endured by the Italian American woman has been considerable. Professor Winsey quotes the poignant remark of a solitary old immigrant woman reflecting on her experience of life in America that keeps her children and grandchildren so busy running they have no time for her. "Bread rises," she said "only when it's allowed to stand awhile. The soul, too, has its own yeast, but it cannot rise while it's running. It's certain that I got things here which in Italy I never could have gotten. But I had things in Italy which in America I still cannot find—yeast, yeast for the soul!"[8]

The Italian woman's soul was in her consecration as core of the family, upholder of its traditions and the transmitter of its values. In that role her hardships and sacrifices were repaid, her value was inviolate, and this gave her a positive sense of her self and of her power—a power that was, however, often manipulative and always relative, confined as it was to the home environment and not used in the world at large. In America she was quickly dethroned from venerable matriarch into the image of the old woman in the kitchen stirring the sauce, heart-warming, maybe, but actually a figure of ridicule, a caricature. She and the stern values she stood for were no competition for the seduction of America which beckoned her children away from stern duty, away from tacky self-sacrifice, away from the old way.

Not able to Americanize on the spot, the Italian immigrant woman suffered instant obsolescence (an American invention), and became an anachronism, a displaced person, a relic of a remote rural village culture.

There is no doubt that family structure was an essential aid to the successful transplantation of Italians in America; it continues to provide stability and important verities and a specific Italian American identity. But now it is its tensions that have been explored by such works as Barbara Grizzuti Harrison's autobiographical *Visions of Glory* (1978), the novels *Miss Giardino* (1978) by Dorothy Bryant, *Tender Warriors* (1986) by Rachel Guido deVries, *The Right Thing to Do* (1988, 1999) by Josephine Gattuso Hendin, or the strains of intercultural marriage as in Rita Ciresi's *Blue Italian* (1996) and *Pink Slip* (1998).

Contrary to folklore, humorous stereotypes, and appealing portraits of the traditional Italian woman as pillar of her family, Italian American literature abounds with portraits of other women who are harsh, frequently cruel, crushing, unfeeling. They are embittered and malevolent, and, given the strictures of their own lives, there is plenty of reason why.

Some mothers, as in Jennifer Lagier's poem, "Second Class Citizen," in Marion Benasutti's fictionalized memoir, *No Steady Job for Papa* (1966), or in Rosemarie Caruso's plays, are portrayed with a humor that nonetheless still reveals layers of apprehension or bleak disappointment in their lives, an edge of rancor towards their lot. Or, there is the figure of the angry mother in Jacquelyn Bonomo's poem, "The Walk-In Closet," and the troubled mother in Linda Monacelli-Johnson's "Home Movies":

> When a bourbon bottle
> became the lens, I discovered
> I was born of you to be your
> mother.

In the haunting words of Janine Veto's poem, "Naturally, Mother":

> Freud aside, all our fathers
> do not matter
> A woman bleeds through her mother

But, family in all its facets—not only the dark side—is what gripped the imaginative powers of the first Italian American writers and, most forcibly, women, because their roles were so enmeshed in that powerful mark of their culture. Thus, the family's benevolent warmth and support are portrayed in Rose Grieco's stories and Dorothy Gentile Fields' play *1932* about an Italian American family in the depression years; compulsive nostalgia and life ritual are the subject of Diane di Prima's *Dinners and Nightmares* where she writes about shopping for eels for an Italian Christmas Eve. And Maryfrances Cusumano Wagner's poem, "Preparations for an Italian Wedding," predicts, "You will be glad you followed tradition; / you will at last understand your mother."

More than for men, the displacement from one culture to another has represented a real crisis of identity for the woman of the Italian family, and she has left a heritage of conflict to her children. They, unwilling to give themselves completely to the old ways she transmitted, may end up with burdens of shame and ambivalence or a sour self-hate as the pernicious inheritance gets passed on. Even third and fourth generations feel the remnants of conflict.

For the modern woman it means that traditional power (based upon self-lessness and sacrifice) has been transmuted into a more gratifying autonomy and self-awareness. If not power over her children in the old way, she has instead power of choice in her own life and the possibility of a democratic family style.

And yet there remain valid ties to the past and feminists of Italian American background look for and find strengths in the old traditions, especially in those parts of the model of *serietà*, which Gambino described as assertiveness, committment to work, activism, and practicality—qualities, it turns out, that are identified as normal expectations for *all male* Americans! Utilizing the Old World values of the ideal of Italian womanliness in the service of the contemporary quest for individuation, the evolving and maturing Italian American woman has learned to redistribute the focus of those qualities from the exclusive service to others to herself as well. That is the balance she explores in her writings. The pull back towards family is powerful; the push forward toward self-enhancement is ineluctable. How to arrive at an equilibrium is something that Louise DeSalvo's essay explores in this collection not with the quaint self-deprecating humor of the past, but with pungent and sophisticated insights.

Despite their specific material, Italian American women writers speak for all women: their emergence is that of all women who once lived in the shadows of others.

There was a dark underside to the bright picture of compact Italian American family life so praised by sociologists and onlookers. The professional apologists who extol the Italian American family had better listen to the women and to their literature, to the voices of women writers who are telling it as it is. Home life was never as satisfying and untroubled as the men said it was; it was what it was for historic and social reasons that are now surpassed.

Put Italian American women in the context of their origin, their time and place, and the collective psyche that formed and held them, and it becomes comprehensible why they have taken long to test language and flaunt tradition as writers, long in giving themselves the authority to be authors.

Gay Talese, who wrote a piece on missing Italian American writers, says that Italian Americans don't write about family and that not being able to reveal family matters has kept him from being a novelist.[9] His misperception, however, is that *his* failure of nerve has kept *all* Italian American novelists from writing about family (or whatever) whereas, in fact, the contrary is true: the family has proved their most cogent material. Through willfullness or ignorance, Talese simply discounted past decades of Italian American writing. Nor is he presently aware that the old culture of shame, of not giving up secrets, has been replaced, one by one, by a new Italian American woman writer.

Single-handedly, Cris Mazza revokes shame by the deliberate shamelessness of images in her collection of stories, *Animal Acts* (1988). There is nothing that she and her sister writers (Mary Caponegro, Louise DeSalvo, Anna Quindlen, Jeanne Schinto, Carole Maso) flinch from writing. For them, there are no more shadows.

## Seeds of Doubt: The Internal Blocks

In America, the newly arrived faced the cultural imperative of the dominant society: to "pass" you had to lose your distinguishing identity and somehow become a stranger in your own life.

This part of Maria Mazziotti Gillan's poem "Public School No. 18: Paterson, New Jersey" perfectly catches the dilemma:

> Miss Wilson's eyes, opaque
> as blue glass, fix on me:
> "We must speak English.
> We're in America now."

> I want to say, "I am American,"
> but the evidence is stacked against me.

Evan Hunter, the legally changed name of Salvatore Lombino, made a nomenclatural leap into America's mainstream; he explored in his novel *Streets of Gold,* the transmutation of Ignazio di Palermo into Dwight Jamison and his attempt, in an anglicized persona, to attach himself to the American dream. The realization of the futility of it all comes because, in his self-made Waspness, Dwight Jamison finds he does not exist; he is a figment of the American imagination.

It was the myth that failed. The myth that told us we could and should be equally American in the Anglo mold, but forgot to mention that to force people to become what they are not produces not equality but enmity—enmity with one's self. Gillan, winner of the prestigious May Sarton Award for her writing, states it again:

> Without words, they tell me
> to be ashamed.
> I am.
> I deny that booted country
> even from myself,
> want to be still
> and untouchable
> as those women
> who teach me to hate myself.

By an early age I, too, had a good start on what is a major motif in Italian American writing: the sense of being out of line with one's surroundings, not of one's family and not of the world beyond the family, an outsider in every sense.

My schooling had provided no texts by authors with Italian names, no expectation that people of Italian background had a rich literature. Rather, the illiteracy of the Italian immigrants was stressed without the countering view that illiterate people do have an operative social system and a culture outside of books. James C. Raymond's *Literacy as a Human Problem* stated that neither wealth nor literacy guarantees superior sensibility; either can engender a warped set of values, fashionable vulgarity, and callousness toward the disadvantaged. People who are highly literate, like people who are very rich, are tempted to regard literacy or money as the measure of human worth.

No mention of any Italian achievement in social or humanistic arts was ever provided to dispel the message that Italian Americans were somehow less than the Tom Sawyers and Becky Thatchers around them. This sense of being alien in America pervades other ethnic groups as well. Feminist writer

Vivian Gornick decried what she saw as the squashing of ideals present in earlier generations of Jewish social activists and the overlaying of revolutionary
goals with the white-wash of protestant ethics in order to fabricate stereotypes of middle-class virtues. This is possible Gornick pointed out because
of the overwhelmingly prevalent WASP models in American schools and
colleges.

Schools were aided in the task of imprinting minds with the need to Anglo-
cize, to grow up with the look of America, by movies which projected images
of Shirley Temple and the Andy Hardy character. Italian American homes,
gardens, names, and churches were embarassing, too ornate, too foreign. It
was the pristine, classic simplicity of the white New England church steeple
on the village green to which taste was expected to conform, not to the ro-
cocco excesses of Catholic sanctuaries much less the gaudy, over-wrought pa-
ganized pageants of saints in some parishes with which Italian Americans
annually annoyed their Irish clergy. Lines from a poem by Elaine Romaine
(née Romagnano) state it succinctly, "You were always irish, god/ in a church
where I confessed/ to being Italian.

For the Catholicism the immigrants found here was a stern, puritanical, in-
hospitable version of what they had known in their homeland. In America
everything was tinged by the protestant ethic: worth was measured by material achievement, visible riches, and success, all of which is quite at odds with
the Catholic harmony of everyone having worth in the sight of God and there
being a divine plan in everything with hope eternal for salvation. The Protestant ethic stresses competitiveness, anxiety, struggle to succeed, to move up
fast and visibly. The Catholic emphasis is on acceptance, humility, and having
an internal sense of worth and dignity without the external show of prosperity
that indicates Calvinist grace. It is the difference between a tolerant, live and
let live orientation and a chiding, judgmental one.

In order to become American, one had to learn to be alone. "One had to
*value* being alone," Michael Novak noted.[10]

There is in this mandate the belief in individualism which is the positive
message of Protestantism, an insistence on maturity by facing the existential
predicament of our essential aloneness and the need to form one's self outside of and beyond family.

But growing up is difficult and filled with the traps of self-consciousness
about being different and finding reasons for shame in the taste and smells of
Italian foods, in the look of grandparents, in the decor of home and garden.

Imagine Italians in a Currier & Ives world: sleighing up at Christmas to a
cold and isolated farm on a forest's edge instead of strolling through a village
where houses are all snuggled one against the other and you can mingle in a
piazza thick with people and human exchange. It's a different image of the
world. The American penchant for being off alone in nature, for being
Thoreau, was not what Italian immigrants valued; it is part of the American

mind. Henry Steele Commager's outdated *The American Mind: An Interpretation of American Thought and Character Since the 1880s* viewed that mind as one in which, it has been pointed out, not a Jew, nor a Black, nor a Catholic had a presence nor, consequently, did their particular sensibilities and visions of what this country means.

Sister Blandina Segale foresaw in her journal that Establishment history, as written by "Mr. Bancroft" (in his ten volume *History of the United States*), would not give the whole picture as to what had been accomplished in American life by non-Anglos. Commenting on how the freedom of conscience edicts enacted by Catholic Lord Baltimore in Maryland were frequently overlooked, she charges, "Yet look at the stream of articles constantly given to the public about Plymouth Rock and the Pilgrim Fathers!" Just as those who decry the Mafia as an Italian import forget that the Ku Klux Klan is an Anglo-American invention.

In its presumption of rightness, the Anglo-conformist society determined that every group but theirs was "ethnic." Thus the disingenuousness, for instance, of John Cheever, who refered to his mother as "an Englishwoman" but denied that his writing, though concentrated on a small world of Episcopalian suburbanites of British descent, was ethnic. British-Americans simply take it for granted that the customs, language, and school curricula of this country are anglocentric. To them, they aren't "ethnic," they're natural. It reflects the American imperative of having to give a common frame of reference and unity to the many disparate peoples who make up this country. But its elitist and value judgment overtones are something more—a slur against other ways and cultures that continues to wound the peoples who feel its sting.

The children of the immigrants immersed themselves in the texts the American schools provided, books with heroes and heroines who were unfamiliar in Italian American life. These models were not only alluring, they also gave Italian Americans a sense of displacement and estrangement. The Italian American self-image was never in perfect focus: one could never find who one was, only who the larger society thought one should be.

It is a delicate question of balance. Italian Americans internalized English literary culture and were certainly enriched by it, but in the process were denied knowing that their tradition had, in fact, riches and glories of its own.

America passed through its period of isolationism and since the second half of the century following World War II has inevitably become part of the total world scene abroad and more accepting of multicultural differences at home.

Different origins presume differences in temperament and attitudes. It was psychologically impossible for Italian Americans of earlier generations to fit themselves into the Procrustean bed of Anglo-conformity without, in fact, maiming a part of themselves.

Consider Medea: she, the barbarian princess, the foreigner, was the ulti-

mate outsider to culturally correct Jason, the Greek insider. And her internalized rage was due to his contempt for her being "other." It is the rage which always informs the writing of all those who are perceived as different. It is there
in James Baldwin's *The Fire Next Time* as he grappled with the theme of
American identity. Over and over it appears in much multi-cultural writing. It
is in women's writing. It is in *The Dream Book* as I question why Italian American writers, particularly women, have been left out of the national literature.

"As I grow older, I think more and more about my cultural background
which I unfortunately denied for many years," playwright Michele Linfante
told me. She expresses the prevalence of those internal seeds of doubt,
known to many ethnic groups, as to who she was supposed to be.

Would it have been different if Frances Winwar, sixty years ago, had
opened the door to respect for Italian American writers by letting her highly
successful books carry "by Francesca Vinciguerra" on their title-pages? One
can only speculate as well as recognize that other Italian American authors
underwent the same self-censorship of name or fictional characters and
material.

"I am really Sandra Mortola Gilbert," explained Sandra Gilbert, "and my
mother's name was Caruso, so I always feel oddly falsified with this waspish-
sounding American name, which I adopted as a twenty-year old bride who
had never considered the implications of her actions!"

Names are powerful signals, and an Italian American surname sets up barriers of preconception or even prejudice in those circles of American literature that are hard to scale even under the best of circumstances. Italian
names are analogous to the high visibilty of Black writers—they immediately
signal difference. The Italian American women who have written with Anglo
surnames acquired at marriage are not seen as being who they actually are.
And that is to be regretted for it feeds the notion of the missing Italian American woman writer. Exceptionally, Barbara Grizzuti Harrison has always kept
her Italian birth name along with her married name.

In her review of *The Dream Book,* Anna Quindlen wrote, "I am Italian
American, my father's surname belies my mother's background. Our literature should in part reflect our lives, and mine has not. There is a world that
has not appeared very often in modern American literature, a world of insular
families scorned by an English speaking society, torn by the lure of assimilation and the sure disintegration of tradition that this would bring." In her first
novel, *Object Lessons,* Quindlen looked at that world.

What I find is that we write ourselves to know ourselves; we write of our
differences in order to embrace them. Yet it is hard for society and the literature to accept our differences. It has been said that the very essence of the
creative is its novelty, hence we have no tried and tested standard by which to
judge it. Substitute "different" for "creative" and the conclusion is the same.

Another difference from other woman writers was the degree of isolation each Italian American felt, a degree that seemed to distinguish them from any other group of women writers. In *Black Women Writers at Work* Toni Cade Bambara says, "What determines the shape and content of my work is the community of writers . . . writers have gotten their wagons in a circle, which gives us each something to lean against, push off against."

Not so with Italian American woman writers. Most of those who appeared in *The Dream Book*, thought herself unique as a writer of Italian American background. Very few knew of others. But once collected and named they became aware of each other, held joint readings, formed groups, began to appear in collections, were asked to talk at colleges and at women's history month events. With Emelise Aleandri's 1987 staging of "The Dream Book Revue" at the CUNY Graduate Center in New York, many of the women whose written work had appeared in the anthology were visibly brought together for the first time as a collective presence and voice.

"What is the way out of this dilemma?" asks Sandra Gilbert in an essay on Sylvia Plath, as she considers the paradox of Plath's (or any creative woman's) life: even as she longs for the freedom of flight, she fears the risks of freedom. Interestingly, Gilbert states that double bind in terms that describe the Italian American sensibility: "How does a woman reconcile the exigencies of the species—her desire for stasis, her sense of her ancestry, her devotion to the house in which she has lived—with the urgencies of her own self? I don't know the answer."

Already some of the myths embedded in the culture about women have crumbled. Jean Baker Miller's *Toward a New Psychology of Women*[11] identifies *growth* as the most dynamic quality of being human. Growth means change, and human growth equals psychological change. It means that personal creativity is a lifelong imperative for having a fulfilled life. Miller's cogent insights acutely question the "desire for stasis," which Gilbert had posited as a female exigency and makes it more a social construct.

The assumption about woman's traditional role as static bearer of the past must be rethought in terms of what reality shows, i.e. women are involved through child care in witnessing and fostering constant change and growth. Women, raising children, have absorbed lessons for change not fixity. By twisting reality, and going against the grain of their nature and the very texture of their experience, women have been conditioned by society into falsely seeming to desire stasis and made to appear as compliant upholders of traditions in which men have a major vested interest. That interest is premised on the maintenance of status quo. The price to women has been the thwarting of creative growth and change in themselves.

Can it be, (what societies have long denied), that women are *more* change-oriented than men, more flexible and tolerant, have always longed for the psychological excitement of growth and change rather than their statuary calm?

Italian American women have particularly projected their feelings of worth outward, making affiliation central to their lives. Waiting to be confirmed by others, they often have a woefully undeveloped central core of self. Women's nature has been defined for them by the other sex, and a woman's graceful compliance to male authority (whether in home situations or in public institutions) has been made to seem the measure of her femininity.

Although Tillie Olsen, in her story "Tell Me a Riddle," gave us a glimpse of the myth deflated, Italian American women were still internalizing the myths of the "sacrificial mother" and "everyone else first before me."

Philosopher Martha Nussbaum, in an essay review of *Reclaiming a Conversation: The Ideal of the Educated Woman,*[12] found that past theorists of women's role, since Plato, who imposed on women a male notion of the Good Life, have always described a female life that lacked something. Solutions, Nussbaum says, are not to be found in the past philosophical tradition; rather, a new chapter remains to be written by both men and women trying to live fuller lives in a joint human experience. What she foresees is that we face a plurality of different lives, sometimes conflicting and sometimes enriching each other. In daily choices, we construct new and fuller meanings to the ideal of the "the complete human life."

If this is a dilemma for all Italian Americans, it is more so for the writer, and utmost for the writer who is a woman. As Cynthia Ozick had reckoned, "You can't be the good citizen doing petitions and making chicken soup for your sick neighbor, and still be an artist." Ozick has the self confidence to be the artist. Italian American women writers, according to which generation they belong, either have not had the confidence, acquired it with misgivings, or have never had the problem.

For it is the woman who, at the core of the family, is the transmitter of its traditions and upholder of its values. Can *she* defect from the one institution Italians believe in, the family? Can she at least redefine the ancient laws to her advantage?

This is the paradox: being at the heart of things, it is Italian American women who, breaking the silence imposed on them by family loyalty, thereupon become best suited to make literary use of the material implicit in family struggles. What was in the past an obstacle to the writing now provides the thematic material.

Emerging from the redoubt called Family Loyalty, many Italian American women writers have used writing as an act of public assertiveness. From Di Donato on, Italian American writers have openly aired their family secrets. Family has been their theme more than such "American" ones as angst, personal ambition, spiritual struggle, or the hard working out of the sexual relationship. Italian American women writers, as all writers, use their personal material to crack the hard nut of secrecy by publishing. That sufficiently gives the lie to Gay Talese's perverse "revelation" that there are no Italian American novelists because the would-be authors are in dread of offending family and are thus bound by a code of silence. But it does not explain why the New York Times gave front page prominence to Talese's exercise unless it were a willful editorial decision to perpetuate the negative stereotypes of Italian Americans. "They are the last ethnic group America can comfortably mock," playwright John Patrick Shanley noted about some of his own material in a *Time* magazine interview. This assessment was reaffirmed in the *New York Post* by investigative reporter Jack Newfield who wrote that in America, "Prejudice against Italian Americans is the most tolerated intolerance."

That Italian American women became writers at all is a triumph of assertion and faith over formidable obstacles. Italian American women were taught to keep out of public view: don't step out of line and be noticed, don't be the envy of others, don't attract the jealous fates who will punish success. Italian American women were not brought up with the confidence that makes Jewish women such splendid social activists, such demanding wives, and able promoters of themselves; nor have they had the long experience of self-reliance and expressivity in the English language (oral as well as written) that Black women have had. They are not incited and brought together by ancient wrongs as are the Native Americans and Chicanos.

They were, instead, susceptible to the idea that excelling or drawing attention to oneself was not womanly, not good. This notion was prevalent in a society in which belief in *malocchio*—the evil eye—was present on all levels. One mustn't disconnect from one's immediate group, as a writer must in order to get perspective and unique vision. And one mustn't try to see too much either into oneself or into others. Such would bring upon oneself the curse of separation. The taboo is against being seen as excelling in anything, or in that close seeing which is self-knowledge. Those who see too far—Tiresias, Milton, Galileo—go blind, or, like Cassandra, go unheeded.

Many Italian American women have had a hard time overcoming inner blocks to creative expression because they were not empowered, as female children, to be independent. Typical are women who have had to disengage themselves from internalized messages of unworthiness. Poet Kathy Freeperson (née Telesco) changed her name to indicate her changed perception of herself after leaving her father's tyrannical household. "Shut up, you're not a boy," was what she and her sisters heard growing up. Many Italian American women have heard the same message: "What right have you got to think?" or, "Girls can't have opinions."

Other Italian American writers have undergone a de-ethnicizing influence in higher education and have rejected their own experience (too often portrayed in film and TV as backward and ignorant) in pursuit of so-called "universal" values which are, transparently, Anglo-American ones. It is, in fact, absurd to think that one can universalize only from Anglo-American models and not Italian American, African American, or whatever American. Jewish writing in America has disproved this.

There is another reason, beyond the question of leisure time and education that Italian American women have taken long to become writers: they have not been used to intense self-inspection, to writing their thoughts in daily journals. They expressed themselves only in the condoned relief of the confessional where a male figure exonerates and blesses them.

But now the phenomenon of rising expectations has reached everyone. Italian American women have a generation or more of higher education, economic independence has been reached, and many have moved in adulthood from the working class of their birth to the professional middle class.

It is the era of self-birthing, an experience well known to women of ethnic minorities who, lacking models, have, in fact, made their own by creating themselves. Therefore, Tillie Olsen in her splendid book *Silences* says to all the silent women: create yourselves. There is much that is unwritten that needs to be written. Bring into literature what is not there now.

The words of Native American poet Joy Harjo are pertinent to us: "As I write, I create myself again and again. . . . We have learned to only touch so much. That is why I write. I want to touch more. . . . It frees me to believe in myself . . . to have voice, because I have to; it is my survival." [13]

Italian American women had long been denied the possibility of finding themselves in literature. How could they affirm an identity without becoming familiar with the models by which to perceive themselves? We are what we read, but, in the case of Italian American women writers, we could seldom read who we are.

It is unfortunate that Grazia Deledda, a strong, relevant, and highly pertinent model of an internationally significant writer embodying female values, someone for Italian Americans to emulate, is so little known here. Unfortunately, it was Simone de Beauvoir who became a model for some feminists.

Much more relevant as model woman and writer, especially to Italian American women, would have been Grazia Deledda. It is she who most captures the ideal of accomplishing her life's mission, both in her art and in her personal life. She was a self-motivated, achieving woman whose sense of her personal mission, movingly depicted in her autobiographical novel *Cosima*, was not set aside for marriage and maternity but successfully combined with those womanly roles.

Born in the most backward and isolated part of Sardinia in 1871, Deledda received only three years of schooling, but continued to teach herself and set herself the task of making her birthplace live in literature. She not only produced a steady stream of literary work (thirty-three novels, eighteen collections of stories, and other writings) in the face of great odds, but saw her life's work honored with a Nobel Prize for Literature in 1926.

Not to be underestimated is the equal achievement of Deledda's having combined family and art in her life. Grazia Deledda was not in the Anglo-American style of the childless great women writers like Jane Austen, George Eliot, Emily Dickinson, Willa Cather, Edith Wharton, Virginia Woolf; she had the support of her Northern Italian husband for her writing career. He and their sons, and family life as a whole, were the necessary sustenance to her art. She needed both.

Deledda fashioned her own destiny to become what she was told (by her family of origin and by society at large) was impossible: a great writer and a happily married mother. And she did it on her terms without denying herself either her art or her family. She is an amazing figure of achievement—more generous and honest towards life and work than the deceptive, coldly intellectual de Beauvoir who died telling us she would have been nothing without Sartre.

The name and story of Grazia Deledda was not in school books as I was growing up, but that is hardly surprising. What is surprising is that even with the new surge of interest in women writers and the resurrecting of old and forgotten authors, Deledda remains a forgotten woman.

Ellen Moers' *Literary Women* for instance, was a thick compendium of the great women writers, concentrating mainly on some sixty English, American, and French women of literature, with textual and bibliographic references to world wide women authors. Grazia Deledda is omitted. The only Italian authors mentioned are in the appendix: a line for Renaissance poet Vittoria Colonna, two for contemporary novelist Natalia Ginzburg.[14]

That Deledda should be so little known, so overlooked by publishers intent on rescuing so-called "lost" women writers from oblivion, so missing from the consciousness of Italian American women writers who need precisely and desparately the kind of validation she gives, is just another of the instances of silence in which we have seemed to struggle alone without models, without inspiration.

Unlike Christina Rossetti who wrote from an internal agony of renunciation and whose art was the bitter fruit of a masochistic abnegation, Deledda did not deny herself. She said she believed in only two things, the family and art for its own sake; these were the only beautiful and true things in life. Such a belief has a very Italian ring, and a very sound psychological basis in the feminist theory of Jean Baker Miller, as well as in the earlier writings of eminent psychologist Karen Horney who identified the dubious split in a woman of public versus domestic life (a dichotomy de Beauvoir insisted on) as "The Flight from Womanhood."

Another undiscovered Italian author is Sibilla Aleramo (1876-1960) whose novel *Una Donna* created a sensation in Europe at the beginning of the twentieth century, anticipating feminism and women's liberation by many decades. It was, in fact, in this autobiographical novel that the word "feminism" was used for the first time, and the author's personal suffering was related to the condition of all women.

Aleramo's novel has been translated into English[15] and is a gripping account of the psychological anguish of a creative woman's marriage to a small-minded and stultifying oppressor and her flight from him at great personal expense. It is a story of courage in a time and place that made her action and subsequent book utterly remarkable. But Aleramo, too, has been missing from the Italian American woman's resevoir of models.

Poets Jean Feraca and Rita Signorelli-Pappas are among a growing number of Italian American writers who have journeyed to Italy and have brought to bear on the ancestral land the unique vision of the American Italian. Feraca's collection *South from Rome: Il Mezzogiorno* is a strong evocation of a deeply felt archetypal Italy as veritable motherland, not merely a tourist pleasure land. And so, too, are Signorelli-Pappas' delicately incised "snapshot" poem-memories of Florence, Venice, and Sicily.

Even the relatively few literate and educated Italian women who emigrated to this country would have brought few models of women writers from their culture and few incentives to imitate them. This lack of a literary ancestry from the original culture has presented a significant problem to Italian American women. Whereas English and French women writers have always been strong within their national literatures, the tradition of women writers in Italy, noted by critic Sergio Pacifici in *A Guide to Contemporary Italian Literature*,[16] is relatively recent (notwithstanding those Renaissance exemplars who are often cited to prove that Italian women have long had voice and stature as authors but prove only that women writers in Italy were an isolated class phenomenon, not a national trend). The emergence of nationally known women authors coincided in the late nineteenth century with the unification of Italy as a nation, and the limited social emancipation of women. The liberated post-war Italy of the late 1940's, and the later feminist movement saw an increase of notable women writers and, says Pacifici, "Their increasing popularity with the public and the critics represents a significant cultural phenomenon, that may well herald a new era." Previously, relatively few women attained literary distinction and this, Pacifici asserts, was not surprising in a country where the social order was shaped so exclusively by men. The lack of critical attention he ascribes "Less to an objective question of artistic merit than to critical negligence or a pronounced prejudice against female talent."

This is no longer true in Italy where some very notable women have attained critical acclaim, but it was, until recently, notoriously true of Italian American literary men and scholars towards women of their background. The shadows into which Italian American women writers seem to have been cast come not only from the spotlight being thrown elsewhere by male critics, but quite surprisingly also from feminist critics.

In Annis Pratt's introduction to her *Archetypal Patterns in Women's Fiction*, she acknowledges having done, for that study, "close readings of more than three hundred women's novels." [17] Not one of those novels is by an Italian American woman. Writing on the novel of development, Pratt notes that in women's fiction it is more often the story of women "growing down" rather than "growing up." Yet Italian American women are writing of rising expectations and the quest for self-realization. One of these is Dorothy Bryant whose novel *Ella Price's Journal* is a classic example of the novel of growth—in this case, not of a young male, but of a middle-aged wife and mother.

Bryant's married name, under which she writes, cloaks her Italian American background, and her character, Ella Price, is an Anglo-Saxon Everywoman. But just as the outsider experience is heightened when told from the point of view of the double outsider (the Black, or the Jew), so, too, the woman's experience of being stifled in a male world might have been made even more compelling if Bryant had used her own Italian American background from which to create the story of a woman's growth towards autonomy. The weight of her tradition makes the Italian American woman's experience in moving out of marriage towards autonomy even more dramatic than that of the more assertive Anglo-Saxon woman. Did Bryant feel that her book would be given more consideration if she made her characters more "American?" That is a kind of self-censorship to which Italian American writers could be particularly susceptible.

Diana Cavallo's sensitive and introspective novel, *A Bridge of Leaves*, is written in the first person voice of a young man whose thoughts and memories record his inner journey from an early self-contained world to full immersion in the world of others that brings him to the crisis and resolution of his maturity. It is a true *bildungsroman*, and yet the opportunity to narrate it in the female voice to reflect the experience of the Italian American woman was not taken.

Many non-WASP writers have come to the fore brilliantly: Jewish women writers, African American, Asian American, Native American, Chicano. All have been collected, given critical attention, and, thereby, given presence. The Italian American woman writer seems to belong nowhere—not minority, not mainstream as Jewish and Black writers now are. She remains without champions or advocates or interpreters. The Italian American woman writer seems to have been stranded in a no-woman's land where there was small choice: either follow the omnipresent models that do not speak to her own particular experience, or write of her experience and know that it will be treated as of no importance, too "different" for critical attention.

All is not family; it is a dominant theme but not an exclusive one in Italian American literature. Present also is the same theme of alienation in an uncomprehending society that has been so well used by Black and Jewish writers. Cultural dichotomy, divided loyalties, the problems between generations, intermarriage, the problems between the sexes as men and women search for new roles, the tragic consequences of self-doubt and self-hate, placing honor before truth and possessive "love" before understanding, the stress on "catching up" with America, the loss of heritage—the Italian American experience has it all, and it has all to be told.

Italian American women who write are in the process of redefining themselves and family patterns; they are writing to create models that were never there for themselves; they are writing to know themselves. They write with positive affirmations. The personages they write about are afflated with hope, with the sense of change, with inspiration. They are not in the "deflation" style of many Anglo-American women writers whose work documents a long period of emptiness and futility in the wispy, stylish voice of minimalism. Italian American women write from the passion of the outsider experience, as women whose time has come. They are emerging, not receding, writers.

In a very true sense, the Italian American woman writer had to be a self-made person. Lacking a literary tradition, she worked in isolation without models and interpretive critics, struggling with an internal dialectic that was not only a barometer of inner doubts but also of subtle discrimination and rejection. She struggled to become an author, sustained only by the need and impetus of what she is doing.

Why this is so has to do not only with the inner blocks of her tradition, but very much, also, with the external obstacles of the surrounding society and its prevailing literary hegemonies.

## Literary Hegemonies and Oversights: The External Blocks

It becomes usual to hear that there are no Italian American writers of any value. Established critics make it so by not noticing them, professors of American literature say it in defense of why Italian American writing is not presented in course work, and an Italian American author of some prominence like Gay Talese says it in the confidence of being the exception. Readers believe it for the simple fact that except for *The Godfather,* they've heard of no other work; no author has been made familiar enough to them to come to mind. It is easy to dismiss what one doesn't know.

The spurious and circular reasoning is this: if there had been any Italian American first rate authors one would have heard of them. But once that was said of women as a group, too. Women writers and women's experience were by definition minor; the male experience was presented as the universal human one. Now we know better.

It is not that Italian Americans have not written work of value. It is that the dominant culture, working under its own rules and models, within a tight network of insiders who are editors, agents, salesmen, reviewers, and critics, is not eager to recognize and include in its lists that which does not reflect its own style, taste, and sense of what is worthwhile, or, more basically, the stereotypes that sell. After *The Godfather* phenomenon, mafia themes proved profitable, therefore the rash of books like Nicholas Pileggi's *Wiseguy: Life in a Mafia Family* and his cousin Gay Talese's *Honor Thy Father* on crime boss Joseph Bonanno that in turn spawned the editorial decision to have wife Rosalie Bonanno "write" a mass market book, *Mafia Marriage: My Story*. *Mafia Princess: Growing up in Sam Giancana's Family,* by Antoinette Giancana and Thomas C. Renner, *Mafia Wife* by Robin Moore with Barbara Fuca, Richard Condon's Prizzi books, and others belong to this sub-genre; they were then spun off into feature films and television mini-series. Thus a skewed and stereotypical vision linked to market potential drives out those books that do not deal with the Italian American experience in market-determined ways. Having first created a mafia market for the general public, publishers then defend their rejection of worthy Italian American material by saying there is no Italian American market for it!

Italian American novelists are not generically second-rate; they handle different material and handle it with the newness, and perhaps rawness, but also drive—of the just-born and self-made writer. Referring to the vividness of her heritage, a Jewish character in Rita Ciresi's title story from the collection *Mother Rocket* says to her WASP boyfriend, "You're so normal . . . so *American*. I mean, what do you people who aren't ethnic think about all day?"

Literature is not only in the great and practiced writer. It is also in the new voices which add to the store of human experience—the voices which, by enriching and extending the national literary achievement, become of permanent value.

Italian Americans who accept, uncritically, the estimate of their denigrators that they are unworthy of attention, have let themselves be defined in a way that writers of other ethnic groups will no longer tolerate. Rather than examine an excluding system and question its premises, critics have accepted that Italian Americans don't read, therefore they don't buy books, therefore publishers are justified in not publishing Italian American writers. This is not valid reasoning; it is prejudice camouflaged as market research.

We are long past the stage of Italian Americans being represented by hordes of illiterate just-arrived immigrants. At the start of the twenty-first century it is egregiously discriminatory still to single out an ethnic group and say its members don't read or buy books. Yet publishers continue to use this worn out red herring to justify not publishing more Italian American authors, even though Italian Americans do not write to be read only by Italian Americans any more than the West Indian American author Derek Walcott writes only for West Indian Americans. When Amy Tan's *Joy Luck Club* was published and became an enormous best seller, it was not because it was aimed at a restricted Asian-American market—*everyone* bought and read the book. It is inconceivable that the publishers of Richard Rodriguez or Sandra Cisneros think only in terms of a Hispanic market for their work or that Louise Erdrich's books are only for a Native American market. The fact is that all those writers are Americans, writing for the whole American public and not just parts of it. The same is true of Italian Americans.

A sub-category of "ethnic writing" was contrived as the catch-all for what wasn't mainstream. This is itself a peculiar notion: a mainstream is not a body unto itself but exists by being fed from tributaries and in literature those tributaries are the feeders that contribute to the whole body of the national literature. That the writings of some American writers are considered marginal and not given entry to the cultural mainstream of the American literary world but exist, at best, in a backwater of folklore and curiosities, is an outdated concept that is finally being addressed in the outpouring of multicultural writing. In 1992 this was officially recognized when Derek Walcott was awarded the Nobel Prize in Literature for his "multi-cultural vision and commitment." The opening may have come at last for many writers who had been overlooked as ethnic or marginal because of the homogenizing tendency to mirror a society of uniform values rather than the lively cultural pluralism which is the reality of American life.

It can be fairly claimed that Italian American writing in a limited amount *did* and *does* get published and that there is no concerted effort to keep Italian American authors from being published. Thus, John Fante's inspired production (*Wait until Spring, Bandini!, Ask the Dust,* and *Dago Red*) and other novels did get published. But they were not really noticed or taken up in any way. They languished and died for want of advocates.

It can also be said that there is no concerted conspiracy of silence on the part of reviewers or literary critics to exclude mention of Italian American writing. How could there be! To organize a conspiracy would imply recognition of a body of literature that is, instead, more conveniently emarginated by simply being ignored.

A novel using Italian American material, when written by an Italian American author, is all but invisible while the use of that material by authors of other backgrounds seems to receive attention as, for instance, *The Immigrants* by Howard Fast, *The Little Conquerors* by Ann Abelson, *Principato* by Thomas McHale, *Household Saints* by Francine Prose, *Fly Away Home* by Marge Piercy, and the very successful stage and screenplays *Moonstruck* and *Italian American Reconciliation* by John Patrick Shanley.

In a country this size, comprised of such rich and varied strains, there is room for all facets of literary expression and there should be the opportunity to become familiar with them. But that is not the case. There are hierarchies and hegemonies which, consciously or not, promote and decide what is literature and what is not. The facts of literary life are elementary: it is not simply publication, but attention before and after that counts.

Mary Gordon once told an Authors Guild symposium, "Reviews have a tremendous impact on book sales . . . books which are not reviewed are buried." [18] And that is what happens to the overwhelming majority of books that are published without being signaled for attention by powerful names; they die. Unfortunately Italian American authors have no national advocates either from within their group or from without.

Nothing exists comparable to the so-called Jewish family of editors and critics who promote their own; or the group of Black writers who, feeling that Toni Morrison was not receiving adequate recognition, published in the *New York Times Book Review* a "testament of thanks" to Morrison for advancing "the moral and artistic standards by which we must measure the daring and the love of our national imagination and our collective intelligence as people." *That* is support.

Books that are not reviewed in the *New York Times,* the closest thing we have to a national paper, are seldom picked up elsewhere along the tightly linked chain of literary life. Literary achievement is gauged by appearance in required reading lists, literature course outlines, textbooks, anthologies, critical appraisal, book reviews, bibliographies, and even jacket blurbs. All things that Italian American writers have been largely excluded from because they lack the interest and support of well-placed people to boost them.

Strategies exist to exclude writing that is considered marginal. Jules Chametzky, a scholar of cultural pluralism as reflected in American literature, has shown how the publication of regional literature became, toward the end of the nineteenth century, "a strategy for ignoring or minimizing social issues of great signficance." [19] Regional novels substituted for those dealing with race, class, the new money-power, America's new ethnic composition, and the challenges to engrained social assumptions and mores. Ignoring the themes that called for serious literary treatment but could upset notions of a unified national culture, local color and regional literature which reinforced notions of a basically homogeneous rather than a conflicted nation and culture was focused on by editors and accepted by the public.

Katherine Newman, an ethnic literary scholar and critic, has proposed discarding many of the old theories of American Literature "since they were fitted to a specific body of literature: that of the Anglo-American seaboard culture." [20] Taking a wider view of the whole oeuvre, other characteristics can be discerned, and she sees one characteristic of American literature (particularly relevant from the ethnic perspective) being eccentricity in its exact meaning of being off-center, asymmetrical, irregular, uneven. This explains the uniqueness and marvelous strangeness of Pietro Di Donato's powerful 1939 novel, *Christ in Concrete.* It explains, also, other facets of Italian American fiction, with its "extraneous" material, eccentricity of style and language, distortions of character like the raging father in John Fante's *Brotherhood of the Grape,* and the often ambiguous attitude of the implied authors. That is not to be wondered at; Newman quotes other studies to show that implied authors of ethnic novels tend to be schizoid, that is, in conflict between the values of their ethnic groups and those of the majority group.

This very off-centeredness (and it is relevant to note that Barbara Grizzuti Harrison's collection of intelligent essays is aptly entitled *Off Center*) of Italian American literature should be valuable in itself. Ethnic literary scholarship stands for understanding material that, before, in a policy of literary apartheid, was often excluded because measured by non-applicable standards.

Like the feminists, ethnic literary scholars opt for a humanist criticism that transcends narrow views of what people are or should be; it should breach the Establishment walls that Mario Puzo, in his own way, set out to scale by writing *The Godfather.* For it was when he made the deliberate effort to embrace the condoned formulae and stereotypical characters of mainstream writing that Puzo was admitted to the club of visible writers. Applauding him for playing the game was Rose Basile Green in *The Italian American Novel* when she noted, "An Italian American novelist, Mario Puzo, has pried open the box that has secreted the sacred blackballs of the American literary club." [21]

But it is not that kind of pandering to violent themes nor the deliberate commercialization of the story that should relate Italian American fiction to the American mainstream. Rather, it is another characteristic of American literature that Newman identified as deriving from the pressure of pluralism: "The chief preoccupation of our writers is *choice-making.*" [22]

The necessity of choice—the old ways or the new, one's loyalty to family or self—has always been implicit in the main thrust of Italian American writing. Italian Americans are laden with conflicted choices in loyalties and roles, with contradictions within the tradition, with ambivalence in life. It is not always a cause for optimism—seeking resolution of conflict is painful—but it *is* affirmation, it is using one's native strength and wit, it is autonomy. And that seems to be the direction toward which Italian American writing is propelled.

The women authors of Italian American background who had dealt with their ethnic material have been the ephemerids of literature, fated to have a creative life-span as brief as that of the mayfly. They were born, in a literary sense, already out of step by virtue of their themes. They were given no notice by reviewers, which meant they went out of print swiftly and receded into the silence from which they came without having made a ripple in the mainstream of American writing. It is a demoralizing and chastizing experience. A writer must be given the opportunity to publish at least two or three books in order to have a substantial voice, a presence. Many Italian American women never get beyond the first book because the lack of response and attention makes a publisher unwilling to risk further. Frequently a complete literary oeuvre remains unknown, unavailable. Italian American male authors have undoubtedly faced these same barriers as well.

Literary history is falsified if it doesn't record all voices and give access to these voices by publishing, keeping in print, and making part of study courses those writers who are not merely the commercially prominent ones of the dominant tradition. As Newman says, the critical function is to examine works on their own aesthetic terms, to relate them to the entire corpus of American Literature, and to overcome the internalized stereotypes and cultural myths that have caused critical myopia.

Publishers have been slow to receive Italian Americans outside of the safe stereotypes of a warm people with comical behavior *(Mount Allegro, Brotherhood of the Grape)* or mafia criminals and connections. They are cool to the complexities of human nature portrayed in minority or ethnic groups. They prefer racial tensions for Blacks, gangsterism and family solidarity for Italians, and complicated emotions or angst only in WASPs or Jews.

Genevieve Belfiglio, publisher of *Real Fiction,* explained that she founded that publication of short stories out of frustration, because her experience was that "Major publishing firms attempt to mainstream fiction, at the expense not only of writers, but readers as well since only a narrow range of experience and style is acceptable."[23] This is confirmed by publishers who accept material that conforms to their notion of what the market wants; it fosters sales, not literature.

Publishers say they cannot afford to be crusaders. But black writer Zora Neale Hurston replied that she refused to be humbled by second place in a contest she never designed, and she identified what comes out of safe, marketable publishing as candidates for the American Museum of Unnatural History, i.e., a weird collection of stereotypes and non-dimensional figures that can be taken in at a glance: the expressionless American Indian, the shuffling Negro, the inarticulate Italian, etc.[24]

Before it was published in 1986, my novel *Love in the Middle Ages* was rejected by one publisher because it didn't "seem right" that the Italian American woman character was the achiever and her Jewish lover was not; it was said to appear anti-semitic and it was suggested that the roles be reversed. Of course! then the formula would have been observed, the same one that John Sayles used in his film, *Baby, It's You,* the story of two high school lovers: he's an Italian greaser who takes woodwork and she's a Jewish princess who's the president of the Drama Club and headed for Sarah Lawrence. She, it's understood, will get over her transitory sexual attraction to Sheik (his nickname derives from a condom) because she is going to be someone and he isn't. Hardly anyone of Italian American background hasn't encountered the use of that slur in real life. With Dorothy Bryant (who was then Dorothy Calvetti, and at the top of her class), it occurred when a teacher said to her, "You can't be Italian, where were your people from?" "Near Turin," said Dorothy. "Then," said the teacher, relieved, "they could be of Germanic origin."

The exclusionary practices in the publishing world where Italian Americans are not perceived as literary writers but, at best, writers of romance, suspense, or Young Adult books, seem to parallel the school's tracking ones: Italian Americans were routinely tracked into vocational courses rather than college oriented ones. In her lead essay in *Crossing Ocean Parkway: Readings by an Italian American Daughter,* Marianna De Marco Torgovnick described her high school experience: "Although my scores are superb, the guidance counselor has recommended the secretarial track; when I protested, the conference with my parents was arranged. . . . My father also prefers the secretarial track, but he wavers, half proud of my aberrantly high scores, half worried. I press the attack, saying that if I were Jewish I would have been placed, without question, in the academic track. . . . I am allowed to insist on the change into the academic track."

Publishers do not like Italian American characters to be individuals, to be complex, to be alive and contradictory, subject to the pulls of tensions and defeats of doubt, subject to losses and gains and changes. Instead the cultural myth perceives them in very rigid, demeaning, stick-figure dimensions. And so Italian American authors often get around this by giving their characters non-Italian names, disguising their material.

That Italian American women writers have been underpublished is undeniable. Just as exclusionary, however, is that the few who are published are not kept on record and made accessible, even bibliographically, in libraries and in study courses. Not only do Italian American women writing their own stories publish with great difficulty, but once in print, they must confront an established cadre of criticism that seems totally devoid of the kind of insight that could relate to their work.

Italian American names were notably missing in essays such as the *New York Times'* "Women Playwrights: New Voice for the Theater" where no mention was made of Donna DeMatteo, Karen Malpede, or even Nina Faso, producer of *Godspell.* In the *Times* piece "Brooklyn, Borough of Writers," a lot of names were dropped but not those of authors Barbara Grizzuti Harrison or Daniela Gioseffi who were both published Brooklynites at that time.[25]

It is not only in reviews and essays, but also in feature articles and in letters it chooses not to print (as compared to what it does) that the *Times* can emarginate authors and practice a kind of censorship.

Herbert Mitgang began a *Times* review of Italian stories with this statement: "Sicily is better known as the spawning ground of the Mafia than as the home place of an unusually large number of pioneering novelists, poets, and playwrights." Certainly a back-handed way of acknowledging (without naming them) literary giants like Verga, Pirandello, Vittorini, Sciascia, and

Lampedusa. And even as Mitgang managed to slip in the *Times'* favorite M-word.

*Times* film reviewer Caryn James wrote of the film *Once Around,* "It is too obvious to say that Francis Ford Coppola and Martin Scorsese capture the texture of Italian-American families more sharply than Lasse Hallstrom (director of *Once Around).* What matters is that *The Godfather* and *Goodfellas* create *believable* ethnic characters instead of shallow ethnic types."

This weighted verdict on "believable" Italian American characters is all the more offensive since Ms. James had previously been on record as sensitive to poor depictions of other ethnic groups: reviewing the Spike Lee film, *Mo' Better Blues,* she called the seamy characterizations of Mo and Josh Flatbush "disturbing Jewish stereotypes." It is not unusual that the prevailing climate at the *Times* allows a double standard for what is "good" stereotyping as against what is "disturbing."

By not reviewing authors, by the almost zero presence of Italian American surnames on bylines, and even by neglecting our letters to the Editor, the *Times* contributes to a perceived lack of Italian American status and a negative cultural image. This, in turn, reinforces the low self-esteem that has been documented among Italian American students as contributing to a high dropout rate in the New York City school system.

On the other hand, coverage of Italian American affairs becomes full when a reputed Mafia godfather or an incident of racism is being covered. It was apparent in reading the reportage of the Bensonhurst or Howard Beach incidents that there was a peculiar slant in the way Italian Americans were depicted and their speech reported, while no probing effort was made to understand the complexity of their community fears and frustrations. Disconcerting was the *New York Times'* emphasis on Italian Americans' poor use of language on the one hand, while on the other it seems to exclude many of us writers who are practiced users of language from its pages.

Then there were the weighted descriptions of people in the neighborhood: "Young women with baroque hair and their names spelled out in gold necklaces wear tight slacks and spike heels." Were there ever equivalent stories on Blacks or Hispanics or Jews or Koreans so peppered with odd words and phrases, or such personal descriptions, to single them out in a deprecating way? Such personalizing has even appeared gratuitously in a theater review where critic David Richards took note of "Laura San Giacomo's vulgarity" and "native sullenness" and then decided that this fine actress (just think of her in *Sex, Lies, and Videotape)* has little acting skill to accompany those offensive personal attributes.

Multiplied inexorably, year after year, author after author, and never redressed, or even acknowledged, this kind of press adds to a general misperception and mockery of a whole group that is coupled with a reluctance to review their books.

After the reviewer, it is the critic who takes the long view and decides what becomes part of the canon. The African American critic Henry Louis Gates, Jr. has done extraordinary service to the career of Toni Morrison. He wrote of her and brought her to national attention. There has been no equivalent Italian American critic either with a national audience, or with an agenda to further the career of an Italian American writer.

Next in the ring of exclusion, editors of collections and bibliographic tools, like the powerful H. W.Wilson Company, close admittance into their bibliographic retrieval tools to those who have not been reviewed in the publications which the Wilson Company chooses to scan. Its *Book Review Digest* lists fiction reviewed in at least four journals on Wilson's approved list of some one hundred sources (compared to the Gale Company's *Book Review Index,* which reports on any book reviewed, no matter how often and no matter where, from four hundred twenty-two sources.) The Wilson Company effectively discriminates against ethnic, counter-culture, or minority writers who are reviewed in journals outside conventional sources. In effect, the reviewing media, not the book itself is being judged. Omitted from the *Book Review Digest,* for instance, have been books by Mary Caponegro, Cris Mazza, Jeanne Schinto, and Mary-Ann Tirone Smith. Such distortion of what comprises writing by and about a particular ethnic group as part of the national literature is another aspect of literary apartheid.

When teachers, editors, or compilers consult the Wilson volumes for, say, the names of authors who are writing about Italian Americans so that they can be included in syllabi, presented at conferences, studied and commented on, they are naturally led to the conclusion that there are pitifully few Italian American authors, and of those few, *no women at all.* Without entry in Wilson's *Short Story Index, Fiction Catalog, Book Review Digest, Standard Catalog for Public Libraries* etc., the non-listed author becomes a "lost" one—difficult for a teacher, compiler, or reseracher to pick up except by hearsay.

I would never suggest that only Italian Americans can write of themselves. But to emphasize, as the *Fiction Catalog* does, that the "the best fiction" on Italian Americans is done by non-Italian American authors is to create a record that is skewed, biased, and eminently flawed.

By ignoring the multicultural literary reality of the second half of the twentieth century in the United States, the Wilson library tools have made themselves irrelevant to what is happening in American Literature and cannot be consulted as a reliable guide to what fiction is being produced, published, and read in representation of various American ethnic groups.

William Vance who produced the notable two-volume work *America's Rome* (1989) included only three Italian American writers (William Murray, John Ciardi, and Dana Gioia) in his examination of American fiction writers and poets in Rome noting that a lack of visibility led him to conclude that possibly there weren't many Italian American writers.

The lack of visibility Professor Vance refered to is directly affected by exclusions from the *Fiction Catalog*. From the inception of subject listings in 1941 through the thirteenth edition of 1996, the listings under the subject heads "Italian Americans" or "Italians in the United States" have been quite ludicrous.

The Wilson Company persists in demeaning the category "Italian Americans" with its longest running entry (listed since 1957!), Max Shulman's outdated satire of suburbia, *Rally Round the Flag, Boys*. Even when available Shulman's slight novel was entirely inappropriate as representative of Italian Americans, using them only as stereotypes along with the two other groups being lampooned, New England Yankees and New York commuters. The only other entries in the *Fiction Catalog* category "Italian Americans" were for Reynolds Price and Anna Quindlen.

Almost equally equivocal is a previous listing under "Italians—New York, NY," which lists Jimmy Breslin, Bernard Malamud, Howard Fast, Mario Puzo, Francine Prose, Richard Condon, and Robert J. Waller as having written on the subject. One has to wonder why only one Italian American—Mario Puzo, represented not by his most respected book *The Fortunate Pilgrim* but by *The Godfather*—was thought to have written meaningfully on the subject. Or why, in one edition, Mary Lee Settle's book about Italian coal miners in West Virginia was featured, but not Denise Giardina's well received works on the same subject, *Storming Heaven* and *The Unquiet Earth*. Or why there was a heading "Jews in Vermont" but none for "Italians in Vermont" overlooking Mari Tomasi's novel *Like Lesser Gods* on the Italian granite workers in Vermont.

When law professor Thomas Shaffer sent me a reprint from the *Notre Dame Law Review* where novels on Italian Americans were mentioned, he wrote, "I turned up *Umbertina* as soon as I began to do research on Italian Americans. I cannot remember who recommended it. . . . If I were asked today where to begin such an inquiry I would recommend *Umbertina* above all else." And yet, if he had tried to locate source material through reference guides such as the Wilson *Fiction Catalog*, he would never have found my work listed.

Novels by Italian American women writers on Italian American subjects have never been listed by the Wilson Catalog excepting one by the unidentifiably Italian American, Anna Quindlen.

It is, again, for Italian American women writers like never having been published at all except for that minute inner circle of friends who may have heard personally of the event; certainly such work is not "published" in the true sense of being made public and accessible. It's as if the writing of Italian American women were some fastidiously secret pursuit, a distilling of a rare liqueur not to be shared.

There are other areas of bibliographic oversight:

- no Italian American novels were listed in the category of family chronicles in the bibliography of *American Historical Fiction* until the fifth edition.

- through the fourth revision of the *Literary History of the United States*, which is still the current edition in library holdings, no mention is made of authors of Italian American background except for the 18th century political writer Filippo Mazzei and Mozart's librettist, Lorenzo Da Ponte.

- *Contemporary Literary Critics,* St. Martin's, 1977, lists 115 American and British critics. Missing, along with the eminent critic Bernard DeVoto, is any other Italian name.

- in *The Ethnic American Woman* (1978), a collection of writings of ninety-five women authors from twenty-four ethnic groups, the Italian American group is represented by one entry, the writer of a scholarly paper, as compared to other groups amply represented by literary writers of novels and poetry.

- *The Columbia Literary History of the United States* (1988) is woefully inadequate in citing two 19th authors of "ghetto" novels and then skipping entire generations of Italian American writers such as Di Donato, Tomasi, Fante et al to arrive at the "new journalism" as practiced by Gay Talese.

- *American Women Writers* (1979–82) in the four volumes edited by Lina Mainiero, includes only one Italian American woman writer and that one, Frances Winwar, is quite unidentifiable by her pen name. Mainiero told me she was predisposed to include Italian American women in the collection but said there were none that she could find; unless writers had been carried in anthologies or mentioned in literary criticism, or had won awards, there was no way to locate them. That rationale is not at all credible: Mari Tomasi had already been named one of ten outstanding novelists of the year in 1940. *Buying Time: An Anthology Celebrating 20 Years of the Literature Program of the National Endowment for the Arts* was published prior to the time of Mainiero's compilation and lists these National Endowment for the Arts recipients, all of them of Italian American background: Helen Barolini, Diane di Prima, Joan Castagnoni Eades, Rina Ferrarelli, Michele Linfante, and Leslie Scalapino. Other Italian American women have been winners of state Arts Council grants and other literary awards. Did the preconception that there were no Italian American women writers, cancel out the motivation for a search? In the 1995 supplement to *American Women Writers,* three authors from *The Dream Book* appear: Diane di Prima, Sandra M. Gilbert, and Mary Gordon.

- *American Women Poets* (1986), of which Harold Bloom is the editor, and *Modern American Women Writers* (1991), edited by Elaine Showalter, both omit Diane di Prima, the most important counter-culture woman poet of the 1950s and still actively writing.

These examples reinforce the self-perpetuating myth on the part of readers, editors, professors (and the demoralizing perception among Italian Americans themselves) that Italian American literature *is* second rate because if it weren't, it would be included in reference tools and collections; would be issued in paperback or series; would be anthologized, collected, selected, recommended, discussed, analyzed, and put in course offerings.

Exclusion leads Italian American writers to the Kafkesque conviction that their writing is not worthy of being included. To emerge from this dismal swamp requires enlightenment on the part of denigrators; an end to stereotyping Italian Americans in the media and in publishing; a wide diffusion of the literary contributions made by Italian American writers; an increase in sensitivity on the part of reviewers and critics and their ability to explicate the particular experience and relate it to the dominant culture; and teachers who will promulgate the work because they need it and want it but have to know *it is there!*

Among ethnic groups, Jews have become excellent critics, literary scholars, and tastemakers. The officially recognized minority groups—Hispanic Americans, Asian Americans, African Americans and Native Americans—have benefited by grants and the critical attention of liberals, eager to right the wrongs of racism, and are doing some of the most interesting work that is being published today. There is an abundance of anthologies and collections of multicultural writing done by minority authors. They have been championed by the Before Columbus Foundation, which has been giving out American Book Awards since 1978 that, for the first time, respect and honor excellence in American literature without regard to best-seller lists or publishers' promotion.

In the wake of the feminist movement, the lost women writers of the past have been exhumed, explained, reprinted and made known. They have been published by The Feminist Press and university presses, and have become entries in the volumes of *Notable American Women* and other sets. Naturally, Anglo-American women predominate, but entries from other groups can be found, that is except for the Italian American group. One is left to ask why Sister Blandina Segale or Renata Brunorini, a playwright and actress at the beginning of this century, or novelist Mari Tomasi are not entered when many more marginal women of Anglo-American background are. The Feminist Press, since its inception in 1970 has had a mission of recuperating women authors who were lost or neglected, but it wasn't until 1997 that Tina DeRosa's *Paperfish* became the first Italian American novel on their list.

Editors and publishers used to engage in a great deal of "vertical" expansion with still more diaries and autobiographies of unknown "American housewives and writers," predominantly of Anglo-Saxon origin, and always documenting the same experiences. Attempts to go horizontally into truly new areas to find other American voices has resulted in the inclusion of many minority women writers, but not yet an Italian American writer although we have recently had Louise DeSalvo's memoir *Vertigo*, Barbara Grizzuti Harrison's *An Accidental Autobiography*, and the re-issue of Diane di Prima's *Memoirs of a Beatnik*. In the almost two decades that have followed the first publication of *The Dream Book*, I trusted that omissions of Italian American women authors from collections would be redressed. Yet two works of 1999 continue the exclusions: despite their focus on grandmothers, no writers of Italian American background are included in *Grandmothers: Granddaughters Remember*. And again, in *The Norton Anthology of American Autobiography*, the single entry by an Italian American woman is not from any of the writers mentioned above, but by a Norton editor.

In the last decade and a half of the century, Italian American women writers have received awards for work of distinction: Mary Bush and Cris Mazza received PEN/Nelson Algren awards for Fiction; Jeanne Schinto's story "Caddies' Day" was among the twenty *Best American Stories 1984* where Mary Caponegro was listed in the Honorable Mentions. In 1991 Caponegro won the American Academy's Prix de Rome; Agnes Rossi's first collection of short stories was awarded New York University's first fiction prize and publication by that press; Rita Ciresi's collection *Mother Rocket* won a Flannery O'Connor Award for Short Fiction, and Donna Masini's poetry collection *That Kind of Danger* was the winner of the 1993 Barnard New Women Poets Prize. The May Sarton Award to Maria Mazziotti Gillan was not only in recognition of her poetry, but also for efforts to difuse poetry to unreached audiences through her founding and directing of the Paterson Poetry Center.

The difference between neglect and respect can be the network of support which one has: in the academic world, in the publishing industry, with reviewers of people in the media; recommendations for writers' colonies, panel appearances, grants, and readings all count. It is an America still to be discovered by Italian American women writers.

## Affirmations

Though the exclusions for Italian American women as writers have been great and the barriers formidable, still there is an answer. If others have not taken the subject of Italian American writing seriously, the writers can do so by becoming themselves the teachers and critics of their experience. That is what Black women writers have said and done. And that is what our own tradition counsels: in the Sicilian version of the Noah's Ark story, after God chose two of all His creatures to go aboard the ark, the fleas found they had been forgotten. So they slipped on by getting into Noah's beard. As the Sicilians say, "If God forgets us, we must use our own wits."

An answer also lies in time—time for Italian American women writers to become economically able to support their writing; and time to add depth to the habit of writing, to explore and experiment stylistically with the language, to re-tell old stories with new insights, to articulate in an authentic way in literature the Italian American experience.

The evidence shows that an Italian American literary record exists and that women are part of it. Yet that body of work remains largely unreissued by publishers and unexamined by critics; it has still to be made known to a wide public and put into libraries and on reading lists. For Italian American women it is a continuing "ordeal of the woman writer"—the words identifying a tape recorded conversation by Erica Jong, Marge Piercy and Toni Morrison to discuss the difficulties *they* faced in getting recognition. Each of them was published and reviewed at the time, and if those three prominent authors could speak of "ordeal," it makes all the more compelling by comparison the hurdles faced by disadvantaged Italian American women writers. Earlier, Virginia Woolf, though privileged by birth with connections to the English literary milieu and intellectual elite, had lamented the obstacles and self-doubt inherent in being a woman writer. How hollow those laments sound to the aspiring writer with the wrong name, with no contacts or associations within the publishing network, and with few or no literary antecedents! For Italian American women who have been struggling upward from distances of poor education, dependency, the burden of traditional roles, and prejudicial stereotyping in the publishing world, the obstacles to their acceptance as writers are still formidable.

A whole new form of literary criticism based on psychoanalyst Karen Horney's theories, and the new insights from ethnotherapy, could most appropriately be applied to developing Italian American writing. Horney had a comprehensive approach to experience, and, proceeding from her studies of alienation, her work focused on the unblocking of neuroses that hindered growth of personality and the full maturation of a person. Her concrete focus is extremely relevant to an analysis of realistic literature and very applicable to the feelings of unworthiness, low expectations, and self-doubt experienced and revealed by Italian American women. Dr. Bernard Paris, applying Horney's theories to the study of literature, has identified a Third Force psychology that goes beyond Freudianism and behaviorism to recognize a third principle—the evolutionary and constructive force in human beings that represents the drive toward self-actualization.[26] This seems extremely applicable to the growth-oriented direction of Italian American writing, which often proceeds from a sense of alienation to reach toward newly articulated self-awareness. Further, cultures themselves can be evaluated in terms of a universal norm of psychological health, for misguided values can also manifest in societies as a whole. As Dr. Paris has stated, "Those things are good in a culture which satisfy the basic needs of its members and foster their full human growth, those things are bad which frustrate the basic needs and induce self-alienation."[27] Some cultures, in effect, demand too enormous a ransom to release the individual from benevolent captivity.

Depth psychologist Angelyn Spignesi set out on a bold new track in her first book, *Starving Women.* Exploring the female psyche, she finds the anorexic woman enacts a war against traditions binding her to earth, food, body, and reproduction. In wording seemingly colored by her own background, she identifies the anorexic as "the carrier of the starving woman in every person, the female starving to be nourished by the underworld from which she has been cut off for centuries,"[28] confined as she was to the world of matter *(mater)* and the literal kitchen, and identified exclusively with aspects of emotion and nurturance, while men were free to scale the heights of intellectual soaring or descend to the imaginative night realm of the other "under" world. An unwitting affirmation of Spignesi's starving woman theory was given me by the novelist Kenny Marotta when he observed of the female characters in *Umbertina,* "all those psychically malnourished, starving women, all women with a doomed wish for a nurturing mother, all with the painful vacuum they must mourn."

More recently Donna Masini's poem "Hunger," in her award winning collection *That Kind of Danger,* reiterates the theme:

> Deprived of a kind of salt I grew
> to an insatiable craving.
> I tried to eat rocks. I snapped
> shut on a terrible hunger.

Spignesi's search for the female self is quite opposite to Camille Paglia's defense of a patriarchal vision of culture; in Spignesi's view, an artifical opposition between Mother and Father resulted in the male-female dichotomy that is at the bottom of Western civilization. The culture has been set up to perpetuate oppostion—the separation between Father and Mother and all that it implies in right/wrong, good/bad.

Spignesi does not propose destroying Father to enthrone Mother, but of reviewing the narrow domination of one psyche (the male) and its one 'way-of-seeing' while more deeply exploring the female psyche. She suggests (quite in contrast to Paglia's old-fashioned and contentious system of opposition between Apollonian male and Dionysian female) that we no longer imagine the female as opposite; by refusing to think in opposites, we can, instead take "Mother and Father as continually in motion, without hierarchy, within one another yet with precise distinction and differentiation."[29]

Spignesi, more original and independent than Paglia, ventures into the new realm of women's unconscious rather than seconding what has been predetermined by previous *male* texts. Spignesi's work is an incisive insight into the position of women vis-à-vis their mothers, and especially pertinent to Italian American women who are less focused on by their mothers than are sons, first, and then husbands—a finding reinforced by Dr. Aileen Riotto Sirey's work in ethnotherapy.

Spignesi's is a clear call to creative women: "an invitation to all of us "hysterics" to begin to write on our own from the psyche which is our own and inherently that of woman. . . . It is time for women to enter the unfamiliar chasm of our own psychological terrain and to carry this up in aesthetic endeavour."[30] Her emphasis on that goal is very much in the tradition of those who articulated the bridge from the dream realm to literary imagination.

Among the theoretical questions that scholar Katherine Newman poses for a critical frame work by which to evaluate ethnic literature is this: what are the causes that bring about the production of literature by writers of an ethnic group? To which Italian American women could answer: the need to know ourselves, to create our models, to write the stories that need telling, and to bring into being the works that are missing and that need to be read.

In the broadest sense, that is the function of literature. Literature gives us ourselves.

As a group, Italian American women have angles of vision and particular perceptions that are a needed part of the revitalizing multicultural factor in this country's national literature. Using the same strengths of their foremothers, but now for artistic rather than economic growth, Italian American women can authorize themselves to give their story to waiting readers.

Perhaps the first step is the keeping of journals, the writing of autobiography or memoirs. The volume *Women's Autobiography* contains a whole chapter entitled "In Search of the Black Self," affords much material by Anglo-American and Jewish women, but has not a single entry for an Italian American woman such as an excerpt from Sister Blandina's Journal, Bella Visono Dodd's *School of Darkness,* Barbara Grizzuti Harrison's memoir of growing up as a Jehovah's Witness, *Visions of Glory,* or Diane di Prima's *Memoirs of a Beatnik.*

A body of autobiographical work has still to be developed to illuminate points of contact with a common past as well as to reveal the inner lives of Italian American women. Black women have realized the importance of the personal voice as part of the long, united march toward recognition. Black autobiographies, they say, help rend the veil of white definitions that misrepresent a person to him—or herself and to the world. Creating a new identity can create a new literature.

In the past the Italian American woman expressed herself orally. The oral history narrators were natural poets as in the case of "Hands: A Love Poem," transcribed from his mother's spoken words by Ross Talarico and appearing in Janet Zandy's collection, *Calling Home: Working Class Women Writing*.

The great range of poetry by Italian American women extends from the oral tradition to today's stylistic sophistication and eroticism, from the intimate revelations of poets Daniela Gioseffi and Maria Mazziotti Gillan, to Sandra Gilbert's accomplished and warmly personal family recollections in her collection *Blood Pressure* (1988) and to the recent poetry collection so aptly titled *Campanile* with its Italian echo of one's home place by Southwestern poet Linda Monacelli-Johnson. Or, a poet like Rose Romano might be her own publisher and focus on separatism. Like a stand-up comedian, in a collection called *Vendetta*, Romano stresses a blue-collar past and present, writes fast and smart, and presents herself defiantly vaunting all her differences ("I'm an olive Sicilian-Italian-American Lesbian / the scum of the scum of the scum"). At a total stylistic remove is the superb linguistic and surrealist transcendence of the more accomplished poets Ree Dragonette and Leslie Scalapino.

Unique in her half-century of writing is Diane di Prima who, having started on an academic route, dropped out to use her drive in a highly original way. She has become the most enduring of the '50s counter-culture poets, a Zen teacher, an activist in social causes, and the founder of a school in San Francisco. Even when not specifically evoking an Italian American milieu, Diane di Prima's prodigious material has a rich thread of her Italian American background running through it—her preoccupation with the children, the meals, the honoring of her anarchist grandfather.

The Italian American woman is more confident now of her place in the world and this is mirrored through the emergence of an educated and emancipated generation which is more given to looking out at a world greater than that mirrored in family. These are the young women who continue their education, have careers, marry outside their group, and ecumenically fashion a mode of living from both traditions.

They signify a new school of young women writers of Italian American background who easily "pass" into the American mainstream of writing without overt ethnic tones in their material to keep them emarginated; some, despite Italian surnames, are only partially of Italian heritage as, for instance, Tina De Rosa, Carole Maso, Leslie Scalapino, Mary Caponegro, Anna Quindlen, and Agnes Rossi. Intermarriage has bequeathed a new generation of writers who bring a differing viewpoint to their material.

Carole Maso's acclaimed first novel, *Ghost Dance*, introduced two Italian American grandparents portrayed with remarkable insight and understanding, who nonetheless remained free of the emotional overlay either of reverence or bitterness with which an older generation of Italian American writers might have imbued them. Maso writes with great literary mastery, deliberately eschewing the linear narrative mode (associated with male dominance of the novel form) for a more circular weaving and interlacing—female skills—of tempi and themes.

Mary Bush (originally Bucci) writes obliquely of the Italian American experience, but it can be intuited in her short fiction collection *A Place of Light*, which was called "compelling stories of everyday existence . . . a treasury of the working-class American voice." Also in that voice are certain nuances and overtones in the family ties that are strongly Italian American. In her collection, the story "Bread" centers on a young girl's impressions as she recovers from an operation, not yet convinced she's survived, and set against an easily recognizable Italian American background. Ole Papa in her story "Difficult Passage" has all the resonance of the old Italian patriarch. Both stories are not Italian American per se but the authenticity of tone identifies them.

Jeanne Schinto (the spelling of whose surname, Scinto, was remedied to help Americans pronounce a soft "c" in the Italian way), is a fiction writer of great promise, who moves easily between stories of an Italian American milieu such as "The Boathouse," "The Disappearance," and "Before Sewing, One Must Cut" from her collection *Shadow Bands* to those of the larger experience as exemplified in her novel *Children of Men* with its focus on a black-white relationship.

Anna Quindlen's fiction focuses on family relationships in a very contemporary way. Ellen, a character in *One True Thing*, reflects, "How much of family life is a vast web of misunderstandings—a tinted and touched-up family portrait, an accurate representation of fact that leaves out only the essential truth." *Object Lessons* deals with a young girl's coming of age, and in *Black and Blue* a battered wife strives to reinvent the idea of family for herself and her son from the sorry remnants of what went before.

All these younger women are stylistically adept, and some more detached from narrative than others. The old robust vitality and passion of story telling, of telling and retelling the story of the Italian exodus to the new world and what happened to displaced peasants in the great urban ghettoes, and what became of their dually conflicted children seems to be gone now. The focus is more on interior life; little moments are prolonged and evoked in a minimalist manner more attuned to mainstream writing.

Mary Caponegro's "Sebastian," from her collection *The Star Café*, is a story of an Englishman and his disconcertions. The writing is certainly crafted, brilliant, and given attention in reviews, but it is also mannered and studied and the sense of struggle that moved the earlier women to write is now absorbed into the writing itself. The themes of earlier novels—how to make one's place in a seeming alien society, how to become educated and evolved enough to move into that society, how to combine work and family how, in fact, to separate from family in order to hang onto one's self without losing everything—have almost been put aside in favor of internal moments told in polished prose.

It was creativity itself that captured the imagination of Carole Maso in *Ghost Dance*. As it does in Mary Caponegro's story "Materia Prima," a finely written, well-conceived parable of the will to creative expression, which brooks no constraints as it is related in the story of a young girl whose obsession for ornithology is the metaphor for any creative passion. Paralleling Spignesi's "starving woman," Caponegro's character, when sent away to boarding school by her parents in an attempt to curb her obsession, stops eating and finds with satisfaction that she has also stopped her menstrual cycle; she becomes anorexic and thus attains the control over herself that her parents had thwarted.

The allusions to birds intersperse the narrative with great acuity and design and early establish the importance of "learning to fly on one's own . . . Then, when it is on its own, there are no confusions. The break is clean; independence is clarity."

Again, as with Maso, the art form is strong in Caponegro. They both express the need for freedom that is realized in the service of self to art. Both are supreme stylists for whom the *materia prima* of background has indeed been transformed into a universal art with surrealistic and mysterious overlay. Curiously, the title of Maso's novel *Ava* also suggests bird flight and freedom.

Some Italian American women writers have a specific Italian American frame of reference; for others it is so attenuated as to seem non-existent except as a muted echo. For Agnes Rossi, the Italian American background is attenuated into accents of detail and character. Marie Russo, the character through whom the title novella is narrated from her collection *The Quick,* is grounded in an Italian American family where the father still rages against children who don't fulfill his expectations, but the larger story is one of loss and has resonances for all families.

The new younger writers have a commonality, a boldness of voice and sureness of style that signals a true liberation from whatever roles and stereotypes of Italian American women prevailed in the past. They write of a gritty reality where women have faced the violence of today's life and survived as in Jeanne Schinto's novel *Children of Men;* or they write with a new humor, which is not the self-parody of the old stories that made comic characters out of Italian Americans who acted and talked funny but is now a controled and knowing irony as in the accomplished auto-erotic fantasy of Mary Capognegro's title story from *The Star Café*. The Italian American is no longer the object of humor but the distanced distiller of it, and what is nightmarish is filtered through an ironic eye.

In the imaginative story-telling of Cris Mazza's fictions, a story entitled "From Hunger" features the heroine as a striving artist who is so hungry for her art (and human attention) she literally eats the paint from her canvas, another one of Spignesi's starving women. Mary-Ann Tirone Smith's characters are strikingly free-wheeling young women who challenge the notions of prescribed conduct, and one of whom, from *The Book of Phoebe,* is named for Holden Caulfield's younger sister in the cult book of the 1950s, J. D. Salinger's *The Catcher in the Rye.* Taking as her subject matter the strains and hardships of a rural Vermont family who have no connection whatsoever with her Italian American background, Dalia Pagani has made an impressive debut with her first novel, *Mercy Road,* which received a great deal of advance praise for its lyrical style.

These newer Italian American writers have mostly taken a stance away from direct ethnic identification, one that engages in free imaginative roaming. Mary-Ann Tirone Smith had put it this way in her letter to the *New York Times* in response to Talese's "Where are the Italian American Novelists?": "As an Italian American novelist, I haven't any interest in creating fiction centered on Sicilian goatherds and crowded ships poignantly pulling away from Neapolitan docks; or Ellis Island, or men carrying a statue of the Virgin through the streets of Little Italy, or the canonization of Joe DiMaggio"; rather, Smith states, what is explored is "the inevitable tragic consequences we must suffer when loyalty and honor are placed above truth. *That* is the Italian American experience."

Like other American writers, the contemporary Italian American woman writer transcends her ethnic and gender group, writing in the fullness of her exposure to, and experience of a national literature which mirrors a many cultured society. American literature is an ocean, says Black novelist Ishmael Reed, and it's large enough for all the currents that run through it.

Referring to her first book, *Gone Primitive: Savage Intellects, Modern Lives,* Marianna De Marco Torgovnick wrote, "Eventually I write the book I like best about primitive others as they figure within Western obsessions, my identification with "the Other," my sense of being "Other," surfaces at last."[31] Her sense of otherness, of course, is that of being Italian American, and this is pertinent to the Italian American position in literature as Outsider.

As Torgovnick disclosed in her book, the civilized West's attraction to the primitive reflects a shiver of transcendental homelessness—a form of absolute alienation from the self, from society. It is easy to have those feelings growing up Italian American and, from the personal, to be able to project them more generally. Noting throughout *Going Primitive* how primitivism has been colored by being conceived and applied in our culture through the masculine view, Torgovnick also seeks to redress that imbalance (much as Spignesi does in identifying the feminine psyche through female material) by looking for the female mode and by making her work accessible.

Again, as in the manner of Spignesi (and contrary to Paglia), Torgovnick stresses the importance of alternate stories to the Western one; unlike Paglia who is beholden to male mentors and has internalized their dominant, masculine values and attitudes, Torgovnick has an independent female outlook. Her refuting the colonist denial of the complexity of primitive societies can also be translated into a refutation of the dominant American culture's hitherto denial of minority culture as important.

Though Tirone Smith and others have transcended their background to range imaginatively where they will, it does not invalidate the contribution of the previous generations of Italian American women writers. Each generation has its story to tell; each will find its own version of the Italian American experience or, contrarily, will not find it relevant any longer because it is so embedded in the total American experience.

Italian American women have always been hard workers; in the past they worked at home—taking in lodgers, making artificial flowers, doing piece work and embroidery, cooking for others. Now they are teachers and lawyers and have added to their work at home the practice of writing. To admit intellectual and artistic endeavour as "work" is a revolutionary change in attitude and class advancement.

"Non-productive" work such as writing was once the activity of a leisured class who could afford the indulgence. But as both Katherine Arnoldi (*The Amazing True Story of a Teenage Single Mom*) and Beverly Donofrio (*Riding in Cars with Boys*) relate, once they had willed themselves an education, their life changed; they were empowered to consider writing, an intellectual endeavour, as a legitimate occupation, something that moved them from working class to middle and triumphed over the *miseria* mentality that told them they would never make it out of welfare or a factory job.

To achieve balance between one's inherited culture and the other culture into which one is born is a feat of what sociologists call "creative ethnicity," that is, using one's ethnic heritage as the starting point upon which to build one's own identity in a selective and critical way. There is choice rather than unquestioning acceptance of tradition. And there is anxiety in choice. The hardships now are not the primitive ones of survival, but the more complex ones of uncertainty of direction, how to choose, weighing self-expression and autonomy over bonds to others.

Pellegrino D'Acierno who edited *The Italian American Heritage* volume in Garland's encyclopedic series *New Ethnic American Literature and the Arts*, has a positive evaluation of the two cultural forces implicated in being Italian American: "The maintenance of two identities, two cultures, two languages," he says, "should make us dissentious within ourselves, should make us into artists."[32] He feels that in their zeal to take on a monolithic American identity, Italian Americans once let the prevailing culture deform their own life experiences and so failed to make the most of their identity crisis and to use the experience as the crucible for artistic production.

Cultural duality is not only ambivalence, it is also advantage—to draw upon two identities, cultures, and languages is to draw riches as well as dissentious-ness once it is recognized in a positive way and so used. Aileen Riotto Sirey's findings in ethnotherapy confirm that those who identify as Italian American conceive of themselves as part of something dually glorious—the magnificent long heritage of Italy plus the unique promise of American freedom to achieve one's best.

Women are in a unique position of being able to use the dichotomy of two cultures as the crucible for artistic production. The Black women writers have been particularly fine at this, for as Nikki Giovanni put it: "Our alien-ation is our greatest strength."[33] This is what lies at the base of Italian Ameri-can women writers using strong themes; they use the paradox of their lives, which has militated *against* expressivity, *in* expressivity. As Barbara Grizzuti Harrison said regarding her past submersion as a Jehovah's Witness, "Women are good at turning their desolation to their advantage." From wait-ing, from patience, comes intensity of focus, words straining to be heard, pas-sion, conviction, an inner voice.

The opening words of the *Decameron* of Boccaccio are *Umana cosa*—"Something human." And that encapsulates the Italian American woman writer's particular sensibility—very human, the stuff of life. She tilts toward life, bringing realism, vigor, specificity, humane understanding of the emo-tions and respect for the human verities to her material.

Italian American women writers were late in coming to the fore of literary writing for historical, social, and personally inhibiting reasons having to do with the culture they came from. It is not surprising that they have taken long to give voice to that experience, nor that their numbers were not greater, but it does remain surprising that recognition of them is still so illusive.

Cynthia Ozick in an essay on feminism wrote, "Cultivation precedes fruition. It will take many practitioners of an art to produce one great artist."[34] And the emergence of the Italian American woman as writer, scholar, intel-lectual is new, incredibly new to the national literature and built on a base of all the "lost" or unthought of writers who wrote without notice or encour-agement.

A start is made and then, like reverberations, one work will set off another: each new literary work responding to a previous one, provoked into being by answering something left unsettled in the other work and, in turn, provoking new responses to itself as each writer stand on the shoulders of another.

It has already happened that Italian American women see themselves as writers, not simply as upholders and transmitters of a patriarchal culture through their roles as wives and mothers. To evolve from that old and potent image has taken the whole of a century that began with the great migration from Italy.

Women are in the unique position of being able to use the dichotomy of their two cultures as the crucible for artistic production, to engage in aesthetic endeavour; from a long wait comes intensity of focus, words straining to be heard, passion, conviction, a firm inner voice. What unites the women is that, at some point, they all derive from a common cultural context and tradition, one in which women had a strongly defined role; it is important to see them whole and to hear in the cadence of their voices the echo of the larger group. That is not to isolate them to a separatist ethnic drawer in the bureau of American literature, but to identify them as an important source of American writing that has been overlooked.

Once the missing pieces have been fitted into the national literature, the unheard voices listened to, the contributions of a large group of American life attended to, the emphasis on ethnicity, per se, will have been transcended. Each Italian American woman writer is what she has always been: an American writer in her own right.

## Notes

1. Olga Peragallo, *Italian American Authors* (New York: Vanni, 1949), p. xi.

2. Frances Winwar, in *Twentieth Century Authors,* ed. Stanley J. Kunitz and Howard Haycraft (New York: H. W. Wilson, 1942), p. 1536.

3. Marie Hall Ets, *Rosa: The Life of an Italian Immigrant* (Madison: University of Wisconsin Press, 1999).

4. Mario Puzo, *The Godfather Papers* (New York: G. P. Putnam's, 1972), p. 179.

5. Andrew Rolle, *The Italian Americans: Troubled Roots* (New York: Free Press, 1980), p. 111.

6. Dorothée von Heune-Greenberg, "A *Melus* Interview: Pietro Di Donato," Melus14, nos. 3–4 (Fall–Winter 1987); p. 34.

7. Ets, *Rosa*, p. 253.

8. Valentine Rossilli Winsey, "The Italian Immigrant Woman Before World War I," in *Studies in Italian American Social History,* ed. Francesco Cordasco (Totowa, N.J.: Rowman & Littlefield, 1975), p. 203

9. Gay Talese, "Where Are the Italian American Novelists?" in *New York Times Book Review,* March 14, 1993, p. 1.

10. Michael Novak, "The Nordic Jungle," in *Divided Society,* ed. Colin Greer (New York: Basic Books, 1974), p. 128.

11. Jean Baker Miller, *Toward a New Psychology of Women* (Boston: Beacon Press, 1986).

12. Martha Nussbaum in *The New York Review of Books,* January 30, 1986, p. 7–12.

13. Joy Harjo, "Bio-Poetics Sketch," *Greenfield Review* 9, nos. 3–4 (1981): 8–9.

14. Ellen Moers, *Literary Women,* (New York: Doubleday, 1976).

15. Sibilla Aleramo, *A Woman,* trans. Rosalind Delemar (Berkeley: University of California Press, 1980).

16. Sergio Pacifici, *A Guide to Contemporary Italian Literature* (New York: Meridian Books, 1962), pp. 133–34.

17. Annis Pratt, *Archetypal Patterns in Women's Fiction* (Bloomington: Indiana University Press, 1982), p. 5.

18. Mary Gordon in *Authors' Guild Bulletin*, September–October, 1982, p. 16.

19. Jules Chametzky, "Our Decentralized Literature," a paper presented at John F. Kennedy-Institut für Amerikastudien, Heidelberg, June 4, 1971, and published in *Proceedings*.

20. Katherine Newman, "An Ethnic Literary Scholar Views American Literature," *Melus*, Spring 1980, p. 6.

21. Rose Basile Green, *The Italian American Novel* (Cranbury, N.J.: Fairleigh Dickinson University Press, 1974) pp. 367–68.

22. Newman, "Ethnic Literary Scholar," p. 10.

23. *Real Fiction* 1 (November 1982); see introduction.

24. Zora Neale Hurston, "What White Publishers Won't Print," in *I Love Myself* (Old Westbury, N.Y.: Feminist Press, 1979) p. 109.

25. *The New York Times Book Review*, February 6, 1983.

26. Bernard Paris, *A Psychological Approach to Fiction* (Bloomington: Indiana University Press, 1974).

27. Bernard Paris, "Third Force Psychology and the Study of Literature, Biography, Criticism, and Culture," in *The Literary Review* 24, no. 2 (Winter 1981).

28. Angelyn Spignesi, *Starving Women* (Dallas: Spring Publications, 1983), p. xi.

29. Spignesi, p. 3.

30. Spignesi, p. 3.

31. Marianna De Marco Torgovnick, "Being White, Female, and Born in Bensonhurst," *Partisan Review*, Summer 1990, p. 460.

32. Pellegrino D'Acierno, from the transcript of the Conference on Contemporary Fiction Writing in Italy and America, held at Columbia University, October 14, 1981.

33. Nikki Giovanni, in *Black Women Writers at Work*, ed. Claudia Tate (New York: Continuum, 1983), p. 70.

34. Cynthia Ozick, "Women and Creativity: The Demise of the Dancing Dog," in *Women and Sexist Society*, ed. Vivian Gornick and Barbara K. Moran (New York: New American Library, 1971) pp. 431–51.

# MEMOIRS

# Sister Blandina Segale

Sister Blandina was born Rosa Maria Segale in 1850 in a village near Genoa, Italy, and arrived in the United States as a young girl, settling with her family in Cincinnati. There, at age sixteen, she entered the order of the Sisters of Charity and at age nineteen was sent by superiors to Trinidad in the Colorado Territory. She spent the next twenty-one years on the Western frontier doing mission work among the Indians and founding schools and hospitals. The journal she kept consisted of letters to her sister, also a nun. Eventually Sister Blandina was relieved of her public school teaching duties at the school she helped found in Trinidad when she refused to discard her religious garb, as the secular authorities demanded. She was then recalled to Cincinnati where she worked thirty-five years ministering to the needs of the growing population of Italian immigrants. Sister Blandina's journal was originally published in installments in a Catholic magazine, receiving attention for its historic value. The journal was then published in book form in 1932 as *At the End of the Santa Fe Trail*.

## *from* At the End of the Santa Fe Trail

On Train from Steubenville, Ohio, to Cincinnati. Nov. 30, 1872. My Darling Sister Justina:

How interestedly you, Sister M. Louis, and myself read Eugénie de Guérin's Journal and her daily anxieties to save her brother from being a spiritual outcast! This Journal which I propose keeping for you will deal with incidents occurring on my journey to Trinidad and happenings in that far-off land to which I am consigned.

The Journal will begin with the first act. Here is Mother Josephine's letter:

Mt. St. Vincent, O.
Nov. 27, 1872.

Sister Blandina,
Steubenville, O.

My Dear Child:

You are missioned to Trinidad. You will leave Cincinnati Wednesday and alone. Mother Regina will attend to your needs.

Devotedly,
Mother Josephine.

This letter thrilled us both. I was delighted to make the sacrifice, and you were hiding your feelings that I might not lose any merit. Neither of us could find Trinidad on the map except in the island of Cuba. So we concluded that Cuba was my destination. I was to leave Steubenville quietly so that none of my obstreperous pupils might cause the incoming teacher annoyance. Hence I went to Sunday Catechetical class as usual—2 P.M. I was to take the 3 P.M. train for Cincinnati. I said to my hopefuls, "Instead of catechism, I'm going to tell you an Indian story today." The schoolhouse roof was not disturbed, though the hurrahs were loud enough! The moral of the story was "Indian Endurance." Dismissed them at two-thirty without one word of goodby except the daily one. You remember how surprised I was to see a crowd at the station to wish me "Godspeed"; I thought I was to slip away without anyone's knowledge except our own. Mr. Tait and Mr. McCann wished to speak to me alone. Both had been in the West. "You will have a long travel on the plains," they said, "before you reach Trinidad."

"Where is Trinidad?"

"A little mining town in Southwestern Colorado." So then I knew my destination, which of course, I would have been told at Mt. St. Vincent. Both gentlemen said they have traveled on the plains on the Santa Fe Trail, and they seemed to have made it a matter of conscience to inform me on the subject of cowboys. This in substance was their conversation with me:

"Sister, you may be snow-bound while on the plains." I looked my assent, I knew I could not stop the snow.

"Travelers are sometimes snow-bound for two weeks, and you are alone. This, though, is not the greatest danger to you."

Mentally I was wishing both gentlemen somewhere else.

"Your real danger is from cowboys." I looked at the speakers.

"You do not seem to grasp our meaning. No virtuous woman is safe near a cowboy." Both gave up trying to make me understand what they considered danger. Why should snow or cowboys frighten me any more than others who will be traveling the same way! So you see, dearest, I'm not going to so long a distance as we thought. At three o'clock A.M. the baggage checker came through our coach. I looked to see how much the pocketbook contained—just twenty-five cents. If I used it to ride to the Good Samaritan I'd be minus the fare to Mt. St. Vincent, so I made up my mind to skirt around from the Little Miami to the Good Samaritan Hospital.

At four A.M. I rang the front doorbell—no response. I sat on the stone steps and waited till I heard the rising bell, then I waited another fifteen minutes when again I rang the doorbell. Sister Anthony came.

"Why, child, where did you come from; how did you get here? I'm sure you are cold." I said I came from Steubenville.

"Oh, yes! dear Father Bigelow died there. He was good to this hospital. Last year he sent a barge of coal to us." I said he was good to anyone in need. He died possessed of three dollars and fifty cents. His hand was always open to any kind of distress.

I did not mention to Sister Anthony that I walked from the Little Miami Station.

After Mass, breakfast and smiles of sympathy and "God Bless You" from the Sisters at the Good Samaritan, one of the nurses accompanied me to Fifth and Vine Streets, where I was to take "Barney's Bus" for Mt. St. Vincent. The bus was to leave at ten A.M. I waited till three P.M. then asked one of the clerks if he thought Mr. McCabe would run the bus that day.

"I fear no bus will run to-day. There is an epidemic—epizootic among the horses." I asked if Mr. Segale's place of business was anywhere near. He pointed to Wood's Theater and I started to the place indicated. Brother Henry managed to find a "hack" to send me to Mt. St. Vincent. On the way, between the first ascent of the hill and the Seminary, I met Sisters Gabriella and Delphina walking in the slush and cold on their way to the Orphan Asylum. I stopped to take them in. They returned with me to Cedar Grove, from there the driver was to take them to the Asylum in Cumminsville. Sister Gabriella said to me, "I would gladly go where you are going instead of shouldering this heavy burden." Sister is to be mother to three hundred orphans, taking Sister Sophia's place.

The Sisters are showing great sympathy. I heard Sister Benedicta say, "She does not mind going so far and alone—I've not seen her shed a tear." Nor will you, my dear Sister. The tears will flow where none but He and myself will know. Still, I'm delighted to go. I did not tell you, dearest, that one year ago last November I wrote to Mother Regina saying I envied the sacrifices the Sisters were making who were sent far away to do God's work. I've received my answer with compound interest. You know that up to date the Sisters going on distant missions were consulted and none were sent who had parents living. I am pleased that that record is broken in my case.

Mother Regina told me to spend a day at home.

Dear Lord! Give me strength. I anticipate a scene.

I spent Wednesday, December 5th, at our old homestead. Mother kept open house all day. Friends came in groups. Mr. Leverone and bride, his mother and the bride's mother, Mrs. Garibaldi, the Misses Gardelli and a host of others. Mrs. Garibaldi threatened to take off my habit. I said, "Hands off! Have you any right to detain Mary if John wishes to take her to California?"

"Oh, that is different."

"Yes, as different as heaven and earth. I have chosen my portion, Mary has chosen hers, each abides by her choice."

John Leverone's mother acted most sensibly all day. She was soothing oil to all the protests made to my going. Our dear mother kept quiet. When we were permitted a lone interview she asked, "Do you want one of your sisters to accompany you?" I answered, "I prefer to do just as my superiors have told me."

"Well, then I will give you a thousand-dollar check so that in case you desire to return you will have the wherewith."

"No, no, dear mother, I fully realize the responsibilities I assumed. As you are aware, I realized them from the first day I entered the Novitiate."

Mother replied: "And I want to tell you I never doubted your vocation. I agree to your sacrifice, my dear child, keep on serving God, I will never interfere. Now that I have your explicit answer, friends cannot urge any logical reason to prevent your going."

All day the visitors reminded me of a disturbed ant hill. When mother and I were alone she spoke the Genoese dialect. It was like hearing sketches of a favorite opera. Wednesday at 2:00 P.M. I went to visit our Ecclesiastical Superior. The Most Rev. J. B. Purcell offered me several gifts. But St. Francis Xavier is my patron, so I'm not going to possess any superfluous article. I only regret I could not pass our home without going in, as St. Francis Xavier did. If I aim high I surely must reach some upper strata of detachment in His service. One thing I take with me, the impressive blessing given me by His Grace, part of which rings clear—"May angels guard your every step." He was extremely sympathetic at my having to go alone.

I went to confession to Rev. Dr. Callaghan. You may recall how we enjoyed his lecture on the "School Question" delivered in Steubenville. After mother had a short interview with me, father managed to see me alone. He took hold of me and asked, "Have I ever denied you anything?"

I signified no.

"You have never disobeyed me in your life?"

I assented.

"Now I command you—you must not go on this far away mission! Are you going?"

"Yes, father." He let go the hold on my arm and walked toward the door. Not without my seeing his tears falling fast. He did not realize his hold on my arm gave me pain—not to speak of the heart-pain for him.

In the railway station at St. Louis between train time, I got off to purchase a pair of arctics. I saw several Italian women selling fruit. One of them had a daughter standing near. I asked the mother if she would permit her daughter to accompany me to the shoe store, which was in sight. The mother looked at me earnestly then said to her neighbor peddler, "How do I know who she is, she looks like a *monaca* (sister) but she might be a *strega* (witch)." I thanked the true guardian of her daughter and went to make my purchase alone. I spoke English to the peddler.

If good Sister Benedicta who thought I did not mind—because I did not cry—had seen me during the greater part of last night she would but too truly have said, "That heart is human in every fiber." That I succeeded in dignifiedly getting away from home is Thy Grace, oh, my God!

Forty-two persons accompanied me to the train, among them friends of old, but my purpose never faltered, not even in shadow. Such tactics as I executed yesterday! I see one trait strong in me, the straight service of God. Not the father whom I had never seen cry, nor the most patient, dearest mother whose heart is crushed at my being sent alone, much less the friends who used every argument to make me say I would not go—could elicit the faintest trace that I was not more pleased at my going alone than if I had had a dozen with me.

Sisters Antonia and Gonzaga came to the waiting room. I asked the company to permit me an interview with the Sisters. When going toward them, one of my dear old friends said, "Look, we cannot doubt she is happy." This was not intented for my hearing, the noise caused the speaker to raise her voice. Sister Antonia asked me how I had spent the day. I narrated some incidents. "I'm an ancient religious, but I could not have gone through the ordeal as creditably as you did." What if I had mentioned all the heart sighs I had witnessed! When it was time to board the train I asked that my last interview be with my mother. Cannot you picture her sad, endearing look of appreciation? I'll skip the last talk with mother— some of it was in silence.

Trinidad
Dec., 1873

We are preparing for Christmas. The Vigilant Committee now composed of ten in the senior class is making secret preparations to supply a Christmas surprise for certain families and children who only know of Santa Claus by hearsay. In my turn, I suggested to the pupils not on the Committee to surprise the Seniors. Clothes and shoes are put in new dress suit cases. Candy boxes are hung on the Christmas tree. The young ladies of the Academy gave their last season's dresses, which are almost new. These will be sent to some families that have been reported as "Needy." Two of the convent girls each received diamond clustered rings and, because the diamonds were not set to their liking, they discarded them. I could not refrain from saying, "I hope I will never see the day you would be glad to possess them."

After the Vigilant Committee has distributed the prepared boxes to the different families, all our pupils will assemble in the Christmas tree room and receive their surprise. Then those who have to go to confession will do so. Those who remain will contribute Yuletide facts or legends.

Then preparations for midnight Mass. The choir will render Mozart's
12th Mass; organ, harp, and first violin will accompany. Quite a change
from the time of an untuned instrument and nasal singing. As you will
notice, we are progressing rapidly, though Trinidad is not yet on the map.

What came to my mind just now is: "Will the frontier missionaries in the
South and West, Franciscans and Jesuits, fare any better in public records
than did the first missionaries who staked all to bring the knowledge of God
to those who inhabited the newly discovered lands?" True, Mr. Bancroft
did narrate in his History of the United States some of the hardships and
heroic sacrifices made by the first Jesuits, but I have been told on excellent
authority that bigots are determined to have Mr. Bancroft omit the praise
given the first Indian missionaries when he issues the next edition. If he
does so, I predict that he, with his history, will sink in the estimation of
every honest reader of history, and the result will be a change of Bancroft's
U.S. History in many of the schools now using it.

How much is there made of Lord Baltimore giving freedom of conscience
to those who lived where he controlled! Yet look at the stream of articles
constantly given to the public about Plymouth Rock and the Pilgrim
Fathers! "Oh, Justice, where art thou!" . . .

Santa Fe
Spring of 1877.

My dear Sister Justina:

The last entry made in the journal I'm keeping for you gave a brief
description of the journey of the first band of our Sisters form Cincinnati to
Santa Fe Territory, New Mexico. They traveled by rail, water and stage.
The second band of our Sisters, traveling by caravan, had some stirring
encounters as novel and dangerous as any experienced by Kit Carson, or
Uncle Dick Wootton.

Both these men have been intelligent guides to avoid warring with the
roving Indian tribes. Kit Carson was, for a time, General Fremont's "Power
behind the throne" in scouting and guiding over trails, and places where
foot of civilized man had never trod. He acted in the spirit of a Free Lance.
Military discipline must have been galling to him. Carson saved the life of
General Fremont on two occasions, and the General saved Kit Carson's life
at least once. Is that not cementing friendship for life? Mr. Wootton (Uncle
Dick) is an entirely different character from Mr. Carson. Mr. Carson is
astute and daring; Mr. Wootton is kindhearted and depends much on
"Luck," as he terms it. I am acquainted with all his children, and have often
met Uncle Dick. His life at present is very quiet. His present occupation is
keeping the tollgate near the dividing line between Colorado and New
Mexico. He still has enough excitement to live on. "Wootton's Place," as it

is called, is a refuge for many outlawed characters. Not that he wants it so, but it is the inevitable consequence of present conditions.

The second band of our Sisters left Mt. St. Vincent May 10, 1867. They were Sister Augustine Barron and her sister, Sister Louise Barron. At the time Sister Augustine was missioned to Santa Fe, she was assistant-Mother of the Community. Previous to this time, she had had charge of two of our largest establishments, so you can at once surmise the middle post of life had been passed. Sister Louise is two years younger.

In the fall of 1866, the beloved Bishop Lamy stopped at Mt. St. Vincent and pleaded for an addition to our Sisters already doing mission work in Santa Fe. He wanted to establish some industry by which the native girls might, in time, make a living for themselves. He strongly emphasized "Industry for the Native Girls." He was then on his way to France, where he hoped to find recruits from the seminaries and financial aid from friends. He returned in the spring of 1867 with a reinforcement to help him carry out plans approved by the Holy See for the betterment of the inhabitants of his vast diocese. Twenty-six souls accompanied him.

When, at some future day, the Church in New Mexico will find a historian, no greater names will be written than the heroes of this pioneer band: R. Rev. J. B. Lamy, Rev. D. M. Gasparri, S.J.; Rev. M. Bianchi, S.J., and Rev. M. Leone, S.J. The life of each of these pioneers was made up of self-oblation and heroism so sublime by the side of which the most notable characters in Tasso pale as meteors before the sun.

Rt. Rev. Bishop Lamy wrote from France to have the Sisters meet him in St. Louis. Three Loretto Sisters and our two Sisters proceeded in company with the Rt. Rev. Bishop Lamy and his twenty-six recruits to Leavenworth, Kansas. In Leavenworth, the Rt. Rev. Bishop manned a caravan of about one hundred covered wagons and started on his famous journey on the Santa Fe trail on the 14th of June. On the 18th, the caravan reached St. Mary's of the Potawatomis. The Jesuit Fathers and students came several miles to meet the travelers. Sunday was spent at St. Mary's, from which the caravan left June 24th.

On the 29th, the Feast of St. Peter and St. Paul, the caravan camped a few miles from Junction City. At noon four Indians visited the camp. This did not portend any good. After a consultation with some of the experienced drivers, the Bishop gave orders to return to Leavenworth at which place all the mules attached to the caravan were sold and replaced by oxen, as having more endurance.

From Leavenworth the Bishop ordered a detour from the Santa Fe Trail. The Kiowas—the most rapacious Indian tribe of the plains—had sent scouts to visit our travelers when camping near Junction City. The Bishop who understood Indian tactics and Indian warfare, changed the animals and the route, in hopes that the Kiowas would be thrown off the scent. The caravan continued its slow travel until the latter part of July. The eagle eye of the Bishop was constantly on the watch for any sign which might indicate the near approach of Indians. The Comanches and Apaches had also free scope on the plains, but the Kiowas were feared the most. When victorious in their attack on white men, they were most ferocious. The men were first scalped, then killed, the children were also killed; the women were made prisoners—a fate far worse than death.

On the 30th day of July, without any apparent reason, the Bishop ordered a corral to be made. Every wagon in the caravan was arranged to form a circle; the oxen were driven inside the circle. The travelers and teamsters ran inside the circle none too soon, for the Kiowas' death whoop preceded the sling of hundreds of arrows which fell harmlessly for some time. This was kept up until sunset, when the Indians retired. The order from inside the circle was. "Be on the alert, hands on guns, no fires to be lighted."

The day's travel had been arduous for want of water. All were suffering from thirst, and, though the water of a river could be seen distinctly not more than a few rods from their improvised corral, to attempt to satisfy their thirst, or to water the oxen, would be certain destruction to all. The Sisters prayed their beads and the men kept a vigilant watch, not to be surprised by a night attack from the fierce Kiowas. At daybreak it was discovered that cholera had broken out in the caravan! Soon after the Indians renewed their attack! Word was circulated that one of the Sisters of Loretto had the cholera! Whether it was cholera or fright the victim gave up her soul to God. Meanwhile, the Indians flung their arrows in quick succession. The travelers were well protected by the circle of wagons, from which vantage ground their guns carried death to some of the attacking Indians.

Some kind-hearted messenger came to Sister Augustine and said: "A young man under a wagon on the opposite side of the circle has the cholera and is pitifully calling for his mother." The words were scarcely uttered when Sister Augustine said, "I'll go at once to render what help I can."

Sister Augustine crawled under from one wagon to the next, while arrows were thickly showering above her, and some arrows fell near her, but lost their force by striking either wagon hub or cogs. When speaking of this to me, she said, "I could only compare the flying of arrows around me to a disturbed beehive." Sister Augustine reached the dying young man and tried to soothe his last moments as his mother would have done. So he and the dear Sister of Loretto were buried, strangers in every way. Months afterwards, all efforts to find their resting place were unavailable.

Meanwhile, the Indians continued the aggressive fight. The weather was intensely warms, all needed water. The Indians had the advantage. The cholera was doing its work, but no more victims succumbed to death.

It is said that one of the leaders of the party called a few of the men with well balanced minds and gave them his orders: "If the Indians continue the attack for twenty-four hours we are doomed. Make no mistakes in the directions I now give you, but let no man act until I give the order. When I see death is inevitable for us I will give the signal. Then you, Mr. ———, shoot Sister Louise, you, Mr. ———, shoot the elder of the Loretto Sisters, and you, Mr. ———, shoot the younger Sister of Loretto. I will shoot Sister Augustine."

Some people, many hundred miles away, asserted the man could not morally give such an order. This is true, but knowing the treatment of women prisoners in the Kiowa tribe, I would have preferred to have been shot rather than to have been made a prisoner.

The sun was declining. The Kiowas disappeared. The leader of the party asked: "Are any of you men willing to practice strategy by wading the stream and land some boxes of provisions and a barrel of liquor on the other side of the stream? Apparently, it is taking your life in your own hands, although I see no danger. My only regret is to use such means to save ourselves." The freight was safely landed on the other side of the stream. As the sun disappeared, the freighters discontinued their work.

The Indians fell into the trap. They suddenly appeared from nowhere and rushed for the barrel of whiskey. They soon chopped off the top of the barrel with a tomahawk, and each, with scooped hands eagerly drank the liquor.

Word was quietly passed to "Start fires an hour later." By this time the Indians had their fill and were dropping off in a dead sleep. Our travelers, like the Arabs, "Stole silently away." The caravan was safe and on its way to Santa Fe. The men and large boys of Santa Fe and surrounding villages formed a cavalcade and met their beloved Bishop about fifteen miles from Santa Fe and escorted him to his adobe cathedral. Meanwhile the Sisters, priests and seminarians arrived in Santa Fe and all proceeded to the cathedral, the *Te Deum* was sung, with what heartfelt gratitude you may imagine. This was the 15th of August. Since our Sisters left Mt. St. Vincent on May 10th, it is evident it took them three months and five days to reach their destination. The details of the journey on the plains have been omitted. The attack of the Kiowas on the caravan was interpreted in the states as that all males were killed and all females made prisoners. You remember the anguish the news caused our Sisters East, especially Mother Regina.

Albuquerque
1886.

"Vanity of vanities and all is vanity."

Fortunately for my peace of mind, dear Sister Justina, neither praise nor unjust criticism affects me. At this period, it is praise. What does it all amount to? If the laudation is given actions performed and those actions are accompanied by single-mindedness, and the direction is straight to God— He will be the recompense. If flaws are found—may the mercy of Christ cleanse them.

As complicated as is the frontier life (and I've lived it fourteen years— from Kit Carson to Trinidad, Colorado; to Santa Fe, New Mexico; to Arizona—by trips) yet I have never turned aside from the purpose for which I was missioned to the Southwest, viz.: to teach and meet emergencies as I saw them. "To meet emergencies as I saw them" is my interpretation of the Superior's wishes.

# *Rosa Cassettari*

The great outpouring of oral memoirs that became *Rosa: The Life of an Italian Immigrant* is the story of Rosa Cassettari (1866–1943) as collected, preserved, and published by Marie Hall Ets, a social worker at the Chicago Commons settlement house where Rosa was a cleaning woman. In Mrs. Ets's account, Rosa is given the surname of Cavalleri. A foundling, Rosa was brought up by a foster mother in the Italian village of Bugiarno near Milan and made to work in the silk factories from childhood. At fourteen she was forced into an arranged marriage with a brutal older man who was going to the iron mines of Missouri. Rosa arrived in the United States in 1884, and after the birth of several children, left her husband and went to Chicago where she found work, eventually remarried, and told her stories, invincible in will until her end.

---

## *from* Rosa: The Life of an Italian Immigrant

---

The year my Leo was born I was home alone and struggled along with my children. My husband went away because he was sick—he went by a doctor in St. Louis to get cured. That doctor said he must stay away from his home one year and gave him a job to do all the janitor work around his house for five dollars a month and his board. So me, I used to go all around to find the clothes to wash and the scrubbing. The city hall was helping me again in that time—they gave me a little coal and sometimes the basket of food. Bob, the sign painter downstairs, he helped me the most. He was such a good young man. He used to bring up a big chunk of coal and chop it up right in my kitchen and fix the stove.

I was to the end of my nine months, but the baby never came. So I went by one woman, Mis' Thomas, and I got part of the clothes washed. Then I said, "Oh, Mis' Thomas, I've got to go. I've got the terrible pains!"

She said, "You can go when you finish. You've got to finish first."

"No, I go. Otherwise I'll have to stay in your bed." When I said that she got scared I would have the baby there, so she let me go.

I went by the midwife, Mis' Marino, and told her to come; then I went home. When I saw it was my time, I told Domenico something and sent him with all the children to the wife of Tomaso. I told those people before, when they see the children come they must keep them all night—it's my time. It was really, really my time, and I had such a scare that I would be alone a second time. So when I heard a lady come in the building—she lived downstairs—I called to her. She said, "I have no time." And she didn't come up.

I was on my bed all alone by myself and then I prayed Sant' Antoni with all my heart. I don't know why I prayed Sant' Antoni—the Madonna put it in my mind. And then, just when the baby was born, I saw Sant' Antoni right there! He appeared in the room by me! I don't think it was really Sant' Antoni there, but in my imagination I saw him—all light like the sun. I saw Sant' Antoni there by my bed, and right then the door opened and the midwife came in to take care of the baby! It was February seventh and six below zero. There I had him born all alone, but Mis' Marino came when I prayed Sant' Antoni. She washed the baby and put him by me, but then she ran away. She didn't light the fire or nothing.

Oh, that night it was *so* cold! And me in my little wooden house in the alley with the walls all frosting—thick white frosting. I was crying and praying, "How am I going to live?" I said. "Oh, Sant' Antoni, I'll never live till tomorrow morning! I'll never live till the morning!"

And just as I prayed my door opened and a lady came in. She had a black shawl twice round her neck and head and that shawl came down to her nose. All I could see was half the nose and the mouth. She came in and lighted both the stoves. Then she came and looked at me, but I couldn't see her face. I said, "God bless you!"

She just nodded her head up and down and all the time she said not one word, only "Sh, sh."

Then she went down in the basement herself, nobody telling her nothing, and she got the coal and fixed the fire. Pretty soon she found that little package of camomile tea I had there on the dresser and she made a little tea with the hot water. And that woman stayed by me almost till daylight. But all the time she put her finger to her mouth to tell me to keep still when I tried to thank her. And I never knew where that lady came from! I don't know yet! Maybe she was the spirit of that kind girl, Annina, in Canaletto? I don't know. I really don't know! I was *so* sick and I didn't hear her voice or see her face. All the time she put her finger on her mouth and said, "Sh, sh." And when the daylight came she was gone.

About seven o'clock morning my children came home. And Mis' Marino, that midwife, she came at eight o'clock and said, "It's so cold I thought I'd find you dead!"

Then here came the city hall, or somebody, with a wagon. They wanted to take me and my new baby to the hospital. But how could I leave all my children? I started to cry—I didn't want to go. And my children cried too—they didn't want me to leave them. So then they didn't make me. They pulled my bed away from the frosting on the wall and put in the front room by the stove. And my baby, I had him wrapped up in a pad I made from the underskirt like we do in *Italia*. But that baby froze when he was born; he couldn't cry like other babies—he was crying weak, weak.

My Visella was bringing up the wood and the coal and trying to make that room warm. But she was only a little girl, she didn't know, and she filled that stove so full that all the pipes on the ceiling caught fire. I had to jump up from the bed and throw the pails of water so the house wouldn't burn down. Then God sent me help again. He sent that Miss Mildred from the settlement house. She didn't know about me and my Leo born; she was looking for some other lady and she came to my door and saw me. She said, "Oh, I have the wrong place."

I said, "No, lady, you find the right place."

So she came in and found out all. Then she ran away and brought back all

those little things the babies in America have. She felt sorry to see my baby
banded up like I had him. She didn't know then, Miss Mildred, that the
women in *Italia* always band their babies that way. And she brought me
something to eat too—for me and for my children. That night another
young lady from the Commons, Miss May, she came and slept in my house
to take care of the fire. She was afraid for the children—maybe they would
burn themselves and the house. Oh, that Miss Mildred and Miss May, they
were angels to come and help me like that! Four nights Miss May stayed
there and kept the fire going. They were high-up educated girls—they were
used to sleeping in the warm house with the plumbing—and there they
came and slept in my wooden house in the alley, and for a toilet they had to
go down to that shed under the sidewalk. They were really, really friends!
That time I had my Leo nobody knew I was going to have the baby—I
looked kind of fat, that's all. Those women in the settlement house were so
surprised. They said, "Why you didn't tell us before, Mis' Cavalleri, so we
can help you?"

You know that Mis' Thomas—I was washing her clothes when the baby
started to come—she wanted a boy and she got a baby girl right after my
baby was born. When I went there the next week to do the washing I had to
carry my baby with me. When she saw him she said, "Well better I have a
girl than I have a boy that looks like your baby! He looks for sure like a
monkey!"

In the first beginning he did look like a monkey, but in a few weeks he
got pretty. He got so pretty all the people from the settlement house came
to see him. After two or three months there was no baby in Chicago prettier
than that baby.

When the year was over for him, my husband came home from St. Louis.
He didn't send me the money when he was there—just two times the five
dollars—so he brought twenty-five dollars when he came back. Oh, he was
so happy when he saw that baby with exactly, exactly his face and everything—the same dark gold hair and everything—and so beautiful. But he
saw that baby was so thin and pale and couldn't cry like the other babies.
"Better I go by a good doctor and see," he said. "I've got twenty-five
dollars—I'm going to get a good doctor." So he did.

But the doctor said, "That baby can't live. He was touched in the lungs
with the cold. Both lungs got froze when he was born."

And sure enough he was all the time sick and when it was nine months he
died. My first Leo and my second Leo I lose them both. Oh, I was broken-
hearted to lose such a beautiful baby!

I have to tell about another good thing the settlement house did for me.
That winter my Leo died we were still living in that little wooden house in

the alley. All my walls were thick with frosting from the cold, and I got the bronchitis on the lungs, with blood coming up. So one of those good ladies from the Commons, she arranged and sent me to a kind of home in the country where people go to get well. They had the nice nurses in that place and they cured me up good. I had a good time there too—I was all the time telling stories to entertain the other sick ladies.

In those two weeks I was gone, Chicago Commons helped my husband take care of the children, and my family moved into a good building. That building in front of where we were living had the empty rooms good and dry. But when my husband asked the manager, he said, "No, I don't let no Italians in!"

So Dr. Taylor, he went himself downtown, or someplace, and saw the owner to that building. The owner said yes, the manager has to let my husband in. The rent was no more, and there we were in a nice dry building. I was no more sick after then. We were the only—or almost the only—Italian family in the neighborhood that time, and the Germans and Norwegians were afraid to let us come in their buildings. But Chicago Commons took care of us. In that time all the streets by the Commons were the Norwegians and the Lutherans. And on the next street were all the Irish. But then the Italians came and the Norwegians moved away. Most of those Italians, they were not Italians—they were Sicilians. Oh, the Irish and the Sicilians they didn't get along together! They were all the time fighting. The Sicilian downstairs put out the tomato sauce to bake in the sun—all the yard covered up with those boards for the tomato sauce—and the Irish upstairs she hung up her clothes above with the paper between so the cord don't dirty the clean white shirtwaist. When she took off the clothespins, the paper, and sometimes the pillow case, went in the sauce. Then they both got mad and started the fighting.

Pretty soon after my first Leo died that darling Miss May got me a job to come every day to do the cleaning in the settlement house. Then Gionin got the good job sweeping the floor for the electric company. And after not long we got to be the janitor in that building where they didn't want the Italians. I had to scrub down the stairs once a week and do a little work like that, and we got the rent for half. We went along good that way. But I had a lot of worry too, because I was all the time gone to my work and my children were alone on the street. My Visella was eight or nine years old and she had to be the mother to the other children. And I had more trouble because the landlord in that new building was so mean. He was all the time beating the children. One day he kicked Visella and beat her terrible because she was playing house in the back alley and moved some boxes he didn't want moved. I was afraid to tell Gionin because he would start fighting with that boss. But I was crying one day when Miss May came in my house. I said, "If only I can have a little house of my own so those men can't lick my children."

She said, "How much do you think it would cost, Mis' Cavalleri?"

I said, "Oh, it costs lots—about a thousand dollars!"

The next week she came back and she said to me and my husband, "If I borrow you the money to buy a little house do you think you can pay me back like rent?"

"Oh, no!" Gionin said. "That much money I can't take for a debt!"

And I said no too. I can't sleep with the debt. But she meant it, that good Miss May. She trusted us and wanted to do it. She was a rich lady but she used to love me. She was the one who slept in my house the time my Leo was born. And later she'd give me much pleasure when she'd come in my house and eat. She'd come in and see the onions and she'd say, "Oh, Mis' Cavalleri, I just love the onions! I want an onion sandwich." And she'd go out and buy a lot of butter and some bread and come back and eat with me.

The residents in the settlement house now are not like in those old days. Now they all have their own work and go their own way. They're all pleasant and nice. They come in the kitchen Sunday night and say, "How you are, Mis' Cavalleri? If we help with the dishes will you tell us a story?" But it's not like in the old days when everyone was one family.

Me, I was always one that liked to entertain the people. So every noon I used to tell a story to the other cleaning women in the Commons when we were eating our lunch in the kitchen. In that time I didn't talk much English but I acted those stories so good that they understood anyway. I made those women bust out laughing when I told some of those funny stories from the barn in Bugiarno. One day Mis' Hill, the housekeeper, came in and heard me telling. She was so crazy for the way I told the story, she went and told Dr. Taylor. Then Dr. Taylor found me one night and said, "Come in the parlor, Mis' Cavalleri, and tell the story to the residents."

Me, I felt like one penny the first time I went in before all those high-up, educated people, and I had to talk half in Italian. But I was so reverent and acted the story so good that when I was the sister seeing the Madonna come alive all those residents raised up from their chairs with me. And oh, I wish you could see how they laughed when I told the funny stories! After then I all the time had to tell the stories to everybody—to the Woman's Club, to the man's meeting, to the boys' party, to the girls' party, to everybody. Sometimes when they had the big meetings in Hull House they would tell me to come there. One time that university in Evanston made me come there and tell stories to those teachers who were going to school to learn the storytelling. I went everywhere. But always some resident—one of the teachers from the Commons—had to go with me, because I didn't know how to go alone. I loved to tell the stories. I never said no.

Gionin, oh he was glad when I told the stories. So for practice I used to test them on him first. If he listened good—if I made him laugh or made his tears fall, then I knew I said them good. Sometimes he went with me to those parties in the settlement; but when I went up to tell the story, he went out of the room. He couldn't stay in, he was so afraid I'd make a mistake. He was more excited than me. But then after a while sometimes he used to stay in too. And he was proud how the people were enjoying to hear me tell.

Me, I was always crazy for a good story. That's why I love so much the dramatics. If somebody says to me, "Leave the supper and take the show," I'll take the show every time and let the eating go. I just love the drama! After I got the job to go every day to the settlement for the cleaning, and Gionin had the job with the electric company, we got along better. My children got bigger too. So then I used to hide a little money from the food so I can go to the shows. That one afternoon in the week I had home from the scrubbing I hurried up and did my washing and prepared the supper; then I'd run. But sometimes the show was long, and I'd see it start to get dark. I'd have such a scare I'd run all the way to get home before my husband came. I was going in the front door and quick put on the apron, because Gionin came in the back door—from the back street through the alley. Once he caught me. It was that time he was working in the night. As soon as he started for his work, I put on my shawl and I beat it. The snow was to my knees, but I didn't care, so long as I could see the show. But Gionin came back again—he forgot his little knife. He said, "Where's Ma? Where's Ma?"

Visella said, "Oh, she'll be right away back. Probably she ran to the store."

I used to go to the drama on Clark Street. I walked way out on Clark Street near Grand Avenue. The first drama I saw was *Hamlet*. I always did like that drama. Laura Alberta, she was the actress that made all those dramas in that New America Show on Clark Street. She used to play good plays—only good plays. Oh, all the shop girls were going behind by the stage door and watching to see her come out. And she used to talk nice to those poor girls. Then she used to come to our church. Sunday morning after the mass the people were outside waiting and looking, like she was God coming out.

Once I begged Gionin so much to take me to a show, and I was doing this, and doing this, and everything he liked to please him and make him go. So when we came out it was late, and I was hustling up so we can get a good seat. He said, "To other places you can't walk, your leg hurts you so much; but to the show you can run."

*The Folding of the Flag*—something like that—it was a kind of a war show, we saw that time. But my husband was not like me; he didn't care so very much for the show. In that show they had beautiful scenery—beautiful! I remember they had all that paper scenery. Now no more. After that big fire the government won't allow it. Me, I took my Visella and went to see that big fire—the Iroquois fire, where the theater burned up. We didn't see the fire but we saw after, when they were shoveling the dead people on the wagon. And then we had the nerve to go right away to the show on Clark Street. (I'd like to know what they did with that New America Show. It's not there anymore.)

Yes, I was always a friend with the shows. I used to go over on Milwaukee Avenue and see the nickel show. Oh, I remember one little bit of a place with two rows of chairs and no air—but that was later when they made the moving pictures. After five or six years the police found out it was not a fit place to go in, and they locked it. Some of those other places where I used to go the police came and closed too, because they were dangerous for fire. Then there was one show near the settlement house that was not right. There were some Italian men that came out on the stage and said jokes to make everybody laugh. But they said wrong things too—all kinds of dirty things that the men like. Two of those teachers from the Woman's Club they told me one day to come with them to that place. They wanted me to interpret so they know what it was. They thought it was not right, but they had to know it to tell the government to shut it up.

But me, I didn't want to snitch. Those men were Sicilian, but they were Italian people anyway, and I was thinking maybe they didn't want to say those bad things—probably they had to say them to get the living for their children. So I said to those ladies, "Better you take somebody else, because those men are talking the Sicilian, and I don't understand very much."

So then I went to that Maurice myself—he was the boss of the show—and I told him he'd better look out and stop those dirty jokes. But he kept on just the same, and the government came and closed his show.

That Jew man that has the little moving-picture show across from my house now, he's good to me. When it's a nice picture he comes by my house and says, "You want to come tonight or tomorrow night, Mis' Cavalleri? It's a swell picture." And when he sees me come, he lets me buy the ticket and go right in the door ahead of everybody. He knows I can't stand in that line of people with my bad leg. When it's a bum picture, he doesn't tell me to come. He never tells me to come to those pictures where they won't let the children in. In those pictures I have to close my eyes almost the whole time to not make a sin.

# Fran Claro

Fran Claro has been a free-lance writer and a managing editor of a magazine for teenagers. Currently she is an editor at a telecommunications company in New York City. She and her husband Joe live in Little Neck, New York where they entertain their five children and nine grandchildren often. Her reminiscence, "South Brooklyn, 1947" was one of UNICO's prize-winning essays in the publication *A New Day*, featuring the literary work of young Italian American authors.

## South Brooklyn, 1947

My mother's name was Mary. Maria Luisa was her given name. It was a beautiful name—it could have been contracted to Marisa—a very fashionable name for girls today.

Instead, she chose to call herself *Mary*—good old American *Mary*. I remember my father singing to her:

*Mary . . . Mary . . . plain as any name could be . . .*

My mother delighted in the song, until she heard the lines:

But with pro-pri-e-ty,
*So-ci-e-ty*
*Will say Mar-ie.*

77

Then she'd say, "Oh, I hate that 'Marie.' My name is *Mary*."

When we went to the stores, she'd meet her old classmates. "Hello, Marie," they would say, because this is what the nuns in school used to call her.

When she started elementary school, she spoke only Italian. She was the oldest child in the family, and she would eventually be responsible for overseeing the education—and the Americanization—of five younger brothers and sisters.

Her introduction to formal adult English started when she was about 11. Those were the depression years, and she would translate into Italian for my grandparents all the letters they received from the bank.

Years later, she remembered reading them the letter which told them that their mortgage had been foreclosed.

She escaped from her Italian world by reading. *Rebecca of Sunnybrook Farm* became her favorite book. For long hours—after she finished helping my grandmother with the younger children and the sewing homework—she would sit and read. Her heroines were fair-skinned, blond-haired, blue-eyed. She could not identify with them, but their world intrigued her.

She wanted to absorb the culture of these American heroines. Because her parents were not educated, she grew up listening to Italian soap operas and being entertained at street festivals. She rebelled against this gaudy, flashy brand of entertainment. As she grew into adulthood, her childhood dreams of American respectability grew into a determination to separate her children from a culture she had learned to despise.

She would never allow her children to get involved in any of the activities which were dear to her parents' hearts. Their culture, she believed, was not one to pass to a new generation.

I remember the Saints' days, especially the parades and the feasts. Early on a Saturday morning, the band would line up outside the church, and the marchers would assemble.

"Open the window!" I would call to my brother. "Quick, I hear the parade coming!"

My mother would say, "Run, get a pillow for my elbows."

We were safely aloof in our second-floor apartment. So my mother could join us in watching the parade, without feeling that she was taking part in it.

As the band passed, my brother would sing along:

> *Oh, the monkeys have no tails in Zambawanga,*
> *In Zambawanga . . .*

"Ma, look! The girls with the collection trays!"

"Hurry," she'd tell my brother, "get some change. No, not a quarter, a dime."

She'd thrust the money into my hand. "Here. Throw it out the window."
I'd toss the coin and yell, "Look, Ma, she got it!"

The girl would look up and smile. She was always a little too fat for the blue rayon dress she wore.

We never watched the parade from the curb. If you were there, you were expected to give a dollar. The maids on the Saint's float would pin the bills to the sash on the statue and give you a holy picture.

My brother and I concentrated on the parade. My mother watched, keeping her distance. She was safe in our little apartment.

The committee came first. These were the men who collected money all year to pay for the affair in honor of St. Lucy—St. Michael—St. Ann—it depended on the province they came from.

They wore red, white, and green sashes and a lapel pin printed with the word COMMITTEE. The median age of the committee members was 65. The parish's Italian-speaking priest walked with them.

The band played. (There were many tubas.) After the band came the float, pulled by the strongest—and, often, the most simple-minded—young men in the neighborhood.

Of course, it wasn't called a float. It was The Saint. Ripe young virgins in cheap party dresses pinned the money on the overpainted statue amid a setting of fake grass and fake flowers. It was a living Woolworth's window, decked out for Mother's Day.

The widows followed The Saint. They were dressed in black, with black rosaries wrapped around their hands. When they caught your eye, they would perform an elaborate sign of the cross, kiss their fingers, raise their eyes, and point the kiss in the direction of The Saint.

In the row of committeemen, I would see my grandfather, his face flushed, sweating, and proud. This was *his* parade. His good grey suit—with the COMMITTEE pin prominently displayed—was used for this one time every year.

Oh, how I wanted to be part of that parade. I wanted to be on that float. I dreamed about pinning bills on The Saint. But my mother was becoming an American.

"That's not for you," she would say. "Even when you're old enough, we're not gonna let you do that."

My father did not interfere. he deferred to her in all decisions about raising us.

My father was the local high school graduate, and he took some pride in being a man of letters. He could be counted on to fill out alien registration forms and to address the tags for the packages everyone sent overseas.

"Mike, you got any boxes?" my mother would ask the grocer. "I'm making a package for Italy. I need a box."

These packages were not "for the relatives," or "for home." They were *for Italy*.

I used to think that a man stood on the dock in Naples and gave all my old clothes to everyone in Italy.

My father worked very hard, but I was never impressed with his civil service job, or even with the time he spent in Korea during World War II. All of it never impressed me the way my grandfather's work did.

My grandfather—and almost all his friends—*dug*. I was never really sure just what they dug, although I knew it had something to do with buildings.

At five o'clock, my brother and I would walk the six blocks to meet him at the subway. His heavy shoes would be caked with mud and plaster. His hands were hard and brittle, like plastic. His complexion was almost Indian red. On the way home from the subway, he would joke with us, half in English, half in Italian.

As soon as we got to his house, we would bring him hot coffee with milk and sugar. We would sit on the window sill in his kitchen, lean out on the fire escape, and see the back of our own apartment.

My grandfather smiled most of the time. He liked to play with us, and he felt proud when we walked with him. We loved being with him.

But what I found charming about him, his daughter—my mother—found embarrassing. It was to please him that she had to attend the feast that followed the parade.

Oh, the feast.

The street from avenue to avenue festooned with curlicues of colored lights and Italian flags. In the middle of the block, a bandstand erected on a level with a second-story window.

The smell of the grease, fried, refried, and refried.

The Saint's dais—a storefront where the statue stood, guarded by members of The Committee.

"*Zeppole, calzone, salsiccia forte!*" shouted the vendors.

My mother, in her patented stage whisper: "Don't eat from those stands! Look, they're filthy! He just blew his nose! Oh, it's disgusting!"

This was her litany, as she unwillingly soiled herself by dragging us through the crowd on a Saturday night.

"Please, Ma, let us stay a little while," my brother would beg.

"Only until we see your grandfather. So he knows we came."

"Here's a dime," my father would say to my brother." "Go try that game."

"No, you do it, Dad." My brother stepped aside so my father could wind up with the small, soft ball.

My father, the almost-ballplayer, winding up. For a minute, he forgot he was 27 and the father of two. He was 16, and trying out for the high school team. He made the team, but he never played a game. He had to work after school.

"C'mon, Dad!" my brother cheered.

The man with the greasy black change apron: "Here, Mister. Pick your prize."

"Take the snake on the stick!" my brother said.

The snake was black and silver and white crinkled paper with one rhinestone eye. It twirled around a skinny dowel. We waved it at each other.

"Ma," I said, "I'm hungry."

She hesitated. Then, "All right. When we walk up the street, we'll get a lemon ice. At least it's clean in the pasticceria."

"*Canta, canta Napoli,*" beseeched the voices of the widows, who brought folding chairs to set up under the bandstand. The music followed us up the street.

If we slowed down, my mother tugged at us.

"Don't dirty your dress. Watch out for that hot grease."

"Look," my father said to us, "there's your grandfather."

"Grandpa, Grandpa, look what we won!"

"*E bello,*" he beamed at us. He turned to his friend. "*Luigi, questo mio nepoti.*"

"*Una bella ragazza,*" Luigi said.

"*Maria,*" my grandfather said, "wait. *Zia* Caterina is coming."

"No, Pa. The kids want a lemon ice. Tell her I'll see her next week. Good night, *Cumpari.* Good night, Pa."

On the way up the street, we met the priest. My mother looked as if she might die. She felt naked. She had come to the feast to please her father. Now she had to face the Irish priest.

"Hello, Mary," he smiled.

"Hello, Father. The kids wanted to walk down and see what was going on," she said, blushing. Under the lights, I could see a tear in her eye.

I felt her stiffen and grab my hand. To herself, she was saying:

> Good Irish father, forgive me, but my children don't know what they're doing. You can be here because you're not one of us. You can be here because *Cumpari* Sal will put a table and chair from his bar at the curb for you and bring you a free cold beer. You can be an observer. But my kids, they want to listen to the music and eat the food and play the games. And my father, he's proud. He thinks this stinking, filthy display will do honor to a saint.

She continued to blush and smile at the priest.

"Well," he said, moving on to greet others, "I'll see you all at the nine tomorrow."

"Good night, Father," we all said.

The walk up the street to the pasticceria was my mother's Gethsemane.

My father met an old bachelor friend. "Hey, Frankie," my father called, "is Sonny here with you?"

"Yeah. He's over there with *Cump' Angelo*. You and Mary leaving already?"

"Yeah, well, you know—the kids. Tomorrow's church and all." My father was embarrassed.

*Cumari* Amelia, Frankie's mother, approached my mother. "Maria, you see *Cumpa* Giuan? He's with your father, no?"

Just being talked to here was humiliating for my mother. "They're over there, *Cumari*, by The Saint."

Didn't these people realize that she had to get off this street? She didn't belong here. Her children must not enjoy this!

"Listen," Frankie said, "don't forget stickball tomorrow at 11 on 18th Street."

"Yeah," my father answered. "I'll be there after we stop up and see Nana."

"G'night, Mary," Frankie said. "G'night kids."

My mother said, "Good night, *Cumari*."

"*Sta bene, Maria.*"

Finally, we arrived at the pasticceria. My father bought nickel cups of lemon ice, just for the kids. He and my mother would take only a taste.

The mixture inside the pleated, slightly waxed cup had a snowy-granular-sour-sweet taste. As the ice softened, you squeezed the cup, and the delicious lemony flavor came into the corners of your mouth. It made you lick the corners of your lips.

"Should we stop at your mother's on the way home?" my father asked.

"No, my brother's bringing his girl over tonight. We'll just go home." She sounded very tired.

The lemon ice got softer. If you folded the cup vertically in two and bit down on the waxy cup, the syrup dribbled down your throat.

My brother tried to grab the snake from me.

"C'mon, let me hold it for a while."

"Hey, stop fighting with your sister." My father rolled the snake around the stick and tucked it under his arm.

"Next year," my mother said. "we're not going anywhere near that feast."

The music became vague and distant as we neared home. But I could still hear the voice singing:

*Mama . . . Mama . . . solo per te la mia canzone vola . . .*

The next morning, my father—the usher—led us to our pew at the nine o'clock Mass. It was a front row seat. My mother sent us to Catholic school so we would be allowed to sit in the front of the church on Sunday. Years earlier, she had been forced to sit in the back, because she went to public school.

She was going to Americanize her children primarily through the church. She wanted her children to become Rosarians, to join the Holy Name Society and the Sodalities.

Her children would never walk the streets soliciting contributions for a saint's feast day. But every Tuesday, they might "help the pastor out with Bingo."

The "fine ladies" of the Rosary Society impressed my mother as being modern, secure, and attractive. She thought the way they let their ice cream melt in their coffee was very stylish. She admired their appearance, so different from her very dark and very Italian beauty.

She admired them without stopping to realize that she was in awe, not of Ladies of the Manor, but of Brooklyn Irish Catholics.

The church did its Americanizing well. By the time I was ready for high school—having lived through the Irish nuns under the direction of an Italian pastor—I had no real identity. I acted like all my Irish classmates, dressed like them, and excelled over most of them in grades.

But no matter what I did, I just didn't *look* like them. All the Peter Pan collars and washing granules in the world could not erase my Italianness.

In college, I started thinking about why my Italianness bothered me. Gradually, I came to realize that it bothered my mother, and not me.

I became interested in the language and the music. I learned a lot that I should have learned years earlier, and I talked to my mother about what I was learning.

My mother—because she revered education—began to listen seriously to what I was talking about. She came to realize that there could be beauty in Italian music and elegance in Italian food.

She learned that there was charm and joy and zest in the enthusiasm my grandfather shared with his friends in planning a feast.

After my brother and I became the adults she wanted us to be, she stepped back and took a long look at us. She realized that without the feasts and the church and the dozens of relatives, we would not have been the same people. After all those years, she was ready to learn about and enjoy her own culture.

She had decided to become an Italian.

# Karen Malpede

Karen Malpede was born in Wichita Falls, Texas, of a Jewish mother and an Italian American father, a doubly alienating background that Malpede says meant she did not fit any group, and that has helped her write drama that is free-ranging. She now lives and works in Brooklyn where she is co-founder of the New Cycle Theater and has had eleven of her stage plays produced in the United States and abroad. A past winner of the Fulbright National Playwrights Fellowship, she has completed a screenplay, "I, Emily," based on Emily Dickinson. In addition to her playwriting, Malpede teaches writing and works in human rights, creating and directing theater based on the stories of refugees. For this collection she offers an autobiographical introduction to a scene from her play *A Monster Has Stolen the Sun*.

## Introduction

One year before my child was born, I took the plane from London to Milan to visit Judith Malina and Julian Beck, old friends whose Living Theater troupe was performing a new play in an old flower market turned into a theater for the people by the artistic wizard Dario Fo. It was almost Passover, festival of freedom, time of pogroms for Jews world over, a time of year I had learned to dread quite early in my life without knowing why. Growing up in the white, Presbyterian, affluent northern suburbs of Chicago, Passover was a holiday I had scant knowledge of. I did know that every year at spring, while my little friends were filling Easter baskets and showing off new patent leather shoes, my Italian Catholic father would escalate his rage at his beautiful Jewish wife and their two unbaptized children, and my house became, once more, a frightening place to live.

"The Last Supper was a Seder," my mother used to whisper to us as we were growing up, "and Jesus was a Jew." "Our greatest rabbi," Judith Malina, devout daughter of a rabbi, would many years later confirm. As a child I knew neither Passover Seder nor Easter Mass; I did not know it had been decreed my mother's people had killed my father's God and so I could not begin to understand the roots of the abuse he hurled at us.

Now the small charter plane bumped onto the runway. Its steel doors slid open and I walked down the metal stairway toward the Italian land. "You got cancer, Joey, because you married out of your religion," my Italian grandmother told her dying forty-two-year-old son. He was dead fifteen years by the time I landed in Milan, long enough for the wounds of those early years to mend, long enough for me to have exorcised the wild girlhood love I bore for this hurt and hurting, impassioned man. The airport was lined with young Italian soldiers bearing rifles. Fitting, I thought, to be met by the state's show of violence against its rebellious children, "Terrorists," they're called, terrorizing the terror makers with their wanton, futile acts.

Then my feet touched the ground. And the tears came, followed by the wish, which was a physical impulse, an involuntary muscular desire, to lay my body down upon the ground and kiss the good Italian earth. My father's home, though he, himself, never had set foot here and did not know the name of the town from which his grandparents had come. In the thirty-third year of my life, without meaning to, while traveling to see my friends, their play and spend the Seder with them, I had come back to my father's land, come back for him and to him, as the silent sobs which shook me as I walked to the airport bus explained.

In a year, I would bear the grandchild he never lived to see and write *A Monster Has Stolen the Sun*, the play about parenting from which a scene is reprinted here. A little girl would be born to me, a child more beautiful than I who was known to have been a beautiful baby, my father's special pride. "Dad would have liked her, he always liked little girls," my twin brother remarked in that full, kind, sad voice of his. My brother had another story; he knew too well about our father's inability to parent boys. "Your husband hates this baby," the Black nurse told my mother, a young and frightened army wife in Texas, about the sickly boy-child in the crib whose arm was nearly broken by the father's rage. And in the years of growing up, very little but ridicule for the son escaped the father's lips.

Last summer at my mother's sister's house, she told me that whenever my mother's phone calls were delayed, my aunt assumed we had all been murdered by my father, or had died in the car which he, drunken and distressed, had crashed somewhere along the freeway speeding from his mother's house to ours on Sunday nights. In his mother's house there was one book, the Bible, lying on the marble-topped round table with its white-and-gold-fringed lamp which occupied the center spot in the bay window of this second-floor brick worker's flat. Every house on the street had such a table and a lamp visible between heavy fringed curtains as we drove up. My father's father worked on the assembly line at the dairy and had a black, blistered nailless thumb never healed from an accident at the plant. He grated Parmesan cheese on the *Chicago Tribune* and swore about the stupidity of the "goddamn White Sox." My father's mother wore black shoes, stockings, dress, a small diamond cross at her neck, her gray hair neatly curled at beauty shop appointments, her one adjustment to the fashion of the New World. She looked ancient to me, always, yet lived only to be sixty-six, dying two weeks to the day before my father did. And his broken father, who lost wife and only son so quickly, turned to us and asked us not visit him again. We reminded him of Joe, he said, or of Joe's transgression, and he didn't want to be reminded.

In my early youth, I idolized these two, the dairy worker and his wife, and thought they had a wisdom of simplicity no one in the affluent suburb where I lived could know. They had been on relief all during the Depression. According to my father, he had eaten mainly prunes and worn one ugly maroon sweater. My liberal mother thought it strange that her in-laws and her husband still hated Roosevelt and always voted Republican.

As a child, I loved my grandparents' scrubbed kitchen with its big pots of sauce, the white bakery boxes full of cookies and the endless relatives who drifted in and out, big Rosa, little Rosa, big Joey and little, and Uncle Tiny who weighted three hundred pounds. A sprawling Chicago Italian family, the younger generation all wore hot jewelry and drove hot cars, some had connections to the Mafia, and no one but my father spoke correct English, as my artistic, upper-middle-class mother could not keep from pointing out. No one spoke fluent Italian, either; most had come as children to this land. "All Jews cheat, don't you think so," my grandmother turned to my mother in the presence of company and asked. And she toilet-trained my father by burning him on the penis with a fireplace poker. That was a story he told my mother in dark nights when their passion for each other and each other's hurts had brought them close.

America, how cruel you are to immigrants, ripping away culture, language, land, roots, and whatever sense of self, dignity and kindliness these things provide, all for the lure of wealth, for a chance one's only son might work his way through college and become a C.P.A.

It was brave what my parents did, breaking class and religious lines to marry in 1943. Two despised peoples, consolidating burdens in their rush to assimilate. Because he had been abused himself and had suffered poverty and prejudice, my father became the abusing male. We know now that the battering of women and children cuts across class and religious lines, but Wasps are quieter about brutality, as they are about most things, and in the Wasp suburb where we grew up no one lived in such a tumultuous house as we.

Never since have I heard such hideous language as he used, screaming at his family over fried chicken and mashed potatoes which we forced ourselves to eat so we would not have to look up and meet his eyes. Sometimes my brother would break out in nervous laughter, and that, of course, would increase my father's rage. We had learned not to answer back. Now a playwright who produces ritual plays of transformation, written in verse, I grimace at the innocence of those who write swear words for the stage and think they are being realistic, they would not dare imitate the strings of sexual, scatological invectives he hurled so regularly at us. He had a lyric poet's sense of cadence and internal rhyme, an imagist's finesse, he startled and surprised.

Does one speak this way about the dead? Perhaps it was the Catholicism, or the working class from which he came. Perhaps it was his betrayal of both when he married a kind and gifted Jewish woman and worked his way through college to become an executive. He was in too much pain to live. The cancer which ate him from the inside out seemed fitting in its horror, a gruesome metaphor suddenly run amok.

He went back to the Church a few years before he died. I used to go with him to Midnight Mass on Christmas Eve. Still in Latin, then, the Mass was a great show, and only dimly did I understand his pain, as he knelt alone with me while everyone else filed slowly to Communion and was absolved of sin. Buried, irony of ironies, on Yom Kippur day, the priest intoned, "Joseph Malpede died for his sins," and we three mortal ones sat in the first row, the Jewish wife and two unbaptized children. Once while he was dying, he sat bolt upright in his hospital bed and told us each how much he loved us and how hard he had always tried to show us love; he asked us to care for one another, and spoke like a noble man, a father, about his coming death. But the rages never ended, and once, too, a weak shadow of a man, he came screaming naked through the house brandishing a knife.

When he died, I stopped writing fiction for eleven years, and when I wrote again, it was a play about women wresting their lives back after the deaths of men like him.

I have never met a man more passionate, a man who held more fire in his soul, a man who cried as easily or seemed to love as fiercely as he raged. Without him, I would never have known so clearly the glory of the human soul which hides beneath the gaping scars life makes.

Is this knowledge visible within the scene from *A Monster Has Stolen the Sun* which is reprinted here? In it, a man is put under a spell in which he dreams he has given birth. He dances with the newborn child; he speaks the words to his small son I felt in my heart when my daughter first appeared to me. In this small bundle which he holds, work of his own loins, he sees no rival nor successor but his own great vulnerability revealed, and he does not shrink from what he sees, does not seek to murder it, does not attempt to break its arm, does not scream at it with hate. For a moment, the father comes clear to us as, potentially, a man of love, of warmth, dreamer, poet. Then he wakes from his spell, and smashes his imaginary infant hard against the rocks.

This long play is set in Celtic Ireland, a mystic culture I found because childhood had alienated me from both my Italian and my Jewish roots. But the play's central tales of father/son, mother/daughter, and the fight between women and men belong to me, my father, my mother and my brother. The play ends eighteen years later when the father gives up his power over others and rocks his grown son in his arms, in the sort of birthing motion lived out which is but dreamlike in the scene printed here. My father had this birthing motion in him, driving him; for fear of it, I think, he died. And this is my song of praise for all he was but could not be. And this is my song of praise for that part of him I would have live.

---

# *from* A Monster Has Stolen the Sun

---

*Scene 2 (*BRIGIT*, the midwife, and* OWAIN*, the king of a small kingdom, or tuath, approach an ancient burial spot, which is marked by a dolmen, rising up out of the rocks)*

BRIGIT: Once I carried you, slung between my breasts,
    and danced here through the night.
    Now the rocks pierce the soles of my feet
    and the wind reminds me of death.
OWAIN: Once we danced together in this spot,
    our breath billowing up.
    We were the crystal waves that lept
    from the depths of the sea
    to shatter in brilliant shapes
    for the sake of eternity.

BRIGIT: This much we know, but much is lost,
So I have brought you here as if to dream
the future of some unbegotten race.
This much is known, and not much else:
how I caught you from your mother's heaving womb
to bear you at my breast. How you stood
shaking with desire when I aroused your sex,
then journeyed to the center of the earth
to spill your virgin seed into that scared cave.
How life and death seemed one to you that once.
All this is known, but nothing else,
so I have brought you here as if to dream the future
of an unbegotten race.
OWAIN: Once I knelt in awe before your shape

(*He kneels.*)


I stared at the weight and motion of your breasts
and felt my own shape change.
BRIGIT: Now a passage into yet another form is asked.
The hungry child sucking at my breast,
the long-haired youth delighting in the dance
have grown into a man whose time to father
the unknown is come.
OWAIN: Is Etain already due?
These many months have seen me turn from her.
BRIGIT: I have watched. I have not said a word.
Etain kneels in prayer on the cold stones; she follows
the bird's flight with her eyes. The young girls
you chase have grown wise. You have remained as you were.
OWAIN: Etain grew large and quiet and unknown before my sight;
she changed and, yes, I felt myself remain the same.
So I turned from what I could not understand.
BRIGIT: And sought a new love out.
OWAIN: As you sought me when you, too, felt a need
to bond with something vibrant and untouched.
BRIGIT: I have watched and have not said a word.
OWAIN: You know the charm that would
have kept my love for her alive.
BRIGIT: Three things only do I know:
The love of the life that is over and gone;
the love of what was and will never return;

the torturous love of the unborn.
This last I would share with you.
OWAIN: Come to me for one moment out of time,
    let us be once more as we were,
    a girlish youth gasping with wonder
    and the wise woman he lay under.
BRIGIT: Back, further back in your heart,
    search for what was and has been forgot.
OWAIN: Take me back beyond that midnight spring
    when the moon lay open and full
    to a time I lay snug in your arms
    when the world was an orb of milklike flesh
    and milky smells.
BRIGIT: Back, further back in your heart.
    Back beyond time or regret.
    A creature unborn is all that is left of what was.
    I have brought you here to dream that new change through.
    You will lend your flesh and your bones
    to the greed of what is unborn.

OWAIN *squats on the ground. He feels himself to be pregnant and begins to move in the rhythms of birth.*

BRIGIT *sings the song of the solitary birth and the chorus of crows emerges from behind the dolmen to accompany her.*

BRIGIT: On a windswept hill on a mountain plain
    washed by the salt of the sea and the rain
    a solitary creature, deer, cow, pig, mare, goat,
    woman alone, squatted down to give birth.
    How many times has this story been told,
    how few the listeners. How many times
    has the labor been made to the sound
    of the wind and the song of the birds.
    And she who brought forth the unknown,
    how many times did she shiver and shake,
    caught in the moment of death, the effort that knows
    one release, form out of form, fear birthing love.
    When the lonely work was done, when she had licked
    the infant clean, who was there on that lonely plain
    to marvel at what had been made. A bandy-legged calf,
    a sniveling runt, an unwanted puck, a son to be feared,
    a daughter scorned. The lonely one and the newborn work
    of her heart rage at the welcoming wind.

OWAIN *wakes. He sees the "babe" he has birthed. He cradles and welcomes the "child" he imagines is there.*

OWAIN: Hello, little babe, little beast, little one.
  Where have you been? Where have you come from?
  A moment before you were only the faith
  that the effort would end and a child would be born.
  Your wet head slithers across my chest.
  Your fingers grasp at my flesh.
  Your eyes blink open and stare.
  You are life looking up, crawling up out of your well.
  You have come from the mud, from the ocean's dark you have come.
  A beast flung down from the sky, heaved up from the earth's dark cave.
  How did you dare to trust a love I never have known
  would anchor your heart in my own?

OWAIN *begins to rock the "child" when, suddenly, the crows begin a piercing, jeering call.*

OWAIN: What is that sound? The crowd, the world
  that calls me from the task of birth. Away,
  away, away, you flat-beaked crows.
  away, I am not weak.
  Stop your screeching, jeering song.

  *(He wakes from his dream.)*

  What monstrous trick is done that you would lead me
  through this hurt, this fear, this great exultant
  effort of the heart, to leave me face-to-face
  with mocking sky and barren rock.

  *(He chases after the crows.)*

  Be gone, you evil tribe of birds.
  Be gone, you stinking, ugly things.

  *(He chases them behind the dolmen, out of sight.)*

  Leave me as I was,
  a man whose mute and shuttered loins
  hold fast against unknown, unwanted things.

  *(BRIGIT emerges from the dolmen, as herself.)*

BRIGIT: Hush, Owain, hush. Before the rage
   which is all you can remember now,
   lived an image barely touched, inside you still:
   a wild delight at birth which turned to fear.
   Upon the sudden thought birth takes all you are,
   rips and uses you while the small thing born demands
   a love more pure than any such a torn and shattered thing
   can give.
   Owain, awake, you have been to the source,
   turned and fled, but the source of that devouring
   delight will one day claim you for her own.
   Not the birth, but love of the birth,
   Not the child, but awe of the child,
   Not the effort, but reverence before it,
   are yours.

   *The dawn has come. A bird's song is heard and* MACHA *answers it. She is
   seen in the distance, heavy with child, a burden carried on her back. She
   is leaping across the rocks.*

OWAIN: Who is that?
BRIGIT: It is Macha, the poor shepherd's wife.
OWAIN: She strides with the grace of the wind or the wave
   yet her belly is heavy with child.
BRIGIT: She is half-tamed.
   She sings with the wildest of birds.
   She runs with the hind and the fox.
OWAIN: Why have I not seen her before?
BRIGIT: Her strength bids her keep to herself.
OWAIN: Where is she from? She is not of this place.
BRIGIT: She came down from the mountain last year;
   to ease the poor shepherd, who lived alone.
   She grew fond of the one she had found;
   now she carries a child under her heart.
   Come, the dawn has played itself out.
   Macha is gone from our sight. I am called
   by the light of the sun back to the tasks of the day.
OWAIN: Go by yourself back to the house,
   I would seek out that poor shepherd's flock.

# Louise DeSalvo

Louise DeSalvo is professor of English and Creative Writing at Hunter
College. A noted Virginia Woolf scholar, she is the author of *Virginia
Woolf: the Impact of Childhood Sexual Abuse on Her Life and Work* and
other works on Woolf. DeSalvo's work has appeared in several collections
and she has also written fiction in addition to *Writing as a Way of Healing* and
three books of memoirs: *Vertigo, Breathless,* and *Adultery.*

## *from* A Portrait of the *Puttana* as a Middle-Aged Woolf Scholar

The year is 1975.

I am thirty-two years old, married, the mother of two small children, a
Ph. D. candidate, on a charter flight to England with a friend to do research
on Virginia Woolf at the University of Sussex in Falmer. This is the first
time in my whole life that I am going away by myself. I have no idea where
Falmer is, except that it is near Brighton. We have no hotel reservations.
We have no idea how we will get to Brighton. But we are gloriously drunk
on our third sherry, free from the responsibility of our children for a while.
(We have already had enough sherry so that each child can have her or his
own little sherry bottle as a souvenir when we return home.) We are, at

93

long last, grown-ups, going to do *real* research. The next generation of Woolf scholars, in incubation. We are formidable.

I come from a family, from a cultural heritage, where women simply don't go away to do things separately from men. That is not to say that men don't go away to do things separately from women. They do. And often. But in the land of my forebears, women sit around and wait for their men. Or they watch their children and wait for their men. Or they work very hard and watch their children and wait for their men. Or they make a sumptuous meal and they work very hard and watch their children and wait for their men. But they don't go anywhere without their men. Or do anything for themselves alone without their men. Except complain. To their children or to anyone else who will listen to them. About their men and about their bad luck in having been born female.

A few years ago, I decided, like everyone else, to explore my ethnic roots. It lasted a very short time. I bought a pasta machine. Learned how to combine the ingredients for pasta, to roll out the dough, and cut it. Word got out that I was a terrific pasta maker. Then I began to realize that you pretty well know how enslaved the women of any country are by the kind of preparation their traditional foods require. Any recipe that begins, "Take a mortar and pestle . . ." now drives me into a feminist frenzy. Well, pasta making is something like that. Women who really care about their families make it fresh every day. Purists insist that if the sacred pasta dough is touched by metal pasta machines (i.e., twentieth-century labor-saving devices), it becomes slightly slippery—a quality in pasta that is akin to infidelity in wives. Oh yes, I now remember what women who do anything without their husbands are called. *Puttane*. Whores. I remember hearing stories in my childhood about how women like that were stoned to death in the old country.

Well, given a background like that, you can imagine the way I felt as we flew high above the Atlantic. There I was, a *puttana*, alone at last.

Early on in my work on Virginia Woolf, I thought that I would devote the rest of my life to carefully considered scholarly essays and books on every aspect of her life and art. Those were the heroine worship days when I blanched at the sight of her manuscripts, when I did not dare to think that she had an outhouse, much less that she and Leonard used the typescripts of her novels instead of toilet tissue, that she could be hardy enough or human enough to walk across the Downs in her beloved Sussex. I saw her as an earlier generation of critics had painted her for me—frail, weak, crazy, tortured, looking out of windows, vacant, probing the inside of her troubled psyche. . . .

I loved the sight of myself, briefcase in hand, walking up the steps of The New York Public Library, past the lions Patience and Fortitude (I would have preferred lionesses), thinking that the kid who grew up on the streets of Hoboken, New Jersey, was now walking past the painting of Milton's daughters taking down the immortal words of his verse, now walking down the third-floor corridor to the Berg Collection, now pressing the buzzer. And they were actually letting me into the sacred recess where I would soon sit next to all those famous literary scholars whose work I had read and do work of my own.

The American Dream.

And as I sat there, beginning my work, I thought that if only I could have the good fortune to be able to sit over a glass of sherry at the Algonquin, or even over a cup of coffee at Tad's Steak House down the block, with someone really famous to talk about Virginia Woolf, life would be so sweet, so very sweet, and I would ask for nothing more in this universe.

I got into Woolf scholarship quite by accident. (Or so I thought at the time.) When I was in graduate school at New York University, I took a course with the Woolf scholar Mitchell Leaska. He was in the throes of his work on *The Pargiters*, his edition of the earlier draft of *The Years*. I was enthralled with his classes. I'll never forget the day that he brought in his transcription of Woolf's holograph, the handwritten draft of that novel. I changed my mind about what I would be doing with my scholarly life in the moments it took him to read to us from Woolf's earlier version of *The Years*. Here was a more political, less guarded Woolf. I had never known that earlier versions of literary texts were available. It had never occurred to me before that one could inquire into the process of the creation of a novel and learn about the writing process and the process of revision in so doing. It sounded like detective work. It was meticulous. It required stamina. Drive. It was exciting. I too would be working with manuscripts. I think I understood that I required a grand consuming passion in a project.

I soon decided to work with the manuscripts of *The Voyage Out*, Woolf's first novel, because I wanted to catch Virginia Woolf in her beginnings where I thought she might be least guarded.

*The Voyage Out* is about Rachel Vinrace, a young, inexperienced woman, who accompanies her father on a trip to South America. On her father's ship, the *Euphrosyne*, she resumes a relationship with her aunt and uncle, Helen and Ridley Ambrose, and she meets Richard Dalloway, a former Member of Parliament, and his wife, Clarissa. Rachel becomes involved with two parental surrogates—Helen and Clarissa—but the relationship with Clarissa is complicated because Rachel is sexually attracted to

Richard. During a storm at sea, Rachel and he embrace. That night she has
a dream that she is being pursued.

Later, when she is at Santa Marina, a South American port city, she
meets Terence Hewet, who is spending his holiday there. They fall in love
and decide to marry. But both are extremely reluctant lovers. Rachel dies of
a mysterious illness before the couple can marry.

What I had no way of knowing when I decided to work on *The Voyage
Out* was that I would have enormous difficulty keeping the problems that I
was having in my life separate from the issues that Woolf was discussing in
the novel. I had reached that moment of sexual reevaluation that often
occurs at about thirty. Although I was married, I went through a time when
I identified with Rachel so strongly that I believed I shared her distrust of
intimacy. It was simpler for me to see myself in terms of Woolf's character
than it was to look at my own problems. I vacillated between thinking that
Rachel—and by extension myself—were typical of all women, and thinking
that her hesitations (and mine) were pathological. It took many years for me
to separate myself from Rachel Vinrace. It took many years for me to
understand that part of the reason for Rachel's hesitation was her submerged rage at the misogyny and brutality of the men in her life—all
disguised through the artifice of civilization to be sure, but there nonetheless. In the process of separating myself from Rachel, I learned not to make
disparaging judgments about Rachel's behavior—or mine—but to look for
the causes of that behavior in familial and societal histories. I also saw that I
was letting this very close identification with Rachel hold me back, keep me
in check, because my work was making me feel very powerful. And I was
terrified of feeling powerful.

I wake up in the middle of the night from a dream. The dream is easy to
describe, difficult to comprehend. Ishtar—the many-breasted goddess—
with a face vaguely like that of Virginia Woolf but resembling my mother,
in profile, has placed her hands under my armpits and has picked me up.
Her face is impassive. She does not look at me, does not recognize me,
stares past me. She begins shaking me—not violently, but powerfully and
rhythmically. As she shakes me, all the things that define me as a woman
fall off. They form a pile beneath my feet. As she continues to shake me, still
staring beyond me, impassively and without emotion, what is left of me
begins to shrivel into the baby doll that I remember having in my childhood. The only openings I have, now, are the hole in the middle of the little
red mouth that you put the toy bottle in and the one where the water runs
out, between the legs. I begin saying, in the doll's voice that I remember,
"Mama, mama." Ishtar stares impassively ahead. But she stops shaking me.

Working on Woolf's composition of *The Voyage Out* was my first long project. One that would take years. It terrified me and it thrilled me. Sometimes I would feel immensely powerful, feel that I, single-handedly, might change the course of Woolf scholarship. Or I would feel impotent, wondering how I could make any contribution to our knowledge of Woolf.

I learned what it is humanly possible to do in one day; what one cannot do; that one must trust the times when no work is getting done, because it is in those fallow periods that the unconscious mind is working. I had to change the way I thought about time. I had to scale down my expectations to a human level. All of this was very hard for me to do. Every time I sat down to the project, my infantile power fantasies reared their ugly heads. I always thought that I would get more done in one day than it was possible to do. Then my feelings of potency would turn into feelings of powerlessness and despair. I slowly learned that the work could only proceed as quickly as it could proceed. (I have not entirely learned that lesson yet.) I learned that I have the same trouble that anyone else has in working, in writing comprehensible sentences, in revising them, but that if you work every day, the work will get done. I gradually realized what working on *The Voyage Out* for seven years must have been like for Virginia Woolf. I too was working on a project that was taking a very long time. There was the temptation, too, to work constantly, without interruption, to get it done more quickly. There was the temptation to work incessantly—days, nights, weekends—at the mountain of manuscripts, at the letters, diaries, and journals that Woolf had written while composing the novel.

From time to time, my husband reminds me of a moment in the days preceding our marriage. He was off at work. I was at our apartment. The place was filthy. I was trying to clean it so that we could move in. All the stores in the neighborhood were closed because of some holiday. I decided that I would clean all the tiles in the bathroom. The only thing I had that would do the job was a toothbrush. So, instead of waiting for him to come back to help me, instead of waiting for the next day to get a scrub brush which would speed the work, I took the toothbrush to the tiles. When he came to pick me up, I was exhausted and miserable, but also triumphant because I had finished.

Much of my work on Virginia Woolf's composition of *The Voyage Out* at the beginning was like that day with the toothbrush. . . .

As I recorded the progress of Virginia Woolf's days in order to figure out what she was doing as she was writing *The Voyage Out*, I started realizing that this was one hell of a woman, filled with incredible energy, so different from my original impression of her. Reading about her life in London, her visits to the British Museum, the books she read, the jaunts down to Sussex on weekends, the trips to St. Ives, to Wells, to The Lizard, to Lelant, Cornwall, the walks, the work, the lived life, fruitful beyond my wildest imaginings, her engagement with the most important political and social issues of her day, her teaching of working-class people, I began to revise my picture of her and my hopes for myself. I decided that it would be foolish of me to spend endless days alone inside libraries working on Woolf when the great woman of my dreams had spent no small portion of hers walking around the countryside, cultivating important relationships, particularly with women, taking tea, learning to bake bread, teaching, getting involved in politics, becoming an essayist, a novelist, integrating work and pleasure, and having, what seemed to me, in contrast to my boring scholarly life, a hell of a good time.

That's when I bought my first pair of hiking boots and started walking, first around the lower reaches of New York State and then, at long last, through her beloved Sussex and Cornwall, and later through Kent, Cumbria, Northumbria, Yorkshire. I retraced the trips she took while she was writing *The Voyage Out;* visited the places she visited; read the books she read; began having important friendships of my own with Woolf scholars; started teaching; began writing essays; started writing poetry; wrote a novel. . . .


I am thirteen years old. I have begun my adolescence with a vengeance. I am not shaping up to be the young woman I'm supposed to be. I am not docile. I am not sweet. I am certainly not quiet. And, as my father has told me dozens of times, I am not agreeable: if he says something is green, I am sure to respond that it is orange. I have mastered every conceivable method of turning my household into turmoil. I have devised a method of looking up at the ceiling when my father lectures me that instantly drives him into a frenzy.

In the middle of his fairly frequent outbursts, I run out of the house, feeling that I am choking, the tears hot on my cheeks. It is nighttime. I have no place to go. But I keep running. There are welcoming lights a few blocks away. It is the local library. I run up the stairs. I run up to the reading room with its engulfing brown leather chairs, pull an encyclopedia down from the shelf, and pretend to read so that I won't be kicked out. It is cool and it is quiet. My rage subsides. I think that if there is a heaven, surely it must resemble a library. I think that if there is a god, surely she must be a librarian.

It is 1957.

I am fourteen years old, standing behind the window of the bakery where I work to earn my spending money. Inside the bakery, I have to control my appetite or I will eat everything in sight and become grotesque and obese. You can't let yourself do that because boys only like attractive girls and attractive girls are always slim. What I do inside the bakery is fold paper boxes before I put the pastries and the cakes inside. And then I tie up the boxes with the red and white string that always tears into my flesh. What I'm doing is putting my appetitive self, which I am afraid will run out of control, into neatly packaged, antiseptic, pure boxes—containing it and tying it up.

Across the street, through the window, I see my friends playing endless games that involve laughing, touching, rolling on the grass. I am behind the plate-glass window, looking at life, looking at them having fun, locked away, earning money by putting buns in bags and cakes in boxes.

On Halloween, children come and paint the plate-glass window. They paint witches and goblins in black and in primary colors. Now I can't even see what is going on in the park across the street. But I still put the buns in boxes. It never occurs to me to even fantasize breaking through the window while I'm working or to wash the paint away. Or, more simply, to open the door and cross the street to the playground. Work is work. And work permits no play. I have to work. That is the way it is. Opening the door to let in the sound of laughter while working, crossing that street to the playground after work, learning to enjoy work and learning to be able to play took many years. And psychoanalysis. And work on Virginia Woolf.

Autumn 1963.

I am a senior at Douglass College. In 1963, Douglass College is the kind of school a bright young working-class woman can afford. Douglass, I think, is filled with brilliant women, and I have never seen brilliant women before. I have studied Shakespeare with Doris Falk, the novel with Anna Wells, philosophy with Amelie Rorty. I now have Twentieth-Century Fiction with Carol Smith.

Carol Smith is lecturing on Virginia Woolf's *To the Lighthouse*. She is talking about the relationship between Mr. and Mrs. Ramsay in "The Window" section of the novel. I have never in my life heard such genius. I am taking notes, watching her talk, and watching her belly. She is very pregnant. She is wearing a beige maternity dress. I take down every word, while watching to see when the baby she is pregnant with will kick her again.

I learn to love Virginia Woolf. I observe that it is possible to be a woman, to be brilliant, to be working, to be happy, and to be pregnant. And all at the same time.

# Granddaughters

One of the richest mines of the Italian American imagination is the grand-parent—mythical, real, imagined, idealized, venerated, or feared. The grandparent embodies the whole tribe, the whole heritage for that—in overwhelmingly the most cases—is as far as a present-day Italian American can trace his or her descent. After the immigrant grandparent, or great-grandparent, there are just faceless hordes stretching back into the past—unknown, unvisualized, unnamed. Many Italian Americans embody the paradox of coming from very ancient roots of an ancient civilization and culture, but knowing their past only as far as a grandparent. Most often there are no written records beyond the grandparent to tell us more of our ancestry; there are no photo albums in velvet Victorian covers. In our grandparents is incorporated all of the past, all of tradition and custom, and, we imagine, some archetypal wisdom and native intelligence. We start from the people who came here.

Over and over again, in the writing, there is mention of a grandparent. Sometimes it is a dream, as in Rosemarie Caruso's vision of her grand-mother walking down to her from the moon—a benevolent vision where the harsh reality never enters—and which inspired Caruso's interesting explo-ration of tradition between mothers and daughters in a play called *Shadows of the Morning Moon*. In a poem called "the dream," which was published in *Sinister Wisdom*, Michele Belluomini writes:

> back in the old neighborhood
> cautiously picking my way among
> abandoned houses and broken sidewalks
> I am trying to follow my grandmother
> but clumsy, I fear I will fall
>
> she shouts encouragement to me in Italian
> she climbs a rope to the attic
>
> words float from her mouth like water

The veneration, the awe, the wish for the strength of the grandparent is an enduring topos, ineluctable and omnipresent, a referential for every writer represented in this collection. The following two pieces, poetry by Gigi Marino, and prose by Mary Gordon, stand for the rest.

# Gigi Marino

Having once worked as a deckhand merchant seaman on oil tankers for the Exxon company where she was "writing steadily while out to sea," Gigi Marino returned to Pennsylvania State University to finish her degree in English. While there she won several poetry prizes and now teaches at the University.

## Angelina

My grandmother used to buy
chickens for a quarter apiece
from the people on the hill;
she'd twist their scrawny necks
painlessly with leathery
quick olive hands
then whack off the head
with a thick-bladed hatchet
she sharpened weekly on her
grindstone in the dank,
dug-out cave cellar where
we kept drainpipes stuffed
with paper and rags
so that rats from the creek
wouldn't sneak in at night.

Saturdays we washed clothes
there in the wringer in that
low-ceilinged stone-hole,
far from a child's paradise.
Upstairs noodles dried
on clean white sheets
draped over beds and chairs;
we blessed a huge tub of dough
with the sign of the cross,
then punched it down
and turned it into bread.
For supper she served
broiled knobbly chicken,
a few potatoes, dandelion greens,
and always: bread.
We sweated all day for Sunday,
a clean house and spaghetti.
She'd start the sauce before Mass,
then made sure we ate it all:
"*Mangia, mangia,*" she crooned,
"Tank God you don't got no tb."

My grandmother was always old.
I have a picture of her young,
maybe thirty, in the 1920s.
Already she'd started shrinking,
sitting outside on a footstool,
thin legs tightly pressed,
hands clasped, Mona Lisa lips,
eyes dipped with sadness.
Five babies too many,
not enough time to sew
the aprons that she sold
door to door, saving pennies
to buy the house where
she spent the first month
picking roaches off the walls.

My father, she didn't want—
she punched her belly, as if
dough, threw herself down steps,
still he stayed inside her;

she visited a doctor, with
Nicky, a small boy then, at
her skirts; the doctor said,
If I kill the one inside you,
I have to kill this one first.
Gramma never said that was sin;
but, "Don't let no boys
look under your dress."
That was a sin as bad as stealing—
Gramma called thieves "Black hands,"
men who waited by the tracks
behind her house for men
on payday on their
way to the beer garden.
Booze was sin too, worse,
because her husband drank,
but yearly her kitchen filled
with wine air of boiled grapes
that she grew and picked—
gallons of dago red she jugged,
and let go to vinegar
hidden in the dark cellar.

Her eyes went bad first,
suddenly, glasses, no good,
"I know your voice,"
then she knew everyone,
stopping people in the streets
to hear their voices, to hug
them and say, "I love you,"
to every stranger she met,
swearing it was 1944 yet.
She quit planting gardens,
but the ground, so fertile,
sprang to life each year:
roses, poppies, garlic,
tomato, pepper grew side by side.
Still she knew which was the
flower to place in the vase
in front of the plaster Madonna.
The fig tree out back
quit blossoming, her grape vines

fell, she didn't notice,
tv did her no good, those
voices, senseless to an old woman.
But children's voices she
understood, those, ageless.
She remembered her family's names,
Pearl Harbor, some broken Italian.

Daily she tracked miles,
to church, to town—
towards the end, sometimes
wearing only a slip, coat, boots.
People in church gasped,
called my father to come get her;
she smiled all the way.
My parents finally dressed
her in street clothes each night
never knowing when and where
she'd go, nothing stopped her.
Until the day they laid her
in a strict hospital bed.

The day I visited her
she asked if she was in church;
she looked like an angel misplaced;
her hair, long undone, all silver,
the sanitary hospital smock
floating over her thin body,
she, knowing somehow that I
knew, ran her thin hands across
my face and felt the
tears she couldn't see.
Two days later, my father
walked into the room,
she was screaming,
the angel had flown—
and left the body,
small, calm, smiling.

I waited each night at the wake
for her thin hands to grab me,
hold me close to her, hugging.

But when I touched the fingers,
stiff, like tough roots
growing above ground, I
knew their movement done.
But even as my sisters and I
carried the casket, I thought
she'd jump out, demand to
walk that church aisle by herself
as she'd done for the last
fifty years, stopping
at each pew to tell
strangers, "I love you."

I bless my dough each time
I make bread—
four hands punch it down:
Mine, young and strong,
and two old, skinny ones.

# Mary Gordon

Surely the least known of Mary Gordon's literary achievements is her
debut publication in UNICO's *A New Day,* a literary magazine awarding
prizes and publication to young authors of Italian American heritage. Mary
Gordon's first novel, *Final Payments,* was widely acclaimed and nominated
for the National Book Critics' Circle Award. Her output has remained pro
lific and has established her as the "preeminent novelist of Roman Catholic
mores and manners." Mary Gordon was born on Long Island of an Italian-

Irish mother and Jewish father who converted to Catholicism. A recent work
is her memoir *Shadow Man* about her father. She is a Professor at Barnard
College in New York.

# Zi'Marietta

My grandfather was always afraid of Zi'Marietta, his youngest sister, and he
passed his fear on to the rest of the family. Nevertheless, all the stories in
the family canon that revolved around her were told to make her look
foolish, carping, trivial, or vain. My grandfather never told any of these
stories himself; neither, however, did he prevent their telling by his wife
and children. The burden of feeling inferior to a younger sister was thus
relieved guiltlessly. If his own children could laugh at his sister, grandpa's
thralldom was only a temporary one: it would end with his death; it was a
private, terminal weight, and not a legacy. For Zi'Marietta represented to
my grandfather refinement, distinction, elegance, gentility, and these were
a difficult baggage for the catch as catch can America he had moved into.
Still, Grandpa valued the idea of Zi'Marietta and what she stood for, and he
would never allow his wife or his children to contradict or criticize her—to
her face, that is.

By the time I knew Zi'Marietta, she was in her late sixties, a small woman
who always wore black and indicated, by her posture and her tone of voice,
genteel but final defeat. It was difficult for me to associate this small, aged
lady with the virago of the family stories.

"You have small feet," she said to me. "That is the sign of a lady. No one
else in your family has small feet." She offered me old pairs of her shoes,
worn, but well made. This was the '50's, however, and the demarcations
between the shoes of old women and the shoes of fashionable girls were
clear and final. But I accepted the shoes with the guilt and anger of the
young who receive what they do not want from the old: guilt that I did not
want these gifts, anger that I felt forced to take them, anger, too, at an old
woman who did not know the right things to give. I have always felt the
pressures of politeness, and I kept the shoes in the bottom of my closet until
I left home, long after Zi'Marietta had died.

"If you read," said Zi'Marietta, "read the things that a cultured gentle-
man likes to talk about. Don't read things that no one likes but yourself.
That will only keep you lonely."

I never asked her to explain; I don't remember the titles of the books she read in the room that was always in semi-darkness. I didn't listen to what she said about my nails and my complexion, about what one could indicate to a man by a tilt of the head or a turn of the ankle. She died in 1964, while I was away at college, priding myself that I was above all these tricks, these valueless and illusory skills that women had depended upon for centuries. The style then was to affect no style, and what did Zi'Marietta stand for but style, with all its bald implications?

And besides, I had heard stories about her. She was not a good woman, they had said. There were dark tales about what she had done to *Nana*, her mother. My grandmother said that *Nana* had begged to come and live with her son, even though his wife was not Italian, could not even speak the language, because of what her daughter had done to her. The family said that after *Nana* could no longer walk, Marietta sat her on the toilet in the morning and wouldn't let her move until it was time for bed. Marietta had driven her husband away from her, had killed him with her demands, they said Uncle Arturo, called Uncle "Toot" had had the loudest laugh in New York until he married Marietta, they said. Everyone loved him; he would give the shirt off his back, they said. He worked on the docks and died of a strangulated hernia. Everyone said it was Zi'Marietta's fault, and I didn't understand why. The family said I would understand when I was older, when I could see how a woman could empty the life out of a man with looks, with silences. And she had killed her daughter, they said, poor Rose who was always so sad, who ran herself down to wait on her mother, who was given nothing but abuse for her pains. All the pictures I saw of Rose showed a girl who had been born old, who had dark circles under her eyes even as a child. She had not had the freedom or the time to be even wistful, which might have been her salvation. She looked ill-fed, wearied, not from a great sorrow, but as though her feet had always bothered her. Now, they said, it was well for Marietta to say what a good daughter she was, now that she was under the ground.

I couldn't bring myself to believe that this failed, but glamorous old woman, with her perfectly manicured nails, her thick, coiffed hair, had caused such misery. It was easy for me to ignore her, to visit her in the old people's home at Christmas, to say I would come back soon, and then to forget until the next Christmas. It was easy for me to take part in the family jokes, to use the family expression, "She's pulling a Zi'Marietta attitude," to mean that someone was being high-falutin' or putting on airs. It was easy for me to think of her ornate crystal and elaborate silver as "old country" and irrelevant, like the rest of the family. It was worse than that, they said (and I went along); it was hypocritical, for everybody knew Zi'Marietta had nothing, had been supported by my grandfather since her husband died.

My grandfather had never wanted Zi'Marietta to work. He was a jeweler, proud of his craft, proud of his ability to pay a year's worth of bills in one day at Christmastime, when the rich bought their jewels. He paid for Marietta and *Nana* to come to New York from Sicily in 1905. He had been here three years and had a place for them to live in West Hoboken, New Jersey.

Zi'Marietta was content to stay home for a while, but then she became bored and restless. This was America, she wanted to make money; she wanted to go into the city to work. No, said my grandfather, he was the head of the family; even though their father was dead, he could provide for his sister and his mother. Behind his back, though, Marietta went to work for the local dressmaker, and then went to New York to work for Macy's. My grandfather worked long hours; he never knew that Zi'Marietta went into the city all day, and *Nana* did not betray her daughter's secret. Zi'Marietta kept all the money she earned in her jewelry box, along with the diamond earrings my grandfather had made for her eighteenth birthday. The truth came out, however, when my grandfather had to deliver a bracelet to Macy's, and saw his sister. He was a gentle man, but he felt he had been deceived by his little sister, and so he was furiously angry, Not at all penitent, either for having disobeyed her brother's wishes, or for having lied to him, Marietta assumed a wounded posture. My grandfather, stricken with guilt, said she could continue to work, as long as she kept the money for herself, and allowed my grandfather to pay her expenses and her carfare. She agreed, and my grandfather was relieved that his sister had forgiven his vicious temper with such grace.

It was through Zi'Marietta that my grandparents met. Marietta made friends with an Irish girl whom she worked with at Macy's. My grandmother was a strapping woman, twice the size of the delicate Marietta, and people laughed when they walked together on the street. But my grandfather did not laugh; he fell in love, proposed marriage, but asked for a long engagement so that he could break the news to his mother and sister, the news that the girl he was going to marry was not Italian.

*Nana* accepted the news, if not happily, with loving resignation. Zi'Marietta retired to her bedroom and did not join the family for three days. She would have to quit her job, she said; her health was deteriorating; she was beginning to have fainting spells again. And so, my grandparents put their wedding off for two years, until Zi'Marietta married Uncle Toot and moved to Brooklyn. My grandmother deeply resented this, and remembered it for the rest of her life, as she remembered that Marietta had called her a peasant, and told my grandfather that he was marrying a girl who had spent most of her life with cows. Grandma was clever enough, however, never to express her opinion of Zi'Marietta in direct ways that my grandfather could directly counter.

The most famous Zi'Marietta story presents my grandmother as hero of the cold war with her sister-in-law. Besides the unfortunate Rose, Zi'Marietta had a son named Joe, a repulsive child who grew into an even more unpleasant adult. Joe was his mother's darling. He had been born, to Zi'Marietta's everlasting guilt, with a club foot. He had been spoiled before his father's death; afterwards he was doted upon with obsessiveness common in, if not peculiar to, widowed mothers of only sons.

My Uncle Nick was the same as Zi'Marietta's son Joe, and to bring them together was to guarantee bloodshed, or at least major destruction of property. They were both twelve this day, and they were juggling with oranges. My grandparents and Zi'Marietta sat near them, watching the two boys laconically as they drank coffee. There was the predictable crash. Joe had sent an orange through the windowpane. My grandfather rose, and as if by reflex, took off his belt and thrashed his own son. Nick didn't murmur; he accepted his unearned punishment in dignified and wounded silence, and disappeared discreetly out the back door.

It was obvious to everyone that Nick had been unjustly punished. Zi'Marietta told Joe that he shouldn't pay attention to Nick when he suggested rough play. Joe, she explained to my grandmother, was a delicate boy, and couldn't allow himself to become over-excited. At this point, Joe dissolved in tears, and told his mother he wanted to go home. Zi'Marietta finished her coffee slowly, put on her gloves, and rose to leave. My grandfather said that my grandmother would be glad to drive her home. Zi'Marietta said they would have to go quickly, because both she and Joe had to have a nap in the afternoon; he for his health, she for her beauty.

My grandmother placed the coffee cups in the basin and quietly walked out of the door toward the car. My grandfather stood at the kitchen door waving, waving, as his wife, sister and nephew drove away. Zi'Marietta stared down at her gloved hands; Joey sniffled in the back seat.

When my grandmother came home, my grandfather was contrite, but silently so. He told my grandmother to tell Nick not to encourage Joey to roughhouse.

In silent rage, my grandmother closed her hand around a coffee cup, breaking it in two. She cut herself badly from fingertip to wrist. Blood spurted into the sudsy water in the sink. My grandfather went pale, and bustled to get iodine and bandages. He filled a basin with water and put it on the kitchen table.

"Come here, cara," he said to my grandmother, "let me bathe your hand."

My grandmother walked silently to the table, with the solemn dignity a smaller woman could not have brought off. Still silent, she sat next to her husband and let him bathe and bandage her wounded hand. Her husband kissed her bandaged hand in wordless contrition.

They never spoke of what had caused my grandmother to break a cup in angry frustration. It was much later that the incident became a family joke, an example of Zi'Marietta's meanness, my grandfather's fearful impetuosity and husbandly tenderness, my grandmother's Northern and stoic restraint. No one one ever wondered what it was about Zi'Marietta that inspired my grandfather to punish his own son rather than embarrass her, that inspired my grandmother to wound herself rather than criticize her sister-in-law to my grandfather. What remained was the image of Zi'Marietta looking down at her hands in the car, not even waving to her brother, who stood at the kitchen door. No one realized that my grandmother was implicated in this nexus of anger, fear and silence—it was simply a funny story to illustrate the differences in people's tempers.

When Zi'Marietta died she left me her silver-backed brush and comb. "Brush your hair five-hundred strokes a day," she had said, "and put olive oil on your hair after you wash it. American girls kill their hair. Your hair is alive; it is your glory as a woman."

For many years, I kept the comb and brush in its box, shoved away in the back of a drawer. Now I have begun to use them, not often, but at those times when I most need to feel like a beautiful woman who has come from a line of beautiful women. When I most need that weight, Zi'Marietta's heavy silver comb and brush are there for me.

And this is important: what the family forgets when they talk about Zi'Marietta is that she was a beautiful woman, that she turned heads on the streets of New York for thirty years, that Arturo Cavalcante had married her for this reason: she was the most beautiful woman he had ever seen. This was what gave her her airs: she wanted manners that would make her difference clear, that would preserve her distinction when age had destroyed it. Her plan had worked, but not in the way she wanted. She did have distinction, but it was the distinction of the lonely, not the distinction of the revered. Why did it go wrong? There are a million considerations—of time, of economics, of geography—of the factor that Americans never want to admit is determinative: luck.

The silver comb and brush lie on the top of my dresser, heavy, archaic, ornate as history, singular as heritage. When I raise my arms to brush my hair, I can only go on for a little while. In another time, women brushed their hair for hours with these, the instruments of their craft. These women, like Zi'Marietta, gave their lives, their precious, precious hours, to beauty. I have never had enough hours in my life. I brush, count to one hundred, stop and move quickly to something else. How could I go on longer?

# NONFICTION

# Frances Winwar

Born Francesca Vinciguerra in 1900 in Taormina, Sicily, Frances Winwar arrived in the United States as a young child and soon became fluent in English. She was a precocious writer and at eighteen was contributing to Max Eastman's *The Masses* and reviewing books for the *New York World*. She anglocized her name, upon the advice of the editor for her first book, the novel *The Ardent Flame,* which came out in 1927. Frances Winwar settled into a career of writing psychological biographies, specializing in the great English literary figures of the nineteenth century and in 1933 won the then important Atlantic Prize for nonfiction. She was a very well-known writer of her time and the only writer of Italian American background listed in the multivolume set of *American Women Writers: A Critical Guide from Colonial Times to Present* published from 1979.

# *from* Poor Splendid Wings

When the four Rossetti children were still young, on the evenings when the paternal sitting room had been too noisy with the polyglot oratory of the Professor's visitors they would go to the boys' garret and spend together the hours before bedtime. Sometimes Maria, the eldest, read aloud, while Gabriel and William colored stage prints, and Christina, the youngest, listened, her grave eyes fixed on her sister's lips. Sometimes they would peep into some formidable tome, always whispered of as *sommamente mistico*, over which their father, with his long-peaked cap shading his face, pored for hours at a time. They would shut it with a gasp of awe at the mountains of black-letter and furrows of small type covering the bottom of the page. Their favorite pastime was working out sonnets from end-rhymes, at which Christina excelled. There were nights, however, when the thunderous company overstayed, and serious amusements palled. On those occasions the children played cards. Through some quirk of fancy they had come to identify themselves with the four suits: Maria with the clubs, Gabriel the hearts, William the spades, and Christina with the diamonds. In three cases, at least, the choice was prophetic.

Christina at eighteen showed nothing of the hard, glittering quality of the diamond. James Collinson, tame and shrinking, had not been awed by her, though she did so much resemble Gabriel's Mary, Virgin, for which she had sat,—

> As it were
> An angel-watered lily, that near God
> Grows and is quiet.

Outwardly Christina was soft and womanly, her rare gayety lighting briefly the meek gravity of her face. But within, where Collinson had not the sight nor the understanding to see, there was a keen, white sharpness, protecting, like a coat of armor, something she held above the treasures of the world. Not that she did not yearn for the gifts of life. Her lips were arched and full for the luscious fruit, though ready to tighten at a whisper from within. The wide-winged nostrils, like Gabriel's, sensitive to the fragrance of living, quivering with the breath of her being, betrayed a struggle the set face would not reveal. To Collinson, as to those who saw her with her brothers, she was a good girl ripe for marriage, who would make a virtuous wife and a dutiful mother. That, her household duties over, she would steal away to her room and write verses, such as had already appeared in print, need not have frightened an eligible groom.

Indeed, any fond grandfather with a printing press in the shed of his garden would have done as much for a pretty niece with a penchant for versifying. In 1842 old Polidori had printed a translation of Maria's; two years later the press in the Regent's Canal garden had produced Gabriel's *Sir Hugh the Heron*, which he would not now hear mentioned. Then had come Christina's turn. But Grandpa Polidori had had nothing to do with the publishing of Christina's poems in the reverend pages of the *Athenæum* in 1848.

From the day Gabriel had introduced Collinson to his family there had been a tacit understanding that Christina's affections were engaged. James came of a solid family, Christian and respectable. He attended the same church as the Rossetti women, and in behavior was devout and mild. Nothing could be said against him except, perhaps, that he had none of Gabriel's dash or William's good sense. He seemed too easily led—but then, that was not always a fault.

By the time the *Germ* was talked of, Christina and Collinson were looked upon as betrothed. William had even visited at the Collinsons' for a number of weeks, during which he had indited much informative correspondence to Christina. Nothing stood in the way of the future marriage.

Collinson, meanwhile, roused by his love out of congenital torpor, did what he could to please Christina. He worked long at his portrait of her, in emulation of Gabriel's, but the two paintings were as unlike as if two different women had posed for them. Gabriel's, lit with spiritual beauty, gazed out "strong in grave peace"—the soul itself painted. Collinson's was a simple English girl, gentle, but not burdened with intellect. He saw her, he wanted her, that way—and as Leonardo painted himself in Mona Lisa, Collinson drew a self-portrait in Christina.

Perhaps in those hours when he saw her clearly he may have felt a sense of want in himself; perhaps the activity of his companions stung him to rival them. At any rate, when the brethren were all enthusiasm in the preparation of their magazine, he wrote a long, blank-verse poem, and illustrated it. Gabriel acclaimed both poem and etching. The stunner had at last done himself justice. Christina would be proud of him.

Christina was proud; but also saddened. For some months her love had given her little happiness. James had changed, and she knew what caused the change. It was not that he loved another; that Christina would have

understood, and in herself the image of him would have been treasured as
an unalterable relic. It was the image itself that had altered, superseded by
the reality of the man. He was a weakling. Though she had long hidden the
truth from herself, averting her eyes to fill them with the pleasanter aspects
of his talent and manhood, she could do so no more.

Again she read over the script of his poem, the "Child Jesus":—

> Joseph, a carpenter of Nazareth,
> And his wife Mary had an only child,
> Jesus . . .

She had loved it because James had written it, and because it was beautiful;
but the reading of it gave her pain. Brought up as she had been in the
Church of England,—though with Puseyite leanings,—she had no sympathy, however, with anything that hinted of Rome. Collinson had strong
tendencies in the direction of ritual and mysticism. Lately he had forsaken
her church. Again, he had confessed to her that before their meeting he had
been converted to Catholicism, but that upon learning that the difference of
their worship would have stood in the way of their understanding, he had
returned to his former faith. Christina was a devout member of her church.
Religion was the one thing in which she would neither make, nor accept,
compromise. Scrupulous to bigotry in her morality, she had already given
up the theatre and the opera, arguing that since actors and singers were of
easy virtue, it was one's Christian duty to discourage their performances.
How much more was one to discourage laxity in faith!

She read James's description of what had been their dream of home—an
English home, though he laid it in far-off Nazareth:—

> A honeysuckle and a moss-rose grew
> With many blossoms on their cottage front. . . .

Blossoms like those at her maiden aunts' at Holmer Green, where she had
spent heavenly weeks in her childhood. She could see with James

> The orange belted wild bees when they stilled
> Their hum, to press with honey-searching trunk
> The juicy grape; or drag their waxèd legs
> Half buried in some leafy cool recess
> Found in a rose. . . .

He must have watched those bees in the garden of his home. Yet at the very
time Collinson had been writing of flowers and bees she had been describ-

ing another dream land, in a dirge for an imaginary girl she had wept for in
her heart.

> Where sunless rivers weep
> Their waves into the deep,
> She sleeps a charmèd sleep:
> Awake her not.
> Led by a single star,
> She came from very far
> To seek where shadows are
> Her pleasant lot.

Again and again, then when she had loved most and seemed most happy,
she had written of that one who died in sorrow. In the abundance of a
brooding imagination, she decked bier and funeral chamber with the
flowers of her art. Sometimes she recognized herself in that corpse.

> The curtains were half-drawn, the floor was swept
> And strewn with rushes, rosemary and may
> Lay thick upon the bed on which I lay.

And once, in suffering for which she would confess no reason, she had
written with trembling hand, pressing her breast against the washstand in
her room,—

> Have patience with me, friends, a little while:
> For soon, where you shall dance and sing and smile,
> My quickened dust may blossom at your feet.

Why that gloom at the height of her happiness? Why the incessant
mourning for that unhappy maiden of her imagination? Sometimes when
her mother had tried to look too searchingly into her thoughts, she had
turned away. To *her* she could not have lied as she was lying to herself. Had
she borne that gaze longer, she would have had to avow that all those dead
girls were dead selves, selves that she had wished dead, rather than in love
unworthily. Yet she did want to love. She had given James love that was
neither for mother nor brother. What had come to threaten it? Inquire as
she would, she did not know. Not with her mind. But there were many
things she felt, and in her feeling she had glimpses of clues to which she
hastily shut her eyes.

She was attached to her mother. In that household, the head of which the
children never remembered as other than elderly, Mrs. Rossetti was the

teacher, the guardian, and, in all mildness, the playmate. When Professor
Rossetti came home, his chair would be waiting for him by the fireplace, the
Dante tomes open where he had left his abstruse researches. There he
remained for hours unmolested. Occasionally a volume in Italian would
appear, bearing his name on the title page. Profound, and of recondite
learning, the Professor's studies on Dante were as far removed from Victo-
ria's England as the works of some obscure monk in the thirteenth century.
Only Maria would read them, admiration in her eyes. However, when not
bent over his books or entertaining his nondescript revolutionists, the Professor was a doting and tender father, whom his children treated with the
same respect his pupils had for him at King's College.

Gabriel and William had been sent to school, like other boys. Maria and
Christina were taught entirely by their mother. By a tacit understanding the
girls followed their mother's faith; and, since the Professor was in no sense
religious,—leaning rather dangerously toward freethinking,—the male
members of the family were left to make their choice. Nevertheless Mrs.
Rossetti watched zealously over them all, and, if one of the boys seemed in
danger of straying,—as when Gabriel stood accused of reading such immoral
books as Shelley's,—she pulled him back firmly to wholesome pastures. It
had never been necessary to play tithingman over Christina. Her mother's
word was law; her look, command—not that Mrs. Rossetti had ever had to
command her younger daughter, the most devoted of her devoted children.
It was enough for Christina to give her pleasure. She was eleven years old
when she wrote her first poem—to her mother, on her birthday.

Except for rare absences, when the girls took places as governesses to
sustain the family budget, mother and daughters were never parted. Separation was torture to Christina. She worshiped her brothers, Gabriel especially, though she felt more comfortable with William, nearer her age.
Gabriel had always been looked upon as the hope of the family whom the
others might approach but never overshadow. In Christina's mind standards were set by Gabriel's accomplishments and by William's virtues. She
had had few opportunities for measuring other youths against her
brothers—or, indeed, other men, outside the odd friends who came to see
the Professor. Her life was bounded between home and her family, the
church and her mother.

It was like the discovery of a new realm for her when her brothers began
going out into the world. At first she glimpsed it in reflection, through the
mirror of their reports; little by little she set a timid foot in their domain,
though with her eyes turning backward for maternal guidance. Sometimes
that world was brought to the decent drabness of Charlotte Street, and the
drabness colored through its magic. But it was not for long. Instead, the
world claimed Gabriel, who from then on came home, in the young girl's
eyes, as a voyager bearing strange and wonderful tales of places that were

not hers to behold. She lived vicariously through his adventures, and if at times her cheeks flushed before her mother's gently lifted brows, her lips were quickly humbled to silent apology.

Then had come Collinson and the other young men. They trooped to Charlotte Street—a jolly, well-mannered crew, converting the bare living room into a gay agora alive with youth and ideals. That happened seldom, and then it ceased altogether. Gabriel, however, took to inviting Christina to his studio, where she sat for his paintings. She loved it there; for, even when he drew away to the apartness of his work, life filtered in as persistently as light through his windows. At times she had been at the studio scarcely ten minutes before it was ringing with the voices of as many friends. James came oftenest.

In the beginning she had not been drawn to him. He was retiring in his ways, dull in his speech. Beside Gabriel with his bluff manliness, James seemed weak and pale. But then, few of Gabriel's friends could measure up to him. Millais might be handsomer, in a conventional sense, but he did not possess that fire from within that lighted her brother's face as he spoke and lent warmth to his actions. Woolner was uncouth in his speech: she was a little afraid of him. Hunt she found difficult of approach. Obsessed by his mission, he had little thought for anything else. Collinson was always at hand, with touching, if awkward, attentions. He was hopelessly plain. She had to admit that, whenever she looked from his to Gabriel's sensitive face with its spacious brow and fine, speaking eyes. Yet she took kindly to him, and whenever Gabriel spoke well of him and his work, her lids were moist with gratitude. She was content when she did not make comparisons, and it was then she allowed the joy of love to come into her life.

Unused to the precious gift, at first she had contemplated it in secret, dandled it, treasured it jealously, sharing it with none

My Mother said: "The child is changed
That used to be so still,
All the day long she sings and sings
And seems to think no ill;
She laughs as if some inward joy
Her heart would overfill."

But as the months wore on, an inexplicable melancholy possessed her, and she had no more pleasure at the thought of her love. That something, perhaps in James, perhaps in herself, robbed it of bloom. Oddly, when she was definitely promised to him, she wept for love as dead, made it a grave among the flowers and laid a stone at its feet. Setting the scene for herself and James, she wrote even the words they might say of the present, become past.

To few chords sad and low
Sing we so:
Be our eyes fixed on the grass
Shadow-veiled as the years pass,
While we think of all that was
In the long ago.

"When I am dead, my dearest, sing no sad songs for me," she could say, envisioning the ultimate sundering.

She had to confess disillusionment; but she could not blame James wholly. It was no fault of his if he was timorous and weak; no fault of his if he could not ever approach Gabriel. His home was not the home that could be hers. His mother—what angel could ever take the place of her own? The fledgling dove she had brought out to see the sun shrank back and was afraid. The tremulous wings folded closer to the nest.

Yet her heart mourned for James and for herself. She loved him as much as she could ever love any man not her brother; but that love was not sufficient. She dreamed of a hearth and children of her own; still, the maternal breast was sweet, the home nest safe. Passion stung her, wakening her virgin senses; the curb of devotion to her mother and her faith pulled her away. The months were eternities of struggle that left her weary and with her problem unsolved. Only in the haunting vision of death, with rest at last in the lap of earth, she found appeasement.

# Barbara Grizzuti Harrison

Born in Brooklyn, New York, Barbara Grizzuti Harrison now resides in Manhattan. During her marriage to Dale Harrison of the U.S. foreign service, she lived and traveled abroad. Her *Italian Days* and *The Islands of Italy* depict her experience of Italy. Her articles and reviews have been widely published and her first collection, *Off Center,* appeared in 1980, preceded by her moving memoir of growing up as a Jehovah's Witness, *Visions of Glory.*

# Godfather II: of Families and families (1974)

When my radical friends cottoned to the fact that I was a *Godfather I* junkie, I was quick to anticipate and disarm criticism by arguing that while it was possible for a *lazy* audience to understand from *The Godfather* that Mafiosi went around knocking off only one another in internecine wars, making offers that couldn't be refused only to other pestilential pigs, leaving the rest of the citizenry to go about their God-fearing ways in peace, an *intelligent* audience could easily extrapolate the truth from Coppola's film— which is that the Mafia ruins small lives, destroys innocent grocers as well as rival dope-dealers. *The Godfather*, I said, bore witness to the bitter truth: evil, hydra-headed, renews itself and triumphs in the end; in America, the Corleones win.

To which my radical friends said, *Bullshit:* "Don Corleone and Sonny and Michael were all so damned attractive. They were killers, but one liked them just the same. Their evil was mitigated by their charm." And my brother said, "You liked it because you're Italian." And of course my friends, and my brother, were right. I had not, after all, seen *Godfather I* six times for the pleasure of witnessing the triumph of Evil over Good. I saw it because, in spite of its celebrated violence, it was perversely comforting and warm; it had a uniquely tender, cradling quality. Each time I saw Don Corleone die his rose-garden death, I was set squarely in that fabled place where families honor, respect, support, and protect one another, *touch* one another, forgive one another their sins. Viscerally I understood the Corleones better than, say, the Louds (and I liked them better, too). *The Godfather* nourished the notion that there was someone, some force, who could absolve guilt and make all the hurt go away, someone whose accepted authority could gentle and sustain us.

"Heresy," my feminist friends snorted. "You are talking about patriarchal families who have no remedy for pain, families that smother you, that protect you because you're their property. Step out of line and see what they do for you." My critical intelligence—and my own experience as a third-generation Italian—told me they were right. And yet I returned, as if on a pilgrimage to an atavistic part of my nature, to the courtliness of Don Corleone, to the sanguinity and vivacity of Sonny, to the magnificent reserve of Michael—that eloquent stillness that promised everything, that

promised absolution. *Godfather I* created a world analysis could not sour. I
felt embraced by the film, and not just because I so rarely see the pungent
gestures and rich rituals or hear the rude songs, the lyrical-vulgar dialect of
my childhood, reflected in literature or art: I have a vestigial yearning to
believe, damn it, that there is a safe, redemptive place, a landscape where
everyone knows his or her place, where one follows, with benediction and
grace, the yellow brick road to the shrine of approving family gods.

And then Coppola, in his extraordinary sequel to *The Godfather*, did
more to challenge my cherished conviction that the family can be a Salvation Army than did all the harangues of my radical friends.

Consequently, *Godfather II* gave me an attack of spiritual indigestion
similar to the heartburn I invariably suffer after Italian weddings. I return,
always, from a family wedding blood-warm, warmed by "the blood." I think
of the extravagant assurances we have all ritualistically exchanged: "You are
our blood," we tell one another, "We will love you whatever you do, we are
here for you." And then I think of the work some of those men with whom
I've danced the tarantella and exchanged blood-love do in the world (it's not
pretty); and I marvel at my capacity to be seduced by the passion and
authority and vigor and charm of men whose work I cannot love. And I
think—looking at their wives, who have reaped the traditional rewards of
traditional lives—What would have happened to those warm, smiling
women if they had chosen separate identities, if their paths had violated the
ethic of *la famiglia*? Would, in fact, their men have been there for them?
And then I think of my brother, who is a just and generous man, whose
authority I *do* accept, who can outcharm Sonny any day of the week, who *is*
always there for me, who stills my restlessness and makes me feel safe, as no
one else in the world can make me feel safe. And I think of my gentle father,
who has learned painfully to love his maverick daughter, who defends me
even when he finds my life incomprehensible. And then I think of a few
bitter women, sitting outcast and alone, who are tolerated merely because
they are "the blood," but who are not protected, not loved, because in some
way they have violated the sacred rules of this large, lusty family composed
of good men and bad men, of strong women and selfless women. I think of
the strength of Italian women, of strength perverted and strength preserved. And I am painfully confused. I want all of these people to love me,
to comprehend me; I want none of them to constrain or confine me. And I
know that what I want is impossible.

I would be surprised if Coppola were not also a victim of the hopelessly
ambivalent feelings about family—about the bonds that both heal and mor-
tify—that all second- and third-generation Italians suffer. I think *Godfather
II* must have been a painful film for Coppola to have made.

Politically, *Godfather II* is as explicit and forthright as *Godfather I* was elliptical. It bludgeons us with what its predecessor hinted at. It says, with a specificity that leaves little room for a gentler interpretation, that we are one nation under capitalism, and that under capitalism, the Enemy is One—and the enemy includes corporate business, members of the United States Senate, organized labor, and the Mafia. It is, as Pauline Kael has aptly said, "an epic vision of the corruption of America."

Psychologically, *Godfather II* is kaleidoscopic—some have said muddled. But its confusions are *our* confusions, its malaise *our* malaise. *Godfather I* was an almost elegiac film. *Godfather II* is an ice bath. After three and a half hours spent inside the second-generation Corleones' conspiracies and psyches, I felt as if I'd been savaged, betrayed, cheated. I've spoken to Italian friends and they agree: Coppola, who gave us in *Godfather I* the romantic family idyll we all craved, forced us in *Godfather II* to test all our own troubled, troubling feelings about family. What he gave us was not entertainment, not a mythical romance that released us, briefly, from the oppression of our singularity and aloneness, but necessary pain.

There was a kind of golden aura about Brando's Don Corleone, even as he was plotting to destroy half the population of Harlem. He was a luminous goon. There, but for a few wrong turns of fate, one felt, goes a real sweetie pie of an Italian poppa. One could imagine being caressed by his caring; he was the prototypical daddy of our nursery dreams—the powerful man of the world who wipes the tears from the eyes of his babies and acts always, and only, to protect his cherished family. He was, literally, the God/Father. Don Corleone was a rock against whom one might lean. The Michael of *Godfather II* is a defoliator, a glacier. There is, about Michael, everything dark, dank, and pernicious. Charity is inimical to his nature; he feeds on the blood, not only of his enemies, but of his family. He kills his dopey older brother Fredo, destroys the womanhood of his sister Connie, and shuts his wife, Kay, out of his heart and his life and robs her of her children. As *Godfather II* ends, he is absolutely powerful and absolutely evil, locked in the solitary confinement of his own corruption, without warmth and without pity.

How well Coppola knows that in Italian families the blood calls to the blood; how devastatingly he deals with the fact that a sister needs, above all things, the approval of her brother to remain whole. When thrice-married Connie approaches Michael (on her knees) and says, with palpable self-loathing, Everything bad I have done to myself I have done to hurt you because you killed my true husband and turned me into a whore, she begs to be allowed to return to the family, *to take care of Michael*, in order *to redeem herself*. Now, for one brief (shameful) moment, I felt my heart leap: the family is back together again! Reunion! Fortunately, I was sitting next to my sister-in-law, who has lived through enough Italian melodramas and vendettas not to be so easily gulled. She introduced a note of raucous sanity into mindless sentimentality: as Connie groveled and Michael bestowed his icy benediction, my sister-in-law yelled, *"Right? There's always some woman around to pick up the pieces!"*

I would like to have seen a woman like my sister-in-law protrayed in *Godfather II*—a strong Italian woman, that is, with a built-in bullshit detector. I'm sorry that the woman who *named* Michael (who pronounced him evil) was the quintessential WASP Kay. When Kay can no longer pretend to herself or to Michael that she is innocent so long as she is ignorant, when she aborts Michael's dynastic successor, her bitter reproach is couched in words I find unacceptable: "I won't," she says, "be part of your two-hundred-year-old Sicilian thing any longer."

My Calabrian chauvinism notwithstanding, I wish Coppola hadn't allowed Kay to imply that Sicilian families have particularly bad odor. Clearly *Godfather II* tells us that crime Families stink to heaven. But what about our need for *family*? Coppola's film says brilliantly and unambiguously that the end preexists in the means—that a single small maggot of corruption, given enough filth to feed on, becomes a devouring multiheaded dragon: I gave you Don Corleone, Coppola says, and I permitted you to love him; but you should have been smart enough to know that evil breeds greater evil, and that the end result would be Michael, would be devastation.

But does Coppola not believe that families can heal? My brother and my father—who are good men—inspire me to believe. Does Coppola? I don't know. I don't know because *Godfather II* doesn't tell us. It tells us about a killer Family; its ambiguities spring, I think, from the fact that the bleakness of its vision cannot wholly disguise Coppola's need to believe. But the need to believe is not the same as belief itself. There is a tension between the need and the conviction. *The Godfathers*, *I* and *II*, reflect that tension, that anguish.

One thing is certain: Coppola understands the terrible hunger of second- and third-generation Italians. Caught in the limbo between the old ways and the new ways, we all want what we are quite sure we cannot have: we want to suckle forever at the family breast. I think he also understands the hunger of all Americans to believe in the goodness of human nature. What Coppola says to that is, Forget it. Bad people are bad people.

What men do in the world resonates in their bedrooms. If one's work in the world is evil, one's "love" for one's family turns into something obscene. The Michael Corleone who has a prostitute butchered to compromise a defiled and defiling senator is incapable of loving *any* woman. The protection the Corleone men offered their women was predicated on the ignorance of those women; and those women, who cultivated blindness, reaped their own destruction. The price they paid for being sheltered was the loss of their souls. I have known women like that. As long as they remain mute and unprotesting—as long as they care more for pasta than for politics—they are happy. As one is happy in a dream. The Corleone men created a dreamworld for their women; they locked them into pink and pretty closets. The closets were roomy—there was space enough for laughter and lust and love and fun. I know those closets; I know that it is possible to stay in them forever. But, for most of us, eventually the world impinges. Mama Corleone, who never questioned, never stepped outside her defined and defended world, died relatively happy in her Skinner-box closet; but even she, at the end, had a glimmer of recognition that her acquiescence had helped to produce that which Kay called "unholy, . . . an affront to God."

If *Godfather II* has a moral, it is that you cannot feed evil men and expect to be nourished by them. Evil men are never "good family men." The myth that Italian-Americans have helped to perpetuate ("Joey Gallo brings his mama roses every Sunday") an Italian-American has helped to destroy. Americans have found that myth irresistible; in these lean and hungry times, when people huddle together for warmth, when robust folk heroes are the vivid symbols of our weary desires, audiences may find Coppola's iconoclasm unforgivable.

---

# Carol Bonomo Albright

---

Carol Bonomo Albright was born in the Italian section of Greenwich Village in New York City, received her M.A. from Brown University, and now resides in Rhode Island where she is editor of the journal *Italian Americana*. She has received grants from the Danforth Foundation of Higher Education and the National Science Foundation for Medical Education. Her articles have appeared in the *Journal of American Ethnic Studies, Melus,* and in the book *Social Pluralism and Literary Criticism.*

# Definitions of Womanhood: Class, Acculturation, and Feminism

With the rise of interest in ethnicity which characterized the seventies (especially with the publication of Richard Gambino's impressive and ground-breaking work, *Blood of My Blood*),there is a danger for some to carve in stone a fixed definition of what it means to be an Italian American man or woman. I wish to focus specifically on definitions of Italian American women to suggest that the range of role definitions are myriad, that a woman must know herself as an individual to determine what is best for her, and that she must also know the socioeconomic and historical context of her Italian American tradition, so that she can resolve apparent conflict between the pull of the family and of her individual desires.

I intend to use two novels, Mario Puzo's *The Fortunate Pilgrim* and Helen Barolini's *Umbertina*, to trace definitions of Italian-American womanhood from the perspective of class, acculturation, and feminism, for all three forces operate in the lives of contemporary Italian American women.

*The Fortunate Pilgrim* and *Umbertina* are worth looking at in tandem, because taken together they form a whole in the experience and evolution of the contemporary Italian American woman. These two novels present a range of role models, so that informed decisions can be made amidst an abundance of riches rather than a dearth of choices, thus allowing us to pick and choose as our needs change.

For purposes of clarification, I have devised a construct of four dominant stages in the acculturation process. They are by no means definitive or rigid, allow for some fluidity, and are certainly open to refinement. The first stage is the immigrant stage of trust and hope—trust in one's cultural values—and hope for a better life in a material sense; the second stage gives way to shame and doubt about one's heritage, and a vague desire for new goals in life. This stage gives rise to the third stage of role confusion, where the goals of one's heritage, one's personal goals and the goals of the new culture (in this case America) all seem to be irrevocably at odds with each other; and the last stage which I call integrated autonomy, in which all three forces are resolved in a personal manner satisfactory to the specific individual.

Lucia Santa and Umbertina exemplify the immigrant stage of trust and hope; Octavia and Carla are both beset by shame, doubt, and a vague desire for new goals; Marguerite is an example of role confusion because she fails to discover the significance to herself of her Italian American heritage; and finally Tina who integrates her peasant origins on her mother's side, her intellectual upbringing as the daughter of an Italian poet, her personal goals and her American formation.

1

Briefly *The Fortunate Pilgrim* chronicles the life of Lucia Santa Angeluzzi-Corbo and her six children through their many travails. Lucia Santa Angeluzzi, so poor in Italy that she could not even afford the traditional nuptial linens, leaves for America to form a new destiny for herself by marrying an Italian American. She is widowed while carrying her third child and eventually remarries. Her second husband, Frank Corbo, goes insane, her oldest daughter, Octavia, marries a non-Italian, her son Larry becomes a member of a protection "union," another son, Vinnie, commits suicide, and a third, Gino, who had been a ne'er-do-well, upon Vinnie's death accepts his role in life, namely to work to support his mother and the two remaining children.

At the beginning of the story, we are introduced to Lucia's reality in her first marriage:

> Her feeling had been the feeling of millions of women toward *improvident* husbands. That men should control the money in the house, have the power to make decisions that decided the fate of infants—what folly! Men were not competent. More—they were not serious. And she had already begun the struggle to usurp his power, as all women do.[1] (Italics added)

The passage is interesting not only from the perspective of what it tells us about Lucia and her view as the wife of a poor man, but also from the perspective of style. It is typical of Puzo's blending of interior monologue and narrative voice into almost one voice, and that narrative voice is female in its total understanding and acceptance of and sympathy with the immigrant woman's point of view. The message is that it is up to these women to do what they must do for the sake of their children. This biological bond gives them a fierce strength. We read that "She had an enormous strength, not unusual in women, to bear adversity." (p. 14) "It was always the men

1. Mario Puzo, *The Fortunate Pilgrim* (New York: Lancer Books, 1964), p. 33. All subsequent references shall be made in parentheses in the body of the paper.

who crumbled under the glories of the new land, never the women." (p. 115) If some heroes in Italian-American literature are Christlike and draw upon the symbols of Christianity for their world view, Lucia is Madonna-like, strong in her role of suffering and by enduring triumphing.

Only once—and momentarily at that—does Lucia allow herself to doubt and ask a philosophical question. She is thinking of the deaths of three of Teresina Caccalitti's sons in one year during World War II. Teresina, who was capable of any treachery for her own advantage, was not able to control this fate. "Did nothing help then? Was there no escape for any-one? For if evil cannot prevail against fate, what hope is there for the good?" (p. 282) We can be tolerant of Lucia's musing no more than this. Greater minds than hers have grappled with this age-old problem. Milton in *Comus* shows us that in the struggle between good and evil, evil often triumphs because it uses methods that the good will not allow themselves. Shakespeare, in his emphasis in so many of his plays on blind chance operating in our lives, has in his acceptance of its operation anticipated Lucia's query. But if Shakespeare accepts blind chance or fate, the narra-tive voice in *The Fortunate Pilgrim* cautions that in the face of the cruelty that fate deals each of us, heroism for a cause greater than self is sheer foolishness. We are told that Dr. Barbato's father, upon learning of his son's heroic exploits during World War II, had a stroke "from sheer exas-peration at his son's foolishness." (p. 284)

Although a tragic view of life, namely a desire to do great things and suffer for it, pervades Lucia's *thinking* (she thinks of optimism as dangerous [p. 276]), a comic view of life to do great things and endure informs her actions. Though "she was pessimistic about life . . . she lived like a true believer in good fortune. She rose in the morning with gladness . . . Her hope was a physical energy replenished by her love for her children and the necessity to do battle for them." (p. 166)

Lucia defines this "physical energy" which enables her to "do battle" for her children as *the* necessary ingredient in a mature woman. Octavia's expressed desire to be happy brings Lucia's contemptuous, raging retort, "Thank God you are alive." (p. 17) For all Lucia's wisdom, her reality puts enormous boundaries on her role definition of woman, so that the knell is struck for the tension that will exist between the generations. The older generation, because of their personal history of dire poverty, has, using Abraham Maslow's hierarchy of needs, only the first three levels satisfied, i.e., the most basic needs of food, clothing, and shelter, next safety and security, and lastly love, affiliation, and self-esteem. And *all* of them are satisfied through *family* ties.

But the next generation, again using Maslow, wants the higher need of self-actualization (as opposed to family-actualization), loosely described by them as "happiness" and involving an individuation unknown and impossible to the immigrants. We can also infer from the novel that it is an individuation that is also impossible for the second generation of Italian Americans. Vinnie, who commits suicide, cannot even name what it is he longs for; Octavia wants "happiness," but she needs security too much to venture forth and fulfill herself by becoming a teacher. She does not believe in her mother's values, but she also has not developed a coherent value system of her own, so that she feels an "overwhelming sadness—not specific, but general, as if her stepfather had suffered some fate common to humanity and that some judgment waited for her, too." (p. 197) It is not only Lucia but also the second generation who lacks a structure with which to comprehend these amorphous desires. However, unlike the young who feel a longing for self-actualization, Lucia feels a fear of what she cannot understand. Instead of the "general sadness" that Octavia experiences and a vague fear of the future, Lucia, born to the immediacy of reality, projects her fear onto a specific thing. Since life for Lucia *is a physical* battle every day (a battle for food, for cleanliness, for health, for freedom from accidents), she creates a deadly opposition between the physical and the mental. "They who read books," she says, "will let their families starve." (p. 216) Only her way of hard physical labor is comprehensible to her. She fears that the young "finding life painful will evade battle duty." (p.216) She cannot comprehend that books might enable the young to do battle in this New World, for their battle in life is more complex than hers had been, and needs more thought—the work of the mind—than physical work to succeed. She cautions that youth with its struggles ahead "should not poison its will with fairy tales and dreams that enchanted them from paper pages they turned and turned into the night." (p. 217) Lucia, like all peasants the world over, is excluded from the world of books. We read, "The mother wondered, What could be in these books that stunned her daughter into some magic oblivion?" (p. 150)

Octavia's desire to be a teacher is discouraged. It is something new and the new, being unknown and having no conceptional framework in which to be understood, is frightening to Lucia. Better to tread the familiar path and remain a seamstress. Security is the preferred mode; risk-taking for the sake of self-actualization is incomprehensible to Lucia, unattainable for Octavia, who has also been formed by the financial insecurity of her past and needs economic security above all.

Lucia only knows that a woman's place *is* the home. She "had the power of life and death over the human beings nearest to her . . . She had her duty to her children, big and small. She dismissed love that was personal, an emotion of luxury, of uncomplicated lives." (p. 123)

If this is her definition of a woman's role in life and of her relationship to her husband, her definition of a man's role equally emphasizes duty and responsibility to the family. We read of "husbands, protectors of children, of life and fate, creators of their own world, acceptors of life and fate who let themselves be turned into stones to provide the rock on which their family stood." (p. 235) Gino, like all her sons, is instructed in this lesson, first by Lucia and Octavia and then by his oldest brother. "He had to think of the family . . . he had to stop doing whatever he felt like doing." (p. 268)

Gino's acceptance of his role is poignant. "Trembling," Gino "promised to become another Vinnie, work in the railroad, marry, live in the tenements along the Avenue, wait at trolley stops with a child in his arms, chain himself in the known, lightless world he had been born in." (p. 272)

Obviously the role definitions of these men and women are based on their economic situation in society. They are just entering the working class. In her relationship with her children Lucia accepts as a given that she must be their "boss," an interesting use of a capitalist metaphor in regard to one's children. In *Umbertina* Marguerite will comment on the similar use of capitalistic metaphors to describe family relationships.

Lucia definitely acts in a manner which psychologists would call the "overinvolved" parent. And Lucia would probably even understand this criticism. But, she would counter, she doesn't have the economic luxury to act otherwise. At the end of the book Lucia, for the sake of her own economic security, tacitly colludes with Larry, in his immature relationship with his wife: *Lucia* will be company to his wife while he pursues his affairs. This is the great sadness of Lucia's mode of relating to her children, for she has only created a little boy, not a man, one who will suffer all his life from what is currently called the Peter Pan syndrome.

Unlike the generations who are to follow, Lucia is unconflicted about her values. She knows with surety what she knows. For example, when Lucia learns that Larry has slept with a married woman, she goes to the woman to nip further impropriety in the bud. Children "sleep under my roof," she says, "until they are married. My children do not become drunkards . . . or go to jail, or go to the electric chair." (p. 75) Lucia continues painting vividly the somber reasons for stressing obedience. "He must obey. Am I right? Does a son show respect to his mother or not?" (p. 74) she adds rhetorically.

As in most things, Lucia is no fool. She knows why she must act as she does. If financial ease were her lot in life, perhaps obedience and respect would be lesser values in parent-child relationships. As a matter of fact, Lucia can even let go of some of her deepest values if it is in the interests of her children to do so. For example, she is secretly pleased that her daughter has not married an Italian. She thinks what mother who had suffered under the masculine tyranny could wish on her tender daughter those guinea tyrants . . . who locked up their wives at home, never took them out except to a wedding or funeral; who made an uproar . . . if spaghetti was not steaming . . . at the precise moment their baronial boots crossed the doorsill; who never raised a finger to help their pregnant wives. . . . Thank God Octavia was marrying a man who . . . might show mercy to womankind. (pp. 217–18)

Octavia shares her mother's view of Italian men, and marries a Jew who, like her, likes to read. The most acculturated of all Lucia's children, Octavia has purchased her measure of independence at a great price. She rejects a central value of Italian American womanhood, and decides not to have children. She views children as that which enslaves women and precludes individuation. Octavia doesn't wish to repeat her mother's life, so that at the end of the book, Octavia, pursuing her career, has risen from seamstress to forelady.

On the other hand, Lucia wants her sons to marry a "good Italian girl who knew from the cradle that man ruled, must be waited on like a duke, fed good food that took hours to prepare; who cared for the children and the house without whining for help." (p. 217) What is not included in this definition is a significant as what is.

Implicit in the first statement is the lack of appreciation of some Italian men for the unpaid work of their wives in the home, a "he who pays the piper calls the tune" type of tyranny. The implications of the second statement are even more interesting. Lucia cannot imagine a different sort of relationship for her sons to their wives. Certainly she must hope that her sons will be benevolent tyrants, a more humane type, where service springs from love and appreciation, instead of despotic tyranny. However, the harshness of poverty cannot really give rise to gentler conceptions and definitions of relationships, no less cause different actions. As a matter of fact, since the economics of the working class allows for little individuation, and prizes adherence to role division and function, the concept of emotional intimacy between husband and wife, as stated earlier, is absent from Lucia's world view, and perhaps explains her total emotional fusion with her children. It is a fusion which serves well the parent willing to make a lifelong commitment to emotional nurturance in exchange for economic survival, but it does not serve well all children. For the child wishing to individuate beyond the family and its definitions, and risk losing the security gained from such fusions, attempts at separating can be more difficult than need be. And even for those working-class families who have risen beyond their working-class roots (as we shall see in *Umbertina*), a devotion to total dependency upon family, beyond economic need, remains. Even with a better economic situation, new definitions of familial relationships and role definition are slow to be born in such a cultural environment.

Perhaps there are more than just economic reasons that make new definitions difficult for both Italian-American children as well as parents. Perhaps still operative is the ancient Roman concept of *damnatio memoriae*, namely that the worst punishment for a Roman was to have his memory erased from future generations. Anyone who visits the ancient Forum can still see the arch from which Geta's name was erased. Septimius Severus had the arch built for his two sons, Geta and Caracalla, and had their names inscribed on it. After Septimius's death, a power struggle arose between the two brothers. Caracalla triumphed; he had workmen use water to "wear away" Geta's name from the stone. This was thought of as the most terrible aspect of the power struggle, because, by erasing Geta's name, his memory was also erased from future generations.[2] Perhaps the Roman concepts of family, existing within its structure, and being held in esteem by it down through future generations still operates, causing conflict and inner turmoil in the lives of Italian Americans when it comes to dealing with the concept of autonomy.

The larger meaning of *The Fortunate Pilgrim* involves Lucia's view of America as a metaphor for a "blasphemous dream." (p. 286) The blasphemy echoes a Blakean theme and involves Lucia's wanting the dream without recognizing the realities of the human condition, i.e., that with every gain there is a loss. "America . . . blasphemous dream . . . why could it not give everything?" (p. 286) She had wanted all this, i.e., "enough food and money for an old age surrounded by respectful and loving children" without the suffering, the guilt, the sorrow, "without fear of death and the terror of a judgment day. In innocence." (p. 286)

As a child, Lucia's wildest dream had been to "escape the fear of hunger, sickness and the force of nature . . . No one dreamed further. But in America wilder dreams were possible and she had never known of their existence. Bread and shelter were not enough." (p. 286)

Lucia is the fortunate pilgrim, because her pilgrimage through life did not include "wilder dreams" which would have put existential demands upon her. These are demands that challenge Gino and Octavia and those who follow, because an old dearly held value, namely that of identification of self through family, will need to be challenged and new resolutions, balancing self, family and work, forged.

2. A dear friend, Isabel Pingree, relates a story about her family which corresponds to the Geta story. When her father emigrated to the United States from Italy, he carved his name on the church door, as did all the immigrants, so that posterity would not forget them.

2

*Umbertina* by Helen Barolini traces the role development of the women of one Italian American family. Umbertina is the founding mother, as it were, of the family. She is of the immigrant generation, corresponding to Lucia, and possessing the same strength and courage that Lucia has. Like Lucia, Umbertina has a sureness about her values and her task in life. Although Umbertina knows that she has left behind failures as well as successes, she is too stubborn to regret them. She too has risked all for her children.

As far as role definition is concerned, Umbertina more nearly takes on the man's role of earning money,[3] first by making sandwiches for her husband's fellow-workers, and then by expanding the business to a full-fledged grocery store.

Umbertina and the family pool their labor and their resources and they expand into other lucrative business ventures. Although Umbertina hates waste and is totally utilitarian—there is no room for beauty or even for angst—she "could not tolerate stinginess and was an abundant provider [of food] to her family."[4]

Though Umbertina directs her energies on establishing her own economic independence as contrasted with Lucia, who relies solely upon her children for her financial security, Umbertina, nonetheless, like Lucia, takes on the functions of provider, protector, and worker, having inherent within them the survival and prosperity of the family unit as the priority value. By working together, in imitation of agrarian structures, they will all succeed.

One of Umbertina's daughters, Carla, corresponds to Octavia. Carla's desire to attend college is not taken seriously. Instead, she is pressed into service as a bookkeeper for the family business. Despite the Longobardis' economic success, there are only accidental rather than essential differences between Octavia and Carla. Materially Carla can have whatever she wants—with one big proviso—so long as she maintains the close family bonds. Although there is no economic need for Carla to work for the family, the code still persists, probably due to distrust of anyone outside the family and the tradition of total reliance on the family.

The suggestion, as in *The Fortunate Pilgrim*, is that Carla and Octavia's

3. A Calabrian sociologist tells me that Calabrian women are known to work "like a man." As a matter of fact there is a town in Calabria where role reversal has occurred with the women the merchants and the men caring for the children.
4. Helen Barolini, *Umbertina* (New York: Seaview Books, 1979), p. 96. All subsequent references shall be made in parentheses in the body of the paper.

generation cannot really act in terms of satisfying anything but the most basic of needs. In Carla's case, Umbertina's judgment that Carla's desire for college is a romantic whim is just, for in marrying, Carla chooses not the intellectual non–Italian American suitor but rather the good provider from her own background, evidencing, like Octavia, the great need for economic security. Carla vaguely knows there is more, but she doesn't have a structure to give it definition, and her problem languishes in romanticism.

Since Carla, the youngest of her mother's seven living children, experienced less of the struggle than the others, it is she who asks if Umbertina had been in love with her husband. Again the immigrant generation in the person of Umbertina blames books for such foolishness. Carla connects happiness with romantic love, which Umbertina denounces: "dreams of love and happiness, as if such things could come bound in any one man." (p. 139) Umbertina knows that happiness isn't a prize that is given and that you can hold on to, but rather a "feeling of satisfaction that receded or advanced according to each day's design." (p. 139)

The novel goes beyond Carla and Octavia's generation to explore definitions of womanhood by focusing on Carla's daughter, Marguerite, and her daughter, Tina, named for her great-grandmother. It is Marguerite, Carla's daughter, who finds herself attracted to Umbertina, "that mysterious old woman with whom she couldn't even speak." (p. 150) Umbertina functions as the silent Buddha on whom Marguerite projects all wisdom.

And Marguerite is in need of searching out an inner wisdom that will clear away her confusion about her life, its meaning and her future. If Carla and Octavia have never been able to formulate the right question in order to find an answer appropriate for each of them, Marguerite is capable of formulating the question to the consternation of her parents: the initial questionings surface as a criticism of them, their way of life, and what they have not been able to give her.

As a child, she is thought of as too serious for a girl, because she reads serious books and finds her parents' life of ease, "the American way of progress: college fraternities, Rotary Club, country clubs," empty. (p. 153) Marguerite's parents, Carla and Sam, only want her to be happy, but they have only the definition of happiness that their generation can have: economic ease, marriage, respectability achieved through acquiring the accouterments, "just show" (p. 154) and without substance, or emotional connections, as far as Marguerite is concerned.

As each generation must define itself anew from the previous one, so must Marguerite, who ultimately achieves what Octavia and Carla only indistinctly feel a desire for, namely autonomy from the family.

Marguerite makes an early attempt at separation from family and at individuation which is dramatic and predictable, yet futile. She meets Lennart Norenson, a Dartmouth student, at her brother's wedding reception, and elopes with him that very night. She felt he understood her when he asked what she was doing alone in that big house with her parents with nothing to do. (p. 157) She takes a route common to middle-class women of her generation in an attempt to discover themselves. If nothing else, marriage is the sanctioned way for a daughter to leave her parents' house. In a week she returns home, having discovered that Lennart had to drink to function, and her parents quickly move to have the marriage annulled.

She goes to England and has an affair with a man who introduces her to Alberto Morosini, a poet, whom she marries. She does what her mother could not bring herself to do. She opts not for riches of the world, but for riches of the spirit. She thinks that by marrying Alberto, twenty years older than she, and from an old Venetian family, she can learn from him, mistakenly thinking that happiness would come from his informed and caring guidance, instead of through her own sense of direction.

Marguerite generally has enjoyed their life together partly in Italy among Italian writers and partly in Washington, D.C., among government officials. But we meet Marguerite when she is in her forties, her children almost grown, and she is questioning the meaning of her life and her marriage. Unlike Lucia Santa in her forties, who leaves Manhattan with her two youngest children for Long Island to live in a two-family house with her son, his wife, and her grandchildren, looking forward to the economic security that they have achieved, Marguerite is in the throes of a midlife crisis.

Marguerite has left Alberto in Rome and decided to take "the immigrant's route," seeking her "fortune in the New World." (p. 201) She moves from the feeling of a few months before of not existing and of being detached from people to feeling acknowledged and seen for herself as she talks to people about doing translations in the future. Marguerite tells her family of origin of her decision to divorce Alberto and, in facing them, makes a mature separation from her parents. In a converse of the immigrants before her, whose physical separation from their parents forced psychological separation and autonomous action, Marguerite must return to her parents to declare her autonomy from them and from Alberto.

Marguerite, however, must make one more realization before she can return to Alberto. She goes to Florence looking for a teaching job, and meets Richard, a minister in his forties, who has not followed the bright career back in America that his background destines him for, but rather who serves in this outpost. Realizing that there will be no physical love between them, Marguerite thinks about their coming to an arrangement. And yet Marguerite demands to know of Richard if this is all there is to be had. Richard answers with a quiet fixity that this *is* it. His answer reassures her, for she realizes that part of his attraction is that he has the nerve to accept the human condition. And yet this acceptance is not enough of a basis for a relationship. Ultimately Richard's vapid socializing exhausts her. "To be Mrs. Wareham instead of Signora Morosini when it all comes to the same thing without, however, Alberto's warming physical need of her" (p. 219) seems the height of foolishness. "I can do as I feel" (p. 221), she thinks. She doesn't have to stay in Florence, she doesn't have to prove that she can work and take care of herself, she doesn't have to arrange a new "classy marriage," she doesn't have to prove to her parents that she is as hardworking and practical as her brothers. She doesn't have to be her father or what he wants her to be. She doesn't have to be "the man of the family—alone, or with Richard." (p. 222) She can simply be herself.

This passage marks a freedom to define herself which, for reasons already noted, the Italian American women of the first generation, such as Lucia and Umbertina, did not possess, and the women of the second generation, such as Octavia and Carla, stuck in security, could not utilize. (Actually the first generation were freer to define themselves than the second. However their definitions were to a large extent determined by economic forces.) Coupled with Marguerite's own unique persona, class, acculturation and feminism have come together to make new choices possible for her. But this greater freedom in which Marguerite identifies more with the values of the New World than with the peasant values of *la via vecchia* brings greater problems.[5]

Although Marguerite knows who she is not, she does not yet know who she is, and shortly after returning to Alberto, who understands her confusion, she has an affair with Massimo, a man of literary ambition, as an attempt to find herself. Although Marguerite tries again to define herself through a man, Massimo, even if he weren't married, will not allow her to. She wants to give meaning to Massimo's life. She wants Massimo to need her and thus create meaning for her own life. Though she works on her photography, which Massimo encourages her in, Marguerite has not received the assignments she had imagined, so that she sees working for the recognition of Massimo's novel as her way of giving meaning to her life. Unlike Umbertina, Marguerite did not focus early enough on defining herself. She dully recognizes that she has "relapsed into emotional dependence upon a man who would always survive without her." (p. 274)

5. Actually Marguerite is a richly complex character who is also defining herself by separating from the stasis and deadness of Old World intellectuals with whom she and her husband socialize. However, that aspect is beyond the scope of this paper. Nonetheless, it would make an interesting study coupled with the experiences of and writings about Italian Americans living in Italy as they mold their self-definition, especially as Sartrian existentialism touches on issues of freedom, belief, choice, and life's meaning.

In her diary that her daughters find, we learn that Marguerite was pregnant with Massimo's child, and that the auto accident in which she dies was a disguised form of suicide.

Carla, of course, has no knowledge that her daughter probably committed suicide. Her grief is voiced in these words:

> Her face and shoulders sagged with the burden of being too late to make it up to the daughter she had not understood or approved of, or even, at times, liked. As if speaking to herself, Carla added, "What did she want? What was she looking for? . . . All that moving around. All those homes she set up and then tore down. And moving those girls around so they had no normal life at all . . . What was it all for? To punish us?" (p. 286)

Even with Marguerite's death, Carla has only one way of looking at Marguerite's life, namely from the perspective of her own value system of *la via vecchia*, of roots, family, stability and security. It is almost as if the uprooting of the immigrant generation magnifies the longing for and emphasis on roots of the second generation to the exclusion of everything else. Yet we are told that when Marguerite returns to America to declare her independence, there is an unacknowledged look of envy in Carla's eyes. The illogic of Carla's last remark in which she muses that Marguerite's actions might have been prompted by a desire to punish them almost obscures the sadness of her total incomprehension of her daughter and of the concept of individual autonomy which respects differences.

If Carla's limited acquaintance with other life-styles prevented her understanding Marguerite, Tina, Marguerite's daughter, is the beneficiary of the evolution of role definition among the Longobardi women. Tina has just broken up with Duke, with whom she was living. When she learns after leaving him that she is pregnant with his child, she does not commit suicide like her mother, nor does she return to Duke, but rather she avails herself of the choice to abort the fetus. She also learns from her mother's inability to define herself early (Tina reads in Marguerite's diary how in college, unlike the girls who knew who they were—one of them is descended from Thomas Edison and Marguerite is the only Italian American there—and where they were going—on to become writers, doctors, etc.) to focus on what she wants to do vocationally, and to undertake an odyssey to find out who she is before involving herself permanently with a man, in her case a Wasp named Jason.

Being of the next generation, Tina does not have certain liabilities that her mother had. For example, Tina knows that her mother couldn't achieve autonomy because her family wasn't supportive of that concept. Autonomy represents the luxury of the American tradition of individuation, of life, liberty and the pursuit of happiness. Jason says, "I think too much is made of this whole family business. After all, once you're grown you can live where and with whom you choose and have the life you choose." Tina responds:

> "Yes, sure, but maybe the point is you can't grow up to get out *for good* if the family isn't supportive in the beginning. A strong base is like a launching pad. But a weak one is just a swamp. I think that's why my mother never got wholly away—there was no push upward from behind her. She was meant to fizzle out." (p. 319)

Tina also recognizes that Marguerite existed mainly to provide "life-systems for the men and children" (p. 358), and, feminist that Tina is, she sees clearly that this was not enough for Marguerite at this stage in her life.

Tina also comes to understand why her grandparents couldn't give Marguerite what she needed. They were too caught up with the task of their generation, i.e., of trying to be middle-class American, and this included imitating the vocational idleness of middle-class women of that historical time. Tina is free of trying to be middle-class American. She simply was born into that station in life and is receptive to American feminist concepts. On the other hand, her grandmother, Carla, can instruct Tina.

> "Your mother . . . never knew what she wanted. But you're more like *my* mother, the Umbertina for whom you're named. She was a strong person and she stuck to her guns." (p. 398)

Tina learns how to blend the good from each of the forces of her life. Initially she had ignored her mother's side of the family, because culturally they weren't "up" to her father's side. But once she starts along this search, going back to Castagna, and finally to the Museum of Immigrants display at the Statue of Liberty, Tina receives her epiphany. In a passage that arouses deep emotion within the reader, we learn that, unknown to Tina, she in fact sees on display Umbertina's very own bedspread, which poverty forced her to sell. We read that

> Tina stood entranced at the spectacle of a magnificent bright-hued gloriously woven bedspread that bore the motifs of Calabrian design . . . "Look at that . . . isn't it gorgeous?" . . . Tina stood before the glass drinking in the beauty and warmth of the old spread. Its colors irradiated her spirit; the woven designs of grapes and tendrils and fig leaves and flowers and spreading acanthus spoke to her of Italy and the past and keeping it all together for the future. (pp. 407–8)

The gutsiness of those first immigrants has saved Tina from what might otherwise be the sterility and enervation of her father's intellectual Venetian background. Tina realizes that through doing what she loves (her scholarship) and by understanding her roots, she will be strong enough to be herself.

Because Tina knows who she is, she can quickly still musings which Marguerite prolonged and face the future with optimism.

> Was there more merit in being self-contained, reserved, unemotional, reticent in the Anglo-Saxon way of the Jowerses, and of Jason? Or in her Latin excessiveness of emotion, her flights of fancy, her intensity of feeling?
>
> It was a silly argument, she thought. Comparisons are odious. And futile. (p. 422)

Any life is a personal odyssey, lived out within a particular cultural and historical perspective. These two novels set this odyssey within an Italian American framework and idiom, giving a familiar ring, as it were, to the personal quest which all people must make to become autonomous. I hope that my remarks, in relating the personal quest to the Italian American experience, do not obscure the universality of the themes of these books.

I would also like to emphasize that the four stages of acculturation not be thought of as stages which all Italian American women go through. A slower acculturation process and/or an acculturation process which on an individual basis never reaches the stage of the arts and the intellectual world would not share the role confusion of the third generation. As long as one followed the traditional path of economic upward mobility, there would be no need to resolve the disinterest of a heretofore utilitarian and a-intellectual Italian American heritage, an a-intellectualism which I suspect is rooted more in economic necessity rather than disregard for the intellectual per se.

# Helen Barolini

Helen Barolini, a National Endowment for the Arts recipient and winner of an American Book Award, is the author of seven books and over fifty short stories and essays, which have appeared in many literary journals, anthologies, and *Best American Essays*. Her novel *Umbertina* has been reissued and will appear in an Italian edition. Her most recent book is *Chiaroscuro: Essays of Identity*.

## Turtle out of Calabria

On Cape Cod I have a house that looks west to the bay into the setting sun and its afterglow. The house is on a rutted dirt road called Sunset Drive, the same name as the well-paved suburban street where, years earlier, I had my first house, a husband, children, but no sunsets.

Today, as I sweep, the day is heavy and hot for the Cape. The sky is a grey glaze over grey water. There is no breeze off the bay. Drops seem about to ooze out of the heavy-hanging air.

I sweep a patio that never was—an idea for one that lives only in my head. What actually lies beneath my feet is a rectangular cement pavement into which, before it set, I put a dozen tiles salvaged from the flooring of a previous home, a farmhouse in the Marche region of central Italy. The tiles form a hexagon in the center of the cement with singles at each corner where poles support intersticed strips of wood meant to be covered with flowering vines or grapes.

I sweep, tidying, still hoping, anticipating the bright orange blare of the

trumpet vine planted summers ago but still only green and leggy as it leans towards its support, far, far from the thick, flowering canopy I envision. I keep
glancing at the vine, willing it to grow, to climb, to luxuriate. It does look a little fuller this year. I note tentacle shoots that hold in themselves the promise
of growth shooting towards stupendous bloom, the promise that a shady
bower is perhaps not impossible.

I sweep because the space has an unkept look which offends me; a past
tenant has left old beer cans and his young daughter's plastic playthings all
about; the log pile is every whichway, spilling over and messy; the builder who
had worked on the siding has left his own debris. Last fall's dead leaves are
still heaped, and the torn lid of my once new, bright blue trash can just lies
there.

What strikes me as I sweep is the greenish patina of weathering on the tiles
whose rust-color is called *sangue di bue* in Italian for their characteristic
ox-blood color. I suppose they should never have been put outdoors but I like
having as part of my present life the salvage of a past life. It connects me.

In order to site the patio at the southwest side of the house I had the
builder remove the bulkhead entrance to the basement and wall up the opening. That proved to be a terrible blunder, a colossal jettisoning of good sense
and functionality done only for romantic and aesthetic reasons. I have always
been subject to pernicious nostalgia and acting on impulse. But this time the
lapse in judgment is really bad: it means that the only access I have to my
basement is from the narrow inside staircase off the kitchen. It means that
when the washing machine in the basement goes, I can't get rid of it. If the oil
tank becomes contaminated with water and is useless, it cannot be removed.
And finally when the furnace goes, the problem will be how to get it out and a
new one down those impossibly narrow stairs. To undo my mistake I asked
the builder if the passage to the basement under the cement can be re-
opened. A frugal and practical Cape Codder, he snorts at such foolishness.

My patio was to have been a sitting area on the side of the house looking towards the bay where I, and my guests, could sit in the evening under an inter-
weaving canopy of vines and trumpet flowers and sip a glass of wine, or reach
up for clusters of grapes, as we watched the sun set and the dusk come on.
We'd glide gently on a porch swing; an old trunk (which I had bought years
before at a yard sale, intending to restore it), would serve as a table. It would
be a simple, natural setting, the kind I had loved in Italy and thought I could
easily command on the Cape.

But my outdoor space has not become a patio; it is only dull grey cement
under raw wood supports bare of foliage. And now it is littered and I am
sweeping.

I think of my other homes. Unlike the turtle (snapping, box, mock, or soup)
who carries her home constantly with her and will live and die in it, I have

only carried forward bits and parts of my different homes. Each one a dream house, definitive; and each one relinquished until finally the message is clear: there is no permanent home. That's like a stab in the heart to me for I was born homesick.

Like the turtle, in my slow, determined way I made doggedness (not far-sightedness) my virtue. It's dogged as does it, Darwin said, and he knew his stuff, so I'm not terribly perturbed. I begin to understand that I am of a people, Calabrians, who endured millenia of obstacles, and that *pazienza,* patience, had to be their motto. Patience in the endless draught, patience in the heat, patience in tempests and plagues, patience in fields that grew stones not crops, patience with nature with bad government with fate. I carry the mark of the turtle: stubborn, dogged, patiently carrying on, making do.

From the stoicism of Calabria to the exuberant, intoxicating Excelsior! motto of New York State was the path of one set of my grandparents. Each a *testadura,* hard-head, noted also for an elephantine ability to hold onto an old grudge. "You Can't Go Home Again" was never a slogan coined for them or their ancestors; they were the pre-eminent people of home, family, *lares et penates.* But now I realize: they had no choice nor any notion of other verities. Being stuck in something is not the same as choosing it.

In this promised land where grace and patience count not much, they learned haste, detachment, separation from family, rugged individualism, competitiveness, greed, the right to personal fulfillment. Those words seem harsher than the stones of the old country, harsher than the old *miseria;* they signify hardship not to the body but to the soul.

In my home on the Cape, the one built on the shining sands of hope and blunder, I see the remnants of my other homes: dishes and linens from my first house in Croton; the flowers plucked in Italy and pressed then framed and labeled, "Spring flowers from Horace's Sabine Farm . . ." I see the old Portuguese basket bought in a Lisbon junk store to the scorn of a friend with whom I spent the summer following my husband's death and her divorce; things from the Marche farmhouse where I filled the feeding troughs of the downstairs stable with plants and installed Antonio's family furniture to make it the living room. Did I think I could transplant the bourgeois furnishings of his Veneto family into an out-of-the way farmhouse and expect everyone to come visit me there? I soon realized I had to leave Italy to make a living in my own land and to raise my children where Always Upward is motto and goal.

I sold the farmhouse with most of its furnishings to a woman who lived over the hills in the town of Fermo. But the old credenza and the table with the impress of an iron on it that were used two hundred years ago in a Veneto kitchen were trucked over the Appenines and put into crates to follow me back to America. The new owner wanted the place as a country retreat. Years later I heard that a band the locals identified as "Turks" descended on the farmhouse during her absence and ransacked it, as in the days of old seafaring marauders. They made off with *zia* Giulia's dormeuse, with the leather settee and chairs from *zio* Giuseppe's law studio, with everything I had not been able to take with me. Should I ever get to Istanbul, will I come across those pieces from Antonio's family and my married life in some great outdoor bazaar?

Finished with the patio sweeping, I bike down Bridge Road towards Eastham center passing the old Burying Ground, which is actually the new one of 1754 replacing that of 1660. The cemetery is a venerable and simple place. I like the Christian names—Thankful, Mercy, Albion—and the surnames Dyer, Snow, Nicholson on the gravestones. A sign warns against tombstone rubbing; the stones are fragile, weathered, worn, some reinforced by a polyeurethane backing. They stand, or tilt, in a grassy meadow; in dead center stands one carved with a death's head at its top. It reads: "In Memory of Deacon Samuel Doane who died March 14, 1795 in the 73rd year of his age." Below that are these lines:
> "Death is a debt to nature due,
> As I have paid it, so must you."

It comes to me, considering the gravestones, that the Yankee creed of fiscal responsability extended unto death as well as in life. The old Cape Codders used "debt, due, paid" as a natural vocabulary to the commerce of life and death. It strikes me as completely contrary to the Italian warding off of death with all the *scongiurie*, entreaties, at its command, the imprecations, amulets, novenas, rites of *malocchio,* and prayers to St. Rocco whom the Calabrians (who else?) installed as saint of the impossible when all else failed.

It is not rectitude and the straight, narrow path that interests my paisans, nor solvency, nor liquidity, nor estate planning, nor debts paid up and no liens outstanding. It is the amplitude of life and its contemplation that focuses the Italian imagination. For that I need a hammock not a Puritan graveyard.

In fact my instinct went to a hammock when, arriving from Italy, I settled on a street of tall shade trees and Victorian houses in a Hudson Valley rivertown. There was a small barn behind my Gothic cottage where, according to graffiti on the walls, a sleigh-making operation had been carried on in the 1860s. And in the tiny yard between house and barn I craved a hammock despite the fact that only one tree stood there, and that one not placed conveniently to either structure for attaching the hammock between them. I spoke of my yearning to Jesse, an ingenious black man who worked at many trades including home services and had repaired storm windows for me. He simply said, "I respect your wish to have a hammock."

What he did, then, was to sink two posts into cement at the proper distance to support a hammock. The posts were not the same as trees, but Jesse's honoring my wish for a hammock made me go along with it. Still, the swinging was not the same. I barely used the hammock.

Sweeping the patio at the Cape helps me reflect once again how life is made of accommodations and compromises between the wished-for and the real. Here I conclude that a hammock might well swing between the one tree which grows alongside the patio and a supporting post of my dream arbor. Not ideal, but do-able. I'll buy another hammock and hoist it diagonally from the locust tree to the post where I hope the triumphant red-orange blast of the trumpet vine will yet ring out.

I do not willingly give up things of my past; it is not with my volition but always a sense of force majeure that I jettison and eliminate in order that a portion, at least, can be carried forward. If I do not sacrifice something, I end up with nothing. This has also been true of my writing life. It has never been a straight shot, right on target, but rather decades of persistence, setbacks, renewal, belief, trust, sometimes betrayals. The same *pazienza* required and learned as that which served the old Calabrians in their fields of stone. Something I have always carried forward: it is my survival. My persistence. My hard head. My turtle shell.

# Gioia Timpanelli

Gioia Timpanelli is a writer and poet/storyteller in the tradition of her ancestral Sicily, where the women kept the culture and handed it down in the oral threads of legend and story. She is one of the founders of the revival of storytelling, traveling worldwide to give lectures on the oral tradition and to perform extempore retellings of stories. Her most recent book is *Sometimes the Soul, Two Novellas of Sicily*, about two Sicilian women and the transformative power of art. The book received an American Book Award in 1999. Gioia Timpanelli has lived in Italy and the following excerpts record a few days from her Italian travels.

---

## Italian Traveling

---

### WEDNESDAY

*Saint Lucy, Saint Lucy*
*Flame of our Flame*
*Saint Lucy, Saint Lucy*
*Light of our Darkness*
*Saint Lucy, Saint Lucy*
*Light of our Light*

We miss the mountain road twice and twice we wind up on the superstrada to anywhere. At the same point in the highway, we pass the same sign pointing to a medieval cluster of buildings. When I make the same mistake again, I figure, "Enough! I'll get off this road, see if I can get a cup of coffee, buy some dog cigarettes and start again." Once off the strip highway, I'm on a small rubble road that no one has bothered to pave. The asphalt ends abruptly and my car falls off it with a start. It's like opening up a dream door to discover a place that one has never walked but somehow knows well. It wouldn't have surprised me to meet some old friend crossing the square. But no one is crossing the square; it is empty. The only place that looks public, with its dangling salt and cigarette sign, is closed. Since there is no one to ask, I start to back the car up, look in the mirror and see something moving: It is a large black dog crossing the square. He stops just beyond the car, finding a grease spot to lick, bobs his head up and down in satisfaction. Remembering last night's dinner, remnants still wrapped carefully inside my bag, I get out and give him all my cache. The dog never looks up so I never see his face. Yet, something draws me out. I walk to the other side of the car, look around, and then I spy her, standing so still in a small rounded doorway. How long has she been there staring at me? She is a very, very old woman, entirely black wrapped; her form fills the rounded doorway and for a second I doubt that I am seeing her. Maybe it is a shadow, but no, she is

there, her intense round eyes looking directly into mine. I feel like stepping
toward her but something stops me. "Signora," I call out softly, very softly.
"Yes," she answers, waiting in her place as I take some steps toward her and
stop. "Signora, would you help me? I need a place to stay." Now, another
woman, younger by thirty years at least, dressed in dark green, appears in
the doorway. "Follow us," she says as both of them disappear into the low,
stone building. We all three enter an enormous cavelike room: cold dark
stone room with a slight smell of old hay. They face me and when I walk up
to them, I notice we are in a small circle. There is only one light bulb hanging from the ceiling so far up I don't have a sense of its beginnings. A large
wooden table is directly under the light. The rest of the room is in darkness.
"I'll write it down," says the green woman, and with that she walks directly
behind the table, takes out a piece of paper from a notebook. While she is
writing, I see that next to her crooked writing finger, lying on the table, is a
delicately cracked egg, not in a box or on a plate but just lying there, balanced on the dark table. She taps her finger. I look again and see that just
out of the light is another egg and next to this one there is a nest of folded
paper cradling five eggs and next to them is a low paper box and in it are
more eggs, small and lightly placed one on top of another. I look down and
am surprised to find boxes of eggs not more than a few inches from my left
foot. . . . And then I know that everywhere in this dark cave there are eggs:
eggs in boxes, eggs in wooden crates, eggs in giant glass jars, eggs on the
floor, covering almost every foot, eggs on shelves, on every wall, right up to
the ceiling. Eggs, eggs, and more eggs. An egg cave. Eggs everywhere.

The green woman hands the slip of paper to the old one, who hands it to
me. I read on the slip carefully written Valino Martini Alberto, and at the
exact same time the two women look at me and say, "You should stay at
Martini (says the older) at Alberto (says the younger)" and as if they had said
the same words, satisfied, we all smile and I bow my head.

"Thank you and good day." There is no further discussion as I leave the
place carefully and step out into the gray autumn light; a light rain is
beginning to fall as I walk to the car. The dog is gone, the piazza empty
again except for my car. I get in, but before I start it I read the paper again.
Now, finally, I know where I am going.

AUTUMN: SATURDAY

*Leaving home one goes into the wilds*
*There is no place between*

The highway turns into a provincial road, the provincial road turns into a
town road, the town road narrows into a dirt road which soon is a cart lane,

and that becomes an old donkey trail which falls abruptly to a footpath and finally even this becomes so overgrown the dried brush scratches and taps at the car as we make our way up into the mountains and finally stop. We can go no farther in this machine. Zia Dina (Alberto's aunt is called "Zia" by every young villager) gets out of the car quickly, looks around squinting and nodding, points to a fallen thatched shelter and says, "That's where the shepherds live in summer, up here on the mountain. A casino. Did you know it is called a casino? They are the only ones who come up here anymore. Shepherds and sheep. Well, Mario and I and a few others are here." Her eyes widen playfully and she laughs as she says the last.

She turns and walks across a mountain field and I follow her to an ancient rock pile, white and gray rubble, one story high. From somewhere a teen-age boy appears and Zia Dina takes one of the large bread loaves that she is clasping to her breast and hands it to him. He disappears as quickly as he appeared. The way it takes time for the eyes to get accustomed to the dark before they can see what is there, it takes my eyes time to see this old place. What seemed at first only rock ruin now becomes a marvelous old town: small attached stone houses with a stone front step, small stables and hand-carved stone archways now appear. The street is so narrow that the projection of an architectural detail on one side shadows a part of the doorway on the other. The town seems to have no piazza, no separate church building; here even the Mother and Son have gone back to the land, rocks, to the great sky itself. We walk through the deserted street, no doors open, no voice calls out; toward the end of the street we are suddenly face-to-face with three white cows who come ambling toward us slowly. In the narrow street the five of us fall automatically into single file, making room for each other carefully. The first cow looks me in the eyes as we pass each other and when, for no particular reason, I look back, I see she, too, has turned to look back at me. No one else comes and Zia Dina does not even mention this event. The chickens everywhere get the afternoons to scratch in the fields, the cats at night roam far, and the young dogs travel out from early morning, and so in this town it is natural to find cows free walking the streets. They are going for their *passeggiata*—to find that last sweet mouthful of something good to eat, to that ribbon of pasture at the beginning of town where the stones of the village and the stones of the land mix with the earth and bright sweet grass.

I follow Zia Dina as she leads me to the outskirts of the village where the houses end and a purposeful space lined with many paths leads to an old fountain whose font is made of half found rock and half human-hewed rock; some spigots of unceremonious color and shape but instead of one or two there are five pouring forth a strong flow of water. As we come up to the fountain a marmalade cat is lapping, taking a long drink from a lower basin.

She does not run away or even look up nor do we disturb her. Zia Dina takes a tin cup from behind some rocks and asks me with some ceremony, "Would you like a drink from the fountain?" But ignorant of what I had been asked to take and not being at the moment thirsty, I say, "No, thank you." She drinks and we walk on. But I think it strange that I have been asked so formally to have some of the water from this fountain.

In an hour, we have circled around, gone to the four corners of the village. We have looked in all directions, high on the top of the mountain to valleys and farther mountain peaks. We have seen the bare autumn fields ("Mario had the best vegetable garden once. We always had more than we needed. He would give a lot away."), the chestnut woods below, felt the cloud. "This is our old apple tree. It still has good fruit." An old apple tree of autumn, no leaves but shimmering black bark, wet and rough tiny valleys, bark valleys with dark life in them. Underfoot, the wild grasses cover everything so we touch yellow hair as fine as a child's. The grass grows to the edge of the thick mud road. We have circled around and now pass the old fountain and then I remember . . . the place where the bees sing, an ancient village famous since before Roman times for its fountain of healing water that heals both inner and outer cares. The same fountain, in the same place, the water still flowing.

It is cold and a strong wind springs up; we are cloud wet. Zia Dina leads the way back into town, to the doorstep of the house she and her husband, Mario, refuse to leave completely, even though the upper floor has fallen in during the earthquake of two years before. She knocks at the door and Mario answers immediately. He greets us warmly, smiling and showing the way, all the while saying, "Enter, enter . . ." As soon as we cross the threshold I feel it, something in the room. I can't exactly name it but it is the feeling of old spirit and it touches every corner of this ancient stone room. It is like walking into a presence. One feels it always in holy places and that is what I feel in this simple room. Zio Mario has made a great fire in the hearth for us and we each take our place near it, even the black and white cat, Minio, on the left, and the old dog, Fino, on the right. There is a great sense of peace here. We all sit in silence for a long while; nothing needs to be said or done here. We sit around the ancient fire, drawn to it. Finally, after all this traveling I feel I have found something. We are here, deeply warmed in some center, a place of hidden stone where a constant fire burns, formed so long ago it has no name and it burns not only for warmth. We have circled around and around and finally find this hearth where we all live and no place else and since it is where we are born each day again and again where there is even a strong feeling of protection where else can we go? Where else would we be at home? Since this is the fire that starts all others how can they let it go out?

We sit a long while in silence. Then Zia Dina speaks, "The engineers say the house is not good. We never go upstairs anymore. They say we can never come back here and they have given us a small box to live in for the winter. It's nearby; I'll show you. Maybe you understand it and can explain how things work in it. We sleep with relatives now and come back home each day and have our fire and cook a little something for ourselves and for the creatures. We don't mind sleeping in the box." She says this all matter-of-factly. She rests in what she knows.

In these past weeks I have been in many places where life was fully lived but no home had this feeling of holiness about it. This place where the sacred fire burns. Where can they go? How can they give it up? To another fire, we say. We can say that, for our fires have been found in places as we go and we've heard some holy ones talk of this possibility but we know it is not easy and of the two ways, this traveling fire is the harder to find. Zia Dina and Zio Mario are reluctant to leave their ancient hearth but soon they will leave it.

Why THIS fire? This particular one. Zia Dina says, "It is a humble place. We know that." Perhaps, it is the earthquake which has left it so . . . exposed to only this center but whatever it is, the spirit in this room, near this hearth is unmistakable.

# FICTION

# Mari Tomasi

Born in Montpelier, Vermont in 1907, Mari Tomasi lived all her life there until her death in 1965. She worked for the Montpelier newspaper and also for the Federal Writers' Project in Vermont. When the first of her two novels, *Deep Grow the Roots*, appeared in 1940, she was named by the American Booksellers' Association as one of the year's ten most promising new novelists. Her second novel, *Like Lesser Gods*, published in 1949 and reissued in 1989, depicts the Italian American granite workers in Vermont. Mari Tomasi was an active member of the Poetry Society of Vermont and the Vermont Historical Society for which she wrote "The Italian Story in Vermont."

## *from* Like Lesser Gods

Why, she thought bitterly, why should Pietro be cursed with this ridiculous passion for stone, and why could she not make him see the need for finding other work? Her mind so thrummed with these familiar thoughts that she could not concentrate on the card game nor did she hear but snatches of the conversation, which drifted from one subject to another:

"There should be snow for deer hunting next month—"

"With the sanatorium at the top of the hill the taxes will probably be raised. But it should mean a fine sidewalk." And the *maestro*'s chuckle, "Hah, if they are like the Ibena taxes, don't be too sure. Public money, like holy water, is dipped into by everyone."

Someone murmuring, "Eh, Ronato tells us, Pietro, that you are carving a beautiful memorial."

And Pietro's shy supplement, "The best these hands have ever made. Yet, if it were Ronato's work, I would consider it the least of his masterpieces."

Maria snapped to attention. Pietro was saying, "It is a cross, standing just so high." His stubby, calloused fingers indicated a height in the vicinity of his umbilicus. "And it is nearly smothered under vines. The best job I have yet undertaken, and it will be finished next week."

*The best job—finished next week.*

The words revolved in Maria's mind with the persistence of a catchy merry-go-round tune. Suddenly, their relationship to a former well-remembered threat of Pietro's fired them with potential significance. She well remembered the day when the stonecutter Gateau had been threatened with dismissal if his hands again slipped carelessly to spoil the stone he was working. Better still she remembered Pietro's fervid, "If by accident my hand should sometime err, just let my boss give me hell. I would throw the job in his face, and quit."

*The best job I have done—I would throw the job in his face and quit.*

As clearly and as sweetly as an Angelus calls laborers from their toil and bids them forget fatigue and defeat, so these words dispelled Maria's fruitless years of begging Pietro to leave the sheds. She must take matters into her own hands: *she must ruin that fine stone of Pietro's, make it appear a careless slip. The boss, Gerbatti, would fume and scold. And against such injustice Pietro would make good his threat. . . .*

Maria's mind was made up. From that moment she directed the evening's activities to the success of her plan. "More wine!" she urged her guests, and made sure to pour a brimming glass for Pietro, too. Ronato, watching Maria's face ripen a joyous red, murmured, "Your cheeks, Maria, are as happily red as that dress you wear."

At midnight, Lucia and Ronato were in mellow readiness to say their good nights, yet Maria detained them with a refilled pitcher of wine. Not until Pietro's words stumbled thickly one over the other and his cheeks bloomed a brick-red, did she close the door behind her visitors. And when Pietro's arm lay in leaden embrace around her waist and his deep breathing bespoke a half-drugged sleep, she rose from their bed, dressed quickly, supplied herself with flashlight and chisel, and stole from the house.

That plunge into chilly night air washed away some of the confidence she had enjoyed in the grappa-vaporized room. A palsied moment of indecision held her slippered feet to the porch. She looked right and left on Pastinetti Place, into the silent drama of darkened windows and deep shadows. In the harsh moonlight the Vitleau sanatorium site was a grotesquerie of exhumed maple roots, standing watch over their open graves. Maria's lips tightened derisively. She stepped resolutely across the granite chip walk and ran in quiet flight down the center of the dirt road.

Down Main Street, on the second block, a cluster of lunch-cart habitués was noisily inviting Officer Riley to a hot dog and coffee. She breathed more easily after she had crossed the bridge and tracks to the shadows of Shed Row. A darkened car was parked beneath a sprawling river willow. In its interior a quartet of male and female voices woefully harmonized—"Show me the way to go home—" Maria gained the sheds and kept to their back yards. Under moonglow Maria's practical mind waxed fanciful. The weathered structures loomed gaunt specters. Strewn grout pieces lay on the ground like whiting bones. Here and there oblong blocks of stone became overturned tombstones. She looked defiantly at the moon. Her lips curled their scorn at its eerie attempt to weaken her determination: here beneath her feet was the harsh reality of granite chips; each step was a sharp reminder of what stone could do. . . .

The great front doors of Gerbatti's shed were strongly barred against her. She tried to raise one after another of the high, heavy windows and succeeded only in loosing thick showers of gray dust. She crept around the side to the smaller windows of the office. A wire ripped open her thumb. The muscles of her arms strained to aching agony before a window at last gave an inch. She explored the inside sill with her index finger, and discovered a bent spike holding the window secure. She poked at the spike with the chisel until she could turn it in its pocket and pull it.

The quartet's mournful voices drowned the creaking of the window. Maria climbed into the room. Her flashlight threw a circle of light on the floor and revealed dust-filled cracks between the floor boards. She reflected grimly that even Gerbatti, boss though he was, received his share of the dust. A door opposite her opened into the dark wet room. It was cluttered with giant saws and polishing machines. Wet room, indeed! *Dio*, here was the earthy chill of some subterranean cave. And cloyed with it was a dank smell of rust and oil that constricted her body into a knot of shivers. What was it Pietro said? Ah, yes—the machinists hate water because it rusts their well-oiled machines; and the carvers detest oil because it stains the granite. Yet, in this machine room, water was truly needed. It had to be fed, she knew, in steady, cold streams to prevent the metal saws from melting as they heatedly cut into stone. Ah, if granite could thus torture metal, what,

then, could it do to flesh and blood! But stone was not always the victor.
Maria's mouth twisted into a sly, determined smile: stone could not reason,
stone could not plot as did her brain. . . .

She pushed open another door to the drier, chalky air of the finishing
room. And here she was blind to everything but Pietro's favorite corner
where his little masterpiece stood under a stiff covering.

Maria wasted no time. She pulled off the tarpaulin, studied the granite
cross dispassionately, and set the chisel point to a corner leaf design where a
chip might appear to be a slip of Pietro's hand. With an iron bar she
hammered at the chisel. The sound struck into the lofty room with a hollow,
sepulchral note. Another blow. A small edge of the cross chipped off and fell
to the dirt floor. Another blow. The leaf pattern dwindled to half a leaf.
Another blow. Another.

She straightened breathlessly. Now that the deed was accomplished, its
magnitude temporarily appalled her. Maria's hands trembled; her heart
thrashed wildly against her ribs. And for the first time since she entered the
spacious finishing room, she looked about her.

A half-dozen memorials stared back at her, stonily, ghastly in the moonlight. On the boxing platform three little markers plainly lettered—ALMA,
GEORGE, and ALICE, held her fascinated eyes with their almost human
accusation. She uttered a cry that was half prayer, half scorn. She shook her
fist at them, and fled back to the office window, clambering out in such
haste that when an outside wire caught at her skirt she tugged it away
frantically, undismayed at the tear, only eager to put the river once more
between herself and Shed Row.

It was not characteristic of Maria Dalli to stint a healthy sleep appetite
with worries. Night, she reasoned, was for sleep. It was during the day that
one should worry about getting rid of worries. Wasn't it foolishly inconsis-
tent to nourish the body daily with good food, protect it with clothing, veer
it from injuries—and at night to undo this good by punishing the body with
wakefulness and by teasing a sensible brain into lunacy? And so it was
tonight.

She crept noiselessly into the house. Once again beside the deeply
breathing Pietro, she promptly fell into profound sleep. But asleep she was
no longer mistress of her mind. Before the seven o'clock whistle could
awaken her to reality, it became a shrill police call which gathered together
hundreds of blue-coated police. They were marching toward her from the
four corners of Granitetown. Hundreds of stern police eyes were riveted to
her right hand which clutched a chisel and which was hacking away at the
lifeless face of the man for whom Pietro was carving a cross. . . .

The sound of Pietro's voice came to her from a great distance. "Yours is a
big head, too, this morning?" he was inquiring sympathetically. She heard

the words even as she struggled to wakefulness. He sat in his nightshirt on the edge of the bed, tenderly massaging his forehead.

She murmured, "Big head?" It came to her, then, that he was referring to last evening, the grappa fumes, and the wine. She smiled ruefully, "*Sì, sì*, we were too generous with the wine last night."

As soon as Pietro and his dinner pail disappeared down Pastinett. Place she fed the children and sent them off to school. Mister Tiff left with them; this was the day for mending umbrellas on Willow Hollow Road. Maria did her housework automatically; mentally she was following Pietro step by step. *Now he enters the shed . . . he chats a moment with Ronato and his friends . . . now the shed whirrs with activity, everyone begins work. . . . Pietro draws the covering off his cross . . . he stares at it with disbelieving eyes . . . now comes Gerbatti. . . . Gerbatti gasps, he fumes and storms . . . the workmen gather around curiously . . . my poor Pietro is shamed before them. . . . "Go to hell!" he shouts to Gerbatti. "I quit!" . . . and he walks out of the shed, never again to return. . . .* This dreaming was balm to Maria's heart. She bustled about preparing his favorite dinner, for soon he would be home, dinner pail and all. He would be saddened, perplexed, enraged. She must prepare a good dinner. He would enjoy *salsigi*, and a snappy salad of endive, tomatoes, and onions.

Vetch and Petra ate their noonday meal and left again for school. The *maestro*, she decided, must be at Lucia's table today. But why didn't Pietro come home? Ah, well, he was no doubt fine-combing Granitetown this minute for another job. *Sì*, that was it. He would find a job, work for a month or two while they made plans for the little store they would have in their house. . . .

It was shortly after four when he came in, his round face thoughtful and his head bent, and she saw that in his preoccupation he had neglected to slap the stone dust from his clothes. She knew he must be grieving at leaving this work he loved, but she felt little pity. *Dio*, if an infant were attracted to the color red, would she not remove a red-hot poker from its reach even though the babe screamed as if its heart were breaking? She waited in vain for Pietro's, "Well, Maria, I did it. Today I quit the sheds." He muttered only with his preoccupied air, "The days are getting too brisk for only a kitchen fire." And in a few minutes she heard him in the cellar cleaning the furnace.

After supper when the children were abed she thought: surely, now he will speak. But he shrugged into his coat explaining briefly, "I promised to help Rossi with his grappa tonight."

She consoled herself: Pietro is Pietro. He will say nothing until he has found a new job. He does not want me to worry. *Sì*, that is it. . . .

She was alone in the kitchen darning socks when Mister Tiff entered quietly, the golf bag drooping from a slumped shoulder. He was hanging back with a strangely hesitant air, ill at ease, uncertain. Despite the cold evening his high, pink forehead glistened with perspiration. He handed her a small square of red-and-white checked cambric. He spoke fast, as if to put an early end to this distasteful mission. "Last night you wore a skirt of this cloth, Maria; the skirt was whole and pretty. Last night in Gerbatti's shed, Pietro's stone was mutilated. This morning this piece of cloth waves accusation from a wire outside Gerbatti's office window. And this morning, I wager, your skirt is minus this little square of cloth—" He shook his head, sighed.

Maria stood speechless. Her fingers clenched the cambric square until her nails, cutting into her palm, smarted her to activity. Her voice was anxious, fierce. "Does Pietro know?"

He shook his head in silence.

"No, no. I chanced to be walking the yard on my way to Willow Hollow Road. I saw the cloth—and I remembered." He finished compassionately, "Don't fear, I won't tell."

She gripped his arm in wild hope, and despair. "What happened, *Maestro*? What did Gerbatti say? What did Gerbatti do?"

"Do? Pietro did not tell you?" He was honestly amazed.

"Not one word has he spoken!"

"Nothing happened, Maria."

He felt the trembling of her hands before they fell limp from his arm.

"Gerbatti did not give him hell?" she said tonelessly. It couldn't be true. Her wretched deed in vain. . . . "Pietro did not rebel and—quit?"

The question was a plea. He understood. There might be thousands of wives who blessedly resigned themselves to the hazards of their husbands' work, but it had to be a deeply loving and deeply willful Maria who would try to take matters into her own hands. She was strong of mind and strong of heart; and although strength has its own joys and rewards, it is heir, too, to its own brand of pain. He asked, gruffly tender, "And why should Gerbatti give him hell, Maria? Anyone could see it was no accident. It was the intentional butchering of some malefactor. A beautifully worked stone—in ruin. Gerbatti respects Pietro's love for his work, he had only to see Pietro's stricken face to know he was innocent."

Her shoulders drooped. Her face shrank, beaten, white. Only her black eyes were defiantly burning against this defeat. He shifted awkwardly under their blaze, and he was thinking: if only Lucia could love the poor Ronato as Maria does Pietro. . . .

She whirled away from him. Never had anyone seen a tear glisten in Maria Dalli's eyes, nor would she let the *maestro* see one tonight.

He limped up the stairs after her, his heart fluttering with a great fear. If last night Maria, riding her crest of omnipotence, ruined a costly stone, what greater harm might she do on some tomorrow? And to remind her of what the stone cost Gerbatti would make little impression tonight on her stony mood of defeat.

The door to her bedroom was open. He began timidly, "May I speak to you, Maria?" She did not reply, and he continued, "Forgive me if I repeat what I have already told you—that sometimes for a man there is but one job at which he can be happy. I have seen Pietro at his work. It is as if he has two hearts: one that beats for you and his family, and one that beats for his work. Since the very beginnings of family, the husband's lot has always become the wife's. And justly so. Remember the wise Ruth who even made her mother-in-law's lot her own, when she said—'Whither thou goest I will go.' And the Roman bride of antiquity formally promised her husband—'Where thou art, Caius, there am I, Caia.' In the same measure your own promise 'for better or for worse' makes Pietro's lot your lot, and you must accept it if you would keep his love."

She had turned a rigid back on him and was staring, unseeing, through the window.

He gained courage in her silence. "Think how Pietro would feel if he knew his own wife had damaged his stone—"

Her voice carried assurance, and a trace of mockery. "He won't know—unless you tell him—and you won't do that."

He said quietly, "You are right. I won't do that, Maria. But suppose God had not been so generous with you? Suppose Pietro himself had come upon that all-revealing piece of cloth? Me, I think it would mean the end of everything beautiful and honest between you. Hah, Maria, don't you know that a man is but an oversized boy, and he likes oversized compliments and flattery on the work that is near to his heart? And, instead of flattering him you beg him to quit his work! *Dio mio*, haven't you known men as fine as your Pietro who have fled for comfort to the arms of other women?"

"Spare yourself the lecture, *Maestro*, Pietro never looks at other women."

Mister Tiff weighed the prudence of implanting a seed of doubt in her mind, but fearful of its catastrophic outcome in the hands of the willful Maria he reluctantly compromised with a—"No? No?"

He did not see the shadow creep into her face. And he turned away, nursing but little hope that he may have touched upon a vulnerable spot in Maria.

Alone, she crouched stiffly on the granite step beside the bed. She was not pondering the *Maestro*'s exact words, but rather the poignant associations they stirred, and which now pummeled her, mind and heart. She,

Pietro, and the children were happy. Except for her persistent fear for
Pietro's health—they were happy. If Pietro ever learned that she had ruined his little masterpiece, how could they continue to love here with the
oneness of spirit and body, and the sweet completion that had always been
theirs.

The dismal failure of last night's trip to Gerbatti's shed was losing itself
now in the vital urgency of preserving the happiness that was hers, Pietro's,
and the children's. Her hands clenched over her knees. "God, please do not
let Pietro find out." . . .


Pietro never saw Peter Michael again. A week after the baby's christen-
ing Petra arrived at the sanatorium for her usual afternoon visit and found
her father napping. She sat beside him for a while, watching the tired lids
quiver over the sunken eyes. Then she slipped out to one of the comfortable
wicker chairs in the sun porch. Her own eyes closed drowsily, and she was
gliding into the tranquil days of childhood when she and Peggy tramped
Vitleau's orchard for the summer's first violets. A hand shook her. She woke
to the urgent words of one of the nurses. "Miss Dalli, your father—"

Petra flew past her down the hall. Gino was attempting, with ice packs,
to prevent the ever-widening of those bright patches of red on her father's
pillow. She knew he was dying. It was added torture to see his soft eyes
humbly pleading forgiveness of her: as if he were saddened at causing her
this grief, yet himself were quite willing to go.

They came quickly from their corners of Granitetown: Father Carty,
Maria, Gabbi, Americo, Mister Tiff. Pietro wished wearily that the white-
tunicked Gino would keep his hands from him and let him die in peace. The
boy's efforts were delaying, only for a few minutes, the great and final
moment of release. This business of dying would be a drifting, not unpleasant sensation, were it not for the grief-ravaged faces around him that tore at
his heart.

Of all the eyes about him only Maria's were dry, bright; her face, an
inscrutable mask. He was proud of her. As strong, as unflinching as granite
she was, he reflected, in his last earthly flicker of humor. The same qualities
in these two he loved. . . .

The faces around him blurred. He was soaring giddily above them, out of
and above himself. He could scarcely see his family and friends; yet in a
strange lucidity he was viewing the complete panorama of Dalli life in Italy
and in Granitetown. He was with his childhood friend, Italo Tosti, in the
hills of northern Italy . . . he stood at Italo's grave in Granitetown . . . and
here he was testily suffering Gino's tireless hands . . . he was embarking
with Maria on the blue Mediterranean . . . he was beside her in their bed

at Pastinetti Place . . . he was here at the Granitetown sanatorium watching
her face grow dimmer and dimmer . . . he plowed brown fields under an
azure Italian sky . . . he hunted mushrooms at Peter's Gate . . . he was in
Gerbatti's shed caressing beauty into stone . . . he and Italo were boys,
pilfering eggs from the hennery of the village priest Don Ricardo. . . .

Redheaded Father Carty, breathless from this hurried sick call, stood
gravely over Pietro. Pietro saw him as another Don Ricardo; and he murmured the deathbed plea of the old world *paesani*, "*Gesù, Giuseppe e
Maria!*"

But his last breath did not come. He was in Gerbatti's shed once more,
his hand guiding the steel into the pattern of a slender cross. He sweated
over his work, eager to finish it before the end of the day's work. . . .

A four o'clock whistle began screeching to Granitetown that stonecutters
were through for the day. In Shed Row, another whistle, and another, took
up the cry. Pietro heard them. A smile settled on his gray face. His head
dropped forward in a nod, and then he was dead.

---

# *Antonia Pola*

---

A ntonia Pola is the pen-name of Antonietta Pomilla who was born in the
Piedmont region of Italy, educated there, and briefly taught in a school
near Turin. Immigrating to the United States, she lived in Cicero, Illinois.
Nothing else is known of her since she is one of those legions of "lost" writers
known only by the title of a single book. Pola's novel, *Who Can Buy the
Stars?*, is an account of an Italian immigrant woman that is forceful, non-
sentimental, and sharply different from the stereotypical portraits of silent,
submissive women. Her protagonist, Marietta, comes to America as the "picture bride" of a coal miner. He is no match for her intelligence and ambition
as she starts a bootlegging business during the Prohibition era and earns
money. Yet she finds that money cannot buy back what she left in Italy, nor
could she ever return to the impoverished life she had known there. In the
end she belongs nowhere. Stylistically uneven though the book is, the character Marietta is vividly realized.

# *from* Who Can Buy the Stars?

"But, Mother, why didn't you wire as soon as you got to New York? I would have had a party for you."

"That's exactly what I didn't want, Delfina. Besides, the boat docked on the thirteenth. I didn't like the date."

Delfina looked surprised. "Mother! Don't tell me that you've become superstitious all of a sudden! If that's what a trip to the old country does for you—!" She laughed disbelievingly as she bustled about completing her supper arrangements. "I know, it's just that you didn't want any fuss made over you."

Marietta laughed, too, as if in agreement. No need for anyone to know that the thirteenth of the month, from now on, would always hurt her heart.

She had not wanted to get in touch with anyone when she first landed. She had not wanted to see anyone, and she was suddenly, strangely, not quite sure that she would be glad to get home. But she had gone directly from the boat to the railroad station and had taken the first train.

When she got to Indianapolis the next day, she sent a wire home. Andrea and Mario and Gina were waiting for her when she reached Clifton at five o'clock that afternoon.

"Christ, but I'm glad to see you back!" Andrea said. "An old soldier like me needs his general."

Mario hugged and kissed her, so glad to see her that he almost forgot to release her. Gina jumped up and down with joy at the sight of her mother, but Marietta could tell that the child had not missed her much.

Delfina had stayed at home to start the supper, and now, swelled with importance, she urged them all to hurry and sit down, so that they might eat while everything was at its best.

"How good it all is!" Marietta exclaimed after she had tasted the various dishes. "As fine as anything I tasted while I was away."

Delfina nodded, and Minot blushed with pleasure. The two were getting along, thought Marietta, only Delfina had become too conceited; she was almost patronizing. She had never been very bright, but her sweetness had made her a dear. Marietta hoped she didn't lose that, or she would be a colorless woman.

"I asked Minot's mother," the girl said. "She couldn't come for supper, but will be up later in the evening."

Angelina was using common sense; she understood that a mother should have only her family around her, on her return after a long absence. And still, after the meal was finished, there seemed little that Marietta had to say to them, or they to her. The first greetings were over, and she had not yet returned to her familiar place in their daily life.

"I'll go over to see Celeste," Marietta said, "before Angelina gets here."

She walked slowly over to the Gilbertis', taking along the handmade shoulder scarf, of white wool, that she had brought Celeste as a gift from Italy. Jim wasn't at home, and Marietta understood that. She wouldn't want to be home either if Joseph Gaia were to call at her house.

Celeste was very glad to see her, and they visited for almost half an hour. They barely mentioned the breaking-up of the partnership and the Gilbertis' plan to move to Chicago. When Marietta stood up to leave, Celeste looked at her appraisingly.

"You weren't away very long," she said. "Still you have changed."

"What makes you think so?"

"I don't know." Celeste was carefully folding the scarf. She added as an afterthought, "I like you better."

"It's all to the good, then," Marietta said laughingly. But she wondered as she left.

Later, when Angelina came to welcome her back, Marietta felt irritated as usual by the woman's vivacity. There was in her an element of joy and life almost impossible to define. Antonio had come with her, and there was much asking and answering of questions. It was almost like a party, after all, for Delfina had baked a cake for the occasion. It was nice, only the child was giving herself too many lofty airs.

"Doesn't she know that a really nice person acts simply and kindly?" Marietta asked herself.

Then she thought that perhaps it was her own fault. Maybe she should have taken more time from the business to teach her children the good manners that *Nonna* had taught her. Still, Mario had been brought up just the same as the others, and he was always modest and gentle and kind. Mario was born nice.

She hoped that if she had another baby, it would be beautiful and gentle like her first-born. She intensely wanted a baby; that desire, more than anything else, had urged her homeward with the greatest possible speed. It made her glad when the Musis left early, saying they knew that she must be tired after her journey. She wasn't tired, only eager.

Early the next morning, before the girls were up, Marietta waited in the sitting room between the kitchen and the store. Mario had opened the place and would be coming through. She had to talk to him about his plans.

He started when he came in and found her there, but he didn't seem really surprised.

"I know you're anxious to take hold of things again, Mother," he said with a little laugh.

Marietta shook her head. "One day more or less will not matter. I want to talk to you." He sat down, and she noticed that his wrist was bare. "You're not wearing the wristwatch I brought you for a present. I thought that you liked it."

"Oh, I do like it, Mother." He blushed. "But it's too expensive a piece of jewelry to show around Clifton."

"It's paid for. What makes you afraid of letting people see it?" He must have a reason for not wearing the watch, but she knew it wasn't its cost.

"Well," he said, blushing again, "the fellows I go with, they can't afford a Swiss watch, not like the one you gave me anyway. There might be some wisecracks about it."

"What kind of wisecracks?"

Mario hesitated, looked embarrassed, and finally said, "Oh, just wise-cracks. I'll wear the watch when I'm dressed up." Before she could question him further, he went on, "Mother, did you want to talk to me about my going to Chicago?"

"About your staying here in Clifton," she corrected him, smiling fondly. "You know I don't want you to leave me."

"And I don't want to leave you, Mother. But I have to go to Chicago."

His voice was respectful, but very stubborn. Marietta spoke sharply. "Have to? Why do you have to go to Chicago?"

"To learn to be a carpenter. That's what I want to be more than anything in the world."

"All right, I don't object to that. But you can learn here in Clifton. I'll go myself to Erikson—he's the best carpenter contractor in town—and ask him to take you on as an apprentice."

"Please, Mother, don't go to Erikson!" He got up suddenly and walked to the window. Over his shoulder he said, "He wouldn't have me."

"He would if you were to tell him you're willing to work for less than the scale."

Still not looking at her, Mario said, "I don't want to work for Erikson. I know what he thinks of money that is not on the up and up." As if he knew how much that must have hurt her, he rushed on, "In Chicago, I'll stand a better chance at the trade. Jim Gilberti's going to ask his son-in-law to help me get in."

So that was how Gilberti planned to get his revenge! She might have known he would strike at her most vulnerable spot, just as she had struck at him. She forced herself not to think of that, to keep her voice calm and quiet.

"If you stay here, as soon as you're through with your apprenticeship, I'll finance you to go on your own."

"What difference will that make?" Mario cried, turning around. His hands were clenched, his whole body tense. "It will be the same as with the watch."

Marietta looked at him, a question in her eyes. She was afraid she already knew the answer.

"Somebody is liable to remark that only bootleggers could afford such costly things." The words were the ones she had feared, but the tone was almost unbearably bitter. In a softer voice he added, "It hurts to have a tag like that."

"Since when has it been hurting you so much?"

"From the very beginning, Mother. Only at first I wasn't so conscious of it, or I was too young to feel as I do now."

That was true, Marietta knew. He had always objected to the bootlegging, but she never thought it would come to this. She couldn't let him go. She assured him that there would never be any more bootlegging. By and by, the people of Clifton would forget that the Sassos had once sold liquor. All the while she talked, she fussed with her hair.

"We didn't really harm anybody," she asserted.

"But we broke the law twenty-four hours a day." He was still standing at the window, his back to the light. Sitting upright in a straight chair, Marietta waited for him to go on. "Mother, people in general begrudge us our money. I feel like a criminal."

Again Marietta fixed her tresses. From the sudden look of tenderness, almost of pity, on Mario's face, she realized that he recognized how upset she was. But he shook his head.

"Mother, it was such a mistake."

"I wanted us to be rich."

"We could have got along with the store," he said stubbornly. "The bootlegging money meant only unhappiness."

"Who else got hurt?"

"Delfina."

The bell tinkled as someone came into the store. Marietta motioned Mario to go in and wait on them. She couldn't. Her legs were shaking. She was cold all over. God, to have her beloved son accuse her so unmercifully—this was worse than Joseph rejecting her love.

"How much more can I stand?" she asked herself.

But she had to know exactly what she had lost, and what she still had and could save. She closed her eyes, so as to gather strength. When she heard the customers leave the store, she called Mario to come back.

"I want to know about Delfina," she said.

Mario told her then that Delfina had loved Joe Bailey (the ballplayer, Marietta remembered; he had been coming around quite often for a while, and then she hadn't seen him again). Now Mario said that Delfina had lost him because of the bootlegging. (But I never knew, Marietta silently protested. If she had known—if she had . . . ? What could she have done?)

Her son spoke quietly, but she could tell that he had suffered for his sister. And only two weeks ago, he said, Gina had been left out of the birthday party of one of her best friends. The child had cried bitterly.

"What's one party?" Marietta asked defensively. But she knew only too well the heartache her daughter must have felt.

"There are going to be other parties," Mario said, "to which Gina will not be invited. Eventually she'll learn the reason."

Marietta felt like an animal at bay. The dearest things in her life were breaking all around her. She would pick up the pieces. But now, this minute, she must save Mario's love and respect for her. He was the best of all her children.

"Sit down, please." It was as if she were talking to a judge. "You know, I guess, that when I came to America I was only seventeen years old. You must have heard us talk about that."

"Yes." He sat down in a chair in front of her.

"In those seventeen years of life in Italy, I already had suffered all the privations and humiliations of poverty."

"Were you really poor, Mother? Were you hungry?"

The anxious note in her son's voice gave some comfort to Marietta. Again she smoothed her hair.

"We were really poor. I never went hungry, but our meals at home were poor and always the same. I never was cold for lack of clothes, either, only they were skimpy clothes, patched and homemade and faded. Until I was fourteen, I went barefooted on weekdays, all summer long, I've often wondered how my feet kept a good shape after the way I walked without shoes on dusty highways, rutted country roads, and on the cobbled streets of Nuvale."

For a long minute mother and son looked at each other.

"Italy is a very beautiful place to live," Marietta said slowly and soberly. "Still I was deeply grateful to your father because he asked me to come here as his bride. The day I sailed for America I cried, and leaving the Bay of Genoa I swore that I would get rich or there was no excuse for leaving my country and my family. That's why I've done what I have."

Mario shifted his feet and contemplated the pattern of the rug. He didn't want to look at his mother. She went on to tell him how every time a child was born to her, she swore again to get rich. Finally she asked, "You believe me, don't you Mario?"

"Yes, Mother. You looked at money in your own way. To me, it seems the wrong way."

He wasn't saying he was sorry for her. His own present hurt was much more important to him than all her suffering, past and present. She made one more effort.

"You are good and honest. You should be able to make the people of Clifton like you for your own self. I think it's worth trying, Mario."

"I don't have the courage. I'm too easily hurt, and I've been hurt too much."

How cruel he was! She could only hope he would remember this and in time understand the motives behind her actions.

"All right," she said. "I'll have your clothes ready for you; you can leave whenever you want to."

He looked at her, and she saw tears in his eyes. But he got up and left without a word.

After her son was gone, Marietta didn't move from her chair. She was alone, watching her life and her house crumble into ruins. She felt crushed, frustrated.

She turned eagerly as the door opened again. But it was only Andrea. Poor helpless Andrea.

"Anything wrong, Marietta?" he asked. "Are you sick?"

She shook her head, afraid to trust her voice. Then, recovering her poise and self-control, she told him of Mario's determination to go away, and her decision to send Gina to a good boarding school. He was surprised to hear about the school, but he agreed willingly, not caring one way or another. She said that at least one of their children should have the advantages of an education. She didn't want to discuss her real reasons with him—or the reasons for Mario's leaving, either. He never had been enthusiastic about the bootlegging.

Neither alluded to the past night. It was too painful. Andrea was done, finished, and the money he had paid for the doctor and medicines had been useless. There was never going to be another baby. The certainty of that had kept Marietta awake for hours, intensified her feeling now.

"We will be alone and lonesome," she said dejectedly.

"Delfina and Minot are with us. We won't be lonesome."

She didn't bother to point out that Delfina was already on her own, living apart as a stranger. He wouldn't understand. At heart Andrea was a child. Even the tragedy of his lost virility had been tempered for him by his simple good-natured philosophy.

Last night, after a little swearing, he had looked at the bedroom ceiling and told Marietta that he had felt it coming on for years, had been prepared.

"Jesus Christ," he had said mildly, "no use getting sore. We have had four children, more than many men can get. Some can't even go with a woman at all."

Marietta had wanted to cry out that she was only forty years old, but she knew that her protests would be wasted. Her husband was like certain streams of water, wide and deep, and sheltered by friendly trees, that no storm can ever disturb greatly.

Now he looked placidly at her. "And don't worry, Marietta. We won't be lonesome. There will be little ones to play with. I'm pretty sure something is on the way. Did Delfina tell you?"

"No, she didn't. But a few days ago when Angelina was here, I heard her lecturing our daughter about lifting things, wearing high heels, and climbing too many stairs." He pulled at his mustache with pride. "When Angelina left, she was so happy even her back danced up and down with joy."

He laughed, expecting Marietta to do the same. Marietta couldn't. This was, strangely, the hardest blow of all—that there should be a child on the way, but not her child. Angelina, already looking forward to being grandmother, would be the supremely happy one. That woman seemed to know how to reach the stars, while she had been fool enough to want to buy them.

"Madonna!" she said to herself. "What a mistake and what a waste!" But, somehow, she would still get something out of life. She must. If Nonna were living, she would want her to. Mario. . . . Andrea. . . . Gina. . . . Delfina. . . . Joseph. . . . She was unable to think clearly. Her heart had received too many cruel blows in succession.

Silently, almost unconsciously, she got to her feet and walked over to the desk in the corner of the room. From the top drawer she took out the ledger where the accounts of the store were carefully marked down, day by day. She sat down and took up a pen.

She must check to see what profit had been made during her absence.

# Rose Grieco

The daughter of Italian immigrants, Rose Grieco wrote with warmth and humor of the Italian American world for many years in stories and articles that appeared in various publications. A lifelong resident of Montclair, New Jersey, she won several awards for her interest in preserving Italian folkways and pursued multiple artistic activities in her community. Grieco's *Anthony on Overtime*, dealing with the conflicts and problems arising out of a dual culture and how they can be transformed into vehicles of enrichment, was produced at the Blackfriars Theater in New York to critical acclaim.

## The Sunday Papa Missed Mass

My uncles Angelo and Jim came into our family by virtue of having had the good sense to marry my mother's sisters Mary and Lina. I don't mention Uncle John, because although married to Aunt Rose, he always managed to keep a safe distance from our affairs.

With her four daughters married, Nonna turned her thoughts toward keeping them physically close to each other, so that in times of trouble they would not have far to turn. The girls cooperated beautifully by living within one block of each other on the Upper East Side of New York.

However, when children started arriving rather regularly, except in Aunt Rose's case, the women decided that while it meant venturing into new territory, their growing families should be surrounded by space and trees and gardens. Nonna quietly allowed her daughters to convince themselves, because it was they who were going to have to convince their husbands.

The idea of leaving the city was given fresh impetus when a "comare" of ours went to a wake in a place called Montclair in New Jersey, and was charmed by the giant trees and surrounding mountains. Her enthusiasm inspired the women in our family to want to settle there, too.

Aunt Rose, being the oldest, set the migration into motion by explaining to her husband that at the age of twelve their son was totally unfamiliar with fields and gardens. In Montclair, they could plant fig-trees and tomato plants and grape-vines. Now, Uncle John wasn't quite so concerned about fig-trees or tomato plants as he was about his wife's beauty, which caused many men in the crowded neighborhood to cast better than admiring glances in her direction. While pretending to agree for their son's sake, Uncle John was accommodating only because he fervently believed his rose was safer blushing unseen in the country air.

Aunt Mary was next in line, and should have continued the journey into the unkown, but, as usual, waited to see what Teresa would do. My mother had little trouble persuading my father. She had always been the quiet one, and when she talked for an hour about how her poor sister Rose must be sick with loneliness out there all by herself, with no one to turn to in times of illness, or listen to her troubles on worrisome days, my father said he would think about it, which meant yes. My mother could have spared herself the trouble of saying her little piece, because my father liked green hills anyway.

When my mother said goodbye to Mary and Lina on the day of departure, they wept as if they would not meet again till the next world. Nonna quietly observed her daughters' luxurious weeping, for she realized that this abundance of sorrow in act one was necessary for the happy ending in act three.

My parents were not long in Montclair when Uncle Angelo was forced to listen to Aunt Mary's litany of loneliness. He let her talk it out, and when she was talked out she became silent and sad; and when Aunt Mary was sad it was the kind of sadness that could not be borne. Uncle Angelo capitulated as he knew he would, because he missed my father.

And that left Lina. Her job was relatively simple because the spade-work had been done, the forest had been cleared. But since she never allowed any drama in life to pass her by, Uncle Jim had to listen patiently while she described to him the torment of being torn from the arms of her nearest and dearest. If a husband died, another could be found, but where pray could one get another sister?

It has never been established whether this particular brand of reasoning swayed Uncle Jim, or whether it was the lonesomeness he felt on Sunday afternoons when he thought of his brothers-in-law playing cards, with the gallon of wine always within easy reach.

In any case, the family was soon re-united, as the women knew it would be; for their husbands' thinking was clear and uncomplicated. They knew that happy women breed happy children, the sum of which adds up to a happy man.

The first spring in their new surroundings arrived, and with it awoke the ancient urge to plant. Once the fig-trees and grape-vines had taken root, the talk turned to the planting of tomatoes. The problem was, where to get the large branches that would hold the heavy flowering plants when they grew ripe.

My father had taken to walking up into the mountains every Sunday morning before Mass. There were thousands of trees up there, heavy with strong branches. He talked over his discovery with Uncles Angelo and Jim. As usual, Uncle John stayed safely away from the fireworks.

The plan was to go up into the mountains early Sunday morning, before anyone was awake, even the police, and provide themselves with the means for starting their tomato gardens. Then my mother asked the unhappy question; was it legal to chop branches from trees that were not on one's property?

Uncle Angelo immediately took the floor. Who, he asked, was responsible for all those magnificent trees flowering on the mountain-top? God, they answered. Were they children of God? Of course, they answered. Was it conceivable that God would deprive His own children of something He so liberally allowed to fill up His mountains? No, they answered, all but my mother, who was finding it difficult to figure out just how God had got Himself involved in this project. The men, however, satisfied now that the Almighty had a personal interest in the success of their venture, blithely made their plans to strip the trees of the Orange Mountains.

The next Sunday, long before dawn, armed with axes and a gallon of wine, the gentlemen planters walked the long walk up to Eagle Rock. As I listened to the details of this story through the years, I could never understand why, if their project was so righteous, they should have pursued it under cover of darkness.

However, when they reached the mountains and saw the number of strong, healthy branches growing in wild profusion, all doubts quickly disappeared. For they saw a definite purpose in the growing of these trees; they were expressly created so their limbs could be cut off to hold up tomato plants.

Putting the gallon of wine tenderly aside, they took off their jackets, rolled up their sleeves and lifted their axes. Until now, the only sounds heard were the pre-dawn rustlings of animal-life, and the restless cries of birds whose world had been rudely disturbed. Boom! The sound reverberated through the silent mountains like thunder, and awoke any wild-life that still slumbered.

"Shhh!" Uncle Angelo, with his fingers to his lips, cautioned Uncle Jim and my father. "Do you want to wake the dead?"

"What are you afraid of?" asked my father. "There isn't anybody around."

"And if there was," said Uncle Jim, "these trees are as much ours as theirs. They belong to the world and we're part of the world."

"I know . . . I know," whispered Uncle Angelo, who realized that Uncle Jim was simply mouthing the philosophy he had so firmly instilled in him. "Still, this is a new country, and you can never tell what kind of crazy laws they have. Remember, I'm a citizen. If I get in trouble I have rights. But with you, they'll deport you."

"No, they won't," said my father, as he raised his axe. "My children are citizens, so they can't deport me." Boom! Down came the axe, and off came the limb.

Uncle Angelo's eyes almost popped out of his head. "Gently . . . gently . . ." He was afraid to speak above a whisper.

"I'll show you." And Uncle Angelo cautiously, quietly chipped away at a weak limb, while the two regarded him, unbelievingly.

"If you want to stay here till next week," said my father, "all right. But I'm getting back for ten-thirty Mass." Down came the axe, as birds and animals squealed and chirped in outraged frenzy.

"Listen," whispered Uncle Angelo, hoarsely, his eyes wide as saucers.

"What's the matter with you?" said Uncle Jim. "Get to work so you'll have a nice thirst for a glass of wine." *Boom* and *Crash!*

"I thought I heard a motorcycle," said Uncle Angelo, creeping cautiously toward some bushes.

"It's your imagination," said my father, unconcernedly.

The tree-choppers were so engrossed in their work, that of course, by the time they heard it, it was too late. As the two motorcycles approached, they remained frozen to the spot. All the time, Uncle Angelo lay flat on his stomach, one arm around the gallon, not daring to breathe. As soon as the motorcycles left with their Sunday-morning cargo, he peeped out, and caught a glimpse of his brothers-in-law . . . each seated cozily beside a trooper, wearing an odd look of bewildered importance.

I doubt if anyone ever hustled down that mountain as fast as Uncle Angelo, on that brightening Sunday morn. With his axe over his shoulder, and the gallon of wine safely in his other hand, he moved his big body as fast as possible toward our house.

When my mother saw him, standing alone in the doorway, the gallon of wine not even touched, she knew she was in the face of tragedy. She remained calm as he related the unhappy details of the morning, but broke down completely when told that her handsome husband had been taken to police headquarters in a basket. She took a batch of bills from her bosom, and commissioned Uncle Angelo to bring them back at any cost. Then she went hurriedly to Aunt Lina's house, and while they shared their mutual sorrow, their envoy started riding the infrequent trolleys in the direction of Orange.

Needless to say, my father never made ten-thirty Mass.

The embarrassing details of how Uncle Angelo played hide-and-seek with the questioning police-officer, as to how he knew his brothers-in-law were in trouble if he hadn't been in the act too, are best left unrelated.

With money left over, after the fine had been paid, and a violent hunger beginning to consume him, Uncle Angelo calmly ordered a taxi.

At about three o'clock, a rustle of excitement was heard, as curious neighbors gathered outside our house. The waiting women ran to the window and beheld Uncle Angelo holding the taxi door open for the other two as if they were visiting dignitaries. Nonchalantly paying the driver, with my mother's money, he followed them into the house, looking neither to the right nor left.

When the excitement of reunion had died down, Nonna was heard muttering to herself from her rocker by the window.

"What are you saying?" demanded Uncle Angelo, for there was never any love lost between these two. "Anything that is worth saying is worth saying out loud."

"I said," shouted back Nonna, "that if anybody had bothered to consult me, I could have told them this wasn't the day to go. I dreamed of beans last night, and anybody over the age of three knows that means trouble."

Uncle Angelo gave her a long, searching look, and finally tapped the gallon.

---

# *Marion Benasutti*

---

M arion Benasutti, the daughter of Northern Italian immigrants, pursued a long writing career in Philadelphia where she was born. As woman's editor of Philadelphia's *Italian American Herald* she wrote news and fea-

tures, as well as a column called "Speaking Italian." Many of the family pieces
she wrote for both local and national publications became the material for the
book about her family, *No Steady Job for Papa*, which was published in 1966
by Vanguard Press to enthusiastic reviews and provided, at that time, a break-
through in authorship by a woman of Italian American background.

# *from* No Steadyjob for Papa

Nowhere in Philadelphia will you find a street like the Back street, for it has
since become a wide smooth stretch of asphalt with identical row houses on
either side of it, and unless you had lived there, as we did, you could never
believe that it had once existed.

There was a street called the Front street where the houses stood in neat
squares of green grass, their front porches illuminated at night by lamps on
little wooden posts at the foot of each set of steps. In the dark, the lights
looked like suspended glowworms, the number of each house swinging on a
sign attached to the underside of each elegant little lamp.

The Back street, as far as anyone could recall, had always been there, at
the edge of the city. Both streets had names, of course, but to us one was
simply the Back street and the other the Front street, with a jungle of
overgrown bushes and shaded footpaths between. The streets were like two
separate entities, strangers to each other. The area was known as Goat Hill
because the immigrant Italian families who lived there had kept goats. The
nearest landmark was the Branchtown Hotel on the Old York Road. In 1751
the Branchtown Hotel served as a stagecoach stop for coaches plying the
route between Philadelphia and New York. We knew it only as the trolley
stop on the way to Poplar Street in South Philadephia. From the Branchtown Hotel you walked down a long tree-shaded avenue where the "rich
people" lived until you came to a fork in the road. On one side was the
Episcopal church called The House of Prayer and on the other was the Beer
Saloon. These two buildings faced each other at the top of the hill at our end
of the street.

The Back street was unpaved and it ran up a hill at one end and up a hill
at the other end. We lived in its hollow. The Laceys came to live in the old
farmhouse at the top of the hill at the end of the street, farthest away from
the church and the saloon. After a bad summer storm, the water in the
hollow between the two slopes of the street came up to the windows of the
houses, and the lucky ones, such as we, walked out of our front doors into

delicious swirling water up to our waists. When the waters subsided, little frogs appeared in the mud puddles. Long years afterward, whenever I heard the expression "it rained cats and dogs," I thought of the little frogs in the mud puddles. I remembered the feel of the clean soft rain against my upturned face and the squishy feeling of the mud between my toes.

Although we were the "poor kids" who lived in the Back street, in the long summer evenings in our dusty bare feet we did not think about being poor; we just had fun. In the twilight we played street games, Red Light and Run, Sheepie. We played ring games. We were lean and brown, fearless and strong, and the summers were an endless season of delight and great expectations largely unfulfilled.

Except for an occasional Army truck racing down one hill and up the other, raising horrendous clouds of dust, there was no thundering motor traffic to impede or interrupt the flow of our delight. The doughboys who filled the trucks waved their overseas caps wildly at the kids who waved frantically back, not thinking, or even knowing, that these were soldiers on their way to war, sensing only the immediate excitement.

There were things to hide behind in the Back street: black bushes, mysterious and fearful in the night; tangled gardens; outhouses; wagons, broken and horseless in the empty fields. In the distance, beyond the Front street, we could see the brick towers of the new public school where some of us would go in September. One day there would be rows and rows of new houses stretching from the Front street to the new school and beyond. But because of the war the building had stopped; the abandoned dug-out cellars became thrilling hiding places, treasure troves from which we stole bits of lumber and bricks and bright shiny nails.

At the top of our hill was a great tree. "Under the spreading chestnut tree" meant, for me, that tree, although no chestnuts grew upon it. The tree stood high on the hill, across from the Beer Saloon on the other side of The House of Prayer, its branches spread generously all around. The grass grew right up to its trunk, for it was not like other trees, so jealous of the sun that all beneath them was bare and dead. This was a godlike tree. Under it the grass and moss were thick and green, like the dark green velvet that Mamma made into dresses for the rich ladies of the Tennis Courts, and as soft to lie upon.

Sometimes I would run away from the others and fling myself breathlessly beneath the tree. The voices of the children squealing "Run Sheep-e-e-e-e" were an endless echo in the deepening twilight. "One, two, three, Red Li-i-i-ght," came the faint screams from below. Sometimes, lying under the tree, in a dreaming void, I heard music coming softly from the Tennis Courts, beyond the Beer Saloon, where the rich children played. I would feel myself lifted to the sky, a part of the softness, everything soft, the music, my body, languid and still, the darkness closing down softly.

Sometimes Franz was with me under the tree. He was the German boy next door, the unhappy German boy who did not like being called Hun, and who played the violin so entrancingly that Papa said, "Mark my words, one day that boy will play before the Crowned Heads of Europe!" And immediately in my mind the Crowned Heads of Europe rose rampant, pierced with jewels and glittering with gold and silver, and I envied Franz mightily.

We picked buttercups in the fields and held them under one another's chins. If the buttercups reflected their soft yellow glow, we screamed: "Look! She likes butter!" as though we had discovered a magic formula or a profound truth.

Sometimes the boys, more daring than the girls, grabbed a bunch of brash yellow dandelions (we pretended not to hear them call the dandelions "pee-the-beds") and dashed after us madly. If they tagged us with the dandelions we knew that the dire prophecy foretold in that phrase we pretended not to hear would, at some future time, be shamefully fulfilled, so we ran harder, harder, away from the boys, in a delicious never-ending race.

On Saturday afternoons we washed the dust from our bare feet, put on high sneakers, and for six cents, a nickel and a penny, we went in a body to the movie matinee at the Punk. It was really The New Lyric Theatre but we had long ago given it the more pungent name. There, vicariously, we hung over cliffs with the heroine and lived through the horror of being bound hand and foot in the path of an onrushing locomotive. The rollicky music of a tinny piano punctured the action while villain's fist met hero's chin in a fight to the finish, with never any doubt, of course, as to the outcome. Didn't the good guys always win? But not until the following week, when the action was resumed. Once we saw, because the manager had neglected to order the film changed for the children's matinee, a lurid Cleopatra in the shape of Theda Bara. It was frightfully boring. No cowboys, Indians, death-defying leaps, forest fires, or fist fights. We walked out in a body.

When all other excitements palled, the cry arose: "Let's go to the Tennis Courts!" The Tennis Courts, in our minds, were capitalized, in keeping with their importance. As we ran, the dust of the Back street billowed in gusts under our feet. By squinting one eye, we could watch the games through the cracks in the fence. I would stand endlessly, patiently waiting my turn at a crack. I would push an eye against the crack, squinting so hard the black and purple whorls came, blinding me, so that the rich children running around the courts, the girls in their white middies and skirts, the boys in long white flannel pants, ran together in a great white blinding circle. Almost the best time of all was when the courts were empty. Then

we scaled the high board fence, yelling like Indians, running into the
bushes, burrowing for the lost balls.

In the evenings the grownups came. Music poured from the Tennis
Courts and there was the hard smack of ball against racket and the word
"love" over and over, and I knew that I had to, one day I would have to,
explore farther into this other-world place and that I would do it, alone.

Mamma sewed for the Tennis Court ladies. She had learned her craft
well when, as a girl of twelve, she had been apprenticed to a dressmaker
in Milan. Nobody sewed like our mother and for so little, too, and the
ladies knew this. They came to our house, these fine ladies, stepping
daintily over the dust of the Back street. They did not speak to me, nor I
to them.

Those first years were the most fun, even though we knew Mamma hated
the Back street. She had always been proud, our mother. Not for nothing
did she bear the name of Europa, a mythical Phoenician princess. Her
other names were Elvira Adele. Papa called her *Donna*, the word that in
Italian means woman, wife, but for a long time we thought Donna was
Mamma's name as Papa shouted: "Donna! Where 'ta hell's my pants?"

His pants were always exactly where he had dropped them the night
before, at the foot of the bed. Mamma could never get him out of the habit
of leaving them there, and it was fun to hear Papa shouting in the mornings.

Unlike Mamma, our father enjoyed life in the Back street, as he would
have enjoyed living anywhere, natural hedonist that he was. Papa was
both happy and wise but he did not, alas, inherit from his maternal Italian
ancestors the energy and industriousness that Mamma maintained was
typical of the north Italian. As our mother so often said despairingly, "That
man! He is lazy as a Neapolitan!" Really, it was sad that Papa had to work
for a living. He would have been quite happy puttering about in his
garden, tending to his strays, reading *The North American*, and fighting
with Mr. Leopoldi, our neighbor, about politics and the Austrians versus
the Italians.

But from the beginning Mamma had hated the drab frame house in the
Back street with its dim damp parlor, so unlike our sunny green house in
western Pennsylvania; the black-encrusted range in the kitchen that never
worked properly; the grimy tin-lined sink with its recalcitrant iron pump
that was, as our mother so often bemoaned, as temperamental as a prima
donna. But more than anything, I think she hated the *feeling* of being poor
that the street gave her. It seemed to rob her of her innate dignity; it
demeaned her in a way that we, who were happy there, could not wholly
understand. For how could she know, as we did, the thrill of pushing bare
toes through the hot silky dust of the brown unpaved road; the feel of cool
running water to wade in; the thick green grasses in the fields, with only the

sound of insects or frogs to break the dreaming quiet? Mamma knew only the dirt.

"It is a mean, dirty street," she would complain often, bitterly.

"The dirt of God's good earth," Papa reminded her mildly, puffing on his pipe, his feet propped comfortably against the door of the hated stove.

But Mamma would move her shoulders expressively, as if to shrug off the feel of something thoroughly unpleasant.

"Never fear," she threatened darkly. "One day I shall be free of it, of the dirt and the mud. I shall have 'na bella casa to live in all the days of my life. Like your sister," she would end always on a note of envy. Then she would begin to bang pots and pans about in a fine fury.

"It is the war," Papa said placatingly. "Rents are high. She had no choice, my sister, for, look you, we had to have a place to live in, quickly. And this was all there was!"

"Ma che!" Mamma said disbelievingly. "Would she live here, your sister? Picture, if you will, your sister and that fine daughter of hers living in this horrible place. Not for one moment would she abide here. She would not be dead here, your fine sister! She, with her palazzo made of stone, and the street all paved in front of it. Oh, that ditch! Oh, that monstrous spawn of the devil!"

When Mamma was really frustrated she took her feelings out on the ditch that ran alongside our house. When it rained hard the ditch filled up with water and spilled over into the yard. For us it was just another place to play in, to run in barefoot after the rain. The ditch had originally been an excavation for the installation of sewer pipe, but the war had put a stop to that too.

One day Gran'ma said: "Let us make a rosaria over the ditch. It will please your Mamma."

So we gathered pieces of lathe from the abandoned houses and made an arch over the ditch and Gran'ma planted little red climbing roses over the arbor and we had our rosaria. Gran'ma had hoped to placate Mamma, her natural enemy. Mamma pretended not to notice. Nonna planted foxgloves, with their cluster of little bells, plunging her hands deep into the moist shaded sides of the ditch where they would be sure to thrive. In ancient times, Nonna told us,. these were called Our Lady's Thimbles. She had a fascinating store of knowledge about green growing things and animals.

But even so, the comparison with the stone house of Mamma's sister-in-law, built by Papa and Uncle Dom in those early years before she had come to America, was a festering sore in her breast that would not be healed.

We, too, adored Zia's house, but without envy, and took turns visiting it in the summers. Mostly we loved Zia herself. As a young girl Zia had seen the white horses of Vienna and she would tell us about them so vividly that I could close my eyes and there they were, there in that place that Zia said was like the opera house, with its balconies and flags and crystal chandeliers. There they were, behind my closed eyes, the graceful white horses of Vienna, with their ballet rhythms, their prancing dancing feet, their tails enchantingly swishing like the long hair of prima ballerinas, back and forth, back and forth, swish, swish. The white horses had become a part of the enchantment of Zia's house on Rockland street, where there were other fine houses made of stone that Papa had helped Uncle Dom to build.

"I will not be like those Irish on the hill," Mamma would say, referring, of course, to the Laceys. "I want to live like a human being!"

"Are you not being uncharitable, Donna?" Papa would say in his mild way. "You are not, as the good Lord says, loving your neighbor."

"How right you are, *caro!*" Mamma answered, nothing daunted. "Except for one thing. Have you not heard that cleanliness is next to godliness? Or is this only for the *Protestanti?* The Laceys may be good Catholics but they will have to do a little scrubbing before St. Peter will let them into *his* house, I'll bet!"

Papa had his vulnerabilities too. But only two things threatened his natural amiability—our neighbor, Mr. Leopoldi's, insistence that he and Papa were true *paesani,* and the factual evidence of our indifferent progress in school as shown on our regular report cards.

"What is this 'B'?" Papa would rage, flinging his hands to high heaven in a gesture of total despair. "What is this 'C'? *Mamma mia!* Disgraceful! The top mark is what I expect, *demand,* of you. Your father in school was 'A'—all the way! *This* I expect of you, too, nothing less!"

By nature a scholar, Papa believed passionately in *La Educazione.*

When Mamma insisted, finally, that Trina leave school in the seventh grade and go to work in the knitting mills in Germantown, Papa was horrified, even though Mamma pointed out to him, with admirable patience, that Trina was naturally indifferent to formal schooling and that no amount of prodding was ever going to change her. A book, to our Trina, was something to be used for a doorstop. So, with Papa's bitter disapproval and to Trina's evident relief, Trina went to work in the knitting mills. But, as if in defiance of something she wasn't quite sure of, Trina cut off her hair. It happened the night before she went to work, while we were all asleep. Mamma didn't speak to her for a week, not even on her first payday, when she silently accepted the envelope Trina handed her without giving her the agreed-upon allowance of two dollars in return.

# Diana Cavallo

Diana Cavallo's novel, *A Bridge of Leaves,* was reissued by Guernica Editions in 1997. She is also the author of *The Lower East Side: a Portrait in Time.* Sections of her *Juniper Street Sketches* have appeared in the Special Fiction issue of the *Philadelphia Inquirer* and the anthologies *From the Margin* and *The Voices We Carry.* As a Fulbright Teaching Fellow and Guest Lecturer at the University of Pisa she taught American literature and also, during her years in Italy, lectured for USIS, the United States Information Service. She continues to teach writing at the University of Pennsylvania. She is married to the German artist Karl Hagedorn and they live in Philadelphia.

## *from* A Bridge of Leaves

When I got up this morning and looked in the mirror, I was not in the least surprised to see my reflection, as I always do. It seemed a perfectly natural thing to be confronted by a picture of oneself that doesn't actually exist, or that exists only in relation to other things, perhaps they also assumed. But the whole thing must be got started in the first place, and just by acknowledging that image without controversy, we are already off—so why not?

After all, we believe quite thoroughly every external form. If I tell you I am within months of thirty, am average-sized, have dark hair, deep-set eyes—even embellish it a bit to say what *kind* of dark hair and *how* my eyes are set in my invisible but omnipresent skull—you are very likely, with only that much, to begin to draw a picture of me yourself. If I am skillful enough, I may even convince you of my reality, and we would get along quite well, you feeling satisfied that you already know something of me, and that being far from the case! It would be totally false; you would know nothing of me, and I want more than anything to impart my presence beyond the form of it, although you hardly expected company the moment you sat down with a book, presumably to be alone. And yet, I will be content if you know relatively little of that external me, and satisfy yourself more with those parts that I would not readily show if I did not feel we were as alone as you thought when you settled down to hear me out.

I should warn you, so that you will not misunderstand when I wander off course, that I intend to talk about things quite as they strike me, but with a purpose all my own. You see, despite everything, I am trying to understand myself, a very ambitious undertaking, especially when I am so contradictory. I am sometimes tiresome, stuffy, and the next moment incredibly poetic or surprisingly humorous. It is very confusing to my friends, and so doubly so to me, who must maintain a semblance of order all the same.

I like to talk and I like to write, and I have such an enormous store of impressions and ideas that I feel weighted down with the load of it. Some of them are not meant to be passed on in conversation. Who nowadays talks about the manifoldness of life and death waiting? It would be considered embarrassing, self-conscious, more than a little naïve. Not that I am going to say such things, not outright, in any case, but I plan to go ahead and say what touches me at the moment or what I am reminded of, regardless of its order or disorder. I don't want to give a mistaken impression, because I want to represent myself and this undertaking in their true light. Yet I want very much to make the right beginning.

Do my intentions seem somewhat indefinite, even contradictory? I am different from what I seem, even here, so different that it is mysterious. The different selves I am are what is mysterious, the ones that I have been, that have been discarded somewhere, until I am so conventionally like other people that there seems hardly a difference between my individual form and theirs.

For I am overlaid with what I have become, and to restore any semblance of the past, I must try to enter it as best I can from this present state, incorporating as much of those other selves as still persist somewhere. It becomes all the harder because thoughts and moments sometimes become so separate from one another, and from what I now am, that I barely remember they belong to me. They vaguely resemble some other that was never me, the one that I imagine myself to be, that is fast disappearing even as I try to fold it into the page.

It is off again; perhaps it has lighted somewhere in these musings, remembrances, or more than likely, it will pass from page to page as my pen does, impressing a little of itself on the rough sheets; but that tiny insect, it will fly the cover. It is nowhere tied fast, secure, not even in these poor pages where I hear his faint buzzing and follow the meandering sound into the night. . . .

1

The amazing thing is that man wants to live, that he does not actively wish to die, that he would rather breathe in foul air, propagate imbecile children, spread contagion to his neighbor, and not rebel against such unnatural acts. As for me, I am surprised that, all things considered, I do not find it more pointless than I do.

Certainly, I have expended much less energy and interest in the matter than its importance warrants. But perhaps I think I will have an excess of such feeling when I am old, and should experience it for myself. But then, the old people that I know seem so reluctant to die. There is my grandfather, for example, an incredible old man of eighty-six who is mortally afraid of death. He suffers the most intense pain in his arms and legs, but prefers it to any thought of his eventual demise. He complains that he is the only one left of his generation; each year has taken one or the other of his friends; he feels out of place and alone in a strange world of youth and activity. Does this move him to a monumental death wish? No, he clings to life as though it were a precious thing, too valuable to resign. Fear makes it so, but still, I doubt that I shall have such spirit or such capacity to be afraid when I am old. I even feel a little cheated. It seems young people like myself have less of everything—less contentment, less pain, less serious ambition, less pride of achievement. We have too much of some things, but too little of these others. We do nothing to acquire the worthwhile ones; we only resent not having them. I wonder—if my grandfather had not worked at his trade for fifty years, would he have had them, anyway?

When I stop to consider what my grandfather has to live for, I am at a loss for reasons. What precisely goes on in his mind I can never know. Certainly I cannot ask him. In the first place, he looks at me, already intractable when I address him, surmising that I am an unintroduced stranger or a tax collector. He has become very sensitive about money, and has felt since he was eighty that his Olympian age entitled him to be tax-free. In any case, it is not until I am with him for an hour or so that he realizes I am one of the family. Then he insists I am Lily's older boy, and when I insist that I am David, Helen's son, he sputters that Helen never married. To convince him otherwise is hopeless.

He has lost all his teeth and refuses to replace them. He eats soft foods and becomes so irritated with their taste and texture that he splatters them about the table like a child. He insists conversation helps to pass the time, but he dozes every few minutes, napping fitfully through the day, so there is no

continuity to his hours. But at night, when he is alone and weary, he is afraid
to close his eyes and sits heavy-lidded in a faded armchair, stamping his foot
or waving his arm to deter death and convince himself he is still alive.

In his wakeful afternoon hours he can never find what he is looking for.
He accuses his daughter-in-law of hiding his things, and has driven her
voice up to a shrill pitch, so that her presence is intolerable to him. In
between all these exasperations, he has a traveling pain that attacks a different limb or vital organ each day. It is not localized, so he can never complain of his poor stomach regularly, releasing his antagonism on a single
malady. He frequently writhes or moans as the pain traverses his frail body,
so that it has become intolerable to all of us, each one hoping he will depart
quietly in his sleep that night. This is precisely why he will not go to bed or
close his eyes at evening. He fears death in the darkness of his vigil, as
though it never comes at noon. He is like some parents who take all precau-
tions to safeguard their daughters in the evening, as though illicit love were
banished by the daylight.

I almost prefer the intense striving after death of the early Christian
martyrs, the blessed release, the marriage with God, the return to the
eternal womb, and all of that. Of course, with such religious zeal for death,
it would be hard to rule out suicide as the Desert Fathers did.

It seems that one is always confronted with that choice—one either
wishes it fiercely or fears it intensely! Surely, there must be a middle
course, some ground that someone as modern and conventional as I might
tread—somewhere between a prayerful St. Anthony and a senile grandfather—without feeling one has avoided the issue entirely, stupidly pretended it does not exist. And yet, it is supposed that people who are not
religious give the matter no thought, and that those who are young do not
actually conceive it.

I know I speak only for myself, but I insist such reflections are bound to
occur. Can one really pass to manhood without some jolt, some jar, that
places it squarely before him? One must dislodge the nettle, whatever the
means.

Perhaps, then, my first reaction was hasty and untrue. We are involved
with it whether we wish it or not. Having put aside those questions which
answer themselves, and those answers which frame the next question, one
must prepare to ponder death with questions unformed, let alone answers,
and that takes the greater effort. Perhaps here the largest number turn back
to old paths once abandoned.

And I fear we are burdened too long with an incomprehensible morality,
remonstrated too soon for acts unknown and thoughts unfelt, filled with
vague fears for the world's transgressions, not yet knowing our connection
with the world, Yes, I knew that exaltation as a child, of being dipped in the

concrete of penance, sinking in the swamp briar of confession, disappearing beneath the sin-filled lake, arms outstretched in supplication. To be reclaimed at the bottom of the sea, to be disengaged from the morass of the flood pain, to reappear in the pure waters of the baptismal font a cleansed soul, a purged heart, a resurrected body! But once frame the last question, and all the waters of the world flooding the cavity left bleeding by the moon cannot cleanse our limbs of doubts encrusted by purposeless life. Baptismal fonts run dry, send rusted water, tepid and brown, to drown the unalterable stain fashioned by manhood. Confession consoled the unquestioning child; penance redeemed his sinless heart. They fail the man. . . .

## 8

This is the very present. Rain falling that has fallen for hours, heard now when the monotonous *tap-tap* destroys itself in a sudden hurling against window, and I look up.

I sit in my room, aware my thoughts have been trailing off, the most recent past tapering until, imperceptibly, we are living the new moment, and some rushing against window, some stir in the room, wakes us to it.

Yet the rain was here when I woke, but exiled to that part of morning which says: it is Saturday, it is drizzling, it is a day at home. It blended so inscrutably with the past that the newness seemed continuous with it, remained unnotable, until a lunging like this forced the head up: this is the very present.

The wind gathers, blowing and stamping on rain; the sky sinks from its gray to a blackness; a thunder roll drops from its midst. Somewhere people are running, seeing skies darken, rain quicken, hearing a dreadful thunder. They scatter, searching skyward for a yellow flash that, even expected, comes over-soon, lighting heavy pockets of cloud. Streets, returning to nature, become rivulets; walls are washed clean. Trees tremble for plumage wind has whipped loose. Between sky and earth no margin; all has become one moist descent.

I saw it close, that blurring of forms, horizon slipped so far, it has soaked in the earth. A boy, I lay by a lake, throwing in pebbles, twigs, watching them cut water, drown in rings their splashing had made. Wind blew against water, rippling wide circles, as if an invisible hand, far larger, stronger than mine, were discharging lightly its fistful of stones. The clouds sank as low as they might, horizon dropping, fading before my eyes. One might sleep in it.

But I heard sound: water fallen on water, welcoming its own, the first growl of thunder, and ran with the rain falling, woodward, to reach the clearing beyond, some roof. So many trees. Overhead a bridge of leaves, pelted, borne down upon by this shower of stones, swayed, holding off sky, imprisoning rain. Underfoot those that had fallen clung to the step. The woods darkened; the birch trees became their heavy, black bands. Boughs, whipped loose by the rain, crashed; my own fear that came to my lips dissolved into that single tremor of forest sighs, earth rumbles—my cry indistinguishable from theirs.

Tripping on swollen root, slipping on perished leaves, where was my sound? In the progressive silence I heard it—the *tick-ticking* of feet, like the beating of an insignificant clock in the immeasurable time of the universe. I stilled it to meet the sudden hush that was spreading. Hardly a bird called or cried or sang. There was barely a movement of leaves. The wind abated. Wood voices stilled . . . trees tenantless . . . shrubs unrustled. Only the echoless, the silent, the void.

Then it burst from the heavens—the thunder clap potens—rumbling and rolling, a giant roar and a mighty quake, a lusty reverberation tumbling a yellow sky into forest darkness. There was a flutter among trees; a quiver ran through them in a common swaying. Only the ash tree was still; nothing of it moved or bowed to break its dark silence. I saw an angry finger of light part its leaves, crackling in deep fury as it sundered that majestic head and plunged itself forcefully into its bowels. I saw it die. In an instant the tallest, loftiest tree in the forest—no more, instantaneously disrobed, shorn of its leaves, clipped of its boughs, stripped of its bark. It remained blanched and naked, gripped by a deadly pallor, a corpse already, and I could see the black disfiguring scar where it was disemboweled, gleaming in its chalky flesh. Yet it remained rooted in earth, as though it were yet forest, still of its world, though less tree. Another monstrous crash of thunder shook the sky, and with it the storm lost force, dissipating as quickly as it had struck.

How many trees in the forest are reclaimed by the Nature that made them? Standing without, who sees them, those blunted tops, broken boughs, hollow trunks that fill the forest? There they stand, covered with the sores of a painful blight, still rooted to the fertile earth that conceived them, no less forest for their passing. Their hulks endure until the forest can cremate its corpses, sometimes hundreds of years after death, when they have, at last, worn away all evidence; disintegrated, they are ground back into the earth where they had lain as seedlings, returning to the conception bed to father new life in their turn.

The moist earth that slides through the fingers, how many lives has it been, how many forms has it taken, while histories mix their silt with the river? Bits of root and flat stone, they underlay the forest: ocean beds grow on them. They have become the soft clay of generation, womb of the universe.

Each single life a small instance, each moment an eternity that cries out against the measuring palm. Who is it counts time? The wind flings sand, grinds boulders, incises mountain faces, takes those captive grains and buries them into the earth, or carries them to the soft underside of clouds where they drop unseen in raindrops to the place where the wind sought them. The river bends trees, strips twigs, dissolves roots, lays them at the foot of the forest, where they had dreamed to be in final union with the earth.

The claim of death, how short a thing, almost as short as life. We fear its violence, yet it has what we seek. The crimson berry glitters in the sun, wishing to stay always crimson, always plump, always berry; yet what is there to fear from the bright-eyed bird sent to pluck it from the bough, warming it in the soft belly? The common rosemary knows: she grows more beautiful, luminously white, exposing a bare head to the approaching foot that crushes its life juice.

I am that berry, that sturdy rosemary, that buffeted grain, that tender root, that lofty ash. We live, yet fear not. It is all the same to us. We have loved what we have been. There is no terror in becoming. Let other men struggle, let them deny, resist. I live, hearing the stilling tread, seeing the quieting finger, not cringing at its dark step. I will be ready. My neighbor, screaming, is welcomed; my father, unfulfilled, is beckoned; my son, unborn, is taken. I wait.

# Octavia Capuzzi Waldo Locke

As her name indicates, Octavia Locke was the eighth child of the talented Capuzzi family in Philadelphia. An artist as well as a writer, she graduated with honors from the Tyler School of Fine Arts at Temple University and was a Fulbright fellow at the American Academy in Rome. Her first story was published in *Seventeen* under the name of Octavia Capuzzi. Her novel, *A Cup of the Sun,* appeared under her first married name, Octavia Waldo, and she has since published in magazines and reviews under her present married name Octavia Locke.

# The Rocks

Scott Claus had a way of confusing the day of the first blasting with the day of the first blessing. Maybe he never heard himself. The words would tangle in his mouth and it took a fine ear like Dinney's to tell them apart. But that was before the rocks.

Long before.

On the day of the first blasting Claus witnessed the last sweep of red earth in Marrow County. He thought not of his father or of his father's father who had once owned the land but of a city, conceived and executed as one—brought to light complete in all her parts like Venus from the sea. With nothing less than a smile, Claus watched a time of fields and forests crumble beneath the bulldozers and the dynamite and fold into the past. Futures were not in wheat and not in fruit but in concrete. Urban planning was all Claus could talk about.

Claus couldn't take his eyes off Model City. You'd think he was playing god, working his way toward the seventh day. The seventh day did come, and on the eve of it, when the work was done, Claus borrowed a tradition of the Mohawk Indians and had himself lifted by a crane to wave the American flag above the pinnacle of the Municipal Building. The city stretched beneath him, a vast monotone of concrete and aluminum, as desolate as the city of the dead on the eve of a national holiday. But Claus didn't see it that way. Even when all the cars pulled away, when the doorways were dim and the escalators did not move and no water gushed from Sumpter Fountain, when Claus was standing alone on the highway, watching the sun set over the quiet, he did not see his city that way. He breathed in the last moment of peace ever to touch that place again, and he wept. He wept not for what he had destroyed, but for what he had created. It was the moment he would always remember as the time he touched God's hand.

Dinney told him it was the sunset.

Claus insisted he had seen an image. Maybe that was where the trouble started. Because after Model City was settled and all the TVs were going at

once and all the patio broilers were burning steaks at once and the kids
were running wild and the parents were taking tranquilizers and sleeping
pills so as not to worry about Mary Jane in the schools or the war (even
though NATO kept reassuring them that they were in their 20th year of
peace) or the riots or the next Madison Avenue campaign for President, the
newspapermen began writing that Model City had everything. "Everything," Dinney said. "Except some saving grace to nourish the soul."
Churches weren't the answer. He never expected Claus to listen to him.

In retrospect, Dinney said, it was that image in the sunset that sent Claus
to Columbus. Because the next thing Dinney knew, Claus had convinced
the Columbus School of Arts to open a branch in Model City, and he
returned with a middle-aged lady with twinkle eyes and silver bangs to
direct it in mini skirts and red stockings. She wore a pink rose in her watch
band, and one look at her told Dinney that Claus had met his match. When
she said, "My name's Millah. Miz Millah," with all the lilt of the South
playing on the words, Dinney was certain that Claus had met his match.
"Millah," she repeated. "M-I-L-L-E-R," letting Dinney shake her hand.
His eyes settled on the rose in the wide red watch band. It wasn't plastic.

Claus gave her everything she wanted from art supplies to discount
tickets. The art school opened its classes to eighteen students inside the
Municipal Hall, and when Miss Miller asked for water to spray sweetly from
Sumpter Fountain, by Claus! she had it. Any hour of the day or night.
People began talking about Living Involvement Through Color, saying
things like, "Paint Municipal Hall pink and violet," using words like *kinetic
colors* and *ambience* as if they were tooth paste. It was alive fun, and Claus
never questioned the vitality of it.

That was how Claus came to approve of the *Fall In*. He didn't know what
a *Fall In* was. Nobody did, that was what was so appealing about it. Because
Claus wanted what nobody had ever had. He advanced Miss Miller a check
for $5000.00 and told her to "think big"; and she said, "Man, will I!" and
began structuring a June week-end, alfresco, that promised to give Model
City an avant-garde send off, guaranteed to lift it to the moon. From Canada
to California people began reading about Model City's *Fall In*, which according to the art commentator of the *New York Tides* was to be "a percep-
tual happening, a psychedelic rendezvous with the kings of polar syncopa-
tion and electronic raison d'etre." Claus was tickled silly to see Model City
in print, and if you asked Miss Miller how things were moving, her twinkle
eyes flashed wide open and she said, "Swinging', Man, are they swingin'."

It was hard to know whether it was a question of design or accident that
swung the rocks into her head. All Dinney knew was that she had driven to
Cashew County one day and told the chief engineer of Gain Construction
Company not to worry about stock piling the rocks from the hill he had

levelled, but to *carry* those rocks to Model City and dump them in the fountain.

"Carry them on down," she said.

"Lady," said the the chief engineer. "How many you want?"

"All of them."

"You're joking."

"Nope. All of them."

"Lady," he said, "if you'd just look them over and mark the ones you want with your lipstick," he laughed, "I'll be glad to oblige."

"I want them all," she laughed, and for a good while they laughed at each other till she flashed him one of those special cards Claus had given her to authenticate her position in Model City, and he complied. But he thought she was out of her mind.

People looking down from the office windows of Sumpter Plaza couldn't believe their eyes when they saw five and six trucks pulling into the Plaza and emptying their loads of rocks. They telephoned the City Council, the Traffic Department and the Fire Marshall to find out what the hell was going on. Nobody knew a thing. Scott Claus was out of town till Sunday. But there was Miss Miller in beach hat and owl glasses, directing the men to "Pile 'em high."

"Lady, you tell us how you want 'em," the men said.

"Just dump them. We'll have a delicious incandescent structure, no matter how you do."

Well, they laughed at her and dumped them and she laughed right back. That was Friday night.

By Saturday morning the Mayor's office had issued a statement to the effect that the rocks were part of the *Fall In*, and by noon different trucks were seen zooming into the Plaza carrying people in bands of six and seven, all equipped with electric guitars and zithers and xylophones. One truck was filled with tanks of helium and three electronic chambers and men in lustrous hug-me-tight leotards. It wasn't long before the groups had set up their booths on stilts and the Plaza took on the look of a circus.

A girl from the press drove into town with a camera. She wore bell bottoms with patches all over them, and squinting through the eye of her camera, she followed the heart of the new metropolis with a steady click click click, talking while she focused her attention on the movement. "Looks like you're having a show," she said.

"A *Fall In*," someone corrected her.

"What the hell's that?"

"Stick around."

She did.

Then the carloads of people began heading down the main streets and they were followed by the usual traffic of a city's Saturday. Everybody took one look at that heap of rocks and wondered if they were real.

Rocks, mind you. Blue-black and salt-grey with dark striations. The fountain's mist sprayed them and when viewed from the distance of a city street, they resembled a picture post card of Tivoli. Except neither the urban planners nor Scott Claus had ever been to Tivoli. The girl from the press narrowed her eye on them and clicked her camera, and when someone told her that the rocks were part of the *Fall In*, she asked, "What part?"

"The art part," said Miss Miller.

"Come again," said the girl from the press.

"The art part—you know, they're earth forms. You've heard of found objects?"

"Sure."

"Well, these are *found forms* created by the earth."

"Isn't that rather obvious?"

"Well, I never take things for granted," said Miss Miller. "They're the earth's art, the art of the earth."

"I know," said the girl from the press, "Like 'Fruit of the Loom.' What are you going to do with them?"

"Look at them," said Miss Miller.

"I have," said the girl from the press, grinning at her.

"Pretty, aren't they?"

"If you like rocks."

Miss Miller's mouth opened in a wide O, but the girl from the press said, "When is someone going to do something to them?"

"Like what?"

"Like carve them."

"Do they need it?"

"Well, don't they? Aren't you going to sculpture them?"

"They are sculptured."

"Where?"

"Look at them."

"I am. I don't see anything but rock."

"Don't you?"

"Now look," said the girl from the press. She let her camera swing from the strap around her neck and folded her hands behind her, and with her feet firmly planted on the ground she said, "Don't pull my leg. When is someone going to get up there and cut them so I can get a picture?"

"Scar them?" said Miss Miller, outraged.

"Well, put a chisel to them—a little work."

"Destroy them?" said Miss Miller. "They've already been scarred by dynamite and bulldozers and the ugly hand of man, and they're sculptural as they are, thank you, quite sculptural, and you can just go . . . help yourself to your pictures."

"I have."

That night huge plastic sculptures, inflated with helium, were seen floating above the spot lights in kidney shapes of hot pink and orange. The fountain was strung with Christmas tree lights and the water sparkled like quick silver. Things had the look of a real fiesta. Even the rocks seemed to belong there and people began saying how they understood them now, sitting on them.

Then the electronic boxes began reacting, only people didn't realize it at first. They just kept hearing voices. The boxes would light up like computers whenever someone crossed their paths and they began hissing at people, and the air would fill with whispers of "I see you, seeyou, seeyou. Scared you, didn't I? Scared you. But I caught you at it, caughtyou, caughtyou. Caught y o u." Imagine copping a feel of somebody's wife and that voice sneaking up on you!

At nine o'clock sharp the bands began to play. Although "thunder" might be a better word, because to hear the press tell it, the bands let out one hell of a roar that blasted Model City from there to Kingdom Come. It was so convulsive, the dignitaries went home to put on suspenders.

Four or five bands played at once while singers sang with all of their strength. Their voices whooped into the larger clash of brass against brass and drums and electric strings—forever lost—while mouths opened and closed in measured time, working the motions of sound.

The men in hug-me-tight leotards glowed in the night. Their bodies lighted to the music, their muscles stretched and flexed and trembled like fluorescent beams pulling love to the ground. The crowds thickened and the music rocked them. If you wanted to hear your neighbor, you had to press your ear against his screaming mouth.

Only the electronic boxes kept their equilibrium. They lit up their square faces and the coils of color blushed and ricocheted in neon tubes while a whim wham blurt blip of noises and little voices came out from under the rocks. "I saw you doing what you did. I caught you pickin' your nose."

"Sweet Jesus," Dinney said. "You couldn't make up your mind whether to laugh at them or swat at them. The trouble was they were more real than real. Like the FCI."

But the young people liked them, and the young came from everywhere—from Crystal and Colebin too. Caravans of them, with their long hair and long skirts and long strands of beads and feet looking like the long roots of trees. They came carrying flowers out of the dust. At first sight of them one of the city councilmen hawked, "Lordgoddahosts," and when

Miss Miller began burning incense, he nearly panicked, thinking it was pot. One lady with milkweed hair passed out.

Miss Miller had to seize the microphone to announce that the incense was non-carcinogenic pine and eucalyptus from the woods of Alabama before some people would breathe deeply. But there was nothing she could do to keep the very embodiment of *haute monde* from wagging its head at the love *pavimenti* which the Children were painting in the streets. You might think those representatives of fashion were witnessing words like HATE or SLUT or SNOT. These same people had never batted an eye at the aluminum nipples all over the undersides of Municipal Hall's archways; but now suddenly LOVE and SODA conspicuously offended them. They just stood there on the curbs, wagging their heads as if they were watching their last diamond slip down the drain, not once seeing themselves or each other—the women in see-through tops and the men in gossamer pants.

For a while it seemed that a competition was meeting under the stars, and it was hard to know where to focus your attention: on the Children or on those who watched.

Just when the hoopla had reached its loudest, someone took it upon himself to be literal. A *Fall In* was a fall in was a fall in, he said, squirting detergent into the fountain, and watching till the suds foamed and then he fell in, right into the cool bubbly basin in the night. One by one the Children followed. In and out. They stepped from that fountain like water babies, offering soap bubbles as gifts from the gods. Then dazed and delighted they returned ten times over for more while those prurient sons of Adam, afraid of a handful of bubbles, shrank back on the sidewalks and watched, distorting what was right and innocent into a boiling hell of misplaced dreams.

That audience in all its chic—the fake diamonds set in platinum gold, the poison-ring watches, the 20 years good service buttons and keys to Bentleys—why, they had everything and nothing, Dinney said, while those Children with their hands full of soap bubbles had nothing and everything.

A mist began to fall and the soap bubbles drifted lightly through the air. But the bands kept on rocking and rolling and the Children kept on tumbling in the suds, and the crowds on the curbs watched. Even when the mist thickened and turned to fine rain, people watched in mute fascination as they might have watched the late late show. There was something so compelling about those lithe wet bodies in a night of deafening music and soap bubbles. Nobody saw the rain.

But someone in the crowd began clipping the Children's hair. At first it seemed he was clowning—as if he were part of the show. He slid in and out of the audience with playful speed, and then he stood right out in the open— high boots, brass buckles, a wide chain dangling from his shears to the ground. He began charging after those Children like a lion tamer while the crowds on the curbs didn't budge. They laughed and the Children went crazy running in and out of the snip snip snip of those garden shears while he lunged after them singing, "Three Blind Mice." He snipped off their hair and he snipped off their beards and he sang as they ran, "Three Blind Mice."

When one of the Children took a swing at him, all hell broke loose and the kid with the shears seemed to multiply right there before you in ten, twenty, thirty replicas—all with garden shears and chains and brass buckles. All with the same beef build and faces as distinguishable as unbaked bread. Miss Miller called the police who came and tucked the Children safely into jail. That's how the night ended. As abruptly as a circus, with a huddle of bright booths abandoned in the rain.

When Claus returned from New York and took one look at the morning newspaper and read THE SCANDAL OF THE ROCKS, he nearly called the police, fire squad and sanitation department to Miss Miller's apartment to not only lock her up but to wipe her off the face of Model City. He never read past the first page that told of "a mass swim in and love in" in Sumpter Fountain. Claus's mind was tormented with visions of bubble dancers and daisy chains and pot. He picked up the phone and called Columbus and woke the director of the Columbus School of Arts right out of his Sunday double bed and told him he was sending Miss Miller right back to him. Then he phoned Miss Miller and told her to start packing.

"Where are you taking me?" she said.

"I'm sending you," he said.

"Where?" she said.

"Have you seen the papers?" he said.

"No," she said.

"I'd love to rub your nose in them," he said, breaking the connection in her ear.

Dinney brought her the newspaper. That girl from the press had smeared the *Fall In* with all sorts of inferences and had ripped the heart out of the fun. The Children were still in jail, booked on charges of disrupting the peace with disreputable conduct in the water and on the rocks and flooding the public domain with pornographic suggestions fed through computers.

"Pornographic?" said Miss Miller. "The Children had their clothes on!"

"In the water," said Dinney. "That's the trouble: in the water. And on the rocks."

"Nobody did a thing on the rocks, except sit on them."

"*A scandalous evening of do-nothing-constructive-art to the tune of scurrilous voices,*" Dinney read aloud from the newspaper. "There's the point," he said. "The rocks didn't move a bit. But the voices. . . ."

"The voices they heard were their own consciences," said Miss Miller. "How could anyone accuse those electric boxes of being lewd?"

"I don't know," said Dinney. "The fountain was jammed though."
"Jammed?"
"The detergent dissolved all the grease in the bearings and Claus had to
send a repair man to turn off the fountain and take it apart and fish out all
the hair and line the bearings with grease again. And that police affair. . . ."
"O God, Dinney, nobody was killed."
"No," Dinney said. "Your head's coming off but nobody was killed."
"Dinney, there was no pot, no pornography, no nudity, no drunkenness.
Just rain and soap bubbles and music."
"Loud music," said Dinney.
"Okay, loud music."
"And rocks," said Dinney.
"And rocks." said Miss Miller.
"People can't stand the thought of innocence," said Dinney.

All of a sudden Claus charged through the door. He hadn't knocked. He
bolted across the threshold—his straw hat shading his head—and he said,
"Get those damned rocks out of there." He was wearing sun glasses, and he
didn't lift them or the hat from his face. Neither did he stand still. "Get
those damned rocks OUT. . . ."
All Miss Miller could do was look at him and let her mouth hang open.
She mustered a faint, "I thought we agreed. . . ."
"We agreed on sculpture," Claus said.
"That's sculpture," she said.
"The hell it is! Don't try to con me, Baby, I can see straight."
"Then you'd better take another look!"
"Oh, no, Baby. I've done all the looking I'm going to do. Nobody's going
to try to tell me the hand of creation is in that mess of rocks."
"Well, it's there," said Miss Miller, shouting at him. "If it's anywhere, it's
there."
"What Miss Miller's trying to explain . . ." said Dinney.
But Claus cut him short. "How long will it take you to get those rocks out
of there?"
"I'll get them out," said Miss Miller.
"How long?"
"How do you expect me to know? I've never moved rocks before."
"Baby, you moved them here; you move them out."
"All right allrightallright," she said.
But of course she didn't move them. She never intended to move them.
She just carried herself and her luggage to the train depot and the last
anyone saw of her, she was eating a candy bar, waiting for the Southern
Sunset Express. And that might have been that, except that the Children

were excused from jail and all of them returned to the fountain, taking turns by night and day to guard those rocks.

"Like homing pigeons," Dinney said. You couldn't chase them away. They carried signs: SAVE THE ROCKS. And it was crazy: someone put an ad in the paper, SAVE THE ROCKS. The next day there were two full page ads. By the third and fourth days there was nothing but SAVE THE ROCKS. The New York Tides got hold of the news and gave those rocks so much publicity that Model City was caught in the limelight. Claus was silent as a statue in a floodlight. That New York Tides art commentator must have liked rocks because he wrote: "Man so cruel and primitive had smashed God's land till it was void of everything real. And now it wasn't a statue that was being idolized or a woman's face or a nude climbing up and down an escalator, but simply a group of rocks that caught in the sun and mist-spray of the June rain."

The curious thing, Dinney says, is that people come from all over to see them. They touch them, run their hands over them as if they were handling a relic. Mostly they just stare at them or sit on them, fitting themselves into the sides of the rock. Up close, Dinney says, you can see the master's touch of color running through them in lines that are never straight because their maker never drew a straight line, although He could have if He tried.

Claus never mentions Miss Miller and Dinney hasn't the heart to ask him if she'll ever come back. But sometimes on a snowy evening when Claus leaves his office and turns away from the aluminum walls of the Municipal Hall, he stops dead for a cold minute right in front of those rocks.

# Mary K. Mazotti

Born in California in 1924 where her father was a ranch laborer, Mary K. Mazotti's childhood was spent among Italians who came from the same Calabrian villages as her parents. Married for over fifty years and the mother of seven children, she has been a school secretary. When she began writing, she started publishing in various Catholic magazines and authored the popular "Know Your Bible" quiz for the Liguorian Magazine. She is herself a secular Franciscan who speaks on the ideals of St. Francis.

## La Ciramella

"Nothing in the house to do?" I heard Papa say as I sat reading on the steps of the front porch. He towered before me like a yellow giant. Papa had just finished sulfuring our vineyard across the dirt road and was covered with the yellow powder.

"We did everything you told us, Papa," I answered, speaking for my two younger sisters and myself. He grunted with satisfaction. Idle daughters always set him on edge, as busyness was Papa's way of life. He turned and walked slowly to the faucet trough to wash up for our main meal of the day. I carefully pinched a rose leaf from the trellis to make a book mark and scooted inside to set the table. It was a spring Saturday, 1936, and six long years into the Depression.

Each early spring the sun's bright rising was directly over our vineyard and small house. In spite of the Depression Mama saw the wand of golden rays as a blessing for her and Papa, and their three young daughters born in America. Times in America could never match the poverty of their native rocky villages in southern Italy. And Mama never stopped pouring out words of gratitude for finding a better life.

Papa was famished from spraying sulfur all morning. Now he seemed content that the new grapes were protected from mildew. He sniffed the homemade noodles Mama had prepared.

"*Una festa!*" he spoke through his nostrils. Mama had tossed the noodles with hot olive oil, minced garlic, and fresh basil, and sprinkled over them her grated goat cheese.

"*Pronto,*" Mama said, putting the steaming platter carefully on the round oak table. Making a swift blessing over our food, Mama served everyone.

I watched Mama's flushed cheeks as she ate. I knew she was hungry. Early that morning she had heated tubs of water on a fire pit outside to wash clothes. She stood stooped for hours scrubbing bed sheets and towels on the scrub board, twisting and twisting out suds and rinse water, and then pinning them to wire lines strung on the sunny side of the house, where carnations and hollyhocks bloomed.

Needless to say, I and my sisters, Lomena and Pina, felt hunger rumbles also from doing housework and picking up around the big yard like Papa told us to do.

Papa finished the first dish of noodles and was into his second when he got off on a conversation about how life used to be in his native village of Grisolia where he was born. (Papa and Mama often spoke of their little villages. Mama spoke of San Sosti.) I tried hard to picture it all and liked to share these stories with my sixth-grade teacher, whom I adored and respected. Papa became very nostalgic as he recalled the fun things that happened as he grew up in Grisolia.

"The thing I itch to do most," he said, "is to play a *ciramella* again." My sisters and I stared blankly.

Mama explained, "It's a music instrument—a bagpipe, made of goatskin."

Lomena and Pina giggled. Staring at my father's unshaven face, I scowled, "Goatskin!" What a stinky instrument, I was about to blurt out, and knew better than to make fun of my father.

Papa rushed on, his face rosy, "I tell you, no one could play the goatskin like me." Laying down his fork rolled fat with noodles, he pretended playing one. With both hands uplifted, he made droning bagpipe sounds come from his nose by wrinkling it upward and humming through his teeth.

This time I laughed till the tears came. "I didn't know you were a musician, Papa," I said with amazement.

"By the saints!" he answered. "I think I'll just make one for old-time sake. It will take the place of the one I left behind in Grisolia. What a pity I was talked out of bringing it to America by *cara* Mama. I let her load me up with dried sausage and her bread instead."

My mother stopped eating. She pushed a loose hairpin into her hair bun. "*Ma*, Nichole," she teased, "what do you know about bagpipe making?" Flinging her right hand upward, she went on, "When was the last time you've seen one?"

Papa stuck out his chin and huffed, "Elena, I can remember a sack of things! What is needed? What is needed?" he repeated, and answered for himself, "Just the skin of a young goat and pipes for playing. That's all!"

"*Sì, Sì,*" Mama argued back, with twinkling eyes and still teasing. "What little I remember the skin has to be peeled off carefully—like a sock, not slit down the middle—to make an airtight bag. And curing the skin! It's not something simple, like swatting flies."

Papa couldn't help but laugh. He liked Mama's sharp sense of humor. He then got up to take some food scraps to Primo, his dog, without saying more about the matter. I wondered, as my sister Lomena and I washed the dishes in a pan of hot water, if Papa would really make a *ciramella*.

My mother and father had met and wed in their new country of America, in the early 1920s, when thousands of Italians left families behind and sailed across oceans to find better lives in new lands. They settled in California, in the San Joaquin Valley, where young vineyards, orchards, and farmlands and small shops were already started by friends before them, and by Armenians, Greeks, Mexicans, and French.

Now, in 1936, America was still having bad times called a Depression. People were out of work. Banks were failing and families lost home and hard-worked lands because they couldn't make payments. Worse, crops were not paying much.

Papa and Mama already knew how to make do with little. Fortunately, Papa had his land free of debt before he married Mama. And Nonna, Mama's mother, let them live in the small two-bedroom house rent-free when she moved to San Francisco. There were plenty of fruit trees and vegetables Papa had planted across the road; eggs from hens, milk from the goat, and catches of rabbits and quails by Papa. Sacks of flour and gallons of cooking oil were bought with side-job money Papa made on other ranches. And, Papa was never without a bottle of homemade wine from his own vineyard to help his digestion, and to help him relax from long hours of work.

One evening the whole family walked to the east side of Clovis to visit Papa's *paesano*, Carlo, and family. Carlo and his wife, Amelia, were godparents to Lomena and me. They had a family of twelve children. I liked to visit them because their oldest daughter, Theresa, and I were good friends. We liked to giggle and talk about friends and growing up.

I had forgotten all about Papa making the bagpipe until I overheard him bring up old times in Italy to my godfather. Papa didn't say he was going to make a bagpipe; he just asked clever questions about how to make one. I thought, How wise Papa is. He still dreamed of making one, but wanted to save embarrassment if it didn't turn out right. After our visit, my godfather took us home in his old Studebaker.

As he did every springtime, Papa bought a young goat from a farmer. Besides giving the family rest from eating jackrabbits and chicken meat, the goat provided the skin for the *ciramella*. I was glad that we were in school when Papa did the butchering and skinning behind the chicken shed. Only Primo, the dog, watched. Papa got the dog from a friend and named him after Primo Carnera, an Italian world heavyweight champion boxer a few years back.

Papa had removed the skin as he wanted it—whole, except with openings at top and bottom, and where the legs stood. Then followed many weeks of scraping off the hair, and rubbing and soaking the skin to make it soft.

One day Mama complained to Papa, "*Mamma mia!* What strange things I'm putting up with these days, Nichole. You have used my washtubs to treat your *ciramella* skin and my clothes are drying an ugly smell."

"I didn't know," said Papa. "*Basta*. That's it. I'm finished with the treatments. I'll scour the tubs with wood ashes for you—that is, if you write a letter for me."

Mama pulled her black-and-white-checkered apron above her plump middle and said, "Let me guess. You want me to write to your father in Italy for the blowpipe and sounding pipes for the *ciramella*."

"Please," said Papa, "you know how poor my writing is." So Mama did. I was proud that she had learned to write in Italian before she came to America. She even went to school in America up to the fourth grade. Papa was still struggling with his writing and I was amazed at how fancy he could write when he made up his mind.

Every night my father pinned the bagpipe skin to the clothesline to air out. Not long after, he was heard yelling, "What happened to it? What's happened to It?!!" We all dashed outside. Papa was red with anger. The line was broken and the skin gone. Everyone searched at least three times, every spot of the yard. Just when the skin seemed forever lost, Papa looked in Primo's doghouse. There it was next to him. Papa shook his fist and cursed. Primo ran and hid behind the woodpile. But I knew it wasn't Primo's fault the clothesline broke.

Late October when grape leaves had turned yellow, and some purple red, and the grapes were picked, Papa brought home a package from the post office. "They have arrived," he said happily tearing open the package. Lomena and I jumped up from doing our homework and Pina from her scribbling.

"Can we watch, Papa?" Pina said, jumping up and down. "Sure, Little Squash," answered Papa as he unwrapped the brown pipes. "And after we eat, I'll fit them into the skin."

That afternoon I carried in cut grape stumps to warm up the kitchen. The stumps threw off good heat to warm up the neat tiny living room, two bedrooms and large, kitchen-eating area. Papa worked on a bench that we kept for company. As Mama toasted fava beans for munching, he marked the skin leg opening that would be used to fit in the blowpipe and valve. He fitted the sounding pipes in the neck opening and bound them in place tightly with twisted hemp. Papa neatly sewed up the bottom and remaining leg openings.

"It looks like a giant flat pear with horns," I whispered softly in Lomena's ear. She bent over with laughter.

"What's next, Papa?" said Pina, pulling on the elastic of the flannel pajamas Mama had made her.

"Air," said Papa. "Lots of it." He blew and blew into the bagpipe and rested. Then he blew until the bag got fat. He put his fingers on some piping holes and let air gush out of the others. Wails and squeals filled the kitchen. I ran to the bedroom to hide my laughter. Lomena followed.

"What terrible music," she gasped, laughing and holding her side.

"Shhh, not so loud," I warned. "Papa will think we are disrespectful."

Before supper, each day, Papa went down to the cellar, pulled on the overhead light string, pulled down the double doors, and practiced on his *ciramella*. He played the old tunes of the old country until they came out like he wanted them to. Within days *paesanos* and friends knew there was a *ciramella* in the Bono household.

"Yes, yes," Papa admitted, "I have made a *ciramella*."

"Well, play for us," they begged.

"At Christmastime," Papa promised. So he kept them waiting until then.

School was out for Christmas vacation. My sisters and I took turns wheeling chopped wood to the kitchen door for Mama's baking. First she made the wine and honey cookies and fig bars drizzled with white frosting; then came the pretzel-shaped bread sticks with anise seeds; finally, the fried dough puffs stuffed with preserved sardines and dried red peppers that had been soaked in boiling water. Mama hummed and sang Christmas songs along with the old Philco radio in the living room.

Lomena and I made fringed napkins from bleached flour sacks as gifts for Mama. Lomena drew sweet litle violets on a corner of each napkin and we embroidered six napkins each.

The time was right for Papa. He visited friends and personally invited them for a night of *ciramella* music and Christmas joy. We decorated the living room ceiling with chains of red and green construction paper. A small red candle was lit and placed by the picture of the Christ Child upon Mama's treadle sewing machine. The bare floors had been mopped clean earlier in the day by Mama.

That evening lights shone in every room of our house. They glowed a long ways down the road. Friends with their children walked or drove up in their secondhand cars. The December air stung noses and ears as bright as stars speckled the valley heavens. Our walls shook with laughter and chattering.

"Nichole, come on now! How much longer do we have to wait to hear your *ciramella*?" hollered Rocco, who had left the old country with Papa.

"*Sì*, Nichole, let's see this secret project you kept from us for so long," begged Pietro, the bachelor.

Papa brought in the *ciramella* from the screened-in porch. He held it high over his head for all to see.

It's just like the ones in the old country," marveled my godmother, Amelia.

"*Sì, sì*," they all agreed. "Exactly!"

The men enjoyed sipping Papa's best wine, and took turns blowing air
into the bagpipe, laughing all the while as it grew fatter and fatter.

Then Papa took his *ciramella*. As he blew through the bagpipe, his
fingers moved over the piping holes. Gentle wailing sounds became folk
melodies of a long-ago homeland. Men and women sang songs they learned
before they ever dreamed of seeing America. Tears slid down their cheeks
and it became hard for them to sing.

Suddenly Papa stopped playing. "*Basta!* Enough crying!" he shouted.
"We are not at a funeral parlor. We are in America! Time to be glad. Time
to dance!" He began playing one tarantella after another. Women spread
wide their skirts and danced around their husbands—back and forth, hands
on hips, round and round each other they danced. Children found partners
and did the same in corners, copying.

"*Bravo, Niccolò! Bravo!*" friends yelled.

That night Papa appeared to me as one gigantic happy glow. I never
wanted the night to end.

Winter passed and then spring. As summer moved into July, a heat wave
hit the valley. A terrible odor began to hang in the house.

Lomena complained loudly, "Mama, my stomach wants to throw up from
the smell."

Papa sniffed his way to a shelf in the screened-in porch. "*Dio!*" he
groaned. "Can it be—no, it can't be!"

"I think your bagpipe is beginning to rot inside," said Mama, holding her
nose.

"What a waste," said Papa. "We could have had more fun with it."

We felt sad for Papa. Who could ever forget that Christmas night? Without another word, Papa ripped out the pipes from the *ciramella* and took
the skin to the backyard. He grabbed the shovel standing upright in the dirt
by the water faucet and dug a deep hole. He plopped in the skin and filled
up the hole, stomping on the dirt with his shoes to seal in the odor. I
watched as Papa put the shovel back where it stood before; without looking
up, he strode across the road and into the vineyard.

# Alma R. Vanek

B orn Alma Rattini in 1906 in Telluride, Colorado, and a graduate of Colorado College, Alma Vanek moved to Berkeley, California (where she
still lives) when she married Edward Vanek. When she retired as a social
worker, Alma Vanek took up writing and attended the classes held by fellow
writer Dorothy Bryant. Her story "Zio" appeared in the collection *True to
Life Stories*.

## Zio

Alma hated the snow when it melted into waters that ran wild down the
mountains, because it kept her friend Zio from coming to see her. Next to
Mama, she loved this man she named Zio, best in the whole world. Alma
was happy when he rode down from the highest mine in Colorado. Zio had
a red smiling face and hair like melted copper pennies. He always looked
too big for his horse.

When Alma was small and Zio was still boss at the mine, he would swoop
her into his arms, and the rough wool of his red plaid mackinaw would
scratch her face. From high on his shoulder she would announce with glee,
"Mama, Zio is here, Zio is here."

Mama was always busy with a houseful of boarders and the care of the
baby, who was often sick; but she would stop what she was doing and

welcome him with her glad smile. Big Sister would come running and Baby Brother would bang his high chair to show he was happy, too, that Zio, their best friend, was here.

Zio would laugh and say to Mama, "Anytime you don't want these kids, I'll take them with me."

It was Zio who helped Alma build a tree house by the fern-edged pool, where the biggest lady slippers fitted the feet of her smallest doll. He even came to Echo Rock, to listen to the funny distorted sounds, where his big laugh boomed back accented with her giggles. Zio was the only one who wanted to know what new names she had discovered and given herself, because she didn't like her own name, Alma.

"What's the new name this time?"

"Ecuador."

"Now where did you find this one?"

"In Big Sister's geography book."

"I like this best so far."

When Zio came alone he brought candy and always had time to play games and listen to Alma's adventures. But after his heart trouble, he opened a saloon, because he couldn't work in the mine anymore.

Then everything changed, and when he came down his wife, Sorina, came with him. Sorina was almost as big as Zio and her hair was jet black as the inside of a lump of coal. She never smiled and she wore black because a brother was killed in the World War that was going on in Europe.

Sorina always brought her pack of greasy fortune telling cards and laid them out for Mama. They never showed anything but bad luck. Then Sorina wanted to see Mama's Italian dream book. They would turn the brittle ragged pages carefully, and always Mama's dreams would spell disaster. Mama would be sad for days, sure that something terrible would happen.

Sorina was having bad dreams about Giorgio, a gambler who had just built a saloon, right above theirs.

"This devil Giorgio sees we're doing good business, so he sneaks around and gets The Mine to lease him the ground right above us. I tried to stop him. I knew all his slops and the water would come down on top of us. I saw trouble right away in the cards and now it's bad in the dream book."

Zio didn't like the cards or the bad dream signs and told Mama. "Cards are pieces of paper. How can they tell what is going to happen?" But Mama believed anything Sorina predicted.

Like the time Baby Brother was real sick. Sorina laid the cards and predicted. "Somebody here is going to die soon. Like I always say, we can't escape our fate." Mama began to cry. Alma stood in front of Sorina. "Why do you make Mama cry with your bad cards?" Mama slapped her.

Alma ran to her hiding place in the attic. Hours later, when Zio found her he told her he had brought the doctor and Baby Brother was feeling better. He wasn't angry with her and seemed just the same until the last time they visited.

That last time they had come down to see the doctor, because Zio was having trouble with his heart again. He didn't play games and even his smile seemed far away.

Sorina was rushing him. "You know we have to get back. I'm afraid what that devil Giorgio will do when he knows we're gone. I had a big fight with him, when he dumped his slops in our yard. He called me a witch and ordered me off his property, when I called him a devil. He's so jealous of our business, he'd do anything."

Zio interrupted. "I don't want these fights. We have to get along or it'll get worse."

"You bet it will get worse. Just wait till the snow starts to melt and water runs like crazy down the mountain and into the saloon."

"It didn't run in the saloon last year, when I made the ditch."

"Last year we made the ditch where we wanted, because that devil Giorgio wasn't on top of us. Remember this year the ditch starts on his property and he'd like to wash us right off the mountain."

"Don't worry I'll fix the ditch."

"Doctor told you. Take it easy, no more hard work."

"I'll work it out with Giorgio about the ditch. No fights."

"You can't work with that devil. I told you when he came that the cards showed bad trouble and now the dreams are worse."

"It's always the cards or the dreams with you. Let's go."

Alma was trying to tell Zio her surprise. She was right on his heels. She touched his sleeve and let the words tumble out. "I'm the only one picked in the second grade to play a part in the senior class play. I'm a pony."

Zio bent down and smiled right at her. "They were smart to pick you. You'll make a fine pony. Stand big, so you'll see me right in the front row. If you do fine, I'll treat you at the ice cream parlor. I promise."

"How do you know you can come? By then the snow will be melting and the water running wild."

"Don't worry. We'll have the ditch fixed and everything will be fine."

"You always think everything will be fine. I know there will be trouble. You better not make any promises to her."

"Don't look so sad, little Pony. Remember, I promise, I'll come to see you."

Saturday morning, a week before the play, Alma woke up happy and excited. Today was the day to pick up her new Mary Jane slippers and go to the dress rehearsal. Feet first, she jumped out of bed into a pool of sunbeams. She paused a minute to warm her toes in their rainbow fire.

After rehearsal, Miss Moran, the coach, sewed ostrich plumes on her headgear. Alma confided that Zio was coming down to see her in the play.

"All that way to see you? He must really like you."

"Oh, yes."

"He'll be proud of you. You're my best pony."

Usually Alma was bubbling over with words, but this time she was so overwhelmed with the praise that she couldn't utter a word. She felt happy enough to fly.

All the way home Alma skipped and flapped her arms to make believe she was flying. She lighted for a second to peek into the ice cream parlor, where Zio promised he would take her after the play. She had never tasted a sundae or soda, just ice cream cones. She skipped on, savoring this delicious choice; but remembered in time not to step on the cracks in the sidewalk. Big Sister had warned her not to break her mama's back. She would never do that, she loved Mama so, and had such important things to tell her today.

Alma burst into the kitchen shouting, "Mama, Mama."

But Mama wasn't there. Baby Brother was crying and Sister was trying to feed him. The boarders were standing like statues.

Alma began to cry too. "Where is Mama, where is Mama?"

"Mama went to help Sorina. Zio was killed dead."

Alma screamed, "Zio, Zio. . . . Dead? No, no, not my Zio."

"Yes." Big Sister was crying too, "Zio's dead."

"Why?"

"A fight about the ditch. Giorgio cut a hole in Zio's head."

"Please I want to see my Zio. Not dead . . . Zio promised to come to see me in the Play. I told Miss Moran he was coming."

Sister was trying to quiet Baby Brother who was screaming and choking. Alma was sobbing so hard she began to shake with hiccups. "Zio, Zio. . . ."

One of the boarders took Alma into his arms. He fed her sips of diluted *tamarindo* and whiskey to stop her hiccups.

When Alma awoke Sunday morning she was in Mama's bed with all her clothes on. Her eyes hurt and her mouth was sawdust dry. Then she remembered.

Mama had found Sorina covered with Zio's blood. She had sat in the running ditch holding Zio in her arms, until the Sheriff came to arrest Giorgio. Sorina refused to move until Giorgio was handcuffed and brought down to jail.

Mama brought Sorina back to stay for the funeral. She was sick with a cold.

Sorina kept repeating the story of how Giorgio had chopped a hole in

Zio's head to kill him. When Sorina had gotten up Saturday morning, water
was running through the saloon. Sorina ran out and began to mend the side
of the ditch that had been cut. Zio had fixed the ditch on Friday and the
work had hurt his heart. Sorina didn't want Zio to come now, but he came
anyway. When Giorgio came out with a pickax, Sorina called him bad
names and accused him of cutting the ditch. Giorgio knocked the shovel
from her hands. Zio lifted his shovel to protect her and at the same instant
Giorgio brought the pickax down on Zio's head.

Sorina never stopped crying and talked until her voice was a croaky
whisper. Alma felt too tired to cry anymore, but around Sorina the crying
never stopped.

Alma was glad Mama let her go to school Monday morning so she could
tell her teacher about Zio. "I can't come to school tomorrow, because it's
Zio's funeral. Could I tell Miss Moran that I can't practice today or tomorrow and that maybe I can't be in the Play?"

Alma confided to Miss Moran that she didn't want to see Zio dead with
the big bloody cut that Sorina kept talking about.

Miss Moran asked if she could come home to talk with Mama. Alma
stayed in her room until Mama and Miss Moran had finished talking. Mama
called her. "You don't have to go the funeral. Miss Moran says it wouldn't
be good for you to see Zio dead. You can still be in the Play. Miss Moran
says you practice good and she needs you."

How Alma wished Zio had been there to see her when she pranced out
on the stage, right down to the front. For a second when the footlights
blinded her, she thought she saw Zio. She was wishing so hard. But if Zio
had been there, Mama wouldn't be crying.

Then school ended.

One day Alma asked Mama, "Where is Zio now?" Mama began to cry so
hard she had to sit down. Big Sister scolded Alma for making Mama cry.
Alma never asked about Zio again, but when she was running through the
wet meadows or scrambling up the mountain slopes she began to think-talk
with Zio. She only did this when she was alone out of doors. First, she
would look into the sky, where she believed he might be. To think-talk she
didn't even have to move her lips. It was like saying prayers in church
where she wasn't supposed to whisper or move her lips.

Alma forgot Sorina, until Sister told her she had moved from the place
where Zio was killed. She was living in the Dalla house on the edge of town,
across the river.

One night, Mama made them hurry with supper, because Sorina wanted
them to come. Alma begged not to go. She was afraid because Sister told
her that Sorina had a row of lemons in her cellar, with rusty nails stuck in
them. They were for people she hated and would bring them bad luck, or

make them die as the lemons rotted. "She stuck thirteen rusty nails in the lemon that's for Giorgio, who killed Zio."

Sorina's house was across the old bridge. In the daytime it was fun and scary to play on the bridge. But every child knew that the bridge was haunted at night.

In the Spring, the massive waters of the river would explode against a giant boulder to lift and catapult it against the bridge. The bridge would shake and groan as if every timber was breaking. Alma would shriek, "A giant!" and cling to the railing with all her strength. Sometimes Alma and her friends would dare to close their eyes and pretend they were riding a great ship to the end of the river. But when the river was in flood, a momentous force of rolling waters would sledgehammer the banks, clawing out rocks and pulling down trees, as a foot of water poured over the floor of the bridge. Then Alma and her friends just watched from a safe distance.

Alma tried to tell Mama that she was afraid of the bridge at night. Mama said it was safe now and Alma would have to come.

Sister was just a step ahead of Alma, carrying the lantern. The feeble, shifting light made the black shadows from the heavy timbers move like palpable shapes ready to jump out at them. Alma screamed, "Look out," when shadows like long waving arms reached out to her.

"Shut up. You almost made me drop the lantern." Mama, carrying Brother and walking a step behind, scolded, "Be quiet." Now their footsteps rang out so loudly they sounded like the three Billy Goats Gruff trip-trapping across the bridge. The noise would certainly wake the old Troll, "with eyes as big as saucers and a nose like a poker."

The bridge creaked and a chill wind moaned through the old timbers. Alma's whole body shook.

Sorina's house looked dark and deserted, hunched back in the shadows of the bridge. Alma could hear and feel the power of the river as its heavy waters rumbled in the darkness.

Sorina opened the door, holding a candle. The flickering light from the candle made her face look all wavy, like a moving mask. Alma was so frightened she grabbed a handful of her mama's coat. They moved forward in silence to put Brother to bed. The only light in the bedroom was from the candle Sorina now placed before the statue of the Virgin Mary. Alma stayed close to Mama, still holding on to her coat. Sorina broke the silence to scold, "Get away from under your mama's feet. Let her put Baby down. You're not a baby."

Sorina pulled Alma's coat and cap off and shoved her out into the large dining room, where a dim light bulb hung from a long cord, directly over the round table. Tonight Alma would have to sit at the table. Since she was small, Sorina placed Sears, Roebuck and Montgomery Ward catalogues under her. They were slippery and hard; her feet dangled and the books cut into her legs.

Sorina ordered Alma to put her hands on the table and stretch her fingers to touch Sister's and Mama's. Sorina turned off the light and said the table would move and there would be knocks and maybe voices from the spirits. No one was to talk except her.

The room was shivery cold and almost black. Alma pressed her hands hard on the table to keep it from moving. Her neck hurt and soon both feet were numb. There was a wavering speck of candle light from the half open bedroom door. Sorina sat hunched over the table, wrapped in her black clothing, mumbling a kind of chant.

Alma thought of Zio. He wouldn't have liked this any more than he liked the fortune telling cards or the dream book. He liked bright cheerful colors and hated to see Sorina dressed in black. He always wore his red plaid jacket and colored shirts.

The first time Brother coughed, Mama started to get up. Sorina muttered, "Don't move. You'll break the spell."

Finally Brother was quiet and Sorina stopped mumbling. Alma squirmed and Mama and Sister pressed their fingers hard against hers to warn her to be quiet and stay awake. She opened her eyes wide and began to look around the large room, so she wouldn't have to watch Sorina and could stay awake. Everyone was still. Alma stared into the stillness.

Suddenly there was Zio, clear across the room. He looked so big, standing there. He didn't move. She watched him with all her might. He began to come slowly toward the table. It took him a long time. When he came closer, she could see he was smiling, as if he were happy again. Slowly, slowly he came until he was across the table from her. Then he held out his arms, as if he were going to pick her up and swing her.

Alma cried out, "Zio, Zio," pulled her hands from the table and threw herself toward him. The chair slid, the catalogues slipped and she fell.

Alma was shouting, "Zio is here, Zio is here," even before Mama could pick her up. "Look, Mama, look." But Sorina turned on the light and Zio wasn't where she pointed. The smile vanished from her face, as Sorina took her from Mama, shoved her shoulders back with hurtful hands and forced her face up.

Sorina demanded, "Did you really see him?"

"Oh yes. Zio came clear across the room to see me."

"Liar!"

Alma pulled away from Sorina and turned to stand against her mother. "Mama, Zio was here. I really saw Zio."

From the way she smiled and held her, Alma knew that Mama believed her.

# Julia Savarese

Julia Savarese was a 1950 summa cum laude graduate of Hunter College in New York City. She worked as a journalist and held editorial positions with several publications. After she received a Ford Foundation grant for playwriting, her play *Nest of Echoes* was produced in New York. She also wrote for television and is the author of two novels. *The Weak and the Strong* (1952) depicts an Italian American family during the Depression years of the early thirties as they try to eke out an existence in New York City.

## *from* The Weak and the Strong

There did not seem room enough in the whole world for the noise that filled the streets of the 79th Street market. It was as if the blocks from 79th down to 72nd formed the vacuum of a giant airless bubble, as if the noise would grow and grow until the bubble could contain it no longer, and then it would burst. The noise would cascade into the air and then flow unchecked down and up the side streets where it had never before gone. The hot, unmoving day added to the smothering noise. It was always the same, Gino thought, the same old carts of rough, splintered, water-soaked wood, with tattered, celluloid-framed licenses bearing small, odd pictures of their owners tacked on the sides, the same healthy, round-faced woman who called, "Nice string beans today, honey!" and was always smiling as her plump arms delved into the contents of her cart or through the sagging pockets of the faded apron she wore. In the winter the apron would be a

torn lumber-jacket, and the green string beans might be potatoes or frost-
bitten apples, but the smile, the "honey," the sagging pockets were always
the same.

Fortuna thought they might find some cheap peppers that she could fry
for supper, but so far the only ones they had seen were three-for-a-nickel
and no bigger than shriveled little lemons. But the prices would get
cheaper as you moved farther into the market, where the heat was the
strongest and the noise heaviest. They passed the corner where the old Jew
always stood, wearing the same black hat, the same heavy coat winter or
summer, selling long black shoots that looked like jointed fingers, poking
upward to where the Second Avenue El rattled slowly along. Musty Italian
stores, whose floors smelled of soaked-in oil and sawdust and mice, and in
which open barrels of greasy black and green olives floated oil-drowned
flies, leaned against tiny American shops, the ones that never lasted but
were always changing from candy stores to hardware shops to garment
stores. A house dress, size sixty, billowed like a tent from a hanger above
Sam's Department Store, and pushcarts glittered dimly with buttons and
bloomer elastic and faded sequins. It was a Bagdad of two-for-a-penny.
Rotted cantaloupes like fractured yellow skulls spilled their seedy brains
into the gutters. Watermelon slices in glass cases, wilted white with the
heat until the seeds looked like black flies burrowing into the mush. An old
woman sold tiny bottles of lavender perfume, sickening with sweetness.
The gutters next to each cart slushed with the ooze of decay and rot, but
nothing was given away. Brown, wilted lettuce leaves were stuffed into
horses' nose bags, while bare, naked children with dark eyes and swollen
bellies poked into the gutter's sludge, until a turned-on hydrant swept away
any possibility of food from their filthy fingers and swirled it down a churn-
ing sewer.

While his mother stopped to pinch some tomatoes, Gino stood looking
into a small, glossy store whose shelves were lined with greasy, lustrous
boxes and cans. A bland, lubricious young man stood leaning his foot on
an unopened crate, cleaning his nails with the long nail of his right
thumb, which he occasionally flicked across the sleek surface of his polished hair.

The tomatoes were rotten, Fortuna told the huckster, who cursed her as
she walked away. Besides, she thought, tomatoes were not supposed to be a
meal. They were served with the antipasto that came before the meal:
large, oval dishes of crisp romaine salad and tart capers, fresh tomato slices
and, nestling between, an occasional anchovy or pickle cube, with a season-
ing of fine garlic and imported oil. And after that came the roast and the
spaghetti. No, tomatoes alone were not a meal.

The fifteen cents she held was sticky in her palm. The faces and noise and smells made her hungry and then nauseated, and each was part of the other. Then the hunger took the upper hand, growing and spreading within her, until the child inside her belly seemed not a substance but a cavity, a hunger in the womb.

They were coming to 72nd Street now, and the blocks seemed to be aware of their proximity to shameful trade, seemed to shrivel up toward downtown, losing identity and personality in the fear of contamination. It was almost the end of the market; they would have to find something for supper soon. Gino held onto Fortuna's hand, but they had not spoken a word since they left their house; it was too hot to talk and their eyes were like those of hunters stalking an invisible prey. It was ugly, Fortuna thought, the rot of mankind, and you had to pay for it.

Gino hoped that they would walk back through the market instead of crossing over to First Avenue. A small isolated cart near the corner was a mass of green peppers, separated into three sections as irrevocable as any caste system. The lowest sign read: Cheap! Bargain!! 2 for 1¢!!! Fortuna and Gino approached the cart. No word was spoken during the transaction. A fat, hairy man, whose black armpits spewed a vile odor, pushed open a paper bag and Fortuna dug through the pile, one at a time, until twelve undersized peppers lay in the bag. She put the sweated dime in the hard, outstretched hand, and waited while it delved into the pocket like a derrick, bringing forth a handful of change. The man picked four blackened pennies out of the silver mass and dropped them into Fortuna's hand. There were nine cents left. They needed bread to make the peppers taste like a meal; there would be no milk, no eggs, no cheese.

The bakery store was hot and steamy but smelled wonderfully of bread. There was a small, day-old pumpernickel that the lady let them have for four cents. Fortuna stood in the store, physically unable to move. Her hunger now was a large, lumpy mass, pushing against her throat, against her eyes, swelling waterily in her mouth. Inside, her body seemed empty except for the lump that pulled and dragged. The stout blonde woman who had sold her the bread watched anxiously as Fortuna tried to gather strength enough to leave. The woman seemed frightened, almost sick herself. Finally, Fortuna pointed to a tin tray of shelves, on the top of which there was half of a thick pie, lushly yellow at its gash, its thin, soggy crust almost as white as the cardboard sliver on which it lay.

"How much for the piece of pie?"

The yellow-haired woman seemed surprised at Fortuna's having spoken. She started and then stared for a second. "Oh, the pie's half. Six cents. 'Leven cents a whole one it sells. It's a—" she bent down before the yellow half-moon— "a custard, cocoanut-custard." She stood with her hand resting under the cardboard dish.

"Eleven cents? Not five cents for half? I thought—"

"No, it's supposed to be six. But you can have it for a nickel, I guess."

Fortuna laid the nickel down on the sticky marble counter and stared as the woman sprinkled the pie with powdered sugar and twisted a piece of greasy white paper over it.

Outside, it seemed even hotter than before. "Stop a minute, Gino. Here, hold this."

She pushed the bread and peppers into his arms, and tore the string from the pie. As Gino watched, her strong yellow teeth bit into the quivering jelly. Her throat moved quickly and her breast heaved with a desperate roll. She did not stop until she seemed exhausted from furious energy.

And then she looked down at him, as if before she had not known he was there. "Oh, Gino—" She thrust the chewed remains at him, snatching the two bundles from his arms.

Then they started to walk slowly back. From the window of the bakery shop where they had stopped, the plump blonde woman stood watching. Her fat, red arm lay protectively across her stomach.

# Dorothy Bryant

Dorothy Bryant is a native San Franciscan, the second daughter of immigrants from near Turin in Italy. Her novel *Miss Giardino* uses an episode from her immigrant mother's childhood. Bryant holds a B.A. in music and an M.A. in creative writing and for many years taught in Bay Area schools and colleges—devoted teachers like Miss Giardino are a regular feature in her fiction. She is the author of ten novels, winning an American Book Award for *Confessions of Madame Psyche*. She is also a playwright and four of her bio-historical plays have been produced with *Dear Master* winning an Bay Area Critics Circle Award.

## *from* Miss Giardino

"Ah, good, you're awake." A stout nurse with red hair stood over Anna. "Supposed to take your blood pressure again before I go off." She wrapped Anna's arm and began pumping. "How are you feeling?"

"Is this Saint Paul's Hospital?" Anna asked.

"That's right. You're that accident case, aren't you?"

"My mother died in this hospital. Eight years ago. She was almost ninety."

The nurse nodded indifferently as she read the gauge, then unwrapped Anna's arm. She did not realize Anna's accomplishment: catching, pinning down, placing a memory.

After she left, Anna turned to look toward the window again. Perhaps I am dying, she thought, and, like Mama, will see a vision. "Nonsense," she muttered aloud. She would see no visions, being neither patient, nor saintly, nor believing. And she was not dying, only lying here, wondering what happened, watching the window as if the light rising outside it would gradually reveal her past, her life, herself. *Window. Stay by the window and watch for Papa. Look down the muddy road, up the hill, to where he comes from the mine. I must watch, must see him come over the hill, tall and pale under the coal dust, dark, with an angry face, angry even when it smiles. I wish he would never come. Watch. Soon as I see him, I must run, run up the road to meet him, take his lunch pail and carry it home. If I don't watch, if I read or daydream, he will come crashing and shouting into the cabin.* "No one meets me? No one cares if I come home? I should just send the money to feed all of you? I might as well stay in the mine?" *He will shout until he starts to cough. He will cough until his face turns white and his black eyes dart around the cabin, like the rat Mike caught last week, eyes looking for some way out, some little slit to slip through and escape its death.*

*Mama says I look like Papa. Tall and thin like him, with his black hair and black eyes. I wish I didn't. The others, Mike and Alfonsina and Victorina, all look like Mama. Golden hair and wide blue eyes and small bodies that go soft when there is enough to eat. There never is. Enough for Papa to drink, Mike says. That bad smell Papa has sometimes when he comes home, that bad smell means he will shout and fight with Mike, and Mike will run out. Papa says he works so we can eat. But he leaves the money in the saloon, Mike says. Mama washes for miners who are alone, whose families*

*are still in the Old Country. She hides the money under the olive oil can.
"Don't tell Papa." When the food is gone, Mama takes some coins from
under the can, enough for another sack of polenta.*

*The others say, "Mama, let's go back home." They tell me about home,
but I don't believe them. Home is, the world is, a cabin on a muddy road up
the hill to a mine. It is called Illinois, Colorado, Utah, Montana. We move,
but it is always the same cabin, road, mine. We move west, going to California, always going to California. But it stays the same, always the cold, the
pot of polenta to stir on the stove, the muddy road between the cabins, the
men on the road, walking, coughing. I know them all by their cough. There
goes Mr. Santucci. I know without looking, by his cough.*

*"No sign of Papa?"*

*"No, Mama."*

*She sighs, and we do not look at each other. We know where he is.*

*I try not to think about him. I think about the other end of the road,
down the hill, the long house where the thin lady rang the bell to open the
school. She taught us all to write our names. I draw my name in great swirls
over and over again. Everywhere, with my finger, in the mud outside our
cabin, in the dust on the pipe of the wood stove, in the soap suds of Mama's
tub of clothes, steaming, always steaming, on the frosted window while I
wait for Papa. But the teacher has gone away. No more school till another
thin lady comes. But I can read. Somehow I have learned to read. At first I
only held, hugged, smelled the books, but now I can read them. I am the
only one in the family who reads English. I hold the book the last teacher
left with me, but I do not dare to read now. I must watch out the window.
Watch for Papa.*

*Then it is dark, and Mama says not to wait anymore, come and eat.*

*I am in bed when he stumbles into the cabin. I wake up hearing the
muttering, rumbling words, like the growling of the mine guard's dog. I
crawl over Alfonsina, over Victorina, out of bed, and I go to the doorway.
Mama sits at the table, a blanket wrapped around her. Her eyes look sleepy
but afraid. She stands up, offers Papa some food. He does not answer. She
sits. He says she does not want to feed him. She gets up again, gets the plate
of food she has kept for him. He pushes it away. "Cold, not fit to eat." He
stands over her, over the table. He swells up with anger, and his swelling
chokes me. I see the fight coming, the fury. Nothing can stop it. He wants it.
He needs it.*

*Mama is already crying.*

*"Stupid woman, stupid!"*

*Now everyone is up. Mike puts on his clothes and goes out, slamming the
door. He can do that, he is a boy, almost a man, already working in the
mine. He can walk out, go to a friend, even go to the saloon. Alfonsina hugs*

*Mama, they cry together. Victorina yells, "Leave Mama alone! You're drunk again!" She grabs the heavy iron that always sits on the stove waiting to be heated and then pushed across the wash Mama does for the miners. "If you touch Mama, I'll kill you!"*

*Papa chases Victorina around the kitchen table. She dodges him and laughs when he stumbles and gasps. He cannot move fast without gasping and losing his breath. He grabs a knife from the sink and throws it at her. She ducks. The knife sticks in the wall behind her. Alfonsina and Mama wait. Victorina screams. Papa stands leaning on the cold stove, shaking his fist, at Victorina, then at God, looking up at the ceiling.*

*I stand in the bedroom doorway, watching. He turns to me, stops and looks at me. His black eyes look into my black eyes. I don't let him see I am afraid. I show him nothing but fierce black eyes like his. I don't believe what Mama and the others say about the Old Country, about how he sang and was happy. I don't believe in that man. I only know this one, this cruel, mean man who sleeps in our cabin, this monster like the giants in the book of fairy tales the last teacher gave me.*

*"And you! What are you looking at!"*

*I say nothing.*

*"The hard one, eh? Hard and skinny, eh? You don't cry!" He almost smiles, to give me a small opening, so I can reach in to touch his anger, make it burst like the bubbles in Mama's wash tub. But I don't move. I make my own eyes narrow and fierce, the way I have to do on the first day of new school in each town, when I stand tall and pretend to be older and stronger than the bullies.*

*"Answer me!"*

*I say nothing.*

*"Won't talk? Talk! Answer me! I'll make you answer!" He comes at me. Mama and Alfonsina scream. Victorina steps between us, swinging the iron. He pushes her, and she crashes against the wall. I stand still, saying over and over in my head, I hate you, I hate you. I know if I stop saying it I will flinch, fall, even cry like Mama. I won't let him make me cry. I will die first.*

*He stops in front of me, stands over me, then starts to shake and cough. I do not move while he coughs, breathes great sucks of air, the way I did when I almost died of whooping cough. "Answer me, talk. I'll make you talk." But his voice is already softer. He stands with his hand over me, but does not hit me. His hand hangs in the air over my head. My head bends back as far as it can go, so that I can keep looking into his eyes as he looks down at me, coughs down at me. His hand droops. He shakes his shoulders. "This one is too afraid to talk."*

*"I am not afraid," I say. Quietly. In English. Somehow I know the words in English will hit his eyes like a whip. He blinks. The new language, the*

*language of the people outside the family, outside the cabin. The language*
*of the people who own the mines. It is my language too. I alone in the family*
*speak it without accent, read it, think in it.*
   *I will never, never speak to him again but in English. I will save Italian*
*for Mama. All my life, all her life, I will caress her with the easy, good-*
*humored Piedmontese dialect, the tongue of golden sunsets and sweet*
*oranges, of the place that is forever home to her. But to Papa I will speak*
*only the language of this new country, my country, that promised him a*
*new life but instead brings him to a new kind of death.*
   *After a while he does the same, speaks to me only in broken English,*
*laughing and saying, "You think I am a stupid immigrant, eh, but I speak*
*English too." He stops calling me Anna. To him I am "the skinny one" "the*
*stick" or, more and more, "the American."*

   "Miss Giardino?"
   Anna opened her eyes. It was a different nurse this time, a pale, empty-
eyed girl, pregnant and very tired-looking.
   "You have a visitor."
   Anna looked at the old woman who stood by the side of the bed. She was
fat and fierce looking, as if puffed up with anger. Her hair was dyed reddish
brown and her face was covered by a mask of makeup. Red lipstick ran into
the wrinkles radiating outward from her lips. She wore a heavy brown coat
and a matching hat, very expensive looking, very heavy and ugly.
   "Do you know me?"
   "Victorina."
   "They said you couldn't remember anything."
   "I remember some things. I was just thinking of you, in fact. Did you
come all the way from San Jose?"
   "Where else would I come from? Yes, from San Jose. They called me,
said you were in an accident. You look all right."
   "I'm fine."
   "What happened?"
   "I don't remember that yet." She felt an uneasy quiver, her first stab of
fear, and she wondered how and why she should fear what she could not
remember.
   Victorina pulled a chair to the side of the bed and sat down. "I just got
back from Reno. My feet are killing me."
   Anna could not think what she could say to her sister. They saw each
other at most once or twice a year since their mother died. Victorina's
husband had died at the same time. She had fought with him for nearly fifty
years, as if continuing the fight with her father. When he died, she was lost.
She turned to religion, not the Catholic Church of her childhood but a small

cult devoted to development of occult powers and something called "mind raising." It turned out to be not so sinister as it sounded to Anna. The most important thing it had brought to Victorina was an introduction to a friend, a slot machine addict who was also a medium. When not engaged in seances, Victorina spent her time in Reno, standing for hours before a slot machine, wearing her pink house slippers, her "lucky" slippers, and sipping gin and juice. She was seventy-five years old.

"I'm sorry they bothered you," said Anna. "There's nothing for you to do, no reason to have driven that far."

"I don't mind coming," Victorina said irritably. "You're just lucky you weren't killed. Why you stayed on in that neighborhood all these years I'll never know. Full of those Mexicans and Blacks and . . . perverts! You should . . ."

"It's a very nice neighborhood and I like it," snapped Anna.

"It's not safe!" Victorina persisted. "Things have changed. It's not the same like when we were girls. You don't have to live there, you could live in one of those nice apartments out of town, San Jose, Walnut Creek, Marin, any of those nice complexes. You can afford it, you . . ." Her voice trailed off. She seemed to know that Anna would not listen, would not argue with her.

"I've thought of many old things today," said Anna, looking off into space. "I've been remembering things."

"Remembering things? What things?"

"I started with thinking about Mama, in the hospital, at the end. You know she saw visions?"

"It was the drugs they gave her. Made her see things. She was getting senile anyway."

"She was not! She forgot things, but she was quite rational to the very end." Another argument starting. Anna sighed. It should be possible to talk with Victorina without arguing. "I lived with her, after all," Anna insisted more quietly, "up to the last few weeks in the hospital. She was just the same as always . . ."

"Afraid, superstitious, weak . . ."

Anna shook her head. "Sometimes I think you hated her more than you did Papa. I don't understand."

"Easy. Easy to understand. Do you think I ever let my husband lay a hand on my children? Do you think I would put up with any of that? Of course, we had our differences." Anna smiled at the thought of Victorina's long battle with her husband. Even when he was dying, she nagged him, accused him of not trying to stay alive. "But I would never let him treat the children the way Papa did us."

"What could she do?"

"Walk out! I'd have scrubbed floors on my hands and knees to raise my children, but I'd have left that man."

"So would I," said Anna, suspecting that she would have left while Victorina would have stayed and fought. "But Mama wasn't like us. She couldn't. It wasn't possible for her even to think of leaving her husband. Surely you can forgive her for that. I got the worst of all from Papa, and I don't blame her."

"You got the worst? You were always the favorite. You were the smart one, you went to college. What do you think he said to me every time I saw him, why aren't you smart like your sister?"

"He did? Yes, he would. He knew how to be cruel. Do you realize he was only fifty-three when he died? We've lived so much longer than he did. I'm old enough to be his mother."

"And just like him."

Anna nodded. "The older I get, the more I look like him."

Victorina shook her head. "I mean inside. I don't know what it is. Something driving you. It makes you not need people, makes you do things, like go to college, to make a place for yourself above us, above . . ."

"You still see it that way!"

"Yes, why not say it? Better than others. I still remember his funeral. You, coming back from the university, just graduated, everyone so impressed, talking about you, not about him, talking to you, asking what you were going to do now, the college graduate."

"They were just being polite. They were Mama's friends, not his. They couldn't say a good word for him, so they showed interest in his children."

"Hypocrites. There must have been nearly a hundred people there, none of them who'd speak a word to him if he was alive . . ."

"All there for Mama's sake, and for ours."

"For ours? What did we care? I was glad he was dead. I wasn't a hypocrite, like you."

"Like me? What do you mean? I was as glad as you. I never tried to hide it. Even if he'd been good to us, with his sickness he was better off dead."

"Then what was that scene all about, the great act when you came in?"

"What act?"

"After the funeral, when we all came home. And those people came to my house, you know the way people used to do, we had them come to my house because you couldn't have them all in those crummy rooms over the store. And it was like a reunion, *paisani* who hadn't seen each other for years, been afraid to visit Mama for years, and everybody more relieved than anything else, relieved it was finally over and he was dead." She moved to the window, staring out on the noisy, smoky street with hard eyes, hard voice, not looking at Anna anymore, not even really talking to her anymore. "And you were listening to old man Rossi, the only one who

had a good word to say for him, talking about the Old Country and what a
fine, intelligent, handsome boy Papa was in the Old Country, how everyone in the village said he'd go far. And then you were crying, and everyone
said what a devoted daughter you were, and so smart too. When all the
time, I knew you hated him more than I did, but you had to put on this little
act for the crowd. I always respected you before that, but . . . when you did
that . . ." Her voice dropped to a grating whisper as she muttered to the
window, "You had to have that pose, the dutiful daughter who stayed after
Alfonsina and I ran off and married and left Mama. But not you. Not perfect
little Anna, who stayed by the deathbed and . . ." *I sit beside his bed,
awkward, uneasy, though there is now nothing to be uneasy about, nothing
to fear from him. No more rages, no more threats. Little breath in him now,
no more than a few whispered phrases between long gasps. He whispers
short, carefully chosen English phrases. What makes me uneasy is the
strangeness of him. He is not the man I know, not Papa. Without his anger,
his fury, his cruelty, what is left? A pale, thin man with thick black hair,
gasping for air he cannot use, lying there, his thin, yellowish arms limp on
the sheets. An uncertain man, opening his eyes from time to time to make
sure I am here. Then, quieted by the sight of me, giving a slight nod and
closing his eyes. His face is unlined, gaunt, the ascetic face of a saint. Where
is the man I hate?*

*For a week I have been sitting here, since he could not get out of bed,
since the doctor refused to come and only sent more drugs, since Mama
called and said he wanted me, only me. During my four years at the
university he had refused to see me. The deserter, the American, dead to
him. "You won't see me alive again," he had told me when I left.*

*But now, at the end, he wants me, only me. I must stay beside him so that
when he opens his eyes he sees me. If I move from the rocking chair, he
calls, gasping, "Anna," the name he had hardly ever spoken.*

*"I'm right here, Papa." During the day I sit in the old rocker. At night I
lie on the floor on an old quilt. Mama sleeps on the couch in the kitchen.*

*On the fifth day his breathing grows more quiet. At first it seems
smoother, easier. No more gasps. But there are long intervals between the
shallow breaths. Longer. His skin turns ivory. His fingers twitch. He opens
his eyes, looks at me and whispers, "Ecco," as if summing up everything, as
if looking at me and telling me that I am all he has to show for his life, his
struggle. He closes his eyes again, and does not open them for hours.*

*Later that day he speaks again. "The American," he whispers. But there
is no sarcasm or bitterness in his voice. "Smart." His tone is even proud.
He fixes his dark eyes on mine. "You know," he says, with just a shadow of
the old cruel irony, "you . . . are like . . . me . . . or you could . . . never
done it."*

*That night I stay in the rocking chair, dozing lightly, waking with a start when the interval between his breaths grows long. Soon his breathing is too faint to hear at all. I stay awake, watching the slight rise and fall of his narrow, bony chest. Sometimes there is no motion, only the twitch of his fingers to tell me he is still alive.*

*About three in the morning he opens his eyes and looks directly at me. He is alert, and his breath seems to come easily. He can speak without gaps between words for gulps of air. "How does it go, at the university?"*

*"Fine, Papa."*

*"You are now a Bachelor of Arts?"*

*"Yes, Papa."*

*"Bene. And now, what do you do?"*

*"I will get a teaching credential and become a high school teacher."*

*"What will you teach?"*

*"English."*

*"Ah." He nods and tries to smile. "You still read many books."*

*"Yes, Papa."*

*Now there is silence again, but he does not close his eyes. He seems to be summoning all his strength to do something or say something. Something very hard, almost impossible. What can it be? I watch and wonder what he must accomplish before he dies, what is it that he must tell me.*

*"You know . . ." He is back to short phrases again, barely whispered through his blue lips. "I . . . like you."*

*It is as close as he can get. He cannot say he loves me. Yet, it comes through, like a burst of light, that he does. He loves me. He has envied me and hated me, abused me, resented me. He has projected upon me all his bitterness and disappointment. And yet he does love me. He has always loved me. It is true. It is inescapable. It is terrible.*

*He watches me, waits for my response. I sit dumb . . . hearing, watching, seeing what I have never seen before. My mind sees that here is a new situation, calling for a new response. But my feelings, so long frozen against him, cannot thaw out at once. I sit, stiff, stuck, unable to respond, unable to give him the words he begs for, the simple, "I love you, Papa." Never mind if it is true or not, never mind if it is impossible. I must say it. To hold back will be cruel, more cruel than anything he has ever done to me.*

*But the moment comes and goes too quickly. His eyes close. They do not open again.*

"I guess," Anna said, "I cried because I didn't hate him anymore." But her sister turned from the window and gave her a blank look. She had obviously forgotten what she was saying and had merely been staring out the window, lost in her own memories. "How are the children?" asked Anna, falling back on her last resort for conversation with people of the married, family world. She was beginning to feel very tired again. Now she would be able to rest while her sister sat down by the bed again and recited her complaints.

Her son lived in Los Angeles. Her first granddaughter had married last year and was pregnant. The other two were in college. But no one ever wrote to her. They were only an hour away by plane, but invited her only once or twice a year, and then she didn't feel welcome. Her daughter-in-law didn't like her. Her daughter lived right in San Francisco and had just divorced her second husband. "I told her, at fifty-three she's not going to find another husband. I blame her for the way all her children turned out, all long-haired freaks, one living like a savage off in Mexico, another raising an illegitimate child like she was proud of it. Oh, I never see her, we just fight. I told her, you're getting old now, we're mother and daughter, but we're just two old women now.

"I'll be honest, Anna, I used to think you missed something not having children, but maybe you did the right thing. No matter what you do with your life, when you're old, you're old, and that's all there is to it. So what did I have children for? No one wants you anymore. It doesn't matter which way we went, we end up in the same place."

Anna did not know what to say. Her head was beginning to hurt.

"I'll stay here, take care of you when you get out of the hospital."

"I don't need taking care of. I'm all right."

"I can stay downstairs in Mama's old apartment. Give me the key. I'll go get things ready for you. I'll stay until you feel strong."

Anna said nothing. . . .

Anna thought again of her father. In her mind, she saw him, gasping and shaking his fist at God. He had made the great effort to change life, to bring hope to it. He had endured the horrible wrench of the emigrant, out of misery to desperate hope. But all hope had been eroded away until only desperation was left.

And how had she differed from her father? At first she had hated him; then she forgot him. Now, finally, she understood him. She had learned to understand him by becoming him. He had a vision of a better life and had strained himself to the utmost to go after it. So had she. He had been used and abused by the forces in which he had put all his hope. So had she. He had become filled with hatred and bitterness and despair, and had vented his hatred on the nearest targets. So, finally, had she.

Anna could barely get up from the rocking chair. She made it to the bedroom, keeping her fingertips on the walls, like a drunk trying to steady herself. She stepped out of her shoes, dropping her clothes on the floor, and let herself down on the bed. It took all her strength to pull the blankets up over her. The weight of them seemed enough to crush her. Maybe now she would die. Enough had happened, more than enough in the past few days, to kill an old woman. This exhaustion might be the beginning of dying.

As she sank toward sleep, one last dim thought of her father drifted through her mind. There was one difference between them. It was a difference in what they knew. Arno was wrong. She must not forget what she now knew about herself. If she forgot, if she dulled her consciousness, she would die in the same despair as her father, without even his hope of a new generation to benefit from his sacrifice.

# Tia Talamini

B orn in 1899 in the Dolomite mountain area of Northern Italy, Tia Talamini was brought up in Boston and received an M.A. degree from Boston University. As a retired psychologist and teacher in Cambridge, Massachusetts, Tia Talamini began a new career as a writer. Attending writing workshops at the Adult Center, she was soon producing a number of short stories. Following her death in 1988, a group of her friends formed the Tia Talamini Book Project and had some of her stories published as a book entitled *Mrs. Iacapucci and the Right Combination,* including the story here presented.

## I Learn Three New Words

My stepfather, Dino, who had always been rather frail, took ill. I was then a big girl. I was twelve going on thirteen, so I took care of him. He seemed so very unhappy. He missed his music and so did I. Our friend Alfredo, the phonograph man, lent us some new records and I would play them for him, but when I was at school Dino was very lonesome. So the phonograph man helped me find a little canary—one that sang ever so happily.

Dino and I loved to watch him carry on and we named him Ti-ti-to. We planned the duets they would play together—Capricci by Dino and his Ti-ti-to—when he would be strong enough to handle his violin. But Dino did not gain strength quickly. He worried about it, especially when he had to stop teaching me Italian. He had promised my father that he would teach me at least three new words a day.

One noon my brother Paulie met me on my way home from school and told me not to go home. I became frightened. Paulie threatened me but I ran home anyway. The house was crowded. I heard my mother talking angrily. A policeman was standing by. She was talking to a priest. My brother Tommie grabbed me as I ran into the kitchen. He said, "Ginetta, go way, go way! Paulie, take her away." They didn't have to tell me. I knew. Dino was dead.

But why was everyone there, the priest, the neighbors and the policeman? Everyone was talking and everyone wanted me out of the way. My big brother Tommie said, "You are too little and you will cry and then you will have bad dreams. You better go to Papa." I pleaded with my mother. She put her arms around me, "Please, Ginetta, I have so many worries. *Fa la brava,* be good. It is better you go with Paulie to your papa."

Someone said angrily, "Cover that silly bird so it will stop its noise." I became frightened. I took the birdcage from the hook and ran to the phonograph man. He comforted me, "Dino had suffered much. Now, he will suffer no more." Alfredo gave me a basket of tiny Italian pinks from his garden for Dino's funeral. Paulie came for me. I kissed Ti-ti-to good-bye.

Tommie would not let me go into Dino's room. He kept saying, "If you don't look, you won't dream." I gave him the flowers and he crossed his heart and promised he would put them on Dino's coffin.

Paulie took me by the hand to the station. It was my first train ride that was not a joy. Through my tears, I could see only the telephone poles and one by one they became walking coffins.

Leaving the station, we walked to my father's office and Paulie said to him, "He is dead." Paulie never talked much. My father just stared at him. Then Paulie said, "Ginetta is to stay here."

My father looked funny and said, "Isn't she going to his funeral?" My brother whispered something to him. My father looked shocked, then he shook his head and sighed. He looked from Paulie to me and said, "He was not a bad fellow." My father and my brothers never referred to my step-father by name.

My father tried to comfort me as we walked with Paulie back to the train. Then my father took me to his home. I did not want him or his wife, Gabriella, to know how dearly I loved Dino so I pretended to sleep and wept alone. I could hear my father's wife talking bitterly as she always did when she spoke of my mother. Usually the litany was, "I work night and day for you but after all she did to you, you still love her. *Stupido*. Don't say *no*. I can see it in your eyes." It was such an old story to me and yet this story somehow seemed different. It had new words in it that I had never heard before. They were three long words and perhaps it was just the way my stepmother seemed to spit them out that made them sound like such wicked words.

I could hardly remember the hard sounds but the very next day I asked her what they meant. She seemed to scream out the words as though she were vomiting all the poison she had wished for my mother these last years. She pounded away, for she wanted me to understand.

She explained. Dino had been a good Catholic. He came from a very devout family. His marriage to my mother, a divorced woman, had broken his old mother's heart and she had died. Dino's son had been shocked and gone away. Dino had pined because of his remorse. But he had not died. He was a *suicidio*, and so he could not have the last holy rites of the church as he had been *scomunicato*. He could not even be buried like a Christian. They would take him to the *crematorio*.

My ignorance of these three words infuriated her but she continued to explain. He had killed himself; the church had cast him out. It was all my mother's fault. She had bewitched him into marriage to spite my real father and now Dino would go to hell, a sinner. First, he would be cremated, but his soul would continue to burn for all eternity in hell.

"Cremated? What is that?"

"Burned—he is to be burned in a fire until he is all ashes!"

I felt a pounding in my ears and a sickish sweet taste in my throat and all mixed up; before my eyes came red and black flames around a swollen mass of burns. Oh, Sweet Mother of God! No, not poor Dino. No, you can't burn to ashes, sweet Dino. I tried to cry out to my father to save Dino but I could not.

When I opened my eyes, I was in my father's arms. He was stroking my hair. "*Povera bambina*," he kept saying. I told him I couldn't bear to have Dino all hurt and in ashes. I couldn't stand it if he didn't have a nice funeral with flowers and a High Mass with lovely music and if he didn't go to heaven. Dino loved flowers and music so he should go to heaven.

"*Povera bambina*, do you think the priest and your stepmother know everything? They don't. Sometimes your stepmother thinks because her name is Gabriella that she'll help Gabriel blow his trumpet on the Final Day. *Carina*, if anyone deserves to go to heaven, he will go. God takes care of that. Do you think only the people that are buried in Catholic cemeteries go to heaven? No, no, my child, all good people go to heaven."

"But why did Dino kill himself?"

"No one but God knows, but perhaps he was so sick he didn't want to be a burden. Maybe it was because he loved you all."

Finally, I fell asleep in my father's arms. Was it only my stepmother's spite that made her repeat those three hissing words? My father did not love Dino, so if he said Dino would go to heaven—well, he would. Now, I could again picture him in heaven playing his violin for the angels and nodding his head and smiling as he always did for me.

When I returned home, my mother hugged me, wiped my tears and told me not to cry. After all I was almost thirteen. Besides there was nothing to cry about. Dino knew best. He wanted to go. He had been too sick . . . So I was afraid to cry.

Only once I cried anyway. That was when Tommie told me they didn't have any flowers because Dino didn't have a regular funeral, but Tommie had put some of my little flowers in Dino's hand just before they closed the casket.

*Povero* Dino. Just a few flowers and no music. I had even taken Ti-ti-to away. And somehow I could never go back for the gay little canary.

# Lynette Iezzoni

A former Mirrilees Fellow in creative writing at Stanford University, Lynette Iezzoni has worked extensively in documentary films, specializing in topics involving nineteenth and twentieth century medical history. Her book, *Influenza,* companion volume for the film by that name and produced by PBS's award-winning series, *The American Experience,* was released in April 1999. She is currently completing a novel, *Impasto,* the story of a painter who views her family's immigrant past and her own through the lens of art history. Iezzoni lives in northern India.

# Window Seat

When I was ten, my family's house bordered a graveyard. The graveyard's stone wall was longer than I could see and much taller than I, and on its top, embedded in sandy cement, were pieces of sharp, broken, colored glass. My bedroom was at the back of our house and its dormer window overlooked the graveyard. This window was so wide that when I knelt on its seat and spread my arms I could just touch each slanting wall. Mother hung dotted swiss curtains at my window and tied them back with satin braids, and for the seat she sewed a velvet cushion and ruffled it with dotted swiss. "A woman must have a place to lie," she said softly, emphatically. So I lay on the velvet cushion, being what Father called "a girl," reading and staring out through the branches of the maple tree at the glass on the graveyard wall. On summer days the glass glittered sea green, coral, and lavender; and the ship I was on rolled in a wave. The captain tipped his hat and smiled. And in winter, when weeds shivered like skeletons against the graveyard wall, the gray, the blood-red, the ice-white glass were the captain's uniform, his teeth, his eyes as he steered through a fierce Arctic storm.

I was intrigued by how, in every season, the gravestones looked the same. Even those tangled in ivy or streaked gray with rain or fallen over seemed oriented, composed. Elegant. Like how my mother folded her hands in her gray silk lap at dinner parties as Father leaned against the fireplace and cigar smoke floated across his eyes and he told stories of India, the lost empire. Father was born in India in a house with terraces and fountains. He told how Indian slaves crept in from jungle fields and hid bamboo in meals prepared by a trusted cook, bamboo which became a hundred knives in a man's stomach. He told how he couldn't tell brown, swarming people from vultures; and how incense like thin strips peeled off a human heart burned so raw that it clouded the sun and dazed your eyes. At every dinner party Father told these stories. My eyes would sting and I'd notice Mother's hand flutter across her lids as if her eyes hurt, too.

The night that my summer vacation began, Father's voice fell to a whisper. "Blue blood is for real. Men are animals without it."

I crossed my patent leather shoes and stared at the pink lace on my ankle socks. Suddenly, I saw Father's cigar lying on the Oriental carpet, and a flame licking gray smoke. Voices became loud and I covered my ears until

Mother grabbed my hand and I was in the kitchen with her and Mrs. Donette. The counter was cluttered with dirty dishes.

"How gallant Peter is," Mrs. Donette said, eyeing Mother. "Of course, that British accent and the beard give him a natural advantage. Still, he has a flair for storytelling." She was wearing a red silk blouse and her dark hair was pulled into a knot below her left ear. Mrs. Donette was new to my parents' dinner parties. She had just moved into a house down the street, near the playground.

"Yes, he tells a good story," Mother said.

Mrs. Donette smiled. "Oh, Judith, don't sulk out here with the filthy dishes just because Peter burned your carpet. A woman who doesn't humor a man's faults loses him."

I leaned against the counter. The door swung shut behind Mrs. Donette. Mother ran the water in the sink. I stared at her nose. It was the smallest, slenderest nose, with such tiny nostrils that I wondered how she breathed.

"Women are cads," Mother said. Her pearls swung loose, dipping into the soapy water.

I turned away from the counter and kicked back through the swinging doors, until I was on my stomach on the embroidered, mirrored pillow near Father's feet and Mrs. Donette's laughter.

That weekend Mr. Alta moved in next door. Father and I watched through the lace curtains as a moving van pulled over to the curb. Two men leapt out of the cab, swung open metal doors, and rolled a flimsy bed, a table, a wooden chair, and several packing boxes into the white brick house with the green shutters and boxwood hedge.

Mother walked into the living room and peered over my head. "He probably just wants to decorate fresh in his new house."

"Not new house," Father said. "*First* house. Diane Donette told me about him. Comes to us from Coaltown, Pennsylvania. An ex-*miner*." He rumpled my hair. "Off to the playground, sweet child?"

"Soon," I said. "Eva's at the dentist."

He turned away, wearing his gardening whites. Father was tending the foxglove and lilies-of-the-valley that he had planted along the graveyard wall. Mother stared after him.

I skipped upstairs. I laid down my book and gazed out the window. A ball was being held on board ship. The pink, purple, soft green glass shimmered into a brocade gown that I danced in, fluttering behind my sequined fan, curtsying to the captain. He seated me on a satin chair; knelt down. His eyes were bright. Weakly, I looked away.

Father was bent over his flowers, whistling. He disappeared down the driveway, carrying a bouquet of red roses from Mother's sagging trellis.

Mother walked out the kitchen door. She held a coffee cake.

"Where're you going?" I called down.

"To welcome our new neighbor."

"The *miner?*" I climbed lazily off the window seat and headed downstairs. There was a hole in the lilac hedge where I used to hide. Mother and I slipped through. When I looked up, across the green lawn, I saw an old man sitting on the high, stone terrace. He had no legs.

Beside me, Mother stiffened. She called, "Hello," and walked quickly on. He was sitting in a wheelchair. His white hair was bushy and uncombed. His black eyes glittered and his fists were clenched on stumpy thighs.

"Hello," Mother called again. We climbed the stone steps and stopped in front of him. "I'm Judith Anderson. Your neighbor. This is my daughter, Rachel. We came to welcome you."

"Hello," the man said.

"Mr. I-EE-ta—have I pronounced it correctly?"

"Yes."

"I brought you a coffee cake." Mother's hand fluttered to her collar. "Lovely day, isn't it? Late spring is my favorite time of year. It reminds me of being a girl. . . . This is a beautiful house, Mr. Aita."

"It's my son's house."

"Oh. Does your son live here with you?"

"No, I take care of myself," he said, and Mother responded quickly, politely, "How unfortunate."

The old man leaned forward and undid the top button of his faded plaid shirt. "My son is not unfortunate. My son is a doctor. My son used his brains. I am not unfortunate either. My son bought me a house. I am a very fortunate man."

Mother was staring at her feet, rapidly nodding. "Well," she said, "I guess we'll be going. Now that we're neighbors, you must come visit my husband and me."

She handed him the coffee cake and he spoke again, softly, staring at her. "Yes, I saw your husband. Your husband was handsomely dressed in white. He grows beautiful flowers. He keeps a very neat garden. I shall enjoy watching your husband tend his very neat garden. I am a very fortunate man to have such a gardener to watch."

I backed down the steps. Mother was pausing. "Good-bye," she said in a high voice; then she was beside me, and the spring grass seemed very thick and deep and the hole in the lilac hedge was much smaller than before.

"Weird, weird, weird," I hissed.

"Shhh," Mother said. "Keep walking."

Finally, we were in the dining room and I rolled my eyes, giggled, and fell hard against the table. "Gross!" But Mother's cheeks were flushed and her eyes were very, very blue. "I think I like that man," she said. She threw back her head and laughed.

She chased me around the table until I slipped and screamed, then grabbed my hands; and we spun through the hall, shrieking, into the living room.

I lay on my window seat. Spread open was my fourth novel of the summer. I did not turn the page. Mother stood in my doorway, watching.

"I wonder who invented suffering," she said gaily. "Silent suffering. It's June first. Time to air the cedar closet. Check the sweaters for moths and send them to the cleaner's. A womanly chore. Let's get you"—she pointed—"in practice. I refuse to raise a bookworm."

I slammed closed the book. I followed her.

A bright, naked bulb hung from the smooth beams of cedar. The closet smelled musty, like brown, mildewed flowers. Mother closed the door behind us.

"I was just at the good part," I said.

"Oh." She laughed, pulling sweaters down off a shelf. "Now I see! The handsome hero was just about to take her in his arms and . . . kiss her."

"None of your business. You don't know everything."

"About romance I do."

"Liar!"

She looked at me, tossed a sweater into a plastic bag.

"You don't know that I tortured a girl in the playground today. Tortured her because of a BOY. The girl stole Amy's boyfriend. She made him *feel her up*. We captured her in the jungle gym and bombed her with pieces of paper that had 'slut' written on them. Eva thought it up."

Mother stroked her neck.

"Eva said I should grow up. She said life is war."

"Everyone for himself," said Mother.

"Yes!"

"Repay betrayal with cruelty."

"Yes!"

"Make the other suffer. Demand that he do what you want."

"Yes!"

"*Demand* that he stop hurting you."

"Mother!"

"It's simple."

I pressed my head against the door.

"Simple. Easy as pie. A pie in the sky."

Behind me she was unwrapping something, opening a box. "Look. Ra-

chel, *look.*" Mother held up a pink lace dress. She pressed its shoulders
against her own. She held to her waist a belt beaded with white seed pearls.
"This is my wedding dress."

"It's *pink.*"

"Our wedding was informal. It was . . . hurried. Your father said I was
divinely beautiful. He could not wait. He said I was the most gracious
woman in the world." Mother cocked her head, staring into the corner
above me. "What he mistook for graciousness was that it never occurred to
me to raise my eyes to his." She uttered a sharp, brittle laugh. "Rachel. I *do*
believe in graciousness. That and kindness." The stiff lace brushed my arm.
"Kindness holds you together. It keeps life from being a mess."

Suddenly, Mother smiled. "Look!" She dropped the dress onto a pile of
blankets. "My hatbox. Here, Rachel, my orange hat. My old pillbox hat.
That sexy bow. Try it on."

She tugged the hat down around my ears. "Pretty. Why don't you surprise your father and wear it to dinner tonight?" She turned her back. I
reached out to touch the wedding dress, but it slipped off the blankets onto
the floor. "Go let the hero have his kiss," Mother said firmly.

When I finished the book I lay gazing out my window. The shadow of our
house fell across the graveyard wall and the glass was dull and empty. Then
I saw her. She was sitting next door, on the stone terrace with Mr. Aita.
Their two heads were like one. Mother's hand waved in the air. She leaned
back, laughed.

I swung around. My feet slammed to the floor.

I ran and sank beside my tea table. I arranged the cups and saucers, but
did not serve tea.

Crystal tinkled downstairs and I knew Father would be talking of India.
I knew how the chandelier would rain white drops of light upon the
women's hair and the men's faces and how delicate a knife sounded upon
china and how the women would gently toss their heads back and touch
their wineglasses to their flushed cheeks and their laughter would seem
soundless in the gracious, noisy room. Mother sat opposite Father, at the
end of the table near the kitchen door. A dark curl would be sculpted over
each ear and her eyes would carefully roam and she would be up and
down without anyone noticing and no one would notice her eat and then
her hands would fold in her gray silk lap. Mother often said that Father
trained her well. Father would raise her chin with a finger and kiss her
when she said this.

"Rachel!" Father was calling from the foot of the stairs. "Come down. A
young lady must learn to socialize!"

I pointed one foot after the other down the carpeted stairs. I entered the living room.

The crowd stood in a blue haze of smoke. Mother was kneeling on the Oriental carpet, her hair in her face. She was putting pieces of glass onto a napkin. Above her, Mrs. Donette lit a cigarette and swayed into Father's arms. "Peter, you big *lug*," Mrs. Donette laughed.

Father stroked his beard, rolled his sparkling eyes. "We men lack the delicate manual dexterity of the fairer sex." He pulled an iris from a vase of fresh flowers, closed her fingers around its dripping stem.

"Judith," he cried suddenly. "You'll cut yourself!"

Father lunged forward, knocking Mrs. Donette's drink from her hand. It splattered, staining the carpet red. A cocktail cherry rolled toward Mother. Mother wiped her eyes.

"Men are such lugs!" Mrs. Donette said.

The room exploded with laughter. The fire was spitting ash.

Father gestured for silence.

Mrs. Donette held her glittering necklace to red, parted lips. Smoke from her cigarette curled around Father's head.

"I've wondered if this is also true among ape couples," he said. "Or if it's a blessed difference reserved for us higher forms to keep us bloody infuriated and coming back for more!"

Mother stood up. In a low voice, she said, "Peter, please tend to the fire. A fire anyway—in June? Our guests must be *burning up*."

Gravely, with a flourish, Father bowed.

Mrs. Donette giggled. "Judith," she said. She tapped her chest and cleared her throat. "I've wanted to compliment your taste. This room is . . . *extravagantly* furnished. All the pillows, flowers, mirrors."

"Peter likes to surround himself with beautiful objects."

"Your wish is my command," Father said to Mother.

Mother walked out the door.

"Judith," Mrs. Donette cried. "Judith."

Back in my room, I lay curled on the dark window seat. Laughter came from downstairs. My ears seemed to beat like hearts.

Finally, there was silence. They were coming up the stairs.

"Why can't you just relax and have a good time? You should see yourself," Father said. "Not a woman. A little girl."

On Independence Day I was tired and stayed home. The neighborhood was alive with noise. That night, when I put down my book and leaned to one side of my window, I could just see the golden fireworks bursting against the dark sky.

The next morning Eva called me on the phone. "Howdy, stranger. Ever
heard of the Fourth of July? America?" she said. "Listen to this." I heard
the sound of rushing air, growing louder, rushing—bang! The receiver
shook. "What did I do?"

"You popped your gum," I said.

"Good, Rachel, good. Now come over to my house. My mom bought me
a pair of fishnet stockings. They're *red*. She says I'm becoming a woman."

"I'm *reading*."

Silence. The sound of rushing air—bang! "Nerd," she said, and hung up.

I ran down the stairs. Mother was lying on the living room sofa. One arm
covered her face; the other hung down, her fingers tense like a spider on
the Oriental carpet. I flew out into the backyard. The sun was burning just
above the graveyard wall and in its yellow glare the sharp glass glittered like
a hundred eyes.

"Slut, slut, slut," I whispered, my chest hurting, bursting with strange,
terrible energy. I ran back and forth along Father's garden. I kicked a stone.
It broke a flower stem, ricocheted off the wall.

"Come here."

Mr. Aita was sitting next door, on his stone terrace. His voice echoed
across the lawns. "Come visit an old man."

I ducked through the lilac hedge. Chin high, I walked quickly. I stopped
a yard away from him. His face was sliced with deep, brown lines and his
black eyes glistened like wet soil.

"Are you playing?"

"Well, *school's out*."

"Nothing useful to do?"

I made a face.

He laughed. "Not even any boys to hold hands with?"

"I don't care about boys," I answered loudly. His head nodded to one
side. His eyelids drooped. "Though I tortured a girl over a *boy*," I said.

He gave a little snore.

"And I wasn't punished!"

Mr. Aita smiled and picked a piece of lint off his plaid shirt. His mustache
twitched. "Why do you think you did something wrong? And even if you
had, what makes you think you'd be punished?" He swelled back in his
wheelchair, laughing. He caught my eyes with his. "Let me tell you a story.
I often tell this story. It comes in handy.

"You see, I am a thief. A thief who grew up on a shabby farm in Italy, who
couldn't tell his brothers and sisters from the chickens and the pigs. The
stoop of our house was worn from sons and fathers and sons and fathers
sitting on it and never lifting their feet out of the dirt. Because it is the duty
of strong men to stand up, pretend they're God, and *walk*, I took action, the

only action possible. One night I stole the key to my father's wine cellar from where it hung beside his bed. I packed up all his wine in his sturdiest cart, harnessed it to his best mule, and ran off to Naples. There I sold everything for a good price and bought passage to America. I knelt before the Statue of Liberty and, since this is the land of opportunity and freedom, went right down into a coal mine. For forty years I labored in the dirt. But when a beam fell and crushed my legs, I didn't need them anymore. My son was a doctor. A wealthy doctor. And all because I had seen and done my duty. I had been a thief.

"Do you understand?" he asked.

"Yes," I lied.

He laughed. "There is no justice. It is up to you. Only the very strong see and act. The majority paw away at life like animals."

I backed down the steps.

Suddenly, his arms flung open wide and he shook them as if embracing the sky. "Blue, blue. There is blue sky above the brown earth. Go now. I can tell you are a good girl. You have a good mother. Tell your mother she is a strong woman. So to be a strong woman." His arms fell, his eyes darkened. "Get out of here," he said. "I am just a brilliant old thief talking a useless game, playing God."

By late July I had read nine novels. I never went out. I lay on my window seat. It was so hot and humid that my eyes stung and my skin itched. Mother spent all her time with Mr. Aita. She neglected the house. When I pointed this out to her she ignored me and mumbled something about Mr. Aita, her mouth twitching, happy. "His wisdom is so brutal." She giggled like a baby, clawed her white throat. "So . . . selfish."

I got into the habit of taking cool baths. I ran the water and lay with it lapping my chin. I made my hands rise to the surface, palms up, and tried to keep them afloat so my fingers wouldn't pucker like an old hag's. I asked Mother for bubble bath. She said bubble bath wouldn't be good for certain parts of me. She said I might get infected. When she came home from Mr. Aita's and I was still in the tub, she would point her finger and say, "You're becoming a fish."

One night Father did not come home for dinner. Pork chops hardened in the oven. At nine o'clock Mother said Father had called and would be staying at a hotel in the city to be near work. She pulled the pork chops out of the oven and folded her hands in her lap. She left the table before I finished eating. Carefully, I put our plates side by side in the dishwasher.

Two nights later Father came home. When he entered the kitchen Mother shivered, clapped her hands wildly, and walked out. "Jesus Christ," Father said. He tickled me under the chin.

Mother began spending her days on the living room sofa. She lay with an arm across her face, a hand clenching the rug. I stayed outside, wandering along the graveyard wall.

Mr. Aita watched as I wandered. Often he called, "Come here, Rachel." I sat at the foot of his wheelchair. He told stories. He used strange words—grief, betrayal, wisdom, courage—and everything sounded complex and beautiful. He told me stories about men with rusty picks and axes tunneling through a black stone earth. "In darkness a man becomes only a smell, a pair of hands and legs, a sound of hoarse breathing," he said. "Flesh . . . and blood." He asked after my mother. He said she was doing something useful. Often I stopped listening to Mr. Aita, and daydreamed to the passionate sound of his voice. Vaguely, wistfully, I gazed up at him.

One day at the end of August, Father sat down on my window seat. He ordered me onto his lap. "I'm too big," I said. "You're never too big to sit on your old dad's lap," he pouted. "Come here."

Father told me my mother is unhappy.

Father told me she has not been happy for a long, long time.

Father has tried to protect me from seeing this, because it is not pretty.

A girl should see only pretty things.

Father told me my mother says she is alone and wants to be left that way.

Father is going away for a while, but not leaving me.

I will never be alone.

Father told me that since there is no tear on my cheek I am a young lady.

A young lady doesn't cry, she understands, and her understanding and happiness make others happy.

Without women's love, where would this crazy old world be?

Where would a man like Father be?

I walked down the stairs. The grass in the backyard was yellow and dry, broken by patches of dirt. Mother's trellis leaned against the graveyard wall, littering Father's flowers—the naked, tangled stems—with moldy brown roses. I felt dull and vague, as though I would suddenly laugh. I ducked through the brittle hedge, and approached his house.

"Mr. Aita!" Arms spread like wings, I ran up the wheelchair ramp and flung open the screen door. I entered the house. The large, white room was empty.

I walked through a doorway. Eerily, my footsteps echoed.

His profiled head did not turn. Yellow light filtered through a bay window. Mr. Aita's wheelchair glittered. He sat facing an empty wooden chair. "What do you want?" he said.

"Where's your furniture?" I said.

"The kitchen."

"The kitchen?"

My cot is next to the stove."

"You sleep beside the *stove*?"

"I have all a man needs. Food and a bed."

"Why are you staring at that empty chair?"

"Sometimes my son forgets. The visiting day comes and goes and he forgets to visit his brilliant father. The one who sacrificed his life for him."

"He's probably just busy."

"Yes, my *girlfriend*, you are certainly right. Please sit down and tell me a story."

"You tell."

Mr. Aita wheeled slowly toward me. "Me? But I am just an old cripple with garlic for blood, and my son's wife says I talk too much. She calls me 'Big Mouth.' She says I have 'delusions of grandeur.' Do you think I have 'delusions of grandeur,' Rachel, or do you believe I'm a man like God?"

His finger cocked, gesturing me near. "I'll give you a hint," he whispered. "They're the *same thing*. Now you tell *me* a story."

"I don't know one."

"Yes, you do."

"No."

"Coward. But you are beginning to understand. That all stories are corrupt, just blasphemies to fill ourselves with."

Mr. Aita kissed his fingertips. Gently, he touched my cheeks with them. "Go home," he said. "Go home."

"Mother!"

I called at Mother's door.

She answered, "Rachel, please make your own supper."

I awoke in darkness. My face ached with horror and to cry.

I had climbed out my window onto a branch of the maple tree. My hair flew in the wind. Only moonlight guided me.

I crawled far out on a thin limb. I lay just above the graveyard wall. The shards of glass glittered into an enchanted room. The room was filled with mirrors and velvet chairs and satin pillows and vases of lovely flowers, flowers every color of the rainbow. Women's fiery eyes burned, inflaming the gestures of bowing men. I reached out, and slipped. With one arm I caught myself, but the glass ripped open the flesh of my feet, my legs, and I bled, a bright, luscious, terrible red. My blood coated the glass and flowed slowly down the wall into the graveyard.

The next morning I got up early and was at the library when it opened. I chose a new novel.

When I returned home Mother was standing in the kitchen. She was

naked except for red satin underpants. Breasts hung heavily from her chest
and her brown nipples were thin, like twigs. Her puffy eyes looked at me:
slits. She leaned against the counter, steadying herself.
"The idea, dear girl, is to be a noodle," Mother said.
I laid my book on the table.
"Noodlebrain." Mother opened the cupboard and stared as if deliberat-
ing. She chose a can of beets. Her shaking hands knocked the can opener
onto the floor. I bent over, picked it up, wanting to get away, upstairs, to
my window seat.
"A noodlebrain looks in the mirror and sees what others tell her to see.
She never grows up. She spends her life in a continual state of self-beautifi-
cation, trying to please others. *Not* because she has a big, generous heart,
but because this is how she gets her head patted. This is how she is told she
is sane and kind and good. This is how she makes the world a gracious, a
happy place to live in. But do you know the catch? The catch, Rachel?
Rachel?"
Juice slurped from the can of beets and Mother bent so close that her
breasts brushed my shirt.
My teeth chattered. "If you tell me, can I go?"
"The catch, Rachel, is that after a while noodlebrains *become* noodlebrains. Just bundles of lies. God knows how to begin separating a woman
from her illusions." She gave a little cry, and turned away. "Of course you
can go," Mother whispered, her head against the refrigerator. "This is a free
country, isn't it?"

# Anna Monardo

A nna Monardo holds an M.F.A. degree in creative writing from Columbia
University and worked for some years in the New York City area. Her
written work has appeared in various reviews and has also been read on National Public Radio's "Selected Shorts" series. She now teaches in the

Writer's Workshop at the University of Nebraska and resides in Omaha. Her novel, *A Courtyard of Dreams*, was published by Doubleday in 1993 and has been translated into German, Norwegian, and Danish, and she is at work on a second novel.

# Roman Ruins

Weekdays, Leah brings coffee to the office in a melting cardboard cup from a nearby deli, then pours it into a mug, a gawky, earth-colored piece of ceramic with a brush stroke letter "L" glazed on it. The mug was a gift from her high-school boyfriend. He later became a potter. They only once said, I love you.

Over the back of her chair in her cubicle at work hangs a sweater, waiting for a day when Leah feels chilly. Knitted by her mother in a surprisingly inoffensive, in fact a pleasant, combination of reds and pinks, it is a good background for Leah's wild spread of tan hair. For all the other young editors at the publishing house, as well as for some of the more important editors, the old sweater constant on its peg is a comfort. It calms them to think that even in the midst of the impossible business of putting forth literature there is room for something made by someone's mother and maybe, by extension, for their own soft spots and quirks, their slight imperfections.

The coffee, the mug, the sweater: these are all very important. They are a few of the touchstones Leah is depending on to feel her way from one day to the next.

There was a time, right after Matt left, when sadness took over Leah's life with the persistence and skill of a charismatic lover. It lured her to bed early. In the morning it would not let her leave. Whole nights through, sadness kept her from sleeping, touching here, touching there, in deep regions of emotion, places where she had never had feeling before. Leah's longing for Matt, ignited each night by his monstrous absence beside her, was the strongest desire she had ever known.

Leah thought Matt had the loveliest hands—sharp bones, fine veins, chiseled from the tautest skin; hands that made her think of art history class and anatomical drawings by Leonardo da Vinci. College was less than one year behind her when they met, so that world was still her most immediate reference. Matt was four years out of college and, because he hated working for people, was trying to live as a freelance journalist. "I'd rather be on my own at any cost," he said when they first met at a party. To Leah this had sounded noble and she'd told him so.

When two years had passed and she was alone, Leah became obsessed with trying to separate the features of Matt's face and reassemble them into some graspable vision that would prove he existed and had loved her: the deep slope of his nose, his sharp green eyes circled with dark lashes. All she saw before her, though, were those hands, resting patiently on tabletops as she and Matt tried to decipher what had happened to them.

The view out of Leah's bedroom window is of recently renovated brownstones, formerly abandoned tenements that sagged in a row. One May night, a few years back, not long after Matt was completely moved in, an arsonist's benzined rags sabotaged the old buildings and left them smoking for days. Their stale cinder smell whipped through Leah's small apartment, robbing Matt's possessions—the beet-colored couch, his alphabetized collection of jazz, a splintery desk and boxes of files—of their own unique scent, making them indistinguishable from Leah's in a way that was strangely exciting to her. Love had never, so completely, encompassed her before.

Each night that hot summer, they fell asleep to the sound of vandals picking through the rubble across the street as if through a fruit orchard. During the day, workmen arrived with bulldozers and cranes to chip away the burnt interiors and haul away the debris. At his desk in the living room Matt was doing proofreading between article assignments. When he could find no reason to call Leah at work—no new article ideas, no good-news or bad-news mail—he'd call to report on the work across the street.

"They just knocked out a partition so we can see straight through now. You should see the exposed brick in there," he'd say. Or, "They're stringing scaffolds along the sides. I think they're going to start scrubbing it. Yeah, they're wearing raincoats. Hey, Leah, you should come home and watch them doing this." Once or twice she did go home. Matt began research for an article on tenement renovation. "You know," he said once, "those old heaps over there are incredibly strong structures."

With their stone skins washed white, the scrolled pediments and ornate facades of an earlier time, some classical time, reappeared. Completely gutted, with patches of flat, blue sky filling their gapped windows and doors, the old buildings stood as solemn as ancient ruins. Roman ruins, Leah called them.

Mornings, she would roll away from Matt's chest where she spent the night, ease one thin arm from beneath the quilt, to pull away the long striped curtains, to look.

"Little boy, look," she would say, "we're in Rome."

Into the back of her neck Matt would whisper, "We are, my sweet," and then they'd make love.

From the start Matt was intrigued that Leah bled only when the moon was full. "Are all women like that?" he asked her. She told him, No, every woman is different. It was a natural embellishment of the conceit of those times for Matt to imagine Leah's body as the cycle from which the rest of the universe took its cues.

One year passed, then several more months, then waking in the morning—pulling away from Matt, placing the two of them in what went on beyond the window—began to feel like climbing out of an abyss. By then, Leah and Matt, convinced that together they formed some absolute, were hibernating in a dark and private intensity. An intensity which was, at first, exciting in its exclusiveness. An exclusiveness which turned terrifying in the way it consumed them and was inescapable.

Matt said he had to buy a newspaper before he could sit down to work, and each day, with that excuse, he walked with Leah to the subway. Leaving him at the newsstand, Leah would hesitate a moment before crossing the street, balanced on the curb, feeling anxious as a child waiting for a chance, the right second, to jump onto a carousel or into a spinning jump-rope. Filtered through Matt's constant presence, as distorting as a prism, the world, to Leah, had begun to feel strange.

One morning she caught herself reflected in a shoe store's large window. She was shocked. The hem was torn and hanging from the back of her badly-wrinkled skirt. In the center of her white cotton shirt Leah noticed a gap instead of a button, and a pinch of pale skin. All this time, she thought, I felt really lovely. Matt had said she was.

That second summer, July's moon filled, then ebbed. A new quarter appeared and still Leah wasn't bleeding. They thought she was pregnant.

"Go to the doctor," Matt said.

"No, I'll feel stupid if it isn't true."

"You're not making sense. You're being illogical. How can you go on not knowing for sure what's going on in your body? Listen, if you'd like, Leah, I'll go with you."

"Why? Why should you go with me? You think all of a sudden I'm not capable of doing anything without you?" But Leah knew she had lost that ability long ago.

A few days later, one night in her sleep, Leah felt her stomach cramped and distended, felt the muscles across her back tighten like tourniquets. She held onto sleep for as long as she could, but the pain grew and spread and finally woke her. When she reached the bathroom she was bleeding.

Rocking slightly, Leah wandered through the apartment. The living room at five in the morning looked disconcertingly useless. Usually if she found herself alone by Matt's desk she would linger there, examining his fountain pen sketches on the desk blotter: complicated series of interconnected cubes. She would proofread and make notes on the pages piled around the desk. Matt was getting many good assignments. "Can't talk, Leah," he'd say when she called him from her office. "I'm in the middle of something." Glancing at the page inserted in the typewriter that night, she saw he was working on something new, an article he had never mentioned to her. So things are happening to him, too, she thought.

Passing his desk, Leah walked into the kitchen, found aspirin, orange juice. Then, half way through that act of curing herself, Leah stopped. Sitting on a low stool, she was spotlighted by one naked lightbulb hanging high above her. A pale, oversized nightgown hung around her like a loose skin, barely touching her own skin, a casing for the pain. The grain of the kitchen table was magnified in the bottom of her empty juice glass. Into the glass she said softly, "I wouldn't have had it."

That thought did not feel blasphemous to Leah. Two aspirins were turning gritty in her hand. The cramps were sharp and everywhere, pouring out of some small spot where a baby did not exist, never had. She realized that. Realized, too, that a child would have grown and grown there, all out of proportion, as Matt had throughout the rest of her, and then she, Leah, would have been lost. Instead, she had her aching middle. Leah's pain: private, her own. She dropped the aspirins back into their bottle. Greedily, she wanted to hold onto it.

When she told Matt that her body, unlike the moon, had simply skipped a few beats, he said, "Leah, did you know I would have wanted it? I think the whole time I wished it was true. I wanted us to have a baby." He said that, he admitted later, only because having a child seemed the one act of faith that could bring them, together, back into the world.

They lived on together for a few ambiguous months, slowly drifting apart, yet also, out of habit and fear, looking to one another for comfort and direction. Sometimes, staring across the living room at Matt reading on the couch, Leah willed him to look up. A few times he did, smiled, stood and walked towards her. But the desire in his narrowed eyes looked more like curiosity and Leah felt betrayed: already he was seeing her from a stranger's distance. Later, in bed, they'd move against each other in new ways, dissonantly. Matt's face below her looked so far away, above her he looked savage and too close.

Then, on Sunday night, lonely and hollow as only Sunday in the city can be, Matt's glass coffee pot slipped from Leah's wet hands and broke.

"I can't believe you dropped it," Matt said.

"I'm sorry," Leah told him. "My hands were soapy. It slipped. Hey, besides, I thought it was *our* coffee pot."

"I've had that thing for years. What happened? Couldn't you catch it?"

"Matt, I said I was sorry. You know I'll buy you a new coffee pot. I'll buy two. What do you want?" She was crouched down, picking up the larger chunks of glass. "It was an accident. I'm sorry. I'm sorry."

"O.K. Let's forget it, Leah." Holding his hand on Leah's shoulder for balance, Matt stooped down beside her, leaned over to kiss her.

"Don't" she said and pulled away.

Matt's hand still rested solidly on her back. "Leah, why are we fighting?"

Crying, she turned to face him. "Because we're making each other crazy, Matt. We're not happy together anymore."

Two hours later she was standing, shaking, in the shower with the water turned on hard so she wouldn't hear him packing or the sound of the front door closing when he left.

The next day, he came back. For three days. Then he left and returned again twice. Finally, when it seemed he was gone for good, Leah emptied all the drawers and closets into the center of their—her—bedroom floor, knelt into the pile and wept.

It was February when Matt left, melting into a timid spring, as it had been when they met. Breezes from the river still skidded old newspapers into Leah's ankles in that ruthless winter way, but the air was turning softer, kinder. Walking alone each night from the subway, Leah sifted through, listed, her grievances against the world. She cursed Matt for saying their parting was a good thing—a generous and cautious parting, he had said, because they had given each other time; a respectful parting because they had never been unfaithful. Leah knew better. She knew they had failed. She hated herself for having lost Matt. And she cursed herself for having given so much that in loving him she lost herself. Now she felt alone. When she walked down the street it was with her face raised, her head slightly tilted, as if she were ready to walk into a hug or hoping to catch a kiss from some gentle stranger.

These days, though, Leah climbs up from the subway tunnel at the end of the day, turns toward distant New Jersey and walks home watching the sky. On nice evenings, an apricot sunset might be slipping into the bruise-colored Hudson. Above her knee socks and boots and beneath her wool skirt, Leah's snagged nylon slip licks the back of her knees; this is a pleasant secret. Life seems good. She passes neighborhood kids sitting up on mailboxes. The music they play in their cassette players makes Leah want to spin her sack of manuscripts one, two, three full times, loose it to the wind, and dance, dance. When it feels like hard work to keep from swinging herself down the street, Leah knows she is getting better.

Finally arriving at her apartment, she calls out, Hello. It is not a greeting, because no one else lives there, and not really a warning in case someone has entered. She just wants to hear her own voice in the stillness, throw new air into the home that keeps breathing while she's gone.

Later, through one side of an Earth, Wind & Fire album, she does sit-ups, leg lifts, and sustained body stretches over her knees, while her dinner—chicken, liver, or a nice piece of fish—simmers in a cast-iron frying pan beneath a new aluminum lid.

During dinner she reads the Sunday paper, slowly, all week long. When she sees articles about renovations, architecture, independent business people, jazz clubs, Mexican restaurants, French movies or the Pittsburgh Steelers, Leah knows, for sure, that Matt has read them. Once she saw his by-line and though she thought of calling him she never did. She knows, as he does, that probably another whole year must pass.

Afterwards, she goes to her bedroom and her bed becomes a small universe. She leans back on four lilac pillows and covers herself with a forest-green quilt—soothing is how Matt described the effect of those two colors against each other. Eventually, a red-trimmed bowl of lukewarm cereal and milk will be balanced on the bed. And a manuscript—one stack of down-turned pages which she has read, and another stack of upturned pages to be skimmed the next day on the subway. Rubber bands which held the manu-script together will be bracelets on her wrist. By midnight Leah will be surrounded on the bed: the telephone, pencils, the jewelry she wore to work that day, her checkbook, hand lotion, an aqua chenille robe, the mail, orange peels, her hairbrush, a grocery list, her appointment book, a few magazines, a glass of melting ice, and her purse. More than the luxury of lying amidst the jetsam of the evening, Leah enjoys the organized feeling after she's cleaned it up.

Before clicking off the light when she is ready to sleep, Leah billows up the top sheet and quilt so she can see clear to the bottom of her bed. If you were watching, this would seem a casual enough gesture, but Leah knows she is looking for things that crawl and sneak. Things that shouldn't be there. The night a small mouse skimmed the floorboards in the living room is when this ritual began. (Too often while making this inspection, Leah remembers a man falling asleep next to her—Ben somebody—who said, "That's some phobia you've got there. We should cart you right off to Vienna." Unable to sleep beside him when he began to snore, Leah went into the living room, taking a manuscript with her. Ben has not been invited back.) Then she bunches and positions a pillow so she can lean her back into it, for company, during the night. In the dark her eyes stay open until she sees how the shadows have settled around the room.

On Sundays now, Leah often makes dinner with friends, almost always women. One friend, Hilary, suspects it is time for her to leave her own boyfriend and each week she presents further evidence in her favor. Hilary might say, "I feel he's grown a lot through our relationship. He's less shy, more confident. Isn't he? Everyone says so. But I feel stagnant, as if I haven't grown at all through him."

And then someone, usually Amy, says, "Hilary, it sounds like you know exactly what you want to do. Make a decision and get it over with."

Listening, chopping green peppers and onions for spaghetti sauce, Leah wonders what Matt told his friends when he moved out.

"I'll probably never meet a man who cares about me again." This is Hilary's worst worry.

"It's true, Hilary," Amy says, "you probably won't."

By the time the dishes are done and everyone has left, Sunday has passed with a minimum of pain. Leah takes a book, she reads a chapter, billows the sheets, sets the alarm, clicks off the light. The darkness. The shadows. Eventually Leah falls asleep.

Mornings, she still has problems getting out of bed. It is not depression or sadness holding her, but a covetous instinct to possess the early morning, to give length to a moment of perfect peace. When the windows are clean, the plants on the sill look greener. On the sculpted ledge outside, a few pigeons might be perched, making those throaty noises, those deep, trilled gulping sounds.

Looking out above the brownstones (her new neighbors are less interesting than the ruins were), Leah knows now that although love can be as random and elusive as an intuition or a lucky streak, it is always hoped for and always possible. And she is almost convinced that in a single morning, in the simple shifting of one day to the next, the world, so tired and old, can be born again, even out of sadness.

# Rose Carmellino

Rose Carmellino has Master's degrees from Columbia University in both creative writing and in business management. While a writing student at

Columbia she won a *Transatlantic Review* award and a UNICO literary award. She is currently working in Financial Services in Manhattan, with long-time plans to complete her novel in progress.

---

## *from* a novel in progress

Pigeons gathered at Grandmother's feet. Their necks crooked forward as they snipped crusts of bread. Iridescent colors bristled among the gray feathers. They reminded Nina of grease slicks, the kind she saw floating like sheets of ice on puddles in the street. Grandmother called them "earth rainbows."

"Yes," she would say, bringing dried heels of bread out from the deep pockets of her housedress, "God gives even the poorest pigeon a fine coat to wear. And today, on the holy day, they all wear their best necklaces."

It was the feast day of the Assumption, and leaving the house at ten o'clock they had walked across the long avenues to the church. Nina knelt quietly against the marble altar railing and bowed her head. The black mantilla that she wore fell about her face. Only points of light were discernible through the lace eyelets. Watching her hands clasped in the posture of prayer, she listened for her grandmother's breathy exclamations.

"Ah, God . . . I fear your church, filled with old women . . . and the priests always sending poor souls to Hell. . . . But yet, your world is so beautiful."

She would cross herself hastily, jabbing her fingers from forehead, to heart, to shoulders, and hearing the smack of her lips against the folded knuckles of her index finger, Nina knew they would be leaving soon.

They did not go home. They continued walking, passing open markets. "Fish, fish . . . live and fresh . . . What, too expensive, Signora . . . then *scarola* . . . Sardines for the frying pan . . ." the vendors barked in raspy voices. Muscular boys in T-shirts carelessly unpacked wooden crates. They sang, "*Femmina, tu sei una male femmina . . .*" Onto piles along the stands they jostled vegetables, and musty-smelling melons, and they shouted out their prices. "A good buy, the best buy . . . Fish . . . Apples . . . Sardines."

Taking Nina's hand as they came to four lanes of traffic, Grandmother turned a cold eye upon the streets behind them.

"These are holy hours. On this day we would always go to throw our sins in the water."

Once across the avenue they followed the uneven path that ran alongside the chain linked fence of the Dyker Park golf course. Slowing her pace to match Grandmother's, Nina watched her small feet in their black boots move with careful determination among broken glass and ruptured cement. Grandmother had told Nina Italy was the shape of a "boot, kicking Sicily away," and she imagined it to be like her shiny black shoe, with the stout heel and wiry taut lace.

Running ahead, Nina leaned up against the railing which separated the walkway from the rocks, holding the wet metal in her hands. She gazed out at the water. It was calm and continuous in its splashing against the littered and stunted shore. Soon Grandmother caught up with her. She spoke above the lulling tide, and highway traffic that raced behind them.

"Once a Gypsy woman came to my town, and everyone was afraid of her, because it was said she could cast the evil eye. One day as I was out gathering twigs for the fire I found her resting upon a stile. Seeing me, she called me by my very name, and told me I would cross much water. There were so many streams and brooks up in the hills, I did not think much about her words. And though I crossed the ocean only once, with each new day, each year, every dollar in my purse, I traveled farther away from the knoll that was my village. And was it all my sin of pride? Did I become a pilgrim, only to wear the face of a signorina? I remember the first time I saw these shores. I had two children pressed to my legs, and a year-old promise that your grandfather would be waiting. So many women had their husbands swallowed up by America. At first, letters full of plans and money, and maybe a photograph at Easter. With time . . . less news, little money, and finally nothing. Deathless widows, yet lower than widows. No respect, only pity and half-smiles. I prayed to Saint Joseph every day, each free moment, while threading a needle, scattering grain for the hens, rocking my babies. 'Noble husband, Saint Joseph, preserve me and mine.' " Tears glistened in the creases of her eyes, and Nina knew she was remembering the girl, who had grown to be her mother, and the boy, who had died wearing the uniform of a country he did not belong to in the faraway land he would not belong to.

"We sold everything. Everything we had went to buy three certificates on the black market. The boat was going to Argentina, but stopping in New York. The whole time I kept the papers hidden to my breast. Men would kill for them. America had laws . . . they did not want any more immigrants." Grandmother pointed left, out to the tip of Coney Island.

"You could imagine, after all those days when we first saw land, how happy everyone was. First it was a faraway dot. Almost nothing. Some said America could not look so small. But then it got bigger and bigger, until finally we were coming right through these Narrows."

They began to walk with their backs to Coney Island, retracing the path of the boat, as it voyaged toward Manhattan.

"I was so afraid. I could hardly breathe." Grandmother beat her chest three times, as if in response to the holy chimes. "Afraid that the men to take us off the boat would not come, and that the officials on Ellis Island would know our papers were false. Everyone was on the deck when we passed into the harbor. The children were taunting each other, 'Who will be first to find Papa?' We had not seen him in three years."

Grandmother sat down on a bench. Reaching into her pockets she brought forth scraps of bread and sprinkled them on the ground.

"So many people were at the dock. All cheering and shouting . . . words I could not understand. I looked and I looked, but I saw not even one familiar face. The children were quiet. I was silent. I looked at us three, me in a dowager's rags with my mother's cameo pinned tightly at my throat, and the children in sailor's suits I thought were American. We wore strained masks. We were all afraid. Then, Lucia began to jump and cry, and shout, waving her fists. 'Papa . . . Papa.' On the dock wearing a black-banded straw hat of white, and shaking brown paper bags filled with chocolate kisses, was my husband."

Hands clasped in prayer, eyes turned downward, Francis led our evening grace. Uneasy, he stumbled over the words quickly. Mother smiled approvingly and patted his hand.

"My son . . . blood of my blood," she whispered with pride. "*Figlio mio.*"

At the head of the table Father's chair stood empty. Three salt shakers within a furious grasp and a stack of crusty bread surrounded the plate that for the past two nights had been untouched. Mother and Grandmother exchanged furtive glances, and Nina watched their faces, eager to share their confidences. The clock, the door, the plate, the chair: they were careful to turn their heads and avert their eyes from them, as if a bold stare could somehow summon Father to appear.

"And so, Francis," directed Mother in a cross tone, "I already told your sister Lucy, and now I'm telling both of you. I don't want Nina left alone in the house. This afternoon as Mama and I were coming down the street, we saw Nina open the door for two strange men."

"Oh, Nina." Shaking his head, Francis reached out to catch one of her braids.

Nina's face reddened with shame. She could not understand how Mother and Grandmother could turn away strangers, humbly pleading "*non capisco,*" or pretend to them no knowledge of the people next door.

"Not another word." Mother was impatient, and she looked coldly upon Francis.

"Who was at the door? Insurance men? Jehovah's Witnesses?" Lucy lifted hurt eyes from her plate.

"*Non lo so,*" answered Grandmother in grim Italian. "Men in raincoats with briefcases."

"Remember the time Mrs. DeLessio was looking for someone to rent her basement?" continued Lucy. "A man with red hair and a red beard came to her door, and Mrs. DeLessio thought he was Christ. She started crossing herself and praying."

"If the man had a devil's wit, he could have stolen even the cheese from her mousetraps," Grandfather smiled.

"Enough of this." Mother made another impatient gesture, as if to clear away her children's laughter. "Francis, did you tell Grandma that the monsignor wants you to assist him for Easter High Mass?"

Francis scowled, his pale face darkening with irritation. "Only because this is my last year," he said without looking up from his plate, then adding, "The younger kids always mess things up."

"The holy days will be here soon. Who eats on Shrove Tuesday, starves on Ash Wednesday," instructed Grandmother in Italian.

"Yes, the holidays," agreed Mother. Her eyes darted around the table, brushing past each face, and finally rested upon her hands. Everyone was silent, eating quickly and noiselessly, and shifting in their chairs.

"My first holiday in America I was all alone," began Grandfather with renewed vigor. "I was living in a boardinghouse on Mulberry Street. During the day I worked digging the subway tunnels, and at night I'd go to this rooming house, have a glass of wine and maybe a plate of *scarola* and some bread dipped in oil, and then go to sleep in a room with eight or nine other men."

" *'Cca nisciuno è fesso,*" Grandmother interjected.

"Yes . . . on the wall someone had written in Neapolitan, 'No fools here.' Every man would write something—if only the name of the town they left. Anyway, I was going to spend Christmas Eve with some second cousins, who lived way up in the Bronx. I had bought two enormous eels at the fish market, and I carried them in a burlap sack. After work, I got on the elevated train, sat down holding this bag at my feet, and after a while I fell asleep. Before you know it, the bag had slipped from my hand, and the eels had slithered out onto the floor. 'A snake! A snake!' women were screaming, people running and somebody pulled the emergency brake. Waking up I didn't know what was happening. I couldn't speak two words of English, but I ran out of there so fast, cursing the loss of those eels. They came with fire ladders to get the people down."

"*È vero,*" nodded Grandmother. "*È vero.*"

They laughed with a forced gaiety, and then finding themselves suddenly relieved of the oppressive silence, they laughed clamorously, senselessly.

"Your father comes," whispered Grandmother.

Father stood at the doorway of the kitchen, uncertain whether to enter. He was tall, with an angular face and bristly hair, and his clothes hung crookedly on his thin frame. Sitting stiffly in his chair, his eyes searched each one of them, studying them with a piercing gaze.

Nina thought he had winked at her, his right eyelid opening and closing with a cold protracted sweep. Only Grandmother glared back at him, the one savage eye of the cameo pinned at her collar joining in her reproach.

His plate before him, Father folded his hands and with his lips moving wordlessly said his prayers.

"Thank the Lord you don't find the lock changed." Grandmother hissed.

"My food has turned to stones," Father gasped, holding his forehead with great anguish.

"Vincent, where have you been?" Mother's voice was a shrill soprano.

"Tenafly," he gulped awkwardly.

"*Dov'è* Ten-a-fly?" muttered Grandmother, shrugging her shoulders. "*Che cos'è*"

"Jersey . . . I was in Tenafly, New Jersey," Father cried fretfully with a nervous twitch of his lips. And then overwhelmed, the palms of his hands turned up in supplication, he grieved, "I had the newspaper. I was going to find a job. I was in Manhattan with the newspaper. Everthing was black and white," he moaned, "and I walked down the street . . . brick upon brick, but in my home not two stones left together. I went into an office. The man looked at me, 'You unemployed?' White shirts everywhere. White shirts and black shoes. Suddenly I couldn't breathe. I felt dizzy, *stordito*. I went outside and I saw a bus."

"Three days? What did you do for three days?" Mother shrieked incredulously.

There was a long silence as Father, his eyes unblinking, his face stony, considered the past days. "I walked . . . I looked. There were trees and hills."

"This *cap'ombrell*. Wasting his time when he should be feeding his children. This *pazzo*," Grandmother railed.

Father turned toward her, shaking a slender bony finger in her face. Dark with rage, he shouted with venom, "You put the *malocchio* on me. You're the one! Ever since you came into this house, your black dress at my table, black stockings on the washline, you've put a black curse upon me. It's you twisting Lucia's mind." He pounded his fist, and wailed in a voice overcome with grief, "Am I not the man of this house?"

"*Sì, sì*, Vincenzo," Mother hushed. "You'll make yourself sick." Placing a finger to her pursed lips, she signaled Grandmother to say no more. "Eat your dinner, Vincent. You are tired. You need to rest."

"*Una bella figura*," Grandmother sneered.

*Una bella figura,* a fine figure, was what Lucia first saw when she met Vincent Savino. Newly arrived in this country after World War II, he was tall and slim, with a graceful pallor on his face. Unlike the roughhewn men in her neighborhood, she saw in Vincent's gauntness a religious asceticism, in his nervousness a sensitivity, and she was impressed by his fine *alta* Italian. In reality, his thinness was the scar of his poverty, and his nervousness the result of the bombings of his town. "I would roam the streets like a hungry dog, yet quicker than a dog, looking among the rubble for a bit of bread," he would say bitterly. "And if I found a scrap it was as poisonous as the gall forced between Christ's lips. And the bombs, always coming when you thought you were safe. *Dio Mio, Madonna Mio,* whimpers of the dying in the night."

Vincent had received some training in architecture, and Lucia, the only high-school graduate of her circle, was convinced that this intelligent man should be her husband. She was proud of the fact that he could work with *matita a mano,* pencil in hand, for Lucia's special dream had been to go to City College and become a schoolteacher. Lucia was bitterly disappointed when she found herself working behind a sewing machine, but she tenaciously hoarded her one dollar each week, her share of the earnings, tucking the money in her shoes, between the pages of her missal, under the statue of Saint John. Now, with the chance of marriage to an educated man, Lucia began to plan for the future she had been promised. She would have the neat house and well-schooled children, the kitchen where only the costliest oil and best cheese were used, the dining room with the ornate chandelier. Although there was no one to recommend Vincent, neither was there anyone to speak against him, and Lucia, who was not young, married.

"He's of no use to you, Lucia," began Grandmother, once Father had gone upstairs. "You should turn him out." Grandmother cleared the dishes off the table, leaving only a half-filled glass of wine before Mother. She worked at the sink and spoke with her back to Lucia. "He's crazy."

"No." Mother shook her head. "He just needs a job."

"Lucia, Lucia, don't you too deceive yourself. In all these years has a job made any difference? Always coming and going as he pleases, and finding his soup waiting hot too. And what work can he do? This fine man with his business suits and English newspaper under his arm. Always lamenting over his town—the fountain, the church, the whorehouse, the garbage heap—as if his Godforsaken village was paradise."

"What can I do? What would become of him?"

"What will become of these children?" Grandmother waved a hand in the air, throwing droplets of water as a blessing across the three faces. "He's weak, bloodless. Turn him out. There would be no shame. The shame is in this poor comedy. His wailings and posturings."

Nina wanted to run upstairs into her bedroom and hide. She edged toward the door, dropping her dishrag on the tabletop.

Mother, seeing that, pushed her wineglass toward Nina, offering her a sip. "*Basta*," she said, giving the final word of every argument.

Nina rested against Mother's side and she was comforted to have an arm around her waist. They drank in turn, until there was no more wine left in the glass.

# Tina De Rosa

Tina De Rosa lives and works in Chicago, where she has been a guest lecturer in the Italian American Studies Department of the University of Illinois. As a writer in residence at the Ragdale Foundation, she began work on her novel *Paper Fish* and received an Illinois Arts Council Literary Award for the manuscript-in-progress. Her novel was published in 1980 by the Wine Press and was re-issued in 1996 by the Feminist Press. She is also the author of several essays and a biography of Bishop John Scalabrini, *Father to the Migrants.*

## *from* Paper Fish

The family plot was purchased as soon as they had any money, before any of them had decent clothes. It is big enough for all of them, they will be buried on top of each other like layers of a wedding cake. The family name is carved into the stone, and the negro grave attendants can not pronounce it. The stone is so large, it is visible a good distance away, so that any living member of the family who visits it never gets lost. On Sundays, they pack a picnic lunch and go to take care of the grave. On the way to the cemetery, in the summertime, they stop at a specialty store that sells monuments and wreaths and small plants for the gravesite. Inside the store, stone angels with blank eyes and a look so forlorn it will tear your heart out if you are five years old are lined elbow to elbow on the wall. The angels sit with their legs crossed, their eyes have no pupils. They sit with their heads in their hands. There the family buys plants green as artichokes, flowers red as blood. In the wintertime, they buy an artificial black wreath and set it in the snow. But in the summertime, the entire living family spends Sunday afternoon at the gravesite.

Marco and Sarah help Grandma Doria out of the blue sedan. Grandma is wearing her old straw hat to protect herself from the sun; stuffed under her arms are the long loaves of Italian bread. Aunt Katerina, Aunt Josephina, Aunt Rosa carry straw picnic baskets filled with tomato, with onion. Uncle Salvatore stuffs into his large pockets the bottles of wine. The blue sedan pulls up silently to the curb by the gravesite, the sun shines on them as they all tumble out of the old blue car, tumble out onto the gravesite, telling each other to keep quiet, helping Grandma and her proud old hat, settling Doriana to sleep in the car's back seat, striating the vigorous cemetery grass with their baskets, their wine, their own healthy bodies.

Set into the stone are the small framed pictures of the dead; their faces are set so that they always look directly into the eyes of anyone who looks into theirs.

Carmolina is five years old. She sits and eats tomato sandwiches with Grandma Doria while the family laughs and talks and digs little holes into the face of the grave to plant the flowers. Grandpa is under the flowers; he does not eat tomato sandwiches. Carmolina runs, when she is asked, to fetch water from the pump at the corner to water the new plants. She is careful not to step on any graves when she does this. She stands, holding the heavy watercan over the family grave and watches the cool water spill out over her tennis shoes, wetting them, watches the holes just dug by Mama for the plants eat the water up. Inside the grave Grandpa listens to them sing, but he does not get water on his face. Inside the grave Grandpa Dominic is glad they are there, is glad the old woman Doria his wife and his children are there with the tomato sandwiches. Grandpa had a white mustache; it's with him in the grave. Carmolina sings the Italian love songs which Grandma taught her, *O rosa! O rosa! O rosa gentillina!* her small mouth opens and sings, and Grandma looks up at her from where she is slicing the onions.

The skin of the onion squeaks in Doria's hand when she pulls it away from the white body. The thin yellow paper of the onion makes no sound, but the first layer of skin squeaks. She watches Carmolina singing in her small broken Italian; she is growing up with the music tooled inside her brain. The sound of Carmolina's growing is filled with music in her head, of the laughter and quick tears of her large family around her. The sound of Doria's time was quiet, was patient, the sound of her growing up was slow and deliberate. The time of Doria's growing was marked by usual, small events, but her people had their own way of remembering. They sat in the dusk of Italy and they made their lives slowly, measuring out the days like milk or salt. They kept picturebooks of their lives, and in them they pasted likenesses of themselves. The pictures were bound in corners of black paper. The people in the pictures had skin the color of onion; they were dressed in shades of brown. Their smiles were fixed and faced forward toward the man under the black hood who with his great funny puff of white smoke would seize them. Their skins were not truly the color of onion; their clothes were not really shades of brown.

On the day that the first family picture was made, Doria wore a white dress which was made for her by her mother Carmella from the wool of sheep. It was a heavy dress, much too heavy to wear in the sun that day, but it was her best dress and her mother insisted. After the picture was taken, Doria wiggled out of it and gave it to her sister Sabatina who immediately undressed and got into it while the family looked on. On the day the first picture was made, Doria was eight years old. She lived with her family on a small hill in a town near the city of Naples which they visited on holidays if the year was good. Their town was a small one; the furthest border was a graveyard whose markers went back to the sixteenth century. The white stucco house was Doria's house. It was buffed white by the sun of Italy; there was no glass in the windows. In the summer the glad weather washed through the windows; the trees became part of the family. In the wet season the rain washed into the house; it dripped down the walls. Then Doria's mother set out after the great black waterbugs with her straw broom. Sometimes Doria and Sabatina found a waterbug in their bed and they snapped it open between their fingernails. Outside was a small garden; this garden was the joy of Doria and her mother. The two of them, dressed in black dresses, sat under straw hats and weeded the grasses away from the small green plants. The mother spat into her hands for luck before she began to work. From the garden came sharp white radishes and lettuces for the salad. Sabatina did not like the garden; it dirtied her hands. The mother said that Sabatina was the child of royalty, that she was kidnapped by gypsies who wore golden earrings and stole children. She said she found Sabatina in a basket in the garden, and that Sabatina was a princess who would never do a lump of work in her life. Doria laughed when her mother said this, because in her heart she knew it was true that Sabatina was lazy as the sun and would never amount to anything if she did not wake up soon. It was true that there were gypsies. They roamed the countryside and played music on their dulcimers, they shook tambourines in the dark. The cries of the strings and of the little silver bells enchanted the children. Doria had seen them, the black eyes and black souls of them. The breasts of the women were large, like the udders of cows; they swung under bright red dresses. Their bodies were dressed in golden jewelry; they wore silver combs in their hair. They were beautiful; they were terrifying. They frightened goats in the night so that their milk turned sour; they terrified the chickens so that they went barren. Whenever Doria and Sabatina passed the gypsies on the dirt roads, they crossed themselves and called upon the Madonna for protection from the evil eye. At night the two little girls lay in their white bedroom, on the clean sheets beaten white in the river. Outside the moon was a blue hole in the sky, washing the world blue-black, making the trees black as ash or as death, making the trees stick all out of the world like the broken brooms of witches. Outside the world turned blue from the moon, its enchanted light made the bedroom blue, and the sheets and their toes sticking out from under the sheets turned blue along with the world. It was then that Doria and Sabatina heard the singing of the gypsies, heard the cry of the dulcimers and the strangled chatter of bells, heard the laughter and songs of the gypsies reaching up out of the ground. The gypsies ride black horses, Doria said, and Sabatina curled into her side of the bed, pulled her feet away from the pitiless blue light, hid her face in the pillow. The gypsies ride black horses that once were devils, the devils grew tired of hell and changed themselves into horses. The gypsies find them and ride them, and the horses run faster than the horses made by God. The teeth of the horses are like knives, they can bite through the walls, Doria said. Sabatina buried her pretty brown face in the bedclothes and her legs were stiff. The horses run faster than the wind, faster than the rain, and if a gypsy wanted to catch you, you could never run fast enough, Doria whispered. Outside their windows the trees were black as matchsticks; a gypsy could set them on fire with his curse. Outside the window the trees looked into the bedroom with twisted faces. The voices of the gypsies travel through the ground, Doria said. The gypsies can reach up out of the ground and grab you with their teeth. The devil gave them special power. Sabatina screamed into the pillow and Doria scared herself. The sound of the dulcimer and of the thin tambourines travelled through the night hills. It was magic music, and sad. The gypsies were sad because they had been cursed by God to wander the world; they must live forever in tents, pitched by lonely fires. They sat round the fires dressed in their devil's gold, with gold at their ears and at their breasts, with gold at their waists and in small beautiful rings round their toes. The gypsy women sat with their long black hair and sang out of throats which burned. The men with their hard gypsy muscles listened and wept and grew angry. They revenged themselves. They stole children. They twisted the life of the animals so that goats vomited and chickens gagged. Sabatina rushed to the window, slammed the wooden shutters shut. She slapped out the blue light of the moon and the evil arms of the trees. Under the sheets, she still heard the music and Doria laughed at the way she scared little princess Sabatina. In the dark room, Doria watched the small slip of blue light under the shutters, clean and swift as a fish. She watched the shadows, stuffed like thick milk into the corners. The shadows only seemed to move. When she grew up, Doria would run away to the circus. With her blue eyes and black hair, she saw the circus and loved it. She loved the humped little dwarf with the yellow teeth, she loved the old wagons. There were green babies, flat and floating in bottles. The people of the circus dressed in clothes like jewels; Doria with her laughing blue eyes would be a part of them. The people in all the towns the circus passed would call out, there is Doria run away. Sabatina would grow old and fat; she would be forced to make large dresses to wear; no bracelets would fit her fat arms. But Doria would be beautiful, with slim ankles. She would lead the elephants, smiling.

In their small bedroom, his children were still asleep. Pasquale glanced for a moment at his daughters. He was a rough man. He had learned all he knew at the side of his father now rotting in the graveyard. The skin of his hands was almost as thick as the wood he worked; his eyes and the world they saw were the same. He wrestled with the world and forced it to yield to him all he demanded. He spat in the face of anyone who would steal from him that which was his. Carmella his wife was his; she had been given in proper ceremony. He had taken her properly in bed. She had yielded him two children though neither, curse God, was a son. He hammered and nailed and chiseled the wooden world into place. What would not yield he placed in a vise and then shaved off or sawed off what would not submit. His hands were black from his work; the palms were scarred by small tears in the skin which would not heal and by slivers of wood which were fixed parts of his flesh. His eyes were not the eyes of his brothers the farmers. His eyes were not marked by days spent under the yellow sun. His eyes followed the narrow grain of wood, followed it closely so that it would not deceive him and crack at a vital point. His eyes watched the fine shavings give way to correct proportions. His eyes ran over countless beams, ferreting out failure. The earth and its rooms, its fields and gardens, its houses and sheds, smelled of varnish and turpentine. He had long since lost the smells of his wife's kitchen, of the dishes set before him. Long ago he surrendered the delicate feast of anise in his coffee, the smell of honey in his cakes. The world smelled of turpentine and of sharp black varnish. His hands he had trained to know a slab of wood as a lover's hands know a woman's sex. They

were hands fine in their work, and from them came the cabinets, tables and
chairs which enabled him to marry Carmella his wife. His work had given
him his family and this small house. He would not, like his father, become a
broken doll, lose his trained eyes. He had taken care of these eyes and
hands, the tools given him by God to make his way on the earth a man and
not a shrivelled worm.

He did not know if his children were beautiful. He knew that they were
his. He had made them, he continued making them the way he made a
ladder or stool. When he walked into his daughters' bedroom on the morning when the pictures were taken, he noticed only that they were asleep.
His eyes were trained to see the joints and pinnings of the world, and not its
luster. Behind him, the black hills of Italy were filled with spectacular
creatures, with creatures of myth, of legend, of dreams and nightmares,
squirming out of people's minds, leaping out of their souls. The restless
people looked up from their cooking, from their seeding, working the pulp
of fig against the soft skin of their mouths like squirrels, looked out from
their eyes and seduced from the humps of stone images which nourished
them as the earth could not. They supplemented what the earth failed
them. They provided the mysteries which God in his haste had overlooked.
Thus the hills were peopled by bandits who slit human throats with the ease
with which mothers slaughtered chickens; who slit open and spilled human
life while glancing at the stars. Their taste was for swift and splendid death,
their hands were bruised with blood, and they licked them clean. Headless
bodies floated in the streams, suspended astonished in the water. The air
was rich with the smell of their blood. Travelling through the hills was
never an unconscious act. The people's eyes filled with what they expected
to see; their irises were moist with the blood they might shed. Waiting, the
people believed their bones lacked marrow, like birds. But more than the
thieves filled the heavy pockets of the hills. The unborn, the never-seen,
populated the trees, the small stone paths, and the stories of these as-
tounded Doria. Creatures which had never existed lurked in the tales of her
mother, Carmella, lurked in her words, in the catches of her voice. They
peered out of their red eyes at the small child listening. The mother stirred
beans in the pot on her stove, shredded the cheese and told Doria of these,
the unseen creatures. The mother's face was deeply olive and her eyes
sought the truths outside her kitchen window, as she prepared the meal.
The souls of the unforgiven dead walked the hills at night. They held their
hands before their faces, hiding their rotted features. They marched in a
hard blue line and the sight of their faces could shoot you into madness,
could spit you into hell. On a hill outside the town they gathered in a
blue-black circle and chanted their prayers for forgiveness. They set their
faces towards the stars, searching out the fingers of God which would hold
them safely once again. They dressed themselves in leaves and danced. In

the rain, they turned silver as pond scum, in the rain their secrets were
revealed. It was true according to Doria's mother that each man is given a
secret when he is born. He is meant by God to protect his secret, to hide it
like a jewel throughout life. Each secret is different, and only God knows
them all. The telling of secrets is forbidden. They must be held close to the
body all through life, because they are the only treasure. Without them, a
man is a snail. You must never, Doria, squander the secret. You must,
Sabatina, be careful. Do not tell.

Sabatina is one of the faces on the family stone. Her eyes look out from
behind her glasses; her smile is quiet on the stone where Carmolina is
watering the grave. Her quiet dead eyes smile at her sister Doria. She looks
like Doria who is slicing the tomatoes open so that the seeds will spill into
her hands, but Sabatina is slimmer, and she is dead. She does not have little
whiskers on her chin.

Because Grandma Doria is the only member of the family who has little
whiskers on her chin, like a goat. The whiskers float in the air when she
talks to Carmolina, Carmolina stares at the whiskers, they are like the
antennae of a gentle insect. She laughs from her stomach; Grandma's laugh
has a wheeze in it. It is as though she uses up too much breath, laughing,
and Carmolina is frightened of the wheeze, let God never take Grandma's
breath away. Her skin and her teeth are yellow. When Grandma makes
lunch, it is cheese on Italian bread, or tomatoes on Italian bread, or just
Italian bread. They sit together at the formica table in the kitchen, the
whole world is burning from the heat of the summer, but coolness is on the
table and Carmolina and Grandma talk:

When Great-Grandma Carmella died, she was sick a long time. Then
Grandma was just a little girl and she sat with Great-Grandma who was
dying, and everyone else was asleep. Deep in the night, Great-Grandma
screamed and sat up in bed. Grandma saw a woman dressed in white crawl
out from under the bed; she was a skeleton; she was Death; only Grandma
saw it. Grandma screamed and ran out of the room; Great-Grandma died
instantly. There is a mountain in Italy filled with candles. Some of the
candles are tall and white. Some are short and sputter with the blue flame.
Each person has his own candle. When he is born, the candle is lit; when
the candle goes out, he dies. You can see this mountain, Carmolina, only in
your dreams, but God will not let you see your own candle, even in a
dream. If there is a mistake, and you see your own candle, you will die. This
is how people die in their sleep. Great-Grandma, knock wood, did not die
in her sleep.

Grandma keeps food on the back porch. She hangs long red peppers from
the line with wooden clothespins. She keeps white lima beans in jars of
salted water; she keeps them there until they grow juicy and bloated; then

she salts them more and feeds them to Carmolina, who loves them. Grandma keeps trays of seeds from the pumpkin to dry in the window. When they dry, she salts them and cooks them in the oven until they are brown.

Grandma stands by the window on a hot summer day; the air is yellow outside. She is laughing, she is fat in her black cotton dress. The sun makes her little whiskers precise and obvious; they are white. She is smiling at the little girl called Carmolina and lifting the screen from the window. The sill is cement and the birds are nowhere to be seen, but Grandma breaks the day-old bread and places it on the cement sill. The sun is making her face beautiful. It is doing magic to her face, and here, in the corner where Carmolina sits, the shade is gray and peaceful and Grandma is standing in the spotlight of sun that someone is shining on her because she is feeding the birds. The old woman laughs, she throws bread out the window. The little girl Carmolina can not reach, the grandmother picks her up, holds her high against the sun so that she can feed the birds too. The circle of sun shines on the little girl, she is laughing, her grandmother owns the sun and is calling the birds:

In the sun the sand was hot like nothing else could be hot under her feet, so that her body did little jumping motions when she walked and she looked like she was flying, but she wasn't, she was walking on the hot sand that sent her up and jumping into the world. In the shade the sand turned cool. It was gray there and small things grew with quiet rocks and red lady bugs that flew in the air and landed on her skin, and all that made it cool. Carmolina left the land and went walking off into the water, and before the water began, the sand was ripples, it was rippled by the wind and was packed hard, like a bed sheet, and she went walking into the water, which was blue like an egg, which made long soft breaking sounds out there where it struck against the world, and spilled over. Standing in the sand, she could hear the water breaking from far away, it sounded like thunder only it was sweet and she wanted to go out into it and she did, she ran out, she ran into the blue water and it was cold around her feet and the water was eating her body up, like a little rock or a fish, and she jumped up and down in it, she put her feet into the bottom of the water and she stood on the world and laughed. When she looked back at the sand, she could not find the blanket with her family on it, she could not see her grandmother with the lunch basket filled with sandwiches, she could not find the right colors in the sand, none of the colors were hers. She splashed her hands in the water and her toes dug themselves into the sand, it was packed hard, with little rocks in it, the rocks bit her feet, they were small mean bites under the water, like angry fish. Then a voice called her from the sand, one of the colors was moving, she watched the color float across the sand, it had no feet, but moved towards the water and was calling a sound like her name. Her toes dug into the water, something was coming to get her. The color came into the water, it was big like a tree, it called her name but she could not find its face and the water no longer was cold, the warm skin lifted down for her, in its hands she was warm, and she was lifted from the water and carried back to the sand. Then she rode the horses of the merry-go-round. The horses were painted red and gold and green and black, they had separate saddles and the reins were real leather, the bit was metal. She climbed up on the horses and she was as far above the ground as she would be on the second level of the monkey bars. The merry-go-round started slowly, it made slow circles of light in the hot summer air, and slowly she moved past her mother and father behind the mesh fences. They were small figures, smiling, and she smiled back at them as the horses moved past. Then they turned into quick little blurs of colors, whisked by air into pure colors which were smiling at her. And her horse rode up and down, it carried her up closer to the top of the merry-go-round where she could see the fantastic iron works which made the horse move, the iron bars pumping steadily up and down, making the horse dance. And the music of the merry-go-round was sad, it was the sound of the ball park where people stood straight and sang to the flag, where the wind was so gentle it was like a hand on your face, and sometimes you saw the moon over the grass until someone moved it and you had to watch the game instead. It was the sound of the men at the ball park whose voices called Coke and hot dogs and beer and peanuts, it was the sound of the men running out there. The feel of the wooden horses between her legs was cool like the sand on the beach when the sun is going down and it's time to go home. It was the feeling of the fun house where everything happened and moved and exploded and disappeared in the half-light; it was the sound of her mother calling, calling to her where she drew chalk pictures into the bricks of the alley to come home, because the sun was going down and dinner was ready but she never wanted to leave because she loved it and this was the last day of summer before school started because tomorrow was September. And the music of the merry-go-round slowed down and the funny fat colors turned into her mother and father, and they were smiling because she was laughing so hard on the horses, and when she got off the ride, she couldn't find them for a minute because she was so dizzy and everyone looked like maybe they could be her mother and father and she looked back at the merry-go-round, at the horses, at the man who stood by the lever, the giant metal lever that made the horses move, and he was lighting a cigarette and his face was sweating, he was wearing a dirty T-shirt and one of his front teeth was missing. And the horses were hard like wood, like all the other rides in the amusement park, like the wood of the roller coaster where they strapped you in so you wouldn't fly out and bump into the clouds or blow across the ocean to the other side of the world. And the music of the merry-go-round was the sound of young voices calling at the beach to pick up the blankets and wrap up the sandwiches, to shake the sand out of your clothes and the rocks out of your shoes, to run to the water to wash the sand off, to splash your feet in the water, to watch a bird fly away, to do everything quickly.

# Nancy Maniscalco

Born into a working class family in Queens, New York, Nancy Maniscalco won a scholarship to Goddard College from which she graduated with a degree in creative writing. She has taught writing workshops at Manhattan Community College and was part of Alix Kate Shulman's Women and Writing Group. A chapter from Maniscalco's novel *Lesser Sins* appeared in *Women: A Journal of Liberation*. She divides her time between Greenwich Village and the island of Ibiza.

## *from* Lesser Sins

### Confessions of a Venial Sinner

*In psychoanalysis the mental condition of the patient is important but still more important is the mental condition of the doctor.*

C.G. JUNG, ABNORMAL PSYCHOLOGY

The closest I ever came to a psychiatrist-patient relationship were my weekly bouts with the supreme white-collar worker: my friendly neighborhood priest. Unless, of course, Nurse Telby puts in a word for me at the psychiatric ward when ol' Father Debenedetto (Uncle Nunzie's friend's priest, no doubt) decides I'm a hopeless case and leaves.

The Most Immaculate Heart of the Virgin Mother is a really old church. All the bricks and the marble were shipped here from Italy. The ceilings are about two hundred feet high. There are these paintings of angels and saints and the Holy Ghost all over them. Along the side walls they have paintings of the Stations of the Cross. They're the story of the crucifixion of Jesus. They have *The Agony in the Garden,* when Jesus got scared and God came down and put a crown of thorns on his head. Boy, I really scream if I pick a rose and one tiny thorn pricks my finger. Then there's the three times he falls with the cross, and Saint Veronica puts this towel over his face to wipe him. Frankie told me that the Pope has the towel with the imprint of Jesus's face on it at the Vatican, and when the end of the world comes he's gonna show it to all the people, right before the Russians drop the bomb.

You should see all the genuflecting I have to do. When you walk into church, you have to dip your fingers in Holy Water (it's water blessed by the priest, but it's right from the faucet) and cross yourself and say, to yourself, "In the name of the Father, the Son, and the Holy Ghost," and bow your head each time you say a name. While you're crossing yourself, you have to kneel down on your right knee. Then you get up, and head toward your pew. When you get to the pew, you have to genuflect again, and cross yourself. After Mass, or even if you get up to go to Communion, you have to genuflect, whenever you come in or out of the pew. Plus, when you reach the center isle in front of the tabernacle, where the host is, you have to do it again. I almost forgot, you have to do it three times when the priest takes the sacrament out of the tabernacle for Communion and the altar boys ring their bells. Only, then, you have to pound (not really pound, but that's what they call it) your heart and say, "My Jesus, have mercy." If you don't it's a venial sin, and you'll be punished.

My favorite pictures are the ones on the windows. They're called *The Joyful Mysteries. The Annunciation* is the best. It shows this angel coming down and he tells Mary that she's with child. There's a bunch of doves flying around and she's grinning like crazy. The next picture is *The Visitation.* That's when Mary visits her cousin Elizabeth, and they're sitting around having coffee. Elizabeth's husband, the rabbi, tells Mary that she's going to have the King of the Jews. They're all very happy.

In the back of the church, there's a statue of Mary, it's called *The Immaculate Conception.* She's always dressed in pale blue. Sometimes when people get married, the bride gives her bouquet to the statue. It's really very dramatic, and I usually get the chills, unless the bride is really corny about it.

The candles on the altar give the church a waxy smell. My nose gets clogged up when I wait on line for the confessional. We have to stand, girls on one side of the confession box, boys on the other. The priest sits inside the wooden box on a little stool. He turns from side to side, boy, girl, boy, girl, all day long. The confessionals are dark, so you can't see the priest, I guess. He's supposed to be taking the place of God, so if you saw him close up, you'd be dead or in heaven. Frankie says the confessionals look like coffins standing up.

## The First

There was a girl in my class named Lynn Krutz. She pissed on the floor of the confessional. It was the day we were making our first confession for our first Holy Communion. The fat ladies who take care of the priest's house had to bring buckets of some green stuff to clean it up. I was waiting to go to confession, and started laughing. I knew I'd have to confess laughing in church; that's a venial sin. Catholics are not too big on laughing. I remember thinking, I have so many spots on my soul, it must look like the sift, that's short for syphilis, the disease you get from sex, and dirty stuff.

Wouldn't you just know I had to go to Father Benchslinger? He is the oldest, dumbest priest in the world. He talks real loud, and can't hear a thing. It must have been him and not poor Lynn who pissed on the floor, I thought, and then giggled. But Lynn was the type. She threw up at least three times a week in our classroom. She wets her lips and sits there all sick-looking, while the nun glares at her real nastily. Then, blah! She vomits all over the place.

Then the next Sunday, after our first confession, on the day of our first Holy Communion, Lynn fainted in church. She was sitting in front of me, and all of a sudden I heard a thud and looked over the bench. There she was. First I thought she was dead. Her crinolined white dress was standing up over her face. The whole church could see her panties. I started to laugh. Three nuns came over. They genuflected and picked her up. Then they genuflected again, still holding Lynn. Lynn's hoop hit the floor and her dress flew up. They got up and carried her up the aisle and out. Boy, was she pale. She probably got yelled at for making a loud noise when her head hit the pew. Catholics don't like noise.

Anyway, back to the confession box. I was whispering, so ol' Benchslinger says, "What? Speak up!" He screamed so the whole damn church heard.

"I lied!" I shouted, and it echoed through the church.

"Your penance will be two Our Fathers and three Hail Marys!"

When I came out of the confessional, my friends were laughing like crazy. I went up to the altar, knelt before the Blessed Mother, and said my penance. I knew then that I wasn't going to like this confession stuff.

The general consensus of my fellow confessors was: all you have to do is say, "I missed Mass. And I lied." The priest never asked what the lie was, so it could be that you cursed or some mortal sin like that.

## The Foremost

The most traumatic test for my swiftly moving mouth came each year on Good Friday (to this day, I can't figure out what's so good about it). Between the hours of 3 and 6 P.M., all good Catholics are supposed to observe Christ's demise on the cross by silence. I'm still counting my lucky stars I wasn't hanged for being a traitor, what with my inevitable snickers, whispers, or coughs during the Pledge of Allegiance every morning. Not to mention my anxiety at not wanting to offend God on the day his son was killed (by the Jews, or was it the Romans?). You see, to speak during this time is a mortal sin. For the nonbelievers, a mortal sin is the sin of all sins. If somebody dies with a sin of this kind on their soul, they go directly to HELL. You do not pass purgatory, you do not collect two hundred dollars, and you do not have hope of salvation. Catholics are very unforgiving.

I would have to sit in church with my classmates and the nun in charge, in total silence. On one occasion, I managed to remain close-mouthed for two hours. I kept repeating the "Gettysburg Address" to myself. I was up to "testing whether this nation or any nation so conceived and so dedicated can long endure . . ." when Diane Proccocino nudged me. She mumbled something I thought at the time was important, and I lost my senses, once again, and spurted, "What?" Next thing I heard were Sister Veronica's rosary beads clinking together. Nuns are like cats; they saunter and stalk. When we were still wearing taps, they had rubber "souled" shoes. My ears were attuned to the clink of those beads. Thank heavens, 'cause the way they come up on you, you could have a heart attack.

As a matter of fact, I know at least twenty people who still stutter at the sound of clinking rosary beads. Sister Veronica proceeded to grab my ear and pull me up from my seat. She gave me a deadly look, dragged me over to her pew, pushed me down on my knees and, still holding my ear, went on with her prayers. Eventually she let go. I wasn't sure, since the pressure had numbed my ear, but I saw her make the sign of the cross. I don't believe this, but I once heard of a nun who moonlighted at a jewelry store. The owner claimed that her method of pinching was far better than any anesthetic in numbing ears for piercing.

At six o'clock on the dot, she turned to me and said, "Miss Mauceri, you will have to go to confession tomorrow."

"Yes, Sister," I said.

She then advised me of my rights. "If you don't go to confession, you will not be able to receive Holy Communion on Easter Sunday."

I stood perfectly still as she towered over me. I nodded at all the right times. Then I did it.

"Sister, I was supposed to go shopping for my Easter shoes tomorrow . . . maybe?"

She had the kind of complexion that became Crayola crayon red when she was angry. She spoke in a whisper, and her voice had a steady terrifying hum.

"You cannot receive the Holy Sacrament on Easter if you do not confess. You want to buy Easter shoes?"

I nodded, thinking there was hope.

"Christ's feet were nailed to the cross on Good Friday, for you and your sins."

I peeked up long enough to see the vividly painted feet of our church's Christ on the cross. It was like a childhood nursery character, like Winnie-the-Pooh. She shook her finger and her head, then went on.

"And you are concerned with shoes? Our God, Jesus (she bowed her head, then continued), died for your sins, and you want to buy shoes."

I retaliated with tears. "No, Sister, I'm going to confession . . . tomorrow, first thing."

She made one last gesture (just in case), "If you dare not receive Communion on Easter, you will be excommunicated."

I stuttered, "Yes, Sister, thank you, sis . . . ter" She turned, and I watched her walk all the way up the aisle. Then she genuflected, splashed herself with Holy Water, and vanished.

I knew my Holy Saturday would be spent standing in line with all the old people who went to confession once a year, on Holy Saturday. The church was like Macy's on Christmas Eve. The last-minute confessors dressed in black, all the statues draped in purple, and me. I thought of not going. Then I thought about the repercussions such an act would have for me. Such rebellion could mean only one thing: instant, irrevocable excommunication. I could imagine myself having to write on employment applications, under religion: EXCOMMUNICATED. So there I'd stand, my feet aching, my sinuses clogged, in the stuffy church, waiting to be absolved.

Father Debenedetto's head is hung. He's praying like crazy. Every time I glance over I catch the reflection of the lamp on his scalp. I've never seen a perfectly bald priest before. He probably never took his vitamins. At least that's what Aunt Dora would say.

Looking at him, sitting there with his head shining and his hands clasped, and his lips moving, I feel sorry for him. And, as usual, I feel like laughing.

The same year, while I was still in Sister Veronica's class, I got more trouble. There was this rumor going around about this gang, the Baldies. I didn't start the rumor—Frankie did! He told me they were coming around to our neighborhood, and they were going to take over the school. He said they carved their names into girl's chests, and raped nuns. Well, at first, I didn't believe him. I thought he was trying to scare me, like when we watched horror movies, and he'd make me scream.

The next day I was sitting in class, and Sister Veronica looked real nervous. The Mother Superior, Sister Mary, came into our classroom, and called Sister Veronica out into the hall. Diane Proccocino nudged me, "I don't think it's really Sister Veronica . . ."

"What do you mean?" I said.

"I heard that gang, the Baldies, are gonna take over the school. I heard they're kidnapping the nuns, and dressing up in their habits, and taking over the classrooms!"

"Don't be . . ."

"No really, did you see her face today? She doesn't look like Sister Veronica," she said, her eyes bulging out of her head.

My stomach started doing tumblesaults.

"Yeah, the way she was facing the blackboard all morning. Like she didn't want us to see. Oh, Diane, I'm scared. We'd better tell the other kids."

Diane started crying, and my eyes began to fill up. The lunch bell rang.

"Let's get out of here," I screamed. "Sister Veronica isn't Sister Veronica! She's a Baldy and . . ."

The entire class scrambled, and ran out into the hall, and down the rickety steps, and out into the street.

"Yeah, that's right they kidnapped her . . ." I pronounced. The kids ran off in all directions. "Run!" I screamed, completely out of control.

When I got home I told my mother about all the trouble at school.

"What kind of story is that?" she said.

"Mom, it's not a story, it's true. Please don't make me go back there. Please, Ma."

My mother grabbed my arm, and before I could swallow my peanut butter sandwich, she carted me off to school. As we turned the corner, I was shocked. The streets were packed. It looked like open school day. Frankie was standing on the corner. He ran up to my mother.

"Ma, Denise got the whole school in an uproar! None of the kids want to come back. All the parents are here. Sister Veronica and Mother Superior want Denise in the auditorium right now."

"You liar!" I screamed. "I didn't start anything! You did!"

"I'm not even in your class. How could I?"

"Stop! Denise, come with me. You too, Frankie."

The auditorium was full. Sister Veronica and Mother Superior were on the stage. They were standing by the flag. Mom dragged us up to the stage. Everybody was whispering and talking.

The nuns ran backstage as soon as they saw us. "Well, young lady, what do you have to say for yourself?" Sister Mary, the Mother Superior, said.

I was crying, "I didn't start the whole thing. I just . . ."

"You better not lie, Denise. You'll have to go to confession," Sister Veronica said.

"Well . . . I . . ."

"Denise, you'll have to go out onto the stage and conf . . . I mean . . . tell the children you lied."

The next thing I knew my mother had me by the arm, and Sister Veronica had my car. They carried me out onto the stage. I was crying like crazy.

"Denise has something to say," Sister Mary said, pushing me to the front of the stage.

I stood, knees knocking and tears flowing, I looked out into the crowd of faces, especially Diane's, and said, "I lied!"

## The Last

On the Good Friday before my nineteenth birthday I made my last confession. It wasn't in the form of last rites, obviously. I was attending night school and learning, via Mr. Biasi, in Social Psychology 101, what constitutes an attitude. He informed me that of all minority groups, women are the most easily recognizable victims of prejudice. Mr. Biasi had an uncanny grasp for the obvious. I was an apprentice bohemian and boarding with my best friend Tina Caralanza.

I got off the bus on 57th Street in Manhattan and walked up the stone steps to the big apple of churches, Saint Patrick's Cathedral. Why would a budding existentialist go to confession? Don't ask. I told you, they had me. I tiptoed past the wax mannequin of Pope Pius something or other. The lines at the confessional were short for Good Friday. Anyone who didn't confess today would be excommunicated. I strained to disregard my new-found moral affiliations, and to remember my sins.

I stammered over the Act of Contrition and spoke:

"Bless me, Father, for I have sinned. My last confession was . . . ah, one year ago." I caught a glimpse of his face; he looked like a hardened criminal through the thinly barred partition. I imagined myself as a gun moll, visiting her lover. Preferably, James Cagney or some good bad guy like him.

"I missed Mass." As I waited for a response, I felt a twitch in my privates. It reminded me of my unclean thoughts and how I put my fingers down there. I knew it was wrong, but it felt so good. I'd never done it before I moved away from home. I guess I didn't think it was so bad after all.

"I prolong kissed," I said, fighting a battle against an insane urge to laugh. I thought of Tom breathing heavily and grinding his penis. How good it feels, I thought. I suddenly felt ridiculous. I started grinning.

He shouted, "You're all alike."

I wondered how he knew I was Italian. Must have been the orange kerchief. He couldn't mean what I was thinking. How could he know?

He roared, "Women are the root of all evil!"

I was mesmerized by the sheer contempt in this man of God's eyes.

"All alike, shameless! Tempting men, sinners."

I was paralyzed.

"Leave this confessional!"

Unconsciously or self-consciously, I crossed myself. I stumbled out of the confessional in time to hear the echo of his last words:

"Leave this confessional!"

For the next few months I dreaded opening my mailbox for fear of finding a very formal, gold-embossed, handwritten scroll proclaiming me EXCOMMUNICATED. When it didn't arrive, I realized the full concept of excommunication. It's from within. You excommunicate yourself. And I did. Every time I felt the twitch.

# DRAMA

◆

# Introduction

In the last decade, there has been a vigorous and notable burst of dramatic works from young Italian American women playwrights, some of which have been presented by companies like New York City's Forum of Italian American Playwrights and Il Teatro del Rinascimento, whose stated interests and aims are to showcase playwrights and theatrical artists of Italian American heritage and to stimulate interest in and exploration of the Italianate identity. Both groups have been receptive to the work of women, and Cleveland resident Rosemary Terango's *October Bloom* and *Her Mother's Daughter* have been staged in New York, as well as work by Anne Paolucci and dramatizations of John Fante's fiction by actress Rosemary De Angelis.

Dorothy Fields's *Poppa* was one of fifteen plays (out of thousands of entries) which were selected to be staged at the National Playwrights' Conference at the Eugene O'Neill Theatre Center in O'Neill's hometown, Waterford, Connecticut. Born Dorothy Gentile in the Italian community of New York's East Harlem, Fields has written a warm and humorous tribute to growing up Italian in America.

Rose Grieco's tribute to her heritage was the three-act play *Anthony on Overtime*, staged to critical acclaim at the Blackfriars Theater in New York during the 1961–62 season. This was followed by *Daddy, Come Home* at the same theater in 1962–63.

Donna DeMatteo is an active playwright and teacher of playwrighting at
the HB Studio in New York. Among her plays are *The Silver Fox, Rocky
Road, The Ex-Expatriate*, and *There She Is, Ms. America*.

Anne Paolucci is a talented writer who has worked in every genre, including playwriting. While she was a Fulbright Professor at the University
of Naples, her three-act play *The Short Season* was produced in Italy; a
one-act play, *Minions of the Race*, was staged three times and in 1972 won
the drama award of the Medieval and Renaissance Conference.

Rosemarie Caruso's play *The Suffering Heart Salon* won an award and
was showcased in Los Angeles in 1983. Her first play, *Shadows of the
Morning Moon*, was written while she studied with playwright Karen Malpede. It is Rosemarie Caruso's feeling that the activity in drama by women
of Italian American background is due to their grounding in the real and the
tangible—they like to see and hear what is going on between people; they
like the clash of dialogue; they like the sheer relief of expressing their
feelings *aloud*. After the silence, they want to be heard. Men, she says,
present points of view, and then rebuttals. But women want to explore and
probe into feelings, and dramatizing them feels natural to them.

There does seem to be a natural attraction to the theater on the part of
Italian American women: Virginia Giordano is a theatrical producer, and
Nina Faso was coproducer of the spectacular and enduring *Godspell*.

---

# Michele Linfante

---

M ichele Linfante was born in Paterson, New Jersey in 1945. She moved
to San Francisco in 1969 where she has worked in the theater as ac-
tress, director, and playwright. She has been awarded a National Endowment
Playwriting Fellowship and her one-act play, *Pizza* was first published by
West Coast Plays, a project of the California Arts Council. Currently Michele
Linfante is writing devotional poetry inspired by her meditation practice.

# Pizza

## CHARACTERS

GRACE INNOCENTI: A woman of thirty.
PIZZA LADY: A pizza deliverer.
LENA INNOCENTI: Grace's mother.
SADIE PETRILLO: An older lady and crony of Lena's.
BONSEY: A punk in the original fifties style.
PERLA THE EXOTIC: A Latin nightclub performer.

## SETTING

The play is set in Grace's San Francisco apartment in the present, with flashbacks to a pizzeria in Paterson, New Jersey, in the fifties and sixties.

The apartment, which occupies one-third of the set, stage right, is realistic, whereas the pizzeria, which takes up the remainder of the playing area, is more suggestive and dreamlike.

The apartment is created by two walls with an entrance to the extreme stage right. On the upstage wall are houseplants, a case full of books, a cassette recorder, assorted objets d'art. A faded Oriental carpet is on the floor and some tasteful, handpicked wall hangings serve as decoration. A homey armchair sits in front of the bookcase and a low coffee table holds the telephone. The room is studious and comfortable.

The pizzeria walls, abutting those of the apartment, are suggested by a skeletal structure of metal bars strung with small, colored Christmas-tree lights. A larger-than-life, cartoon-style pinball machine and juke box are along the upstage wall. A shelf above the pinball machine is covered with baseball trophies. Left of the juke box is a curtained doorway to the kitchen. The metal framing angles away from this door to create the storefront. The large window holds a bright, neon "PIZZA" sign which faces the street.

Downstage from the window the metal framing creates the open door to the
street. Below the "PIZZA" sign is a counter which holds all the trappings of a
fifties' pizzeria: telephone, pizza trays, chrome napkin dispenser, large pepper shaker, etc. In the center of the pizzeria space is a table flanked by
three chrome-legged chairs.

*While the pizzeria remains in blackout the lights come up on* GRACE *who
is sitting alone in her apartment. She's dressed in layers of clothes including a robe and slippers. In the opening moments she's holding a pad and
pencil and is anxiously mulling something over. She finally puts down the
pad and dials a phone number, long distance.*

GRACE: Hello, Richard. This is Grace. I've been thinking . . . well maybe it's
not such a good idea to send ma all by herself on the plane. I mean, she's a
sick woman, you know. Yeah, I know you know. But the idea of sending
her with a note pinned on her dress is kind of callous, don't you think? It's a
long way. Can't you arrange a business trip or something and bring her
yourself? . . . Or maybe you can convince daddy to take a plane and he
could come too. . . . Yeah, I know he needs a rest. How's he doing,
anyway? That's good . . . Yeah, well make sure she brings the note from
the doctor about her medicine, and remember to pack some warm clothes.
It's not that sunny here , you know. And tell daddy not to pack any dented
cans or anything, I've got plenty of food . . . I guess that's it. Er, are you
sure there's nothing else I need to know, because I might unplug the
phone and then you won't be able to reach me for a while . . . Uh-huh,
well I guess that's all, then. All right, Richard, good night.

*As she is saying goodnight the doorbell rings.* GRACE *goes to answer the
door and there is a* PIZZA LADY *there holding a pizza. She's dressed in
black trousers and a short-sleeved white shirt. She's wearing a cap with a
winged pizza emblem and on her back is the same emblem in an oversized appliqué with a considerable wingspan, giving her an almost an-
gelic appearance when she turns around.*

PIZZA LADY: Here's your pizza. It's $6.50.
GRACE: Oh sure. (*She goes to get the money.*) You know, I don't know what
came over me tonight. I haven't ordered a pizza in years.
PIZZA LADY: Well, the moon must be in pizza tonight 'cause we sure got
plenty of orders.
GRACE: (*Nervous smile.*) Maybe that's it. I thought maybe it's because I'm a
little nervous. I'm one of those people who eat when they're nervous. I
also eat when I'm not nervous. I eat when I'm depressed. I eat when I'm
happy . . .

PIZZA LADY: Can't complain. Keeps us in business.

GRACE: It's awful cold tonight. Are you sure that jacket's warm enough?

PIZZA LADY: I got a truck full of pizzas to keep me warm.

GRACE: (*Finds her money and hands it to the pizza lady.*) Keep the change.

PIZZA LADY: (*Already out the door and offstage.*) Thanks. Good night.

GRACE: (*As she carries the pizza to the coffee table she is giving herself a lecture to calm herself.*) Nothing to be nervous about. I'm a grown-up person of indeterminate youth. My rent is paid. I have no cavities. My mother is coming to stay with me, but I can handle that.

GRACE *puts the pizza box down on the coffee table and arranges the few things beside it in an elaborate gesture of meticulousness and composure. She then goes to the bookcase and activates the tape player and we hear the strains of Erik Satie's "Trois Gymnopédies." She then sits down, composes herself, and opens the pizza box. As she opens the box the telephone in the pizzeria starts ringing and the chorus (composed of* LENA, BONSEY *and* SADIE*) is singing "Sh Boom." During the opening bars of the song the lights have also come up on the pizza set.* BONSEY *is animatedly playing the pinball machine.* LENA *and* SADIE *are seated at the table playing with a larger-than-life deck of cards.*

CHORUS: Life could be a dream. Life could be a dream.
Life could be a dream
    Sh Boom. Sh Boom.
If I could take you up to paradise up above.
    Sh Boom. Sh Boom.

LENA: (*Calling to* GRACE *over the sounds of the song and the telephone.*) Gracie. Gracie.

GRACE: (*She has gone first to the doorway then to the tape cassette to discover where the music is coming from. She responds to the call inadvertently in the annoyed voice of a twelve-year-old.*) Whaddaya want, ma?

LENA: Gracie, answer the telephone.

CHORUS: (*Continuing.*) And tell you darling you're the only one that I love. Life . . .

GRACE *finally suspects the music is coming from the pizza box and slams it shut, freezing the action in the pizzeria. As she opens it again the sounds and actions continue.*

CHORUS: . . . Could be a dream, sweetheart. Hello, hello again. Sh Boom and hoping we'll meet again.

LENA: Where is she? (*The phone keeps ringing*. LENA *goes to the counter to answer it and the song fades out during her conversation*.) Lena's Pizzeria. Yeah we got some pies left but we can't deliver anywhere tonight. We close in half an hour if you want to come down and pick up your pie. Yeah, that's right. Dominick is here, but the car got stolen. No, we didn't call the police yet. No, my son can't drop the pie off. He's the one that stole the car. (*Hopeful*.) You think so? When does the drive-in get out? (*Whining voice*.) Oh. I don' know. That car is such a junk it wouldn't make it to Hackensack. I'm afraid the engine'll blow up or somethin'. Yeah? Well why don't you call your sister and have your nephew Raymond call me as soon as he gets home. And if you want any more deliveries tell my husband to buy his son a car. All right. Yeah. Good night. (*Calling out the front door*.) Gracie!

GRACE *responds to this last call and enters the scene as a twelve-year-old*.

SADIE: (*Using all her willpower not to peek at* LENA'*s hand*.) Lena, come on. Finish this hand.

LENA: (*To* GRACE.) Where were you?

GRACE: Down by the dye house.

LENA: Down by the *river*? I *told* you not to play by the river!

GRACE: Aw, ma, nobody could drown in the river, there's too much junk in it.

LENA: Look at your clothes. They got all holes. What happened to your clothes?

GRACE: I dunno. We were just playin' with this box a rags. And then we saw our clothes were gettin' all funny. Kind of eaten up.

SADIE: She looks like a swiss cheese.

LENA: It's the *chemicals*! Go wash your hands!

GRACE: I already washed my hands. Doreen took us to her father's store and let us wash. Then she gave us ice cream and let us look at the comic books.

LENA: Why do you play with that girl Doreen?

GRACE: Is Richie back yet?

LENA: No, and I'm worried sick.

GRACE: I brought you a Chunky.

SADIE: Look, Lena. You gonna finish this hand or not? I gotta go before Sam gets home.

LENA: What are you afraid somebody's gonna steal all your money? Don't go yet. Dominick will walk you home. (*To* GRACE.) Where's your father? (*To* SADIE.) Stay and have some pie. (*Phone rings*. *She runs to answer it*.) Yeah, this is Lena. We only make one size. A dollar ten. We got a half-and-half pie with anchovies and a combination with peppers and sausage, or peppers and mushrooms or mushrooms and pepperoni . . . or you can get a garlic pie with just tomatoes and garlic or a zombie with everything on it, that's two and a quarter. (*Pause*.) Yeah, well I'm sorry. We're closin' for the night. We only got two pies left and we're gonna eat them. Call back tomorrow.

*Towards the end of the phone conversation,* GRACE, *who has gone over to the pinball machine, gets into a fight with* BONSEY *which overlaps the last part of* LENA's *conversation.*

BONSEY: Get your elbow off the machine.

GRACE: I didn't do anything.

BONSEY: I was hittin' sixty-five thousand on the fourth ball. That coulda been the week's top . . .

GRACE: Not a chance. Deeker got the week's top. Ninety-five thousand.

BONSEY: Who aksed you, pimple brain?

GRACE: Except for Richie. He got ninety-eight thousand but that don't count 'cause he lives here.

BONSEY: You busted my streak.

GRACE: I didn't do nuthin'.

BONSEY: Tell your mother to give me another dime.

GRACE: I'll tell her you won last week 'cause you put a matchbook under one a the legs.

BONSEY: Shut your mouth, half pint.

GRACE: Who you callin' a half pint? Ya half wit.

LENA: Shaddup, both a you. Bonsey, you go home now.

BONSEY: Come on, Lena. I was on a streak till a certain adolescent messed it up.

GRACE: You're crazy.

LENA: (*Shouting and shutting them both up.*) No more games tonight!

GRACE: (*To* BONSEY, *sheepish and conspiratorially.*) She's in a bad mood 'cause Richie's missin'.

LENA: Aaaaaa . . . (*She bites her hand in a rage.*)

BONSEY: Awright. I'm sorry, Lena. I'm goin'. I'm goin'.

LENA: (*To* GRACE.) What do you fight with that moron for?

GRACE: (*Quiet and angry, wronged.*) I wasn't doin' anything.

LENA: (*Going over to* SADIE.) There's men fightin' and dyin' in stupid wars all over the world and these kids are gonna wind up just like them and there's never gonna be any peace unless people learn how to talk to each other.

SADIE: These kids today are no good.

LENA: I got no more patience. I see them fight and I want to break their heads. (*Phone rings*.) Dominick. Is he still upstairs? (*Phone keeps ringing*.) Gracie, you better get that.

GRACE: (*Answers the phone, singing to the tune of "Bella Ciao."*)

> It comes with sausage and pepperoni,
> and extra cheese if you please,
> on your pizza pie.
> It's hot and tasty
> That's why we're crazy
> About our pizza pies.
>
> (*Lena turns to look at her.*)
>
> Oh yes we're crazy.
> Our future's hazy.
> But there's one thing for sure
> That our sauce is pure.
> My mother made it.
> Sometimes I hate it.
> And I'd like to run away.*

*She hangs up the phone ready to run as* LENA *gets up and goes towards her.*

LENA: What did ya do that for?

SADIE: Look, Lena, I gotta go.

LENA: Don't go yet. Dominick will walk you home. (*To* GRACE.) Where's your father? (*To* SADIE.) Stay and have some pie. Gracie, put a pie in the oven with a lot a garlic like Sadie likes.

SADIE: No, I shouldn't stay. I dunno if I want any pizza.

LENA: Come on. You want a little glass a wine.

SADIE: No . . . Well, maybe just a little glass.

LENA: And a slice of pizza.

SADIE: Well, maybe just a little slice.

LENA: With a lot of garlic.

SADIE: And some anchovies, maybe?

LENA: (*Calling into the kitchen.*) Put some anchovies on the pie, Gracie.

SADIE: And some peppers?

LENA: And some peppers.

*© 1980 by Marga Gomez.

SADIE: (*Calling into the kitchen*.) And don't cook it too crispy 'cause I can't eat it so good.

LENA: (*Returning to the table with a glass of wine*.) You know, Sadie, as much as you eat, that's too much work for one tooth. Why don't you take some of that money from under your mattress and buy yourself a set of teeth. (*Phone rings*. GRACIE *appears from the kitchen and answers it*.)

GRACE: City Morgue.

LENA: (*Frantic, thinking it's the city morgue calling about her son*.) What?

GRACE: You kill 'em, we chill 'em.

LENA: (*Shouting at her daughter for fooling her*.) Shut up!

GRACE: Actually this is Lena's Pizzeria. Home of the world famous Zombie Pizza. Oh, hi, Raymond. Yeah, she's here. Ma, it's Ray Donato.

LENA: (*Grabbing the phone*.) Raymond, were you out with Richie tonight? (*Pause*.) Was Gabe with you? . . . What about Gene Cherini? . . . When was the dance over? And you didn't see any of them? . . . You wouldn't lie to me would you, Raymond? (*Curtly*.) Yeah. All right, never mind. Yeah, goodbye.

GRACE: You think we should call up Missing Persons and they could send out a search party?

LENA: *Be quiet!*

SADIE: (*Now she's getting mad*.) This game's no good anymore. You don't want to come and play 'cause I'm winnin'.

LENA: You probably got all my cards memorized by now. Why don't you finish the game yourself?

SADIE: You can't talk to me like that. What are you mad at me for? You think you can buy me off with a piece a pizza.

LENA: (*Coming back to the table, nervous and distracted. Whining*.) I don't wanna finish the game. I can't concentrate. Maybe Gracie wants a finish or we could play three-handed scope.

GRACE: I don't feel like it.

LENA: (*Nervous, as if stalling for time*.) Why doncha tell us your story, then?

SADIE: What story?

LENA: What story? Your one story. The one about the devil. (GRACE *ad-libs a grimacing remark and attempts to go back to her chair but her mother pulls her over*.)

SADIE: Oh . . . in that case, lemme see. Are you sure that pizza's not gettin' too crispy?

GRACE: I just put it in.

SADIE: Jeez. The time I saw the devil. Can you imagine? It was after my first son was born and my mother was still alive, God bless her. My mother was a saint. I still get masses said for her. How she suffered, poor woman. She never liked Sam, you know. He's the one person she called an *imbecile*. (*With an Italian accent*.) She never said that about anybody. She was such a good woman.

LENA: (*Prompting her*.) Go ahead. Tell us the part about the devil.

SADIE: I'll get to that part. Where was I?

GRACE: Your mother was callin' Sam an imbecile. (*English pronunciation*.)

LENA: It was after your first son was born.

SADIE: Ohhh. An' I got so sick. And in them days they didn't have any medicines like they do now. An' I swelled up like a gourd and I couldn't get outta bed. An' I couldn't eat to save my life. Er, are you sure that pie won't burn?

GRACE: I put it on the top shelf and turned the oven off.

SADIE: An' there was snow outside higher than the doorway. And the wind was bangin' at the windows.

GRACE: (*Incredulous*.) I never heard the part about the snow before.

LENA: Shhh.

SADIE: An' I had such a fever I got so I couldn't see nothin' even with my eyes open. An' I closed my eyes for a minute and I opened 'em an' that's when I saw him.

GRACE: The devil.

SADIE: Standin' at the foot a the bed no farther away than you are now.

GRACE: What did he look like?

SADIE: He looked like a man who was too handsome to be any good. An' he was wearin' a red suit and his hairy arms were reachin' out to me.

GRACE: How could you tell his arms were hairy if he had a suit on? Did he have a pitchfork?

SADIE: No, I don't remember seein' no pitchfork.

GRACE: What did he do?

SADIE: He told me to come with him. He said "Veni qua," and pointed his hand at me. I said, "No," and he got mad an' he said it again. "Veni qua," an' he looked right at me with his black eyes like a couple a coals an' I tried to reach my throat for my crucifix but my arms wouldn't move . . . An' then he opened his cape an' he was naked as a red devil.

GRACE: I thought he had a suit on.

LENA: Shhh.

SADIE: An' I said, "Go away, devil." An' I closed my eyes and started to pray but I felt myself gettin' pulled by my feet to the foot a the bed an I musta wet my pants 'cause I felt wet—down there, y'know—an' I heard a sound like spit on a hot stove. And I made the sign a the cross inside my mouth with my burning tongue an when I opened my eyes I looked right at that devil an' said "*No*." The bed shook but he started movin' away an' the last thing he said to me was, "Tu sei più forte di me . . . you're stronger than me."

GRACE: I never knew the devil spoke Italian.

SADIE: Sure, what do you think?

GRACE: Did the sheets get burned?

SADIE: Black as coal, an' they never did come clean, either.

LENA: Get the pie outta the oven Gracie.

*GRACE goes to get the pie while PERLA enters to the sound of a low wolf whistle from outside. She's in spiked heels and flamboyant clothes.*

SADIE: Speak of the devil.

PERLA: Aren't they a little young to be hangin' around at this hour?

LENA: (*Goes to the door and calls out.*) Bonsey, go home before I call your mother.

PERLA: Are you still open?

LENA: We're closin' up but come in. We were just goin' to have a pie.

PERLA: I thought I'd see if I could get a pizza to take upstairs and maybe rest a minute.

LENA: (*Motioning her to sit down.*) You want a soda? (*Calling back to the kitchen.*) Gracie, bring a couple a sodas, too. (*To SADIE.*) This is the new neighbor from upstairs.

*At this moment GRACE enters with the things from the kitchen and as the action slows down or freezes for a second she acknowledges this new memory, quietly, with a half laugh, as she reminisces.*

GRACE: You too, huh, Perla?

LENA: (*To PERLA.*) What's your stage name again?

PERLA: Perla the Exotic.

LENA: This is Sadie Petrillo from across the street.

PERLA: Pleased to meet you.

SADIE: (*Very close-mouthed and disapproving of PERLA.*) Hello.

LENA: Perla's a dancer. She toured in South America and everything. (*SADIE lets out a whimpering harrumph. To GRACE.*) Did you put the cheese away? (*GRACE nods.*) We gotta put the sauce away too. An' take out the garbage. Where's your father?

GRACE: Last time I saw him he was upstairs calling in the numbers.

LENA: (*Giving GRACE a high sign with her face behind PERLA's back to be quiet.*) Sta zit. (*Which means "be quiet" in Italian. Then to PERLA to make sure that she didn't understand.*) Er . . . you don't speak Italian, do you?

PERLA: No. But a lot of people think I look Italian. Do you think so?

LENA: Oh yeah, yeah, you could be. But you're not, huh?

PERLA: No. My father was Spanish, Castilian. My mother is Puerto Rican. (*SADIE lets out another disapproving whimper.*)

LENA: (*Brusquely, to* SADIE.) Well, what are you doin' just sittin' there. Eat your pie.

GRACE: Eugene next door is Spanish.

PERLA: Oh.

GRACE: He never goes out anymore since the time he tried to drown himself in the river. But he had on t his bulky jacket that made him float until they fished him out, right, ma?

LENA: (*Reminded to be anxious again.*) Don't talk about the river. Look what time it is and your brother's not home yet. Go get your father. (GRACE *leaves to go upstairs. To* PERLA.) Have a piece of pie. Go ahead.

PERLA: Well I was thinking of ordering one.

LENA: Have some of this. It's for us. It's got peppers and garlic. You like garlic?

PERLA: Yeah, sure. Have you got any forks?

LENA: Forks? Eh, sure, if you like. I'll get you one.

PERLA: No. Don't get up. I'll get it. Where are they?

LENA: There are some on the counter back there. (PERLA *gets up and sashays back to the counter.* SADIE *leans over to look at her ass.*)

SADIE: Guarda che culo. (*Loosely translated, "Look at that ass."*) Pizza with a fork like a real American. (*Said with an Italian inflection.*)

LENA: (*To* SADIE *curtly.*) So, what's the matter with your pizza? Is it too crispy, or what?

SADIE: (*Tartly.*) Yeah.

LENA: Then dip it in your wine. Or eat the middle part. It's soft in the middle like the brain of an old woman. (PERLA *returns with a fork and sits down.* GRACE *returns.*)

GRACE: Daddy fell asleep listenin' to the baseball scores. Not only that, but Richie is takin' a shower and the car is parked across the street.

LENA: (*Incredulous.*) No! (GRACE *nods.* LENA *goes to look out the door for the car.*) He musta sneaked upstairs. (*Angry whine.*) Oh, I could kill him. He had me so worried.

SADIE: (*She is starting to grill* PERLA *before* LENA *swoops in.*) Do you let your mother see you dressed like that?

PERLA: My mother knows I'm in show business.

SADIE: You Catholic?

LENA: (*Bustling.*) You finished with your wine, Sadie? You finished with your pizza?

SADIE: (Still to PERLA.) You married?

LENA: (*Hustling* SADIE *out.*) Here, I'll wrap up a piece for you to take home with you. Gracie, bring some wax paper for Sadie.

SADIE: (*Putting her sweater on.*) You told me Dominick would walk me home.

LENA: Yeah, well I don' wanna wake him up now or he'll get started with Richie and wake up the whole neighborhood. (*She looks out the door.*) Hey you, Sheik? What are you still waitin' around for? You walk Sadie home and I'll give you some free games on the pinball machine tomorrow.

SADIE: Lena, you wanna gimme another little piece a pie for my breakfast tomorrow?

LENA: (*She rushes to wrap up another piece of pie from the tray.*) Sure. You want one or you want two?

SADIE: Naw, one's enough . . . er, well, all right. Two. Maybe one with anchovies.

LENA: Yeah, I got it. (*She brings the pizza to* SADIE, *who is still hanging back at the door.*)

SADIE: You sure it's all right to go home with this kid?

LENA: What are you talkin' about? I know these boys like I know my own son. (*Thinking of her son immediately inspires her whining anger again.*) Oh that lousy punk! Wait'll I get my hands on him.

SADIE: All right, I'm goin'. I'll see ya tomorrow. (*She goes out.*)

LENA: Good night, Sadie. (*Calls after her.*) Don't forget to dip it in your milk if it's too crispy. .

SADIE: (*Off.*) Go on.

LENA: (*To* PERLA.) You want to hear some music? Put the juke box on, Gracie, and lock the door. (*She comes to sit down.*)

PERLA: You look as tired as I feel.

LENA: Yeah, I'm always tired lately. Anyway, I think I was born tired. My mother used to call me sheep-eyes because I always had such dreamy eyes. An' my husband still jokes about when he used to come and take me out and he'd hear her yell, "He's comin'. Go wake her up."

PERLA: You do have beautiful eyes.

LENA: Oh, you should have seen them when I was a girl and I'd put on makeup, you know. And with my dark hair, it was long then. Once at the World's Fair in New York they gave me a card to take a screen test.

PERLA: No kidding? Well, I can believe it. What did you do?

LENA: I didn't do anything. I was stupid. Backwards. You know. I never called up.

PERLA: Have you still got the card?

LENA: What for?

PERLA: You could still call up. It's never too late.

LENA: (*Titillated, opening up in a big smile.*) Go on.

PERLA: You got to follow all those leads. You never know what somebody can do for you 'til you find out. I've been in a few movies myself, kind of like an extra.

GRACE: You know how to cha-cha?

PERLA: Yes, but that's not the kind of dancing I do in the shows. I do this special act with fancy costumes. Feathers and sequins. They cost plenty, let me tell you. And I sing, too. Would you like to be in show business when you grow up?

LENA: Gracie, do your Jimmy Durante impersonation for Perla.

GRACE: Maaa, I haven't done that since I was little.

LENA: Then do the Sid Caesar, or the Bette Davis. "Peter darling." Go ahead. She does it so good. (GRACE *shakes her head no.*) Come on, Gracie. Do it for Perla. She does stuff like that all the time in front of the mirror on the cigarette machine. Come on, Gracie. You do it so good.

GRACE: (*To* PERLA.) I wrote a poem, if you want to hear it.

PERLA: Why sure.

GRACE:  Life is a two-pronged fork
        With space in between
        Life is a cold butter knife,
              rather dull
        Life is a napkin ring
        An eternal type thing.

PERLA: (*To* LENA.) She's very bright, huh?

LENA: Yeah, she got skipped once, already. And she draws, too. (*To* GRACE.) Go get the sketch you did of Pinochle with his big mustache. And the comics. (GRACE *goes off.*) My people are all intelligent. Two of my sisters finished high school and they're both teachers. My mother always used to say, "I'd rather be bad than stupid. If you're bad, you can always move to another town. But if you're stupid, people know it as soon as you open your mouth." (GRACE *comes back with various pizza boxes.*)

GRACE: (*Showing* PERLA.) There's comics in this one and this one. This is the little match girl and this one's a story about Niccolina; she's a wicked girl scout who's mean to everybody all the time and she gets hit by a car. See, these are her legs under the car. I've been practicing how to draw cars. This one's an Impala. This is old stuff, the animals in the movie house and the talking peppers. And this is a paper doll I made and these are all her clothes. They don't fit so good now 'cause I got mad one time and ripped her in half and now she's got all this Scotch tape around the waist and she can't really wear two-piece outfits anymore.

PERLA: You're really good. I should have you design some of my costumes sometime.

GRACE: No. I don't know. I don't design clothes anymore really. I'm getting ready to throw all this stuff out.

PERLA: Are you sure? I'm working on this new act and I've got to come up with something really special, you know. (*She is pulling them in to her with her energy.*) It's got to be a costume that when you come out on stage in the nightclub you can hear their eyeballs fall in their glasses. Now it's a challenge to design a good costume when all the clubs really want to show is your body, let's face it. But I got this idea for a number and the costume is going to be important.

LENA: Well, what do you need? Maybe I could think about it too?

GRACE: Yeah, she's good at that stuff.

PERLA: Well, you know Sonja Henie the ice skater, right?

GRACE: I *love* her movies.

LENA: She's got a fat face though, doncha think?

PERLA: Well, it's going to be like a Sonja Henie number, except without the ice.

GRACE: (*Excited.*) Oh, I do that all the time. (*She jumps up and "ice skates" around.*)

LENA: Yeah, that's how I get her to polish the floors when we wax 'em.

PERLA: Then you got the idea perfectly. I want to come out as an ice queen, I want to look so cold that they will have to put on their fur capes and order hot toddies. And then the number will be so *hot* that the costume will start to melt and by the end of the song they will be fanning themselves and ordering rum coolers.

GRACE: What's a rum cooler?

PERLA: You don't need to know that.

LENA: (*Thinking.*) So you want something like a big ice cube maybe.

GRACE: What's the song going to be like?

PERLA: Here, I'll show you. (*She takes* GRACE's *hand and takes her to the middle of the pizzeria. Then she goes to get* LENA *by the hand.*) You too, Lena. Play these. (*She takes maracas out of her bag.*) And when I tell you, you sing the chorus, it goes "Turn up the heat." You got that?

LENA: (*Sheepishly.*) Oh, I don't know.

PERLA: Come on, you can do it. (*She poses, readying herself for the song. She skates forward.* LENA *and* GRACE *join in and eventually get carried away by the end of the number.*)

> My story is sad.
> But I don't feel so bad.
> Romance was a thrill.
> Now it gives me a chill.
> I'll be icy 'til I meet
> Somebody who can turn up the heat.
>
> CHORUS
> Turn up the heat.
> Don't let me shiver.

Turn up the heat.
When I can quiver,
Turn up the heat
*And* raise my temperature.

You better get lost
Or you'll turn into frost
Unless you are sold
On a passion that's cold.
I'll be icy 'til I meet
Somebody who can turn up the heat.

CHORUS . . .*

LENA: Come on, Gracie. Why don't you do one of your impersonations now. Do the Jimmy Durante.
PERLA: Yeah, come on. I'd like to see it. (PERLA *and* LENA *seat themselves and* GRACE *fusses a little and then goes into her act.*)
GRACE: (*As Jimmy Durante.*) I was takin' a bath when the telephone rings . . . And I gets up and I goes to the phone . . .
LENA: I get such a kick out of this one. She looks sort of like him, don't she? She does those funny parts so good.

GRACE *hears what she says and stops, distraught. Then she runs off, back to her chair in the present. The light darkens on the pizza set and* PERLA *walks off.* GRACE *is left breathing hard, remembering this incident.*

GRACE: Don't think I'm ever gonna forget that, ma.
PERLA: (*Notices* GRACE *has run away.*) Gracie, Gracie, come back.

GRACE *finally gets up and walks back into the scene. She talks in her adult voice.*

LENA: Why did you run away like that? Why did you get so mad?
GRACE: Because you said I was ugly.
LENA: I never said you were ugly. What are you talkin' about?
GRACE: It's when I was doin' Jimmy Durante and you told Perla I looked like him.
LENA: No I didn't. I just meant you did it so good.
GRACE: I am ugly.

*"Turn Up the Heat" © 1980 by Marga Gomez.

LENA: You're not ugly. Don't talk like that. You got nice features.

GRACE: Perla's beautiful and you were beautiful and I'm ugly.

LENA: Who says I was beautiful?

GRACE: You say it all the time. Daddy says it.

LENA: (*Sheepishly.*) I wasn't so beautiful. I just wore a lot of mascara. You shouldn't think so much about beauty. Do you think beauty is every-thing? I got news for you: a lot of beautiful people are unhappy.

GRACE: Yeah, well as long as I'm gonna be unhappy, I'd rather be beautiful and unhappy.

LENA: You got brains. That's more important. And you got a good person-ality.

GRACE: That's what you always say about people who are ugly. You hate me because I'm not beautiful like you.

LENA: (*Crying.*) Don't talk like that. That's not true.

GRACE: And I hate you. I didn't ask to be born. I'm gonna die and you'll be sorry.

LENA: Don't say that. Never say that.

GRACE: Die, die, die, die. I wish you'd drop dead. (*There's a gasp between them.* GRACE *reverts to her twelve-year-old voice.*) I didn't mean it, mommy.

LENA: I never wanted to hurt you.

GRACE: I'm sorry, ma. I didn't mean it, honest. (*She goes over to* LENA.)

LENA: I'm sorry, Gracie. I didn't mean nothin'. I just meant you did it so good. I love you so much. You gotta believe me. I love you more than anything in the world.

GRACE: I know, ma.

LENA: Put the lights out, Gracie, and put the juke box on. (GRACE *goes to put the lights out.*) Come and sit by me. I like to sit here sometimes with just the light from the juke box on and the sign light from outside. It's cozy. (*Opening strains of "In the Still of the Night" can be heard faintly.*)

GRACE: Richie wants me to massage his arm. He's gotta pitch tomorrow.

LENA: Keep me company a minute. (GRACE *goes over to her.*) Gracie, let's have a Halloween party here. We can turn the lights out like this and have a stuffed dummy over in the corner. We'll make it scary. I kind of like that. To scare people, you know. Even when you and Richie were in the baby carriage I used to make those big scary eyes at you. You think that's normal?

GRACE: Probably not.

LENA: Is the oven off, Gracie? (GRACE *nods.*) We better go upstairs or I'll never get you up for school in the morning.

GRACE: (*Going into a subtle performance.*) Oh yeah, that reminds me, ma.

You know I had this funny dream that I was hit by a truck right down by
the playground on the way to school.

LENA: (*Scared; the anxious voice again.*) What are you saying? You're kid-
din' me.

GRACE: No, I just remembered. I think it was a Wonder Bread truck.

LENA: Don't go to school tomorrow! I'll write you a note.

GRACE: I really ought to go. I got that editorial due for the paper.

LENA: You can take it in on Monday.

GRACE: Well, if you say so. I think I feel a little sick anyway. You think I got
a fever? Feel my face. (LENA *feels* GRACE'*s face with her face.*)

LENA: I don't know. You feel a little warm. But you were back by the oven.

GRACE: Maybe you can make me some tea and toast tomorrow and some
Lipton soup and I'll take my blankets and go lie on the couch in the living
room . . . and you can help me write my editorial.

LENA: I thought you said you wrote it.

GRACE: It's almost done. I got the idea . . . And we can watch the afternoon
movie on Channel 5. It's a Fred Astaire movie.

LENA: I don't like Fred Astaire. He's got no sex appeal.

GRACE: Then we can play cards, and I'll draw your picture. Or we can play
Modern Art.

LENA: What's that one?

GRACE: Tessa and me invented it. I'll show you. (GRACE *wraps herself
around* LENA *in a bizarre pose, then shouts.*) Modern art!

LENA: (*Laughs, but acts annoyed and tough.*) You're chokin' me. (*They poke
at each other playfully.*)

GRACE: Gimme a kiss. Oh, let's play the kissing game and see if I can catch
you. (LENA *shakes her head slowly from side to side and* GRACE *moves
her head until she zooms in and plants a kiss: This is a game that they are
obviously familiar with.*) You're gettin' too slow. See if you can get me.

She starts shaking her head while LENA tries to plant a kiss. When they
start the kissing game the sound of "In the Still of the Night" drifts in
while the lights fade and LENA backs out of the scene. As the song fades
out GRACE slams down the pizza box and dials the phone again.

GRACE: Hello, is this Suicide Prevention? This is Grace Innocenti. I used to
work there, answering the telephones? Oh, you're new. Well I've got
this pizza over here that I can't eat and I thought maybe I could bring it
over to you. No, it wouldn't be any trouble . . . You did, huh . . . Oh,
yeah, that's all right. I could always freeze it or something . . . No, this
isn't the kind of mood I feel like sharing with a friend right now . . . Oh
no, I've just been reading too many psychology books. You read them

and you start thinking about how messed up your parents were and then you start thinking about how messed up you are and how messed up the world is and you get to feeling how you just want to crawl into somebody's armpit and feel safe, you know. And then you start thinking about all the people you've ever loved and wonder where they all are and you wonder who's going to care if you die and then you get mad and think about dying just to spite everybody that doesn't care, and you start thinking about how nobody needs you. But as soon as you find out somebody needs you you start worrying about your freedom. You know what I mean? . . . (*Repeating what the other person has said.*) You hear what I'm saying, huh? (*Sharply.*) Of course you hear what I'm saying, your phone's working, isn't it? Anyway, I just thought you might like some pizza. I better let you get back to your phones. Good night.

*During the last two lines the doorbell rings and it's the* PIZZA LADY *with another pizza.*

PIZZA LADY: Here's the pizza you ordered.
GRACE: (*Slightly bewildered.*) Thanks. (*She goes for her money again and brings it back to the* PIZZA LADY.)
PIZZA LADY: You know, it's a good thing you don't like pizza or we're liable to run out tonight.
GRACE: (*Smiles weakly.*) Yeah. Look, I'm sorry to make you come all this way again.
PIZZA LADY: It's all in the line of duty. (GRACE *pays her.*) Thanks. (*She exits.*)
GRACE: (*Calling after her.*) Be sure to lock your car door. (*Then, coming back into the room, she talks to the pizza box in a whining tone.*) What did I say that for? (*As she carries the pizza box over to the table she talks to herself in the voice of an Indian guru.*) Nostalgia is a dangerous thing. Too much mooning over the past, like too much mooning over the future, may not leave enough time for living in the present. (*She sets the pizza box down delicately and then speaks in a normal but dreamy voice to herself as she goes to open the second pizza box.*) One must, however, acknowledge certain modes of receptivity where the slightest provocation . . . a melody, a scent, the look of your own aging hand, a wad of tissue in your pocket . . . brings on the deluge.

*The lights come on in the pizza set while* LENA *summons* GRACE. *This is a quick and delicate change.*

LENA: (*Quietly.*) Gracie.
GRACE: (*From her apartment.*) What, ma?

LENA: Something's wrong with me, Gracie. I can't remember how to make the dough. (*A bowl is on the pizzeria table in front of her as if she were standing over the dough.*) I don't remember what to do. My mind is trying to tell me but it doesn't work. (*There is crying in her voice.*)

GRACE: (*Slowly enters the scene as a fifteen-year-old.*) Don't cry, ma. Maybe you're just nervous or something.

LENA: No, it's not that. That's what Dr. Pellicone says. He thinks I'm just nervous, but it's more than that. Something's happening to me, Gracie. I don't know what it is.

GRACE: Well, maybe we ought to take you to another doctor.

LENA: You think maybe I had a stroke? Is this what happens when you have a stroke?

GRACE: I don't know, ma.

LENA: They think I just complain. Nobody understands. Nobody believes me. Your father doesn't believe me. Take me to the hospital, Gracie. Something's wrong with me.

GRACE: I took you to the hospital last week. They said they couldn't take you, that you had to go through a doctor. They can't tell what's wrong.

LENA: Take me to the state hospital, Gracie. I think I'm losing my mind, Gracie.

GRACE: (*Nervous, trying to cope.*) Come on, ma, you just forgot how to make the dough. It can't be that hard. I'll help you. You showed me before.

LENA: I got this terrible feeling I can't explain. I don't understand. I'm scared.

GRACE: Don't be scared, ma.

LENA: Take me to the state hospital, Gracie. We'll get Katy's son from across the street to drive us. I've got five dollars in the underwear drawer.

GRACE: Ma, I don't want to go to the hospital again. They're shitty. They ask you all these questions and then they say they can't do anything for you. Anyway, you can't be so bad if you remember you got five dollars in the underwear drawer, right?

LENA: No, something's wrong, Gracie. You gotta believe me.

GRACE: I believe you, ma.

LENA: Promise me you'll take me to the state hospital, Gracie. Make them do something for me.

GRACE: I promise, ma. We'll take you to a specialist.

LENA: I can't make the pizza anymore. I never feel good anymore. Who's going to make the dough?

GRACE: I'll help you, ma. (*As she says this she starts backing out of the scene towards her apartment.*)

LENA: I can't clean the house anymore. I get this lousy nervous stomach all the time, I can't do anything right anymore. (*The lights eventually fade to a blackout on* LENA *by the end of their exchange.*)
GRACE: Don't cry, ma.
LENA: Do something for me, Gracie.

*The lights are up on* GRACE *standing behind her chair. She is shaken, not wanting to cry, trying to look tough. She crosses her arms in front of her and looks down at the culprit pizza box.*

GRACE: For six lousy dollars you'd think they'd at least sell you a pizza that makes you forget. (*To the pizza box.*) People pay to forget. Who wants to remember anything anymore? Who wants to feel anything anymore? What do you think I'm a chump? (*She has sat down nervously and is giving sidelong glances to the pizza box as a real enemy. Petulant and trying to sound tough.*) A person could starve trying to get a bite to eat around here.

*She goes through an elaborate strategy of trying to sneak a piece of pizza out of the box. As if stealing something, she has sneaked her hand into the pizza box and sneaked out a piece of pizza. As she raises it to her lips we hear the strains of the first lines of "Mama," a sappy Italian-American song that Connie Francis used to sing. A look of comic despair and defeat crosses over her face through this first bar of music and as she opens the box to replace the slice of pizza the second "Mama" swells out.*
*The lights come up on the pizza set, but the lighting is different to indicate a change in the place. The colored lights are dark on the outlined pinball machine and juke box, leaving just the bare construction showing. There is a large James Dean poster over the pinball machine, a cloth over the table, a colored spread over the counter to give the place a look of abandonment, of a closed resort, besides indicating that it is* GRACE'*s living space now. There is a typewriter on the table. Some books and cardboard packing boxes are scattered about.*
LENA *is standing, leaning on the table. She is stooped, aged; one arm is bent and her leg drags. She's wearing a soiled housecoat, slippers, and stockings drooping around her ankles. She has a handkerchief or a wad of paper towel in one hand that she twists nervously during the scene. It is obvious that she is sick and has deteriorated from the first scene. She has a certain bright-eyed, tic-like animation because of the medication she takes.*

LENA: Gracie, where are you? You in the bathroom? Don't squeeze your face. What are you doin'? Where are you?

GRACE: (*Entering the scene as a twenty-year-old*.) Ma, you know you're not supposed to come down the stairs by yourself.

LENA: You wanna come upstairs. Daddy bought some cold cuts.

GRACE: Not right now, I'm busy.

LENA: What are you doin'?

GRACE: I'm getting some of my things together.

LENA: "Animal Kingdom" is on.

GRACE: Yeah, so what?

LENA: Put it on and watch it with me.

GRACE: I don't want to watch "Animal Kingdom."

LENA: You know I like to watch it when the animals fight. You think that's normal?

GRACE: (*As if in disgust with the human race*.) Probably.

LENA: I like the way you got it fixed up here now, Gracie. Like Picasso.

GRACE: What do you know about Picasso?

LENA: I know. He's a painter, right. What do you think I'm stupid? (*She has been walking around, crotchety and childlike at the same time, looking at things like a visitor*.)

GRACE: All right, ma. I want you to sit down here, okay? So you don't fall down. I want to talk to you. (*She guides* LENA *to a chair*.) Did you take your medicine?

LENA: Yeah, but it don't make me feel so good anymore, this new medicine.

GRACE: Well, I was reading about it. It's all experimental, you know. They don't know that much about it. It's important that you don't take too much or you get these weird side effects.

LENA: I got to take the medicine, Gracie, or else I can't do nothin'.

GRACE: I know, I know.

LENA: Daddy got some rolls, too.

GRACE: All right, all right. I'll come up and eat later. I want to talk to you first.

LENA: Put the television on, Gracie.

GRACE: (*Getting a little angry*.) Not now, ma. In a little while. I want to have a talk with you, ma.

LENA: What's the matter? Somethin's the matter.

GRACE: Nothing's the matter, ma.

LENA: Gracie, you wanna make me a sandwich?

GRACE: That's one of the things I like about you, ma. Your dedication to the à la carte school of philosophy. "I eat therefore I am."

LENA: Yeah go on. What do you want to talk about?

GRACE: My friend Jay found me an apartment in New York.

LENA: What are you talkin' about?

GRACE: I found this great rent-controlled apartment and I'm gonna move to New York.

LENA: *You're crazy*. What do you want to move to New York for?

GRACE: Lots of reasons. I got my friends there . . . and, and there's lots of museums and lots of theatres and . . .

LENA: Lots of murders.

GRACE: Yeah, well I don't plan on getting murdered.

LENA: You're crazy, Gracie. All the relatives used to live in New York. We all left. Now you want to go back and live in New York. It's stupid, stupid.

GRACE: (*Petulant, angry*.) It's not stupid. Living in *this* dying, polluted city is stupid. Living in this dying neighborhood with its boarded-up, broken-down corner stores and its broken-down pizzeria is stupid.

*A light comes in on* SADIE *in a corner of the set. She's an apparition. Only* GRACE *sees her.*

SADIE: A girl ought to stay home and take care of her mother.

GRACE: You shut up. You're dead already.

SADIE: The devil's gonna get you.

GRACE: He should be so lucky.

LENA: (*Who hasn't acknowledged this interchange*.) Don't go, Gracie. Stay here. You don't have to pay any rent.

GRACE: Ma, I gotta live my own life. I need to . . . gather my rosebuds, sow my wild oats.

SADIE: What's she gonna do? Go live on a farm?

GRACE: I can't stay here living in a closed-up pizzeria, reading old magazines, writing letters to dead authors.

LENA: But you got it fixed up so nice.

GRACE: I want to *do* something with my life. (*Quieter, half-assured*.) I want to be a beatnik.

LENA: What do they do?

GRACE: (*Shrugging her shoulders*.) Nothin' . . . (*Brusque and defensive*.) I don't know. They write, they paint. They make love.

SADIE: She's gonna get in trouble and then she'll come back.

LENA: What do you want to move to New York for? It's so expensive. It's so much trouble.

GRACE: Give me a break, ma. Nobody sticks around here. Even Perla moved back to New York.

SADIE: At least she got married. She's respectable.

GRACE: (*To* SADIE.) She's bored.

LENA: There are no jobs. What are you gonna do? You can't find a job.

GRACE: I'll do something. Anything. You think I can't live on my own.

SADIE: She thinks she's better than everybody here in the neighborhood.

GRACE: (*To* SADIE.) Just different.

LENA: You can stay here. You don't have to pay any rent.

GRACE: Look, ma. Nobody said anything when Richie left us, right?

SADIE: That's different. He's a man.

LENA: He's got his own family.

GRACE: He got married and got his ass outta the ghetto and nobody made a fuss. He wasn't around when your brains started leakin' and we didn't know what was happening. It was me you used to talk to, right? Well my brain is leakin', ma. I've got to get out of here.

LENA: (*Whining voice.*) You won't come back. You just want to be with your friends. You'll never come back.

GRACE: Ma, it's only thirty minutes away. I can come back a lot. Or you can come and see me.

LENA: (*Still whining.*) Oh, it's so much trouble. You got to take the bus and the train.

GRACE: (*Blowing up.*) Jeezus. Life is too much trouble, right? Let's face it. I'll go turn on the gas on the pizza oven right now and we can stick our heads in it. Is that what you want?

LENA: (*Angry, sullen.*) All right. Go on, go on, go on.

GRACE: I'll come and see you a lot. I'll take the bus. . . .

LENA: Yeah, sure, sure.

GRACE: Jeez, ma. You could be happy for me.

LENA: (*Still sullen and sarcastic.*) Sure, go ahead. I'm happy.

GRACE: You don't look happy. Why don't you try and get happy about it?

LENA: (*Curt and standoffish.*) I don't feel good. I feel lousy. I never feel happy. I feel lousy.

GRACE: (*Trying to get through to her mother, who is sitting there rigid and angry.*) If you just think about it and try to accept it . . .

LENA: (*Angry and sharp.*) I don't think about nothin'. I feel lousy, that's what I think about. I think about nothin'. I feel lousy. (*More quietly.*) I'm gonna die. (*She whines on the last line and rocks back and forth in a series of short moans.*)

GRACE: (*Blows up and swats her mother impetuously on the head.*) I'm gonna die. Everybody's gonna die!

LENA: Go on, hit me. Like your father. Like your brother. Everybody hits me. (*The juke box starts playing "Mama" again; GRACE goes over and kicks it. It stops and SADIE disappears, too.*)

GRACE: (*Trying to get through to her mother, holding her shoulders.*) Ma, you're not gonna die from the Parkinson's disease. Especially now that you're taking the medicine. You just got to help yourself.

LENA: Go on. You sound like your father.

GRACE: You're just afraid to die because you never lived enough, ma. I got to go out and live, ma. I gotta find out about things. Why didn't you tell me anything, about anything? About girls. About boys. About getting married or having babies. Or being normal.

LENA: I never knew much.

GRACE: I can't stay here like this, ma. Afraid to leave the pizzeria. Being sickly all the time. Never leaving the family, like the girl next door. Like the whole family next door.

LENA: (*Whining cry.*) I want you to go, Gracie. I know it's no good for you here. I only care about you. I don't want you to be like me. I want you to go and have a good time. I want you to be happy.

GRACE: I want *you* to be happy.

*GRACE and LENA repeat this phrase, each in her own inflection, simultaneously as GRACE backs away. Lights fade on LENA. We eventually hear only GRACE's voice as she returns to her set.*

GRACE: I want you to be happy. I want you to be happy. I want you to be happy. . . . Is everybody happy? That's what I want to know. Because it seems I can't be happy unless everybody's happy. (*Looking over to pizza set.*) I know you're not happy. But it's you who got sick. I didn't make you sick. Why are you making me sick? You're making me sick, ma. I'm supposed to have it together by now. I had to leave you. Can't you see that? I couldn't hang around trying to keep you alive with every breath I take. I still do it. I keep everybody alive with every breath I take. (*The doorbell rings. She thinks it's another pizza delivery.*) Oh no. Cancel my order. No more pizzas tonight.

*The bell still rings incessantly until GRACE gets up to answer it. As she moves to the door LENA enters from the kitchen door in the pizzeria and crosses over into GRACE's apartment. She's an apparition of a younger LENA, more youthful and graceful than we have seen her in preceding scenes. Her hairstyle may be different and she is dressed in heels and a stylish, classic coat suggestive of a twenties' style. Her opening lines startle GRACE, who's standing at the open doorway.*

LENA: Hello, Gracie.

GRACE: (*Stunned.*) Ma?

LENA: What a nice place you got. Real cozy. (*She turns to GRACE, who is still dumbfounded at the doorway.*) Gracie. You should close your mouth or you might catch a fly.

GRACE: (*Starts to look suspiciously at LENA while she closes the door.*) All right, who are you?

LENA: I'm your mother.

GRACE: You are *not* my mother.

LENA: I surprised you, didn't I?

GRACE: This is crazy. Come on, who are you? What is this?

LENA: I'm telling you. I'm your mother, Lena. You were thinking about me and waiting for me, weren't you? Who, then?

GRACE: How come you're not drooling?

LENA: (*Indignantly.*) I don't feel like it.

GRACE: You're not moaning. You're supposed to moan. You're sick. You feel lousy. There should be food stains on your clothes. I don't know who you are, but you are *not* my mother. *What did you do with my mother?*

LENA: Look at me, Gracie. It's me. You want to see the mole on my neck? Remember how you used to want to bite it off?

GRACE: (*Grilling her suspiciously.*) Where were you born?

LENA: The Bronx.

GRACE: How many miscarriages did you have?

LENA: Two.

GRACE: Who won the World Series in 1955?

LENA: (*Sharply.*) How do I know? The Dodgers probably lost is my guess.

GRACE: Where do you keep your money?

LENA: Well I used to keep it in the underwear drawer but I got it all with me now. I thought maybe we could go shopping.

GRACE: (*Shouting, beside herself.*) What are you talking about? We haven't gone shopping in twenty years.

LENA: (*Calmly.*) That's why I thought it would be time for something new.

GRACE: (*Whining cry.*) Where's my mother?

LENA: Gracie. You shouldn't get so upset. I hate to see you agitated like this. What are you making a big deal about? You wanted me to be different all these years, didn't you? You're the one that always used to say anybody can be anything they want to be. If you don't peg people a certain way anything is possible. Right? Isn't that what you always say?

GRACE: Yeah . . . but *this isn't possible*. You're not like my mother.

LENA: How do you know what I'm like? Besides, I'm not all that different, I'm just more like I was before you knew me. Isn't that what you always wondered about? Who I used to be? Who I could have been? Well, here I am. And maybe tonight we could go dancing?

GRACE: *Dancing?*

LENA: Yeah, I love to dance. Before I knew you I used to like to go to Roseland Ballroom. You got someplace like that out here?

GRACE: But you're sick. You moan all the time.

LENA: Jeez, I wish you wouldn't be so morbid. I came all this way to see you and I went to all this trouble so you could see me looking good.

GRACE: (*Still stunned but wanting to accept it.*) It's a miracle.

LENA: (*Casually and skeptically.*) Maybe. Whatever you think.

GRACE: (*Dejected, skeptical.*) It's no miracle. (*Hitting on in.*) It's jet lag. That's what it is. It's some kind of cosmic jet lag . . . (*Getting anxious.*) You better go and lie down, ma. Don't you want to lie down? I'll fix up a bed for you. Don't you want to lie down and watch television?

LENA: No, I don't feel like it.

GRACE: Now look, ma, I'm gonna make your bed and I want you to lie in it.

LENA: What I might like to do is go out and take a walk, look at the sunset.

GRACE: By yourself?

LENA: And why not?

GRACE: But you never like to take walks or look at sunsets. You've never been alone in your whole life.

LENA: That's not true. Sure, I lived with my family until I got married, but when I was a girl I used to like to take long walks in Crotona Park, right near my house, especially in the winter when the snow made everything so clean and quiet. I used to wear this big brown overcoat that I loved and it was like I could look down from above and see myself standing there against the snow and think, "This isn't just the second-born daughter of the shoemaker, or the pretty one, or the lazy one, or the girl on the end of the line at the candy factory that got all the jokes a little late." I'd think, "There's a part of that girl that nobody knows. That nobody will ever know."

GRACE: (*Stunned and then grumbling.*) Yeah, well this neighborhood is kind of tough. Maybe you'd better not go out by yourself.

LENA: It don't look any worse than the Riverside. I can take care of myself.

GRACE: You might fall down or something. (LENA *is walking around the apartment and* GRACE *is following right behind her with her arms out as if waiting for her to fall down.*)

LENA: (*Turning to her daughter abruptly.*) I feel fine and I'm not gonna fall down.

GRACE: (*Whining voice exactly like her mother's in the first scenes.*) Nooo, I don't know what's going on but you're really old and sick and sooner or later you're going to fall down. (*Last lines are especially wimpy.*)

LENA: Stop it, Gracie. Stop it.

GRACE: (*Same whining voice.*) And I'm going to have to pick you up.

LENA: Yes. But why don't we worry about that when the time comes?

GRACE: (*Sits down.*) What's the matter with you? I'm worried. I'll call this friend of mine. She's a doctor. (*Picks up telephone.*)

LENA: (*Sarcastically, crossing to* GRACE.) Good, ask her if she wants to go for a walk. (*Still behind chair.*) And you should· come too, Gracie. You look a little pasty.

GRACE: (*Slams telephone down.*) What are you so anxious to go for a walk for? You just got here. I've been thinking about you all this time. I've been worried sick.

LENA: What for?

GRACE: Worrying about you. I don't know. I worry about you all the time.

LENA: Well what good does that do? You should worry about yourself. Or better yet, you shouldn't worry at all. And do me a favor, Gracie. Quit thinkin' I want your blood. Just because you're a bleeding heart don't make everybody else a vampire, you know.

GRACE: (*Looking at her mother mildly, quietly, incredulously.*) Who are you anyway?

LENA: Come on, let's not go through that again. Listen, Gracie. I smell pizza. Is that a pizza you got there? Maybe we could have a piece before we go for a walk, huh?

GRACE: You are my ma, aren't you?

LENA: That's what I been tellin' you. You got some with sausage?

*They lean down towards the pizza box together.*

B L A C K O U T

# POETRY

◆

# Severina Magni

Severina Magni was born in Lucca in 1897 and came to the United States in 1921, experiencing a hard life as a worker in a flag and banner factory. Her only known book of verse was *Luci Lontane,* in Italian, from which a poem was translated into English as "Poetry" by Rodolfo Pucelli and appeared in his *Anthology of Italian and Italo-American Poetry.* She was married to John Magni and contributed her poetry to several Italian-language periodicals but nothing more is known of her. She is emblematic of those Italian women of sensibility who came to this country, lived hard lives, wanted to express themselves, and then passed on, unheard of and unknown.

## Poetry

When in my heart resounds the tone
Of poetry, so dear and sweet,
I'm like a beggar to whom someone
Offered a necklace in the street.

I'm like a sleeper in a garden
Who wakes up at the fall of white
Petals that whisper, dance, and wander
Lightly before they, tired, alight.

I'm like a prisoner full of grief
To whom one a love-letter hands.
The jail is no more dismal, if
With harmony my heart expands.


# Pacé Nicolino

**B**orn in Barre, Vermont, in 1917 of Italian immigrant parents, Nicolino was named for peace during World War I by her Socialist father. Orphaned at an early age, she went to night school for drawing lessons and put herself through college by teaching cake decorating. She lived in the region of Italian granite workers all her life and worked as a speech therapist with handicapped children. She was also a member of the Poetry Society of Vermont for many years and is represented in the Society's anthology, *Second Harvest*. A frequent contributor to the review *Troubadour*, her poetry was often accompanied by her artwork.

## Goodbyes and Hellos

My consciousness quietly
unfolded in the super market
as if
by remote control.

Two gray heads
one, Silver Pearl No. 17
simultaneously turn,
handshakes that set
the pressure soaring,
aeronauting as if
I were handing out
my flaming heart;

That last night
of adolescent youth,
the moon ballooning,
dip-needling the clouds
spanning the cosmic display
of hidden destinies
flooded with expectancy.
We almost did—
but didn't—

Carriages filling
with beans and carrots,
honey and forbidden fruit
as we exchanged pleasantries—
the distance between
two parts of the brain
controlling them forever
on different planes
but still back-tracking
forty years.

What if we had?

## Dandelions

Out of the rain-sopped ground
I dug
enough for a salad
while
the May-like sun scorched
and
the March-like wind chilled.
In proper time
I'll brew my wine.
From gold to gray
leftovers by the millions
I'll puff away
childhood fantasies
now grown
to old necessities
rounding out a circle.

# Kathy Freeperson

Born Kathryn Telesco, Kathy Freeperson's new name reflects her rebirth as a person in her own right. She has vocally orchestrated her work as a poet for stage performance and has directed productions in Florida, where she lives, as well as other parts of the country. Freeperson writes a column for a publication of opinion and commentary for the contemporary/progressive woman called "Nobody Asked Me but I am Telling You Anyway."

# Italian Bread

Exorcise the little Italian
devil who makes fat and
mucus.
As grandma and ma
shove it towards me
in a paper wrapper still warm
from the local Italian
bread pushers.
The monster emerges from its
long envelope and rears its
ugly but beautiful crispness
and smell
warm and sweet like
blankets of childhood.
Dad rips off an end.
It heaves a visible sigh and
gives
with the sound of crisp
spilling little brown
bits of gold around the
wrapper like sand.
The white soft center yields
stretches like the soft
olive thighs of a plump
Italian.
I am trying to reduce.
This loaf has a (w)hole like a
mouth saying "oh"
like the tongue's response
when it hits slice
after slice
the hole continues
but in a little different size
dunked in gravies, juices

it gets sloppy drunk and
wavers before the
open mouth bent close to
receive it.
Soggy with the taste of whatever
else is served
and somehow against
what I know is right it
makes its way to my mouth
and the mellow ballet my
lips and teeth play
has nothing to do with
the sermon with the fishes.
These flour clouds
cannot reproduce unaided.
The last sound is the heel
of the bread that crunches like
soft glass
and that hand that pulls the rest
away before your nose
gets stuck in its shape.
My willpower disappeared like
rising dough after a poked finger.
The pillow fight is finished.

# Elaine Romaine

Elaine Romaine (née Romagnano) was born in the Bronx, New York and
now lives in Oregon where, she says, she hasn't eaten *sfogliatelle, cannoli*, or even an Italian lemon ice since moving. She was co-editor of the poetry journal *Gravida* and also taught in the Poetry in the Schools program.

She is a poet and fiction writer and her work has appeared in several journals
and anthologies. She has completed a novel, is currently working on a collection of short stories, and is the recipient of a grant to study Mary Shelley and
nineteenth century science.

# fan letter

ah marcello marcello I love you because you are Italian. No.
I love you because I am Italian and you wear it better
than me whose only green growing plant in the kitchen is a
clove of garlic suspended in water, hanging by toothpicks and
that is not wearing my Italian melancholy well if I can't laugh at
the irony and Yes I do love you and your weary mouth, your
sallow skin, your heavy-lidded visions that finally
make me laugh/love that garlic for now it can green my days,
and I can love that risible miserable symbol, that goddam
garlic. I love you marcello. you wear our Italian well. send
a glossy. I will hang it above my plant.

# Song and Dance Lady

Next to her dance of snare drum and tap
What's stillness but a minor scale?
Now eighty, still the high stepper
jiving across her backyard, this is
her way to raise hell: on its haunches
ready with the kick of a spit-and-polish
hoofer who hears the drum, the music roll,
a harmony she's not forgotten.

To the last beat she's quick with
a rowdy buck-and-wing, brisk
on the stone path, circling her yard.

This is a game where time is her rule,
where she tests like an explorer
each stunt of the heart, refusing pause,
storming the dance that arrives
from the neat center of death.

---

# you were always irish, god

---

You were always irish, god
in a church where I confessed
to being Italian.

But then St. Anthony
had a feast and lights ringed
the street as sausage and peppers
steamed in booths, gambling wheels spun
as the tenor held his stomach, pushing
a note higher. Behind a booth my brother
pitched pennies with a priest, rolling
deep fried bread sprinkled with sugar
in his mouth. The processions began.
My father and his brothers shoulder
the statue through the crowd, hymns
and feast bless the air.

And all the sights of you, god,
were wine-filled.
For these sins we took communion
the next morning, sleeping on each other
in the pews until the altar bell rang
and we filed up to the railing,
opening our mouths for your blood
and flesh. O god,
god, I confess nothing.

# Grace DiSanto

Born in Derby, Connecticut in 1924, Grace DiSanto moved to North Carolina in 1961 where she graduated from Belmont Abbey College. She resided in Morgantown with her husband and three children until her death in 1993. In addition to having been a newspaper reporter, drama critic, and feature writer, she studied with James Dickey in his poetry workshop and had over 180 of her poems published in literary journals and anthologies. *The Eye Is Single* (1982), her first collection, was judged the best poetry collection published in North Carolina that year. She taught poetry at Western Piedmont Community College and in the Poetry in the Schools programs.

## In Defense of Plath, Berryman, Sexton

I used to wonder
how they lost it,
how desperation
got so deep
they overdosed,
jumped the bridge
into fire and ice,
ribboned their brains,
unpetalled their hearts;
now as I salute pain,
the claw and pull
and snarl,
rabid clutch devouring,
understanding starts:

*As soon as one does not*
*kill oneself, one must*
*keep silent about life.*
First, they locked
their ears against screams
of survivors;
then they sewed up
their tongues to dumb
speech; next
they gouged out their eyes,
tucked them,
potato stubs, beneath
the soil to grow the
horror out of light;
last, at the stage
where their guts
spilled out each to each,
they began to choose how
and when: week, day, hour

---

# Last Supper

---

*In memory of my grandparents*

In your chiesa-large kitchen,
at the oak table where
with praise for one another,
we celebrated,
*Lord have mercy*
Christmas, Easter,
we believed,
believed you would breathe on
with time, believed
you would not die.

As we knelt, gave your
ropeveined hands the kiss
of reverence, windowglass blushed
beneath the warm sun.

From the cup,
elevated high,
we drank wine:
blood of Concord grape,
sweat of Nonno's hand;
with each other
we broke Nonna's bread,
*panis, panis angelicus*.

And happy we were
called to that supper.

Today years after your deaths,
in Milano, where Leonardo's
"Last Supper" amazes a wall,
I enter the ristorante,
find spread before me,
ritual of the past,
and an old couple,
ropeveined fingers outstretched,
approaching.

I ache to genuflect,
kiss their hands,
but then I realize
that supper,
the bread and wine of childhood,
was long ago consumed.

---

# The Eye Is Single

*for Mother, July 2, 1896–August 28, 1977*

1.
Mother
I want you young
when
your flesh was unused
tissue,

your eyes Balinese bells,
your hair crackled
wheat
and your mouth spilling
merlin-
magic, kings and knights,
queens and wizards, fairies
and elves.
Mother
I want the time
we both thought death
a unicorn.

2.
Mother my eyes quiver,
my heart stares.
Like an umbrella
death stays a net
above your head.

# Anne Paolucci

Born in Italy, Anne Paolucci finished her education at Barnard College and received a doctorate from Columbia University. Long a distinguished Professor of English at St. John's University, she was also a Fulbright Lecturer in Italy on American Drama for several years and has lectured on literary topics throughout the world. In addition to her teaching career, she founded the Council on National Literatures and edits the *Review of National Literatures*. She has been a prolific writer of fiction, drama, poetry, literary essays, and scholarly articles and translations. She still lectures widely and serves as an Educational and General Culture consultant with a great range of topics.

# Party Overlooking the Narrows

*To Robert Lowell, who wasn't there*

At my age
A party is a routine sacrifice.
Incognito
I stand Olympian
In the midst of critics,
Hounds from printing houses,
Girls from Ohio
Learning how to live,
Professors stretching myopic egos
To the social test.
I wait for food
Wondering if editors
Have time to brood.

Miss Gotham
As delicate a bird-lady
As ever wore a flowered straw
Stands listening to bearded lore.
O beautiful young man,
What's love to birds,
To ladies raised on Schrafft's?
Do they write poems
Sit on grass
Roll over on the lawn
Wait under umbrellas until dawn?

At my age
I'm just a peevish guest.

# To My Fat Friends

A simple theory, mine:
The soul in us
Circles in ever-widening orbit
Until drowsy, tipsy, tired,
It drowns.
Our puppet lines grow limp;
We raid the freezer then
For ice cream
Rip into pretzels
Potato chips
Watch Perry Mason
(The fat-idol of our waste),
By slow stages soothe our flesh.

Or, in Wordsworthian fare:
We brood first, refuse to eat,
Then all our energies burst through,
Find hooks, fly high, and spin
Around our youth!
Falling in love is but a passing feast,
The morning after tells us just how brief;
And when we glance behind
To apple cores and orange peels
Chewing gum wrappers, Glad bags—
The history of our intentions—
We circle sleep to rest
In that point of no dimension
Where Satans burn their blessings.

# Acuto

I am afraid I shall not know
The place, unless it is

Mountains crowned in a mist,
Clean morning sounds,
And the friendly donkey
Struggling up the narrow path
Under my window.

Here in the cold light
Of habit I thread my days,
Smoothing the snags that catch
On inconsiderate memories:
The sun does not reach down
Deep enough here
For recognition. But
In the purple morning
Of Angel-donkeys carting
Fresh apples to market,
I shall know my way:
A child
Running across the busy square,
Down the path below
The open fields,
Past stalls and sheds
To my father's house.

# Back in the Old Country

Back in the old country, a white beaver coat
Would be presumptuous, even in a dream;
I'd dress in black or in a cotton print
And bless the Lord for a warm shawl
On Sunday. In the evening, I'd sit
By the fire, knitting caps and sweaters,
Listening to the scratch of pens
Over notepaper as the children add up
Their days, conjugate the past in two
Neat columns, and dream of the future.
Back in that other world, I might have been
A country girl, singing my mornings
To the fountain's tune, carrying a pail
Of water effortlessly on my head.

In my father's village, shabby urchins
Stare at me and young girls smile
As if they knew me. Among my people,
In my own place, I feel secure—as though
I had not come on a visit from afar
In a magnificent white beaver coat,
An American with a familiar kind of face
And a nostalgic look around the eyes.

# Phyllis Capello

Also known as the Ukulele Lady, Brooklyn-born Phyllis Capello is a writer, musician, storyteller, and part of the Big Apple Circus Clown Care Unit for hospitalized children. She also teaches poetry and fiction-writing workshops for the Teachers and Writers Collaborative and is active in many other community and museum projects. A winner of a New York Foundation for the Arts fellowship in fiction and a 1996 Allan Ginsberg Poetry Award, her poetry and prose have appeared in literary journals and anthologies and her one-woman show, "Careless Love," featuring her poetry and music was staged in New York at The Kitchen Performance Space.

## getting my jazz down

sliding around that thin ebony neck
fingers looking for strings
chord position into chord position
a seventh lays back into a sixth
a major sneaks into a minor

oozing out those thick sweet melodies
that make the air smell like pastries,
skimming the nape with the left thumb
feeling the rosewood hum

fingers jumping like a gymnast on the beam
smoothing it out—playing it until the hands know
reaching for those faraway frets
getting the note clear before the muscle stabs
    in the back of the hand

listening for those sweet, rich sounds
getting my jazz down

## at my breast

his hair is a velvet phrase
a brown nap on his round head,
he drinks
and is drunk in my arms

my nipple like the nib of a pen
writes a poem inside him

his hand
rests in my palm, a tiny starfish
brought in by the tide
to the shore of my skin

## Camping Out

Stars watch us undress;
his face is the moon between my knees.
He is creeping prick first into
my sleeping-bag cunt;
we cling zipped together.

I envelop his penis;
my vaginal canal is lined
with goose-down quilted silk.

Like wolves we sniff each other,
nestling in fur and flesh—
we see-saw rocking horse on our buttocks,

and warm wet orgasms
fall down in me like clitoral dominoes.

# Rita Valentino

Born in New Jersey and still living there, Rita Valentino says she's not going to apologize. She has been writing poetry since grade school and is also a painter. Her work appears in the collection *The Wind in Our Sails*, published in 1982.

## o walt, I had no idea

o walt, I had no idea
it was your world
that I made die inside of me
your tears that rolled down my cheeks
as I expressed thru your hills
in some air-conditioned bus
there was no way of knowing

you were the father
of my unborn children
breaker of my bread
piler of my wood
starter of my fires
how could I
who barely knew your name
know it was you
who leaped out of every blossom
patted every dog
smiled at every child
hugged the earth's equator
tell me what should I do
with your outdated clothes
that have become part of my skin

## the funeral parlor's in brooklyn

I'll get it ma
ma jeanette wants to know
if louie's going to take us to the funeral parlor
no jeanette, uncle lenny said he's taking us
but one of us will have to go with jo ann
ok I'll call you back
hello jo ann
yes I know maryann's car is broke
but she decided to go with bill didn't she
now I told jeanette
o alright I'll call you back
yeah ma I got it
yes maryann jo ann called
but why didn't you . . . O I didn't know that
when did this happen
uhhh. . . . maryann I hate to interrupt but
jeanette and jo ann are waiting for me to call
and I have to find out what's with bill
hello bill

you're not going, well that's nice
put your wife on the phone a minute
at the beauty parlor, of all the
well tell her if she wants to go with me, jeanette and jo ann
to meet us under the big clock at two, got it
you what
are you crazy I haven't the
but I have to
O alright, what are they
go to tenth because there's no eleventh ave, got it, then what
then when I reach ft. hamilton
make a right
for only half a block?
alright I'll try to call you back
hello angela
no bill has to work
but he gave me the direct . . . . .
uh angela, call me back
the dog just ate them

# Maria Mazziotti Gillan

An extraordinarily active poet, Gillan is the founder and Director of the Poetry Center at Passaic County Community College, editor of the Paterson Literary Review, and co-editor with her daughter Jennifer Gillan of
several multicultural anthologies. Maria Gillan has taught the Geraldine R.
Dodge Foundation Poetry Workshops for teachers since 1993, and her own
poetry has been widely anthologized. The winner of many fellowships and
awards including the May Sarton Award from the Poetry Club of New England, Maria Mazziotti Gillan's work has been read on National Public Radio.
She is the author of six books of poetry and is presently working on a memoir
called *My Mother's Stoop*.

# Petals of Silence

The softness which comes to me at dawn
has petals made of silence.
Upstairs, my husband, my children sleep,
dreaming their own shadows.

In these moments, stolen from the night,
no one needs me. I have my own quiet joys.
My notebook page is clean and white.
My pen moves across it almost by itself.
Even the cat sleeps content in the corner.

I collect the edges of myself around me,
curl in the flowers of my stillness
where I find the strength to emerge
into the world of this house,
your bubbling lives.

It is not that I love you less
or would wish you gone;
it is only this need
to gather my forces,
to drink from my own fountain
that causes these retreats from you, my loves.

Someday, perhaps my daughter will read this poem,
see her reflection in its glass,
as she sits alone, in the clarity of early morning,
with the sound of the crickets and her ghosts
and the place inside herself
that nothing, nothing can shatter.

1980

# Public School No. 18: Paterson, New Jersey

Miss Wilson's eyes, opaque
as blue glass, fix on me:
"We must speak English.
We're in America now."
I want to say, "I am American,"
but the evidence is stacked against me.

My mother scrubs my scalp raw, wraps
my shining hair in white rags
to make it curl; Miss Wilson
drags me to the window, checks my hair
for lice. My face wants to hide.

At home, my words smooth in my mouth,
I chatter and am proud. In school,
I am silent; I grope for the right English
words, fear the Italian word will sprout
from my mouth like a rose.

I fear the progression of teachers
in their sprigged dresses,
their Anglo-Saxon faces.

Without words, they tell me
to be ashamed.
I am.
I deny that booted country
even from myself,
want to be still
and untouchable
as these women
who teach me to hate myself.

Years later, in a white
Kansas City house,
the psychology professor tells me
I remind him of the Mafia leader
on the cover of *Time* magazine.

My anger spits
venomous from my mouth:

I am proud of my mother,
dressed all in black,
proud of my father
with his broken tongue,
proud of the laughter
and noise of our house.

Remember me, ladies,
the silent one?
I have found my voice
and my rage will blow
your house down.

# Elizabeth Marraffino-Rees

Although still writing poetry and prose fiction for young people, Elizabeth Marraffino-Rees has also become an exhibiting painter and sculptor and teaches painting at the Crafts Student's League. A recent essay of hers will appear in *Bearing Light,* an anthology edited by Rochelle Ratner on women and childlessness. Marraffino-Rees continues to reside in Greenwich Village where she also maintains a studio.

## Blues After 35¢ Beers in St. Louis

Frank is probably home in Ottawa
It's damn hot here in Memphis
2 hour bus delay

Air sticks deep
    to the soles of my feet
Elvis Presley postcards glow in the dark gift shop

Omens are less frequent
except I wore white again
    last night
Slept in Jobo's room
        surrounded by monster games
            HOW TO BE THE INCREDIBLE HULK
& lots of Indian history books

Was nearly dreamless first time in months

I'm scared I'm pregnant

Would abortion in this case be murder:
Wayne is in Minnesota with his wife populating his future

A couple of years back
    driving home from Great Barrington
I got lonely
    because I was going extinct

---

# Night after night light after light

---

Night after night light after light
goes on in Canaan across the hill
from my house where hours later
dawn will turn on the sky with
a hundred beautiful colors.
I want to believe in unhappiness
but each day there is this joy
beginning out my window
& I find going on alone
is no less no more separate
than being with you.
That the spaces in my life
are not holes but entrances
& I begin at last
to be brave to slowly one by one
step through.

# Linda Monacelli-Johnson

Since 1977, Linda Monacelli-Johnson has lived in or near Santa Fe, New Mexico, but she was born in Pittsburgh, Pennsylvania, and grew up in Cleveland, Ohio. Her three books are *Lacing the Moon* (1978), *Weathered* (1986), and *Campanile* (1999). The last two include drawings by her artist husband, Whitman Johnson. Poems by Monacelli-Johnson have appeared in literary magazines and anthologies throughout the United States. Some of her poetry has also been translated and published in Italy. Holding a master's degree in English literature, she serves the Santa Fe area as a freelance writer and editor.

## Home Movies

In an early movie my godfather made,
you were pretty and shy with the baby
you had prayed would be
perfect.

When a bourbon bottle
became the lens, I discovered
I was born of you to be your
mother.

Drowning in my costume,
I longed to grow transparent,
unfilmed.

# Morning Walks

1.
Dim light. Your horn barely
tapped. First breath of dew. Run
to the car. Hello to you
and April—she licks my hand as I plunge
into the front seat. Off to the woods
around Shaker Lakes.

I've become your nature novice.
My boots are leather and lace up
forever. Yours are rubber—pull on
with a good tug—great for soggy
ground. The smell of wet fallen leaves is bliss
if your feet are dry.

2.
Out here, Joan, I got myself some gum
boots and now walk most
mornings. I often talk
to you in these New Mexico river

woods: suggest that bark fallen on barbwire
looks as limp as wet laundry
on a line; tell of spotting a cactus the size
of an apricot—an intricate

network of spines, thin as hairs, protecting
the succulent. Once when I visited
you on Murray Hill, we gazed beyond Little Italy
at a bell tower lighting

the night—a gentle presence.
From that *campanile,*
a hymn chimed.
Now I pause

beside a certain juniper,
its purple-berried branches scenting
the golden air they comb.
In the distance, centered

beneath the ski basin and framed—
cottonwoods on three sides, green and red
foothills at the top—is the belfry
of a small adobe church, the roof

a pyramid of tin that in some morning light
shines, like snow, over dark arches.
The rounded peaks above,
in winter, are an altar draped

with white linen. When melting uncovers
gray, the *campanile* is still as compelling
as a church bell calling
across a valley on Sunday morning.

# *Anna Bart*

Using a combination of her mother's and father's first names, Bernadetta D'Arcangelo Gorski established Anna Bart as the pen name under which she publishes her poems and does readings. Her story, "Things" appeared in *Nimrod: International Journal of Prose and Poetry,* and she is currently working on a book of fictionalized memoirs as short stories. A graduate of the Buffalo School of Fine Arts, she has also been involved in designing, exhibiting, and teaching various forms of textile arts. She is married to the painter Henry Gorski and they have two grown sons.

# Ravioli

Grandma's long black dress    black iron stove
narrow windows on a narrow alley
the Roma Street kitchen a shadowy cave
but the back door opens to a sunny yard

She breaks eggs into a flour volcano-crater
mixing, kneading, rolling it smooth on the dough board
cutting circles with a coffee can lid
spooning ricotta in each circle
folding them into half-moon pillows

At five I can press the fork tines round the edge
crisp bird tracks in the dough
press my thumb to make a dimple
in the powdered skin

　　Cover them with a towel
　　they need to rest awhile
　　Let's go out and feed
　　the Pee-Pees

Bouyant air bright with sunny ferment
jostling each other hungry chicks
lift red wire legs beaks stretched
in frantic Pee-ee-eep!
Pee-ee-eep! Pee-eeep!

# Preserving

after school as I near home
pungent smells spice the air
red paste drying on a board

propped up netting makes a tent
to keep the hungry flies away
        backyard altar of *conserva*

mother, aunts have worked all day
call out "come down here and help!"
in the cellar summer kitchen
bushels of tomatoes    peaches
quart jars to be washed and scalded
overflow the laundry tubs
        copper boiler's steady chuckle

golden peach halves firm and slippery
pack them down in clean quart jars
pour in sweetened juice to cover
fit the tops with rubber jar rings
twist the metal cap just so
        the sealing twist comes after boiling

and one bleak day in February
"get a jar of fruit for supper!"
in the cellar dark the light bulb
shimmering on rows of jewels
bounces off the grey stone crock
        storing dried tomato paste

---

c. 1896

---

Ermelinda, young wife with two small boys
leaves the mountain village in Abruzzi
        muleback to Naples
        steerage to America
a month it takes
        but Luciano her husband is waiting.

Ellis Island confusions
New York's bewildering mass
endless train ride across that wide state
the blaze of newness stuns
        but Luciano her husband is waiting

Sister, cousins, brother-in-law will ease
the way: Benedetta, Ortensia, Persabella,
Giovanni    how they welcome her! They
have their own land, small house and garden.

Where is Luciano?
    Ah, of course, at work
    Thank God he has a job
    Tonight he will come for them
    Dominic, Donato, play in the yard,
    Papa comes tonight.

Then in swoops grim Ortensia
and roughly drapes a black shawl
on Ermelinda's shoulders,
    *Piangi! Piangi!*
    dear sister    cry!
    your husband is dead.

---

# Giovanni    1854–1940

---

All that remains, this saddle model rifle converted to percussion
    with brass patch box
a J. H. Merrill, patented 1858, bought for $2.00
    from *paesan* Desiderio
immigrant entrepreneur of Vesuvius Paving Company.
    Unskilled laborer
Giovanni never hunted, had no time for sport. What did he
    want with a gun?

A quiet man. I remember him sitting on the porch, resting a lot
    in old age.
Came to America in 1887 with promise of a job. His life
    shaped by jobs.
From Roma Avenue he walked six miles each way to Williamsville
    stone quarries.
In 1900 walked west to Delaware Park to dig for the
    Pan American Exposition.

Walked to Lake Erie, 5¢ ferry ride to Canada, then walked
    to Ridgeway quarry.
Back home again at night, dug his garden. He learned about gunpowder
    in the quarries.
Fourth of July mornings Giovanni stood in his yard, aimed his rifle high
    and fired in celebration.

# Maria Iannacome Coles

B orn in the Abruzzi region of Italy, Maria Iannacome Coles immigrated to
the United States with her family when she was fifteen. Settled in the
Italian American community of Rochester, New York, she says she "came to
know immigrant life, its toil, its wholeness within, and its marginality to
American culture." She studied at the State University of New York at Buffalo but says she acquired her literary education on her own. Her poetry has
appeared in many literary reviews and in the anthology *All We Are Saying*.

## Millinocket, Maine

To repay for their passage
with their aged skills, the weightless treasure
            theirs to bring across the seas,
the fathers built the mill on the Penobscot River and
scratched off the numberless twelve-hour days
            on the towering mason walls.

The sons reproduced unfancifully
up to this son who knows his parents' life
the way a soldier knows the country he fought
the places he bombed with accuracy
the people he shared rations with afterwards.
On the bare spot above the end table
hangs the photograph
a big-shouldered man in *carabiniere* uniform
pushes out his chest like priceless medals.
He was among the hundreds picked up for the mill
right from the Boston Harbor.
On the side of the rushing river stands the white cross still.
It marks the death of the "unknown river driver"*
for all men with see-through aliases
who took refuge on the slippery tree trunks
driven down the wild water to the mill.

The mothers brought dry *camomille*,
handfuls of seeds
in bright handwoven kerchiefs.
Their backs powered the passing
of everyone's season.    Nurtured
in gardens.    Built
no standing walls.    Their names
had the meaning of their days forever gone,
offered up
like the steaming baskets they carried to the mill at noon

*The "river drivers" were the men who in the earlier part of the century accompa-
nied and pushed timber downriver. The job was particularly dangerous because
when the logs got jammed one of the river drivers would be asked to dynamite the
jam and often be unable to run away fast enough. Since men running from the law
were attracted to the isolation in the woods, many of these lives were particularly
cheap to the paper companies for whom they worked.

---

# Gray Waters and Geraniums

---

She raked up some orange leaves
with her bare hands
and dropped them

over the gray waters of the river
where they shined bright, warm.

         walking and leaning
her head for the sounds at her feet,
hearing as many thoughts as there are leaves
and with the same promises,
         she returns home
         the kitchen, the smells,
         the spices next to the stained volumes of poetry
and begins the ceremony maintained
although the kids are gone:
washing the breakfast dishes,
cleaning the counter top,
sweeping the floor.
Against silence
she recognizes in the rasping of the broom,
the sound of festive cleaning,
hears the voices in the language become foreign to her,
and the women in clothes made colorless by time
clean house to house, medieval dwellings some,
somber, haunting, brightened with geraniums,
spices hung to dry, embroidered tablecloths.
There was the smell of woman made spring there.

She looks up.
The front door,
the full length window precisely framed
in the corridor of rooms and doorways
faces her. The front yard tree framed still.
A few leaves hang on it like old christmas toys.
The tree trunk stands defined again, its
leaves are gone.

Taking a book between the palms of her hands,
she sits at the refinished table,
opens to a marked page.
One hand holds the book on her knees
like a piece of cloth,
the other hand inside her blouse,
around her breast as she reads.

# Rina Ferrarelli

B orn in the Sila area of Calabria and orphaned at a young age, Rina Ferrarelli joined relatives in Pittsburgh in 1954 and was educated here, receiving her M.A. degree from Duquesne University. A recipient of a National Endowment for the Arts grant, Rina Ferrarelli's poems and translations have appeared in many journals and anthologies, and she is the author of two books of poetry and two translated works. She lives in the Pittsburgh area where she has directed poetry readings and workshops and taught Italian in the continuing education program.

## Fictions

It's raining hard.
The cat has invented a mouse
to chase across the living-room floor.
She lopes
              hides under a chair
                            crouching
then pounces    lets go
                            pounces again.
With as much gusto as if it were real.
We sit next to each other
the way we do almost every evening.
Absorbed in our books.
                            You have your fictions
and I have mine.

# On the Outer Banks

*To the Wright Brothers*

And life sometimes is on the fringes
a fringe of sandbanks strung along a coast
what relief there is is man-made
the shapes of man's work
the shapes of man's leisure

blending with the pebbles and coarse brown sand
you plover your way in and out
constant motion one way to survive

or you forget about all that:
singleminded about your needs
you incubate your dream in a drafty barn
until it grows wings
then watch it rise above the low landscape
soar higher than gull and sea hawk

# A Georgia O'Keeffe Bloom

The hawthorne hedge by the school
parking lot is in full bloom
tonight, throbbing in the blue of dusk,
blue-white, its aura electric, the scent
a current that pulls me across the street.
                    Early today
I woke with lines to a new poem
running through my head, again
after a long fast, and now this,

and as if it weren't enough, the moon
has just come up above the neighbors' roof
large between silhouettes of pines,
and it, too, seems to glow from within:
a Georgia O'Keeffe bloom
pinned on the breast of night.

# Jacquelyn Bonomo

Born in New Brunswick, New Jersey in 1948, Jacquelyn Bonomo completed her doctorate at Rutgers University in 1980. She is a learning disabilities specialist with a private practice in Manhattan and is Assistant Director of the Program for Academic Access at Marymount Manhattan College.

## Patience in the Endless Rain

Always to kneel like this at the porch edge
With one hand cupped for rain,
The small reserve in my mind filling,
Leaves alert and unalterably patient with the rain.

Days and days of it,
Long grass swaying back and forth
Like a woman's head gone wild with passion.
I think of the rain I must see in your smile,
The alterable truths spilling down
On my naked body in the warm bedroom,
How difficult and necessary the patient yielding to rain.
Always to kneel like this,
Not to judge too much or too little,
To have the right kind of strength,
The long muscles of a swimmer.
"Patience," Grandmother said,
And for once the old seem rightfully wise,
The old one in me from the island seems wise.
There's a sensible way to walk across the road,
To stand above the filling valley until the earth gives way,
To swim above the gravestones.
Patience in the endless rain
That rains on both of us this night.

# Hens

Dry thunder.
Rasp of the hotrod driving the sun to perfection.
10 A.M.
90 degrees.
The heat sits on my body with the cumulative weight of my dream men.
All night they climbed on and off
Yelling at me in panicky whispers,
"No babies!"
Outside the hens are clucking in crescendoes,
Like crickets who have evolved bourgeois mentalities.
Who asked them anyway? my men might say,
To lay their eggs so punctually, so prolifically,
Making such a job out of instinct?
Every day the fussbudgets get me
To set out their corn, their mash,
The water they desperately gobble with their clipped beaks

So they may brood on eggs some don't seem to know
Will never hatch.
This is what a hen does and has to do,
Cock or no.
I'm ashamed to spite their bodies,
To pry one out of her nest with a stick.
Handling her eggs, white, hot,
Even I am tempted to think that soon
Something would have to break through with a life of its own.

# The Ninth Life

Like an old woman searching for the one change
In a house she could walk through blind
Again and again,
You search your life.
Have the homemade constellations on the mantle
Shifted positions in the last second
Before you came down the stairs?
Coming down the stairs! What work!
Eight invisible black cats
Now retrace your footsteps
In every shoe of every size you've ever worn.
It's the ninth life,
The only one that has to make good luck for itself,
God knows.
God crosses the bad luck lines of centuries
To the seeming magic of stardom.
By now he leaps as high as Nijinsky,
Dies with Pavlova's grace,
Defies gravity like Astaire.
One clear-hearted turn from the bed to the window
And your mind's night stars
Dance into view.

Delaware-Raritan Canal, on a walk with
a friend.

# The Flashlight

Trained on the towpath
Makes a light tunnel we can walk through
Without fear of stepping in shit.
It's as if we're underground driving from New York to Jersey.
Every hundred yards I look back for the pale figure
That wants to stay in the city,
Hoping to turn her to salt.
Now the office fluorescence interrogates the night
And my heart still hurts from asking of watches
"What time is it? What time is it?"

I am efficiently bored with thinking
I know what I see.
The flashlight is a bad habit.
When we come to a dimensional darkness
I can say, "It's just a tree root.
It's just shit."
I don't see the spirits caught in the trees
That can't feel when the wind makes them touch.

We are discussing our mothers and fathers,
How you have come to some peace with them,
How you stayed up all night
To hear your father say he was relieved to know
You were not stupid as he had thought.
This is what I too want of the night,
To hear the voice of the owl admitting its ignorance.

Still, I say it's impossible for me
To be free of mourning my parents' marriage,
As if each turning away from my own contentment
Would map out the place and time when their broken trust
Civilized, then buried my feelings.
And I again pull the files, seeming to make the final report
Using the diction of deadlines for two people I saw just once

Kissing at the foot of mahogany stairs, the richest wood of all,
To say this is not worth an investment.

Shit and roots, shit and roots.
The flashlight exposes what's waste,
What's grown away from its source.
Better to imagine in the dark two tree spirits,
One like this one, split to the roots by lightning,
And the standing one it's gashed in falling.

Between husband and wife they call this cruelty,
Because of the giving, the feeling of pain.
I try to think another way,
Hearing how my father always said
Even after the lightning bolt,
"Don't think so much. Don't worry so much.
You'll grow old before your time."

All night the flashlight searches the world
For the mahogany staircase ripped out of the city house
By the new owner.
Who knows where it is? Who cares?
Who who who cries the owl.

# *Jennifer Lagier*

B orn and educated in California, Jennifer Lagier is a second-generation
American of Italian descent. A writer of both prose and poetry, Lagier
holds degrees in English Literature and in Library and Information Studies.
She is a full-time faculty member of Hartnell College and also teaches part-
time at California State University, Monterey Bay. Forthcoming is a collection of her poems, *Second-Class Citizen*.

# second class citizen

*for mom*

we laughed
calling it latent wop syndrome
the compulsive addiction
that triggered your spending
week after week
using layers of i. magnin clothes
t-birds and two hundred dollar a pair shoes
to eradicate the shabby shame of
growing up foreign and poor
being born to farm laborer parents
in a contractor's shack
using bank books to balance
your cheated childhood
that scrawny immigrant's kid
who still squirms uneasily around
behind the elegant vogue dressed facade
scared that someday this
middleclass masquerade
will crack down the middle and fall away
letting a squatty italian fishwife with a
broken womb in black
wearing fat nun's shoes
climb through and escape
you with one foot planted
on the skidding skateboard
of near country club status
the other nailed
back there on ellis island
stuck in quarantine
and waiting official permission
to be let off the boat

# Janine Veto

Janine Veto is the adopted child of an Italian father from Calabria and a Viennese mother. As an adult she found her birth mother (of French, English, and Sioux descent) and her birth father whose family immigrated from North Italy. A graduate of Northwestern University, she worked in television and advertising before moving into arts management and fundraising. Janine Veto is the author of a novel, *Iris* (1983) as well as poetry and short stories that have appeared in small magazines and anthologies. She lives in Sag Harbor and New York City with her daughter Francesca, adopted in China in 1994.

## Body Wisdom

*for Donna Brookman*

out of unknown bodies
  we come
slippery from moist spun space
an echo across light years
from the tunneled silence

we come
out of unknown bodies

our own and its opposite
alien as first breath
grappling on the grave of wonder

out of unknown bodies
we become    our own
unknown body
crying across
                     a loop of time

## Naturally, Mother

1.
I looked for you
spinning the wheel of my horoscope
I lied for you in court chambers
I performed for your benefit in Catholic charities

But you were always with me

every time I loved and left
each time I put my life in suitcases

as I watch the coupling of friends
and know I can not follow

envying the simple faith of the world's majority

with the clairvoyance of daughters
I wrote you five years ago

knowing even then
I was writing myself

2.
No wonder you now wear watches
synchronize every clock
panic when someone seems unconcerned

We are all fleshed out pivots of your time

I am here
but only because discreet phone numbers
were not yet published in underground papers

My sister you sold to Miami Jews
for red shoes and a purse to match

The boys you kept
hoping it would be easier
not to raise your own reincarnation

and the nameless one
decomposing somewhere in North Africa

the final ticking under your heart
before your racing timepiece
was disconnected

Freud aside, all our fathers
do not matter
A woman bleeds through her mother


3.
So tempting to stop sailing

retire to a Zen simple room
washed ashore on contemplative rocks
safe from the question of waves

It is not us

We get sweaty from grappling with this life
there is no hope of approval
no safe drydock

I forced your gaze back, mine inward

But we will not drown

We are buoyed by our own messy faith;
we love

# Theresa Vinciguerra

A poet and writer of short fiction, Theresa Vinciguerra's work has appeared in various publications and anthologies, most recently in *Pillow, Exploring the Heart of Eros* (1998). As founder of the Sacramento Poetry Center and recipient of a New Works in Performance Grant from the Sacramento Metropolitan Arts Commission, Theresa Vinciguerra has contributed to the vitality and growth of the literary community in Northern California. She is the mother of four children and currently works as a technical writer and freelance editor.

## Aftertaste

About this morning lingers
the thin, round sheet of moon,
the aftertaste of you, an apple
cooked down
till the skin thickens and bubbles.
I am full to the sugared rim
from the midnight fruit,
have no appetite
for ordinary breakfasts
and lick the sweetness of peel
and core that circles the moons
and arcs of my fingers.

# This Small Universe

### 1. The Twenty-eighth Day

Our belly swells,
the twenty-eighth day of its cycle colliding
with the full white circle in the night, and
as we look aside in our mirror, its lunar shape
glares at us, its gravity tugging our flesh,
our very expectations.

We wish
we wish to dam this female tide,
push the waters back,
protest aloud the harshness of it
making the bright clots like constellations
shower from our body.

Wearing all the full moon's vestments,
singing the ocean's pitch
this same red-black orbit consecrates itself
the inviolate gift.
We look again with more than a sidelong glance.
We wonder: Can we attend with nothing less than
acceptance to this small universe of mystery?

# Rope

I pull on the rope of your body drawing you in
at the center where there is no struggle
where the unbraiding begins at the tip of the spine
and we unravel strand by strand
the thick twine in the spiral of pleasure
where there are no ends
no letting go.

# Kathryn Nocerino

A confirmed New Yorker, Kathryn Nocerino is a poet and short story writer who has been a writing fellow at Yaddo and the Ragdale Foundation. Three books of her poetry are in print, *Death of the Plankton Bar & Grill*, *Candles in the Daytime*, and *Wax Lips*. She has been widely represented in magazines and anthologies, most recently with a short story entitled "Language Difficulties" in *Identity Lessons*, an anthology edited by Maria Gillan and Jennifer Gillan.

## El Sueño

*for Frida Kahlo, Mexican painter,*
*1910–1954*

one woman, asleep, sees flowers
    start purple from the rib-cage of her
skeleton.    at the foot of the
    bed are tap-roots;    around her hair,
dark water pouring from the pillow,
        bowers of green leaves.

another woman stands at height of
    day before her mirror.    her own hand,
bearing a cloth, rises slowly to her face.
    she erases one eye and then the
        other.    mouth, nose, contour and
expression disappear.    when she screams,
        the sound is made of dust.

# Maria Dominica Lazzari, "L'Addolorata," a Miller's Daughter, Who Received the Stigmata in 1835

*Herodotus, in his description of a temple of Hercules in Egypt, wrote that it was unlawful for the authorities to capture runaway slaves who took refuge there, if they received certain marks on their bodies, devoting them to the deity.*

> she awoke
> to the morning of the ploughed field;
> scrub-brush; washing pail;
> to shoes kept on a shelf till Sunday,
> to the black dress that a woman wears:
> her earth!

> mysteries
> made their home in the sky:
> the saved flew up to heaven, or they rode the chariot.
> the priest's voice:
> "dust thou art, and unto dust thou shalt return."
> sometimes she woke from a dream, crying.
> she had been lying down, hands crossed;
> earth
> had filled her mouth until she could not breathe.

> rise, then,
> like the woman in blue robes, or else be doomed.
> eyes up,
> she saw the ladders of the prophets
> being lowered for her, then withdrawn.
> her smile of secrets brought her gifts of oranges and olives
> from the village boys.

she saw no one.
she was a spring field waiting for first fruits;
   she was thorns and roses:
she was not earth.
   she was not merely earth.

# Empty Factory, N.J.

the train passing and passing these buildings,
   a view persisting long enough to slow our wheels

beyond the shattered panes,
   business in night is booming.
the painted legend on the brick,
     M—s—n Ma-h-ne-y Co.

the broken windows say, "death"
the still freight car in the loading-yard,
   beached in sand, says "death."
death walks the roof-spine,
   cocking its head at foreign movement.

volumes of silent air
   carry a glittering suspension of dust—
gold coin of forgetfulness.

   an instant more,
and we will rest before these walls
         forever.

the forward pull begins at last.
   rounding the bend,
we thrust it into memory.
   the motion of this great, wheeled scythe
parts two halves of spoked earth.

# Sandra M. Gilbert

Born Sandra Mortola in 1936 in Jackson Heights, Queens, New York, Sandra Gilbert now resides in California and is a Professor of English at the University of California, Davis. In addition to her growing reputation as a poet, she is a widely published and acclaimed literary critic. Her co-authored work, *The Madwoman in the Attic,* is the first of several volumes of seminal feminist criticism. Her most recent publications include *Wrongful Death: A Memoir,* and *Ghost Volcano: Poems.* Her most recent book is the poetry collection, *Kissing the Bread: New and Selected Poems, 1969–1999.*

## Mafioso

Frank Costello eating spaghetti in a cell at San Quentin,
Lucky Luciano mixing up a mess of bullets and
calling for parmesan cheese,
Al Capone baking a sawed-off shotgun into a
huge lasagna—
                    are you my uncles, my
only uncles?

            Mafiosi,
bad uncles of the barren
cliffs of Sicily—was it only you

that they transported in barrels
like pure olive oil
across the Atlantic?

Was it only you
who got out at Ellis Island with
black scarves on your heads and cheap cigars
and no English and a dozen children?

No carts were waiting, gallant with paint,
no little donkeys plumed like the dreams of peacocks.
Only the evil eyes of a thousand buildings
stared across at the echoing debarcation center,
making it seem so much smaller than a piazza,

only a half dozen Puritan millionaires stood on the wharf,
in the wind colder than the impossible snows of the Abruzzi,
ready with country clubs and dynamos

to grind the organs out of you.

# Doing Laundry

I am doing laundry in my laundry room
the washing machine grinds and pumps like my father's heart
it is sick      it is well
sick again      well again

behind the round window your shirts
leap and praise God slowly like gentle souls
and my old brassieres bound like the clean breasts
of antelopes

I am doing laundry in Africa
and overhead the parrots shriek
they encourage me to beat harder
beat the dirt out of the flowers

I am doing laundry in Indiana
my husband the insurance salesman comes in
wanting to know if I would like to buy his new
insurance against laundry

I am doing laundry in the river Styx
I pound and I pound
the shirts disappear
the brassieres dissolve to nothingness

I am a heart doing laundry
and I beat and I pound
until I no longer remember
the color of dirt

---

# The Grandmother Dream

---

My Sicilian grandmother, whom I've never met,
my Sicilian grandmother, the midwife, who died
forty years ago, appears in my bedroom.
She's sitting on the edge of my bed,
at her feet a shabby black bag,
and she speaks a tangled river of Italian:
her Sicilian words flow out like dark fish, slippery and cold,
her words stare at me with blank eyes.

I see that she's young, younger than I am.
I see her black hair gleam like tar as
she draws from her small black midwife's bag
her midwife tools: heavy silver instruments
polished like doorknobs, polished—misshapen, peculiar—
like the knob of an invisible door.

# The Thoreau Pencil

*Thoreau's father was a pencil manufacturer, and young David Henry improved the Thoreau pencil in several important ways.*

—*Arnold Biella*

I am not writing with it
right now    you can't buy one
for ready money
anymore    but
I dream    dream of it
(who has not)
the steely graphite
at the center
rock-dark
black-night-lake-surface-dark
inscribing    scribing
the wood around the outside
a fir-tree    a birch-tree
—I don't know the details—
pared down to size

what characters it must write
what clean Romantic
hieroglyphs
pebbles from the shore of Walden pond
(beyond the trailer park)
nut shells    mosquitos wings
tangled branches intricate
and indiscreet
"to glorify God and enjoy him forever"

they say Thoreau could pick up twelve
Thoreau pencils at a time
without looking
like picking up a year    all at once
in a minute

# The Summer Kitchen

In June when the Brooklyn garden
boiled with blossom,
when leaflets of basil lined the paths
and new green fruitless fingers of vine
climbed the airy arbor roof,

my Sicilian aunts withdrew
to the summer kitchen,
the white bare secret room
at the bottom of the house.
Outside, in the upper world,

sun blistered the bricks of the tiny
imitation Taormina terrace where fierce
*socialisti* uncles
chainsmoked Camels and plotted politics;
nieces and nephews tusseled

among thorny bloodcolored
American roses;
a pimply concrete
birdbath-fountain dribbled ineffectual
water warm as olive oil.

Cool and below it all,
my aunts labored among great cauldrons
in the spicy air
of the summer kitchen: in one kettle
tomatoes bloomed into sauce;

in another, ivory *pasta*
leaped and swam;
on the clean white table
at the center of the room
heads of lettuce flung themselves open,

and black-green poles of zucchini
fell into slices of yellow
like fairytale money.
Skidding around the white
sink in one corner

the trout that Uncle Christopher brought back
from the Adirondacks gave up
the glitter of its fins
to the glitter of *Zia* Francesca's
powerful knife.

Every August day *Zia* Petrina
rose at four to tend the morning:
smoky Greek chignon
drawn sleek,
she stood at the sink.

Her quick shears
flashed in the silence,
separating day from night, trunk
from branch, leaf
from shadow.

As the damp
New World sunrays struggled to rise
past sooty housetops,
she'd look suddenly up
with eyes black as the grapes

that fattened in the arbor:
through one dirt-streaked window
high above her
she could see the ledge of soil
where her pansies and geraniums anchored.

Higher still,
in tangles of heat
my uncles' simmering garden grew,
like green steam swelling from the cool
root of her kitchen.

# Leslie Scalapino

Growing up in Berkeley, California, Leslie Scalapino received her Master's degree on a Woodrow Wilson fellowship at the University of California at Berkeley. She has also been the recipient of a National Endowment for the Arts grant in creative writing. She is the author of many books of poetry, fiction, plays, and essays. A reviewer of her poetry collection, *Considering How Exaggerated Music Is,* wrote that she "may well be the most original young poet writing in America today" as she "explores . . . dislocation and confluence between her public and personal selves."

## In sequence

> We cross India in a train, our feet on a cake
> of ice which our father buys in a train
> station.

We take a train which stops at a village by rice when a Chinese girl is killed on the tracks. The villagers come out to the side of the track. I thought they didn't like female children; but they bend over and are crying sounding as if they are laughing.

---

I see a man who is starving lying holding out his cup to beg from me.

In Calcutta my parents are in a building while we sit outside in a horse-drawn cart waiting for them. My grandmother who sits in the cart with us doesn't give money to the beggars because there are too many and they have begun to push holding their hands on their bellies and hands stretched out to take the money. My grandmother is wearing a heavy corset and occasionally removes her hand from mine in order to fan herself.

An Indian doctor examines us at our hotel and thinks that we have smallpox, though he is not sure and a day later we are well. We take the ship from Bombay and Indian women on the ship become ill with smallpox because they have not been vaccinated. The ship is segregated by race and a dance is held but the white people stay on the upper-class deck and listen to the music. We sit by the dance floor on the second-class deck with Indian families who do not dance even if they are married.

We dance with two African men—so that we are the only couples on the floor. My partner's legs shake violently while we dance; my parents sitting beside the empty dance floor with the Indian families, their heads nodding every once in a while.

The Indian women who have smallpox get into an ambulance which is like a wooden paddy wagon. An Indian man goes down the ship's gangplank—his brother has come to Mombasa for him—our parents sit in the car also, and they take us for a ride in the countryside going eighty miles an hour to cool us.

Later we meet them again, drive up after we've been travelling for a while and have come to the town where they live and they're under their car working on it.

We stay with a family. Their servants fan us at the dinner table. We go out for a drive around Manila with the daughter and she buys us ice cream bringing the cones back to the car.

My sister is embarrassed and gives her cone to the chauffeur but then the daughter is angry and the chauffeur refuses to take the ice cream cone. We go by ship to the southern islands, sleeping on deck. A herd of pigs is on the lower deck. The pigs slip to one side of the deck when the ship rolls, then slip back again. It is hot and our parents talk to the ship's mates. Later the daughter visits us, comes on Thanksgiving bringing a dinner though we have already prepared it, and she occasionally addresses my mother as "auntie."

---

The students in the class are black, a student asking to go to the toilet but the teacher not letting her—then he lets her, calls me up to his desk in front of the class asking me to look under the toilet stall to see if she went there.

I say she was there after I go into the hall and wait. I don't realize that I can say I won't do it and the other students don't either. I talk—try to kill myself because I think that I don't have enough ability but I have to continue in school—and so the principal comes to observe our class, the teacher getting fired and the principal is made a math teacher the next year.

---

We get to know a friend even though her father will not allow her to go anywhere usually.

My mother asks the father if we can go to the movies and we walk to the theatre where in front of the doorway a beggar who has no legs wheels himself on a cart like a sled. Our friend speaks in a flirtatious way to my mother and us and the movie starts. It is called *Mother India* and the heroine in it sings wading in mud up to her waist after a monsoon. The son has lost his legs, the husband is crazy so the audience and our friend weep during the movie but my sister and I react by laughing. We laugh wildly. We go back to America and go to school. One of my sisters has a boyfriend and he stays in bed with her by climbing up to a balcony on the second floor.

---

We go to the coast on the motorcycle. We have a minute weaving before the motorcycle turns over since there's a blowout. There aren't any cars anywhere, it's Thanksgiving, and my friend says to hold on so I am on his back when we're thrown from the cycle, sliding several yards. He isn't hurt. People who tell us they are missionaries drive up. They run over to me and take us to the hospital in their car with the cycle lying beside the road, the doctor saying that I should take off my clothes.

I pull off the clothes very slowly since my arms are twisted and she remarks about it when I've removed them.

A boyfriend and I are wild about each other but don't get along, break up and then home on vacation I come in my sleep. I am in school, my father advising a president the other students and I not agreeing with his views— they slam their books on the floor making sounds when I'm talking about something else.

A man who has been hit by a club climbs a pole when I am walking back from class; then later an instructor asks our class to think of any women scholars—an instructor skips me and I decide not to go back to school.

I get married our families coming with us, sitting in the pews in the chapel in Reno with people in wedding clothes outside in line for their turn. I want to laugh when the minister is a holy roller yet my husband almost cries at the ceremony although later we are divorced, my sisters get divorced, my father sees my uncle in a museum embracing a woman other than his wife.

The museum has ramps rather than stairs so my father crouches afraid my uncle will be embarrassed, will turn and see him so he goes up and waits.

I sit in the car in a parking lot of a market, hold up a bottle of wine for a sip, two old men sitting in the front seat of a car facing me—they each take drinks out of cartons of milk with their chins up as they drink the milk. I like music playing on the radio in the car and a friend comes out of the market.

We go back, get into bed, come—I'm entirely concentrated on this—I think everything is the country.

I sit down to write about a man's mother who is killed in a car accident but I make tea before the telephone rings. I hear that my grandmother has been killed in a car and I leave and go there, finding my father in a motel sitting with her clothes hanging up, frantic, and he eats a date out of a package because he is hungry so I take the clothes down and wring the sweater to make the blood and rain water fall into the bathtub in my room.

We get back. Later they go to Java where my mother is carried in a chair on a mountain because she can't walk since the accident and people there sing,

"Americans have gone to the moon. Now you have come. We are glad you are here."

---

I go with a friend to Las Vegas. He and I gamble at the slot machines people gathering around me as money pours out of my machine. I like Cleopatra's Barge in a casino floating in water with gold leaf on the woman's body and we go to Colorado—I realize I have never thought about money—see a man who pumps gas where there are no people who gives us his newsletter and it is all about things like baby shoes dipped in bronze.

We bring a painting to someone's house and are asked to stay to have lunch my friend saying no by mistake and leaving so that we get in the car. We drive and I have a dream when we sleep for a few minutes, reclined in the car seats.

---

I left, was in New York, people came up and told me how to get to the subway; since they saw I was looking around standing on the street—I thought that people have an inner world, associated it with architecture and monopolies.

---

I have various jobs—I make a mistake at the soda fountain and a milkshake doesn't catch on the blender, flies off splashing the counter where the old white-haired men and women have come to have lunch.

I walk looking at clothes hanging in windows—the weather is hot—and sit in a restaurant by myself. A woman is loud at a different table but she throws a bottle of perfume at me all of a sudden and it breaks on the floor—I had been angry hearing her though not saying anything and there are only a few people in the restaurant—the staff standing behind the counter.

---

*In autobiographical sections*

Our parents go to Mandalay leaving us with missionaries who say we shouldn't go around by ourselves.

Water pipes have been bombed, we have a barrel of water to drink from that's in our house, and we take a ricksha around the city getting out near shops. Then we take one back but the man knows where we live—we didn't see him before—pedals very fast not wanting to hear our address and calling to other ricksha drivers who race with him.

Driving down to Los Angeles a man who was in the lane on the freeway beside me began talking to me out his window.

The wind blowing, he went over onto the soft shoulder of the road to get me to drive into the fast lane—since my window on the driver's side wouldn't roll down and he was going very fast. My window—on the passenger's side—being rolled down. He didn't do it just having a sense of liking me, for that reason alone, since he'd just come up very fast beside me—me answering him although not going into a rest area; so he'd then continue his trip.

People were speaking emotionally, in Peking with my mother, and finally she asked you mean that you were the ones who paraded the professors in public—and they said yes we were, upset; another one there says she's one who was turned in front of a stove—she hadn't had clothes on—and then thrown outside; this not being done by ones sitting there.

I had a job, possibly then I got an injury, of working in a restaurant with boys who were the other dishwashers. I washed enjoying it. A boy had been dismissed for being late and two who were there asked me how old I was—I was much older than they—when a friend came back into the kitchen wanting to talk though I had this work.

I woke in the morning—my fingers on one hand wouldn't separate—perhaps beginning prior to this work.

I didn't associate it with injury—I couldn't continue the job—yet I associated it with some people who upset me then.

The weather was hot and I took a job at a soda fountain, the hands not ready yet to clear dishes though time had gone by, above the sink at the soda fountain there was a long window and a house where one of the people lived could be seen from it. I looked out sometimes seeing them going in the house.

---

I rode—seeing pigs on the farms, of surprising size—and six hours away from where I started I feel warm going into the cafeteria where several people are. Coming at someone's invitation, I then perceived that his son is hurt and therefore this meant that the father sees women, the wife isn't there, and I dropped him off in the car as he asks me to do a ways away from their house but not driving there, driving back again instead in the heat with the farm animals on the road sides again; it is getting late and I return after it's night though it is summer-time then.

---

We'd been in bed and then on a ride stopping in front of a record store where there were adolescents standing near some motorcycles, a thought occurring from seeing a man intermingling with the adolescents just in walking by them, only without his having facial wrinkles, and seen to be probably in his thirties. Us having come (sexually) earlier—it having just occurred really—and then being outside there anyway in the particular situation.

---

I was enjoying weeding some of the weeds very tall on a strip of a road. Of the passengers in cars a few looked at me or didn't attend to that, the cars going by very fast up a hill, and someone began speaking to me who lived near there, asking if I were paid indicating the work I was doing.

---

# Jean Feraca

A native of New York state, Jean Feraca derived her love of poetry and strong ethnic identity, she says, from her father who called Italian Americans "people of the heart." She lived in Rome and traveled in Italy after receiving her M.S. from the University of Michigan and now lives in Madison, Wisconsin. The recipient of *The Nation's* Discovery Award for her first book of poems, *South From Rome: Il Mezzogiorno*, Jean Feraca is also Wisconsin Public Radio's Distinguished Senior Broadcaster and host of "Conversations with Jean Feraca." She recived a Wisconsin Arts Board Fellowship to complete her second book, *Crossing the Great Divide*.

## Memorare/8

Maratea, Lucania, 1974

1
Sleepless he rages, fists on the rails
howling for hours . . .

This, the old dream to be martyred
the calling denied
floats up, a kidney in a bowl
carried to the altar, St. Agnes's breasts
Ophelia's face

the procession of Virgins advances, she carries
a candle
she wears a white dress

a thimble rolls out of my grandmother's coffin
I am bound on the hoop sewn into my hem

This is the way, each moment
I mount
ever higher, the life
of the flesh
falls away

*knock knock knock*

upstairs, the invalid thumps with his cane
from the bed

*knock knock knock*

in his three-legged
crib, the infant stands up.

2
I live alone on the edge of town
I keep my father's house

*Remember, O most gracious virgin mary*
*never was it known that anyone who fled*
*to thy protection*
*was left*
*unaided  . . .*

Skull-bald, these mountains hang over us
massive and terrible
leaning like great-aunts over an infant's crib.

3
teeth descend from the cave roof in rows
Mouth
under the Mountain

*O mother of the word incarnate*
*before thee I stand*
*sinful and sorrowful*

a tower extrudes from a hill
salt
laps at the edge, uneasy

my darling, I'll croon to you, I'll coo
I'll carry you for hours
your wails
splash my sides like a tide of acid
you wear me away all white

the sea sucks up, shudders
subsides to a hiss
starfish slide
dead crabs float
belly up
the moon spins upside down

I'll croon, I'll coo, I'll carry you for hours

all the rock pools give up their ghosts
in the sun
white algae heaps up in pockets
petals on the altar
airy
weightless
I drift, I rove, I carry you for hours

O Mountain, O Rose, O Gold

*knock knock knock*

pocked, pitted, this blister of rock

white algae heap up in pockets
*despise not my petition*
*hear me, O mother*
*answer*

# Scirocco/12

At noon, bells crack the air. I climb
into light
clattering on the rooftiles.
Above the slamming of shopfronts, wet sheets
slap like sails. The smell of fishhead,
flower-stem, sweeps up in gusts.
In this dirty wind, I hold
a steady watch
wary as a whore in steerage, traveling alone.

# Vision in the Grove/6

> *". . . and this is the sixth month*
> *with her that is called barren."*

1

Driving to Roccella Ionica, east across the boot
through a forest of hair
rank
as pubic growth. Prickly-pear
erupts along the rockwall, a red cancer of thumbs.
Lizards clash, geranium jetting over the edge like blood.

Suddenly I am sick of it: this harsh landscape
running to extremes
the south, the struggle to survive—
Agave thrusting with its horn
gores
its way out of my side;
honey-coy, the locust hides its thorn.

Let me unlearn these hills
I have loved,
*scogliera* needling the shore; my ancestors
saracen-faced, with your thick black speech
how you tongue me, your eyes brooding under cliffs.
I carry the itch of those looks
under my skin for days.

2

It's april in North Atlantic States, the maples
pushing out their sticky leaves like scouts.
Here, the honeysuckle already brown
the mouth of the rose
blown wide,
it hurts. I close my eyes
dream my way back to olive groves
we passed at dawn:

Gioia Tauro, Laureana, Taurianova
old hags, old crones
I call you like a congress of great-aunts
your crooked trunks unhook
a universe of moss
and rime
that drifts, sinewy smoke. Your wrinkled
rippling flanks unleash black rain
to nets below. You grow like scars
beyond yourselves you dream
you're young again wandering the grove
loose as snakes
weaving each other's necks and waists.

Lulled by the haze, I stay
a long time.
The grove fills. Calves brushed
by dew, I move through dawn-soft air,
wet light mews in the leaves
I pick my steps
with care, until my walk
becomes a kind of swim
through long wet grass
I am drenched
newborn
swimming in a sea without a name.

## Diane di Prima

Diane di Prima was born and grew up in Brooklyn, New York but for the past thirty years has lived and worked in northern California. In addition to raising her five children and becoming a student and teacher of Zen and Buddhism, she has been continuously immersed in literary productiveness as a publisher, editor, and co-founder of the New York Poets Theatre. Recognized as an important member of the Beat movement, she is the author of thirty-four books of poetry and prose, many of which have been translated into a dozen languages. Diane diPrima has received many awards and residencies, and in 1999 was awarded an honorary degree from St. Lawrence University. Her forthcoming autobiography, *Recollections of My Life as a Woman*, will be published in 2001.

---

# Lullaby

---

Rockabye
baby-o
nothing is strange
your daddy cut
for Baltimore
your mommy's
making
songs

Rockabye
baby-o
no one's to blame
your daddy lives
with wife and child
your mommy
doesn't
cry

Rockabye
baby-o
nothing will change
your lunch is hot
your bed is made

your daddy
sends
his
love

---

# Marriage

---

This husband of mine thinks the sea is to visit
In the summer
Whereas I find it the thing to live beside
Desiring as I do to step into it every morning: cold & grey
Or not, as the sun
Rises, before the tasks start,
That my skin and hair should taste salt & I
Could easily live on seaweeds, clams
Breathing that air.
He says it would give him arthritis.
Yet we are better matched than most, we recognize
This as a thing of value, a bone of contention
Between us

---

# Letter to Jeanne (at Tassajara)

---

dry heat of the Tassajara canyon
moist warmth of San Francisco summer
bright fog reflecting sunrise as you
stop out of September zendo
heart of your warmth, my girl, as you step out
into your vajra pathway, glinting
like your eyes turned sideways at us
your high knowing 13-year-old
wench-smile, flicking your thin
ankles you trot toward Adventure
all sizes & shapes, O may it be various

for you as for me it was, sparkle
like dustmotes at dawn in the back
of grey stores, like the shooting stars
over the Hudson, wind in the Berkshire pines

O you have landscapes dramatic like mine
never was, uncounted caves
to mate in, my scorpio, bright love
like fire light up your beauty years
on these new, jagged hills

---

# To My Father

---

In my dreams you stand among roses.
You are still the fine gardener you were.
You worry about mother.
You are still the fierce wind, the intolerable force
that almost broke me.
Who forced my young body into awkward and proper clothes
Who spoke of his standing in the community.
And men's touch is still a little absurd to me
because you trembled when you touched me.
What external law were you expounding?
How can I take your name like prayer?
My youngest son has your eyes.
Why are you knocking at the doors of my brain?
You kept all their rules and more.
What were you promised that you cannot rest?
What fierce, angry honesty in the darkness?
What can you hope who had preferred my death
to the birth of my oldest daughter?
O fierce hummer of tunes
Forget, eat the black seedcake.
In my dreams you stand at the door of your house
and weep for your wife, my mother.

## Prayer to the Mothers

they say you lurk here still, perhaps
in the depths of the earth or on
some sacred mountain, they say
you walk (still) among men, writing signs
in the air, in the sand, warning warning weaving
the crooked shape of our deliverance, anxious
not hasty. Careful. You step among cups, step out of
crystal, heal with the holy glow of your
dark eyes, they say you unveil
a green face in the jungle, wear blue
in the snows, attend on
births, dance on our dead, croon, fuck, embrace
our weariness, you lurk here still, mutter
in caves, warn, warn & weave
warp of our hope, link hands against
the evil in the stars, O rain
poison upon us, acid which eats clean
wake us like children from a nightmare, give the slip
to the devourers whom I cannot name
the metal men who walk
on all our substance, crushing flesh
to swamp

## Backyard

where angels turned into honeysuckle & poured nectar into my mouth
where I french-kissed the roses in the rain
where demons tossed me a knife to kill my father in the stark
       simplicity of the sky
where I never cried

where all the roofs were black
where no one opened the venetian blinds
O Brooklyn! Brooklyn!
where fences crumbled under the weight of rambling roses
and naked plaster women bent eternally white over birdbaths
the icicles on the chains of the swings tore my fingers
& the creaking tomato plants tore my heart as they wrapped their
    roots around fish heads rotting beneath them
& the phonograph too creaked Caruso come down from the skies;
    Tito Gobbi in gondola; Gigli ridiculous in soldier uniform:
    Lanza frenetic
& the needle tore at the records & my fingers
tore poems into little pieces & watched the sky
where clouds torn into pieces & livid w/neon or rain
scudded away from Red Hook, away from Gowanus Canal, away
from Brooklyn Navy Yard where everybody worked, to fall to pieces
    over Clinton Street
and the plaster saints in the yard never looked at the naked women
    in the birdbaths
and the folks coming home from work in pizza parlor or furniture store,
    slamming wrought iron gates to come upon brownstone houses,
never looked at either; they saw that the lawns were dry
were eternally parched beneath red gloomy sunsets we viewed from
    a thousand brownstone stoops
leaning together by thousands on the same
wrought-iron bannister, watching the sun impaled
on black St. Stephen's steeple

# April Fool Birthday Poem for Grandpa

Today is your
birthday and I have tried
writing these things before,
but now
in the gathering madness, I want to
thank you
for telling me what to expect
for pulling

no punches, back there in that scrubbed Bronx parlor
thank you
for honestly weeping in time to
innumerable heartbreaking
italian operas for
pulling my hair when I
pulled the leaves off the trees so I'd
know how it feels, we are
involved in it now, revolution, up to our
knees and the tide is rising, I embrace
strangers on the street, filled with their love and
mine, the love you told us had to come or we
die, told them all in that Bronx park, me listening in
spring Bronx dusk, breathing stars, so glorious
to me your white hair, your height your fierce
blue eyes, rare among italians, I stood
a ways off, looking up at you, my grandpa
people listened to, I stand
a ways off listening as I pour out soup
young men with light in their faces
at my table, talking love, talking revolution
which is love, spelled backwards, how
you would love us all, would thunder your anarchist wisdom
at us, would thunder Dante, and Giordano Bruno, orderly men
bent to your ends, well I want you to know
we do it for you, and your ilk, for Carlo Tresca,
for Sacco and Vanzetti, without knowing
it, or thinking about it, as we do it for Aubrey Beardsley
Oscar Wilde (all street lights
shall be purple), do it
for Trotsky and Shelley and big/dumb
Kropotkin
Eisenstein's Strike people, Jean Cocteau's ennui, we do it for
the stars over the Bronx
that they may look on earth
and not be ashamed.

# Minnesota Morning Ode

*for Giordano Bruno*

The City of the Sun is coming! I hear it! I smell it!
here, where they have made even the earth a jailer
where not even the shadows of animals sneak over the land
where children are injured & taught to apologize for their scars
the City of the Sun cannot be far now—

(that's what you said then, brother, waiting in prison
eight years to be burned, to find the sun at last
on the Campo de Fiori—FIELD OF FLOWERS—yes)
how could it be far?
isn't evil at its peak?
(you asked 300 years ago) has not
the descent into matter reached a nadir? & here
5000 miles later, Northern Minnesota
a forest once, now wasteland
where they mow grass, rake leaves:

I vomit lies like the rest, not knowing
whom to trust, here where betrayal is taught as virtue
I weep alone for the words I would like to say
& silently put the faces of the old gods
into the hands of the children; hope they recognize them
here in this Christian place, where Christ the Magus
& Christ the Healer are both forgotten, where the veil
of the temple is rent, but no resurrection follows. . . .

THE CITY OF THE SUN comes soon, cannot be far
yes, you are right—what's a millennium
or two to us, brother? The gods can wait
they are strong, they rise—the golden tower
flashing the light of planets, the speaking statues
that guard its four gates, the holy wind
that carries the spirit of heaven down thru the stars

it is here! it is here!
I will build it
on this spot. I will build it at Attica
& Wounded Knee
on the Campo de Fiori, at the Vatican:
the strong, bright light of flesh which is the link
the laughter, which transmutes

*Minnesota Home School*
*Sauk Centre*

# Ree Dragonette

Born Rita Marie Dragonetti in Philadelphia in 1918 of an artistic Italian immigrant family that also produced the singer Jessica Dragonette, Ree Dragonette was called by fellow poets one of their finest "undiscovered" talents, the bulk of whose work remains unpublished. Ree Dragonette lived in New York's Greenwich Village where she was a legendary figure as poet, teacher, social and political activist, and mentor for young writers in addition to being the devoted mother of four children. She is remembered as an exceptional jazz poet and performed her poetry in concert at New York's Town Hall in 1962. Ree Dragonette died in 1979.

## This Is the Way We Wash Our Hands

Side by side we sit in a café as if in a trough. Uneasy after long absence we have almost forgotten who we once were. We reach out our hands; our lips touch; our smiles gather ashes. You ask how my life is.

It is season of gale wind. From unimagined parsecs the quasi-stellar clocks unwind, rise on their pulses. It is the hour struck by inexplicable transitions where midnight crosses morning; the hour poised unreal between births and deaths. Moment when the moon, nicked, shudders among its winter phases. Time of sun glittering cold in Capricorn; time scaled faster than light-months, than the familiar order of our days piling and sinking.

A waitress comes to the table; we greet her. You gaze at her, gaze; measure each contour. A look of proud birds overtakes you; you straighten, puff into feathers as if into mating regalia from pebbled arena. The waitress repeats and marks down the items we chose from the menu. She is tall; she displays before us her fluent, delicate body. Her thighs are exquisite, her hips curve flawless between the links of a silver chain belt. In cordial understanding, although unlike one another, she and I become telepathic, our glances and perceptions islanded together where no man can follow.

Her skin is ivory; tinted pale it pales and deepens. Her hair ripples brown, yellow-brown, gold. It sparks under the lamps, under stuttering neon. She is wearing a silk dress, fringed, silvered with flowers. The flowers sigh when she stretches over the table to set glasses and spoons into place. The blouse of her dress ruffles low, almost to her nipples. She is Piscean; her feet make no sound on the floor; she walks filmed. Her shoulders seem ultramarine and lapped with reflectors.

I am mildly jealous of what, palpable, occurs between you. You are quick to conceal it. She and I let it surface. We are calm and ironic, bearing each other no malice. Considerate, we look away from you. I train my mind inward to attend nova explosions; to examine fiery lines in the Crab Nebulae. To read scrolls freezing and fanning out in the spaces between galaxies. On awful summons I return. On sudden arrival of

faces which I recognize, which come into my sight in splinters and
clusters, nearing and receding.

They are brown faces, gray, orange ochre; with cheeks gnarled and
shrunken on their bones. I dream them. Women and children shot out
of huts, out of hovels. They run over fields, over hilled cities. Some of
them stand still, open-mouthed; arms outstretched, bleeding. They push
through my sides, my swelling veins. Their lips are cracked, pressed
together crooked and like insects. Some have mouths which dangle from
gashed jaws. Many of them are infants or babies just learning to walk,
unsteady as foals on their legs. They are not dressed in silk or in flowers.
Rags cover their sexes. Their backs are laced with sores, dried rusting.

You are drained away from me, your conflicted demands yielded up
beyond my concern. I witness plague now. Wars, wars; blaze on blaze,
the whirlwind. Sibilant return of reptiles! I have fallen out of time; I
lodge mesozoic on slime. Fallen on petals and ripped branch blowing
seared; on burnt limbs blowing into red leaves. I have received lost life
to eat unholy eucharist sweated into drops, into glistening brine soaped
under naphtha.

You call me back, aura of you slanting imperative along my being.
Inquisitor, now, you hold me, rake my flesh.

We speak of the present—how glad we should be that we have met
again. We laugh; our laughter casketed, embalmed fragrant. We ask each
other why we parted; why our best plans fell away. Why we were
broken from rapture—our joys redolent and canceled in rain, dissolved
in strict circumstance. Memory coffins us, fills us burdened and contrite;
tugs our senses until arced. Until changed, longing ceremonial, we start
awake, astonished as ancient mummies trying to shake off griefs, to cast
off quivering scarabs. We reach out our hands, stiff to fathom one
another. You ask why we cannot be joined again close, as once we were
close.

We ascend raging to face one another polar over walls, righteous
through impenetrable barriers.

You turn in your chair, hold back tremor, halt the twitch of nerves,
nerve's ache. You turn guarded, cognizant to decipher signs, avoiding
dire surprise. You study my face for omens. You cull your thought to
manufacture a charm, to build gemmed recess in which to catch me and
arrest my thought. You kiss me.

We move apart, linger safely in clearings beyond pull from our
opposite magnets. You are circumspect, unimpeachable with gestalts.
With dry airs, you comb the world's affairs.

I hear you criticize the play you saw last night; ask you if your wife is
well. We share speckles from a text on modern metaphysics. We ridicule

our feckless, rambling statesmen. We deplore judicial systems, rising
prices, national elections. I call for God's wrath to come down and smite
the consciences of those who jail devoted nuns for saying nones, for their
practice of soft mercy. God's wrath upon tycoons who stifle honest
workers' tongues. Who compensate skilled laborers with pity-pennies for
daily struggle in airs of vinyl chloride fumes; laborers who tread
assembly lines whose floors are carpeted in arsenic or braided deep with
thick carcinogens. God's wrath to fall on those who murder
minstrel-priests; who silence poetry.

We debate each raw new filament in theatre, in massage emporia and
sensorium of pseudo-therapies. With eyebrows raised you skim green
scented gardens, approve palaces of flesh and fuming necromancy. How
sad it is, I say, that anyone must shatter old inhibitory rules by
copulating foolishly on stage, cheered on by drums and giggles. Must
wash their grime of hell-fire guilts in scald of oiled pornography.

You beam, applauding Youth Culture, that it rocks the nation. You
praise the young, their somnambulism, their night rise over cliffs in thick
migrations luminous as penguins crossing pack ice. You call them pagan
and gloriously free. Watching their revelry I weep: see their lives
snared, descending between webbed feet, snared! My mind reels on
squalls; my nostrils hurt pinched on fossil fuels, on odorous cannabis and
on cocaine.

Your cigar chokes me; I cough. Your smile twists into grimace.

I tell you our children are in thrall; are seduced by wizened hawks
who sell them apathy. By panderers who cover them in studded shrouds
which bury sexual identity. Who nourish them on spiked drink, on bread
stuffed with submolecular nightmare. Who tell them loudly *live, dance,
flash* like flashing comet tails. But really mean to tell them *die, burn out*
too soon.

You ravel and unravel platitudes about American democracy. Tally its
treasure troves of goods and services, its generous opportunities. You do
not lament as I do, famine spreading pandemic. Do not notice tantalus of
abundant orchards denied the poor, blighted by official ill-intention. You
are placid; you gloss over whoredom of politics and bureaucracy. Murder
by isotopes; the massive, inverted magic show accelerating on human
sacrifice, led by satanic cohort.

Tell me, how do you relieve humiliation of black men, of Caribbean
slaves? How do you comfort the innocent, deranged and roaming the
planet in search of clean meadows? Are you never seized to consider
prisoners mocked by miscarriage of justice? Adolescent boys who hang
themselves, their spirits fierce and wanting to stampede; narrowed eyes

colored topaz, Indian copper, colored striped marble; eyes fixed
sardonic, dull and no longer supplicating.

No, nothing seems to prod you, nothing stabs your vision so that you
anguish. So that you sympathize with mothers wailing against indifferent
fate, their bodies caved like pathetic shields over dying offspring.
Mothers of discourteous sickness—cancer, sickle cells, malnutrition of
lead-paints. They walk like draft horses. They pray; they keep their
children alive by clawing and scrubbing, by shrieking through salt-tears;
by mystical wishes. Have you seen them in welfare centers, in courts
and detention pens? Waiting in hospitals, trying to lick away gunshot
wounds; pawing at needle holes in daughters' skins, where morphine and
meth-crystal have chewed? Or leaping into chasms where rapists have
bitten, have snarled and plundered.

In our city of discothèque, of thug and transfixion, of radiant carousels,
have you embraced wives of killers? At autumn of fire and
transhumance, have you known girls kept from first bloom, made into
concubines for men who judge themselves bestial? Thieves, procurers,
peddlers of powdered death who enjoy only the supremacy of their lust.
Self-devourers taught that to be male is to pillage, to slay or be slain.

You bid me hush and have hope. You weave and shimmer. I cannot
glow in your glow.

We stare at one another; perish under neon's glare. We lock our
trembling hands together. You drowse in rivering warmth, whisper to
me how much we need each other, but I say to protest how much we
love is not enough.

The skies fall. Among cold winds they fall into the spaces between our
skulls. Far away, double stars fly. Blind they tumble, dying in upon each
other. We freeze to the sockets of our eyes, our wrist bones, to the
masks and visor of our smiles. I say:

The world is at shine point near crest before it crashes, before
humanity drops into stillness. Governments are run by men. Diabolical,
they want us docile and grinning under masquerade. They want the
peoples dull, stupefied, if not stupefied then smoothed fat for bathing in
the endless baths. Want us washed into sepulchers, winking under
coined eyes under degenerate brahmins.

The male of the species has studied conquest, has instructed his sons
to study conquest. The folly of women is that we have surrendered too
long, tarnished our nature; let men, monumental with idolatry, tarnish
our children.

My voice drops, my words dwindle into your senses as a snowflake
fades in hard sunlight. I notice that you have aged since last summer.

You are old in your clean, polished fingers, at the top of your spine
where it is bronze and tucked to your neck between bones and
meninges.

The waitress passes our table, goes to sit among friends at the far end
of the room. I watch her closely, catching her unawares. You watch her,
too. We see her through steam and through smoke wreaths. We see her
shadowed auburn into mirage, waving her mutable arms among the arms
of her playmates. Her neck inclines supple on its lengthening stem. You
lean on your elbows impacted, shot with desire. The future descends,
folds in stealth through our foreheads.

You grow tranquil, stretch, drink your coffee. Planning in casual
posture, seeming at ease, you are alerted exact as a gunfighter. I watch
you gaining time rehearsing, hiding battle plans. I read your mind's
blueprint, can predict that, tomorrow, the waitress will become yours for
a time. You can wait.

Tomorrow, in her room filled with incense and enchanted trinkets, she
will jewel your life. Give herself to you for an hour or two, without
pledges or passion. When next you wish to possess her she will refuse
you. Bearing a fresh scar over old scars you will be left hankering, as on
reflection of certain flowers blue and drifting beyond reach. As on the
wake of lake birds wavering, stirring unseen.

Your sorrow veils me, brushes me with small stones.

We are lonely, busying ourselves at dipole moment, breathless with
gesture and abstractions. So that truth will not bolt us into gape, into
dismay. We rest, give off faint resonance. Perplexed, we are beached
surfers trying to understand what force once drove us to ride out huge
waves, to fuse into each other.

You smoke, inquire how I am feeling; have I taken a lover?

You are vain, yet I cherish you. Agonized, dizzied with ambivalance,
fettered with biology and outworn traditions we remain trapped
together. For all our glimmering insights, our needs and ventilations, our
will to converge in pure love is worn effete; is mechanized and debased.
Residual, we inherit our fathers. Will we ever become serene and equal!

Being man among men; among those who, until now, have owned the
world, why do you make no effort to transform it? Privileged since birth,
you are self-absorbed. Placated by rich rewards, by baubles and
indulgences, are you grateful? Blessed by women generous to kindle
your self-esteem—your mother, your wife, loyal and content to bask in
your shadow. Graced with friends, with ardent lovers, do you notice the
misfortunes of others? No, and so I love you but judge you wanting.
Love you, but cannot forgive that you do not labor in vineyards; that

gifted with talents you stint and work only for material profit. Only to
bolster your ego; to satisfy your appetites.

Night chimes around us. It ends on muffled clocks, in radio quiet and
dead stars.

A young man enters the café. He walks slowly and unsteadily. His
eyes hollow his face; he scowls and smiles. I have known him since he
was a small child. If you were not with me I would go to him, cushion
him with my body. But as he passes our table, I ignore him; do not look
up or speak his name.

He is old enough to vote, to compete in business, to be summoned
into armies. He will not maturate in peace; if he sires children he cannot
promise them they will escape neutron bombs or ecological disaster. His
mother abandoned him long ago. She is very glamorous; drinks too
much, vacations too much, changes partners too often. His father
despises him because he does not want to be an industrialist or a
super-athlete. Rich in money, alienated, the young man is dying of
heroin addiction.

I avoid his glance. I do not want to acknowledge him or expose him to
your phallic scrutiny. I tell you I would like to go home. Cunning, you
delay me, question me about the boy; how long I have known him and
what he means to me. You put your palm to your chin, your voice is
dry-husked.

No, he and I have not slept together. But in a realm you will never
even visit he is, indeed, my dear love.

He sends me a message, silent, solitary as a ginger flower, as a wood
anemone. It is a wisp, easily erased, but it scourges me, Ebbed,
dragging himself through existence, he can still think of me, offer himself
should I need him.

Reading your unspoken thoughts I remind you that you never seem
able to transcend your combative gender. Paternal, you will be
chastised. Male, you will meet nemesis; inexorable women. Male, you
have made war, have made numerous poisons. Have ravaged those who
live dreaming, who will not worship your fierce image.

Dawn has come. I stare into your eyes, rise and leave the café. You
follow me. The streets outside are flushed with light, but not light rinsed
or opalescent. Dawn struggles through clouds, through grained layers as
alien as alloys, as cobalt rare earths . . .

We walk together, thin on thin bearings. We meet late troubadors.
They are pallid and smell of orange trees. They smell of weed-smoke, of
loss and patchouli oils. I take your hand. You and I walk like stilted
birds, careful not to fall.

# Daniela Gioseffi

For over thirty-five years Daniela Gioseffi's poetry and prose has appeared in many journals and anthologies and as book publications. She has also edited two important collections, *Women on War* and *On Prejudice*, which have won awards. Her recent book of poetry is *Word Wounds & Water Flowers: Poems* and in prose, *In Bed with the Exotic Enemy: Stories & Novella*. Gioseffi is also a performance artist and has given readings and lectures both here and abroad. She currently edits "Wise Women's Web: An Electronic Magazine of Literature" on the Internet, is a member of the National Book Critics Circle, and together with Alfredo diPalchi has founded an annual poetry award for bilingual poetry in English and Italian translation.

## *from* American Sonnets for My Father

*Written in Edna St. Vincent Millay's studio at Steepletop, New York*

1.
You died in spring, father, and now the autumn dies.
Bright with ripe youth, dulled by time,
plums of feeling leaked red juices from your eyes,
pools of blood hemorrhaged in your quivering mind.

At forty, I climb Point Pinnacle, today,
thinking of you gone forever from me.
In this russet November woods of Millay,
I wear your old hat, Dear Italian patriarch, to see
if I can think you out of your American grave
to sing your unwritten song with me.
Your poetry, love's value, I carry with your spirit.
I take off your old black hat and sniff at it
to smell the still living vapor of your sweat.

# Bicentennial Anti-Poem for Italian-American Women

*"You are one of only two or three Italian-American women poets in this country," said the professor. "You are a pioneer. There are fewer of you than Black women poets."*

On the crowded subway,
riding to the prison to teach
Black and Puerto Rican inmates how to write,
I think of the fable of the shoemaker
who struggles to make shoes for the oppressed
while his own go barefoot over the stones.

I remember Grandma, her olive face
wrinkled with resignation,
content just to survive
after giving birth to twenty children,
without orgasmic pleasures or anesthesia.
Grandpa, immigrant adventurer,
who brought his family
steerage passage to the New World;
his shoemaker shop where he labored
over American factory goods
that made his artisan's craft a useless
anachronism; his Code of Honor
which forced him to starve
accepting not a cent of welfare

from anyone but his sons;
his ironic "Code of Honor"
which condoned jealous rages of wife-beating;
Aunt Elisabetta, Aunt Maria-Domenica,
Aunt Raffaella, Aunt Elena, grown women
huddled like girls in their bedroom in Newark,
talking in whispers, not daring
to smoke their American cigarettes
in front of Pa;
the backyard shrine of the virgin,
somber blue-robed woman,
devoid of sexual passions,
to whom Aunt Elisabetta prayed
daily before dying in childbirth,
trying to have *a son*
against doctor's orders
though she had five healthy daughters;
Dr. Giuseppe Ferrara,
purple-heart veteran of World War II,
told he couldn't have a residency
in a big New York Hospital
because of his Italian name;
the mafia jokes, the epithets:
*Wop, guinea, dago, grease-ball;*
and the stories told by Papa
of Dante, Galileo, Da Vinci,
Marconi, Fermi and Caruso
that stung me with pride
for Italian *men;*
how I was discouraged from school,
told a woman meant for cooking
and bearing doesn't need education.

I remember
Grandma
got out of bed
in the middle of the night
to fetch her *husband* a glass of water
the day she died,
her body wearied
from giving and giving and giving
food and birth.

# My Venus Fly Trap Is Dying

because it frightens me.
I've tried to remember to water it.
I keep saying I'll buy it a new pot,
furnish it with fresh earth.
After all, it is a plant and I do love
greenery. But it's carnivorous,
ingesting raw meat, living
insects, engulfing them in heart-
shaped leaves. Other plants wait
for death to give flesh to roots.
I resolve to become a vegetarian.
I've loved and envied plants
for their peacefulness,
their quiet conversion of the sun,
that first all contingent link
between solar energy and animal.
But this Venus Fly Trap
is too much for me.
It will have to die
tossed into the waste can
with the bright red lipstick,
the blood red nail polish.
I no longer wear.
This Venus Fly Trap doesn't
photosynthesize peacefully.
It's trying to become an animal
and I
trying so hard to be a tree
can't bear it.

# Peace Prospect

Too many people scribbling on each others' tongues
gagging the cities.
Politics muddle the nature of bodies.
Sexual energy, a force confused, wasted.

While sleep plays out the pain in me,
I have a pleasant dream,
a land inhabited by bright animals
who refuse fire
and eat nothing but leaves.
I count the people I have tried to touch;
my hands melt sand into glass.
We can't manufacture food like vegetation
standing in the light. Photosynthesis
is the trees making love with the sun.
A vague intuition blossoms in my stomach,
a chance for a finer love.
We are a mind-ridden race, incompatible with earth.

A better race will come. I feel
bright animals waiting
for the right genetic moment.

# Lorraine DeGennaro

Now living in Pine Bush, New York with her husband Robert, Lorraine DeGennaro has been writing poetry for a long while and publishing in many small-press publications throughout the country. She is now the publisher and co-editor of the Alms House Press, which publishes poetry.

## Table Manners of an Only Child

I covet
The six chairs around your table,
The crumbs you sponge away
After every meal. I am neat,
Leave no crusts behind
No drops of Cabernet
On yellow linen; yet you
Complain about the mess,
Dishes in the sink, brothers
At the door demanding plates.

I unfold my napkin,
Trays pass from hand to hand.
I enjoy the clash of covers on pots,
Opinions on statements
That you find ordinary.

I barely eat, my eyes are
Nourished by connecting lives.
I could grow fat on them
Without ever tasting foreign
Aperitifs and sweet tea
Never minding the thickness of my waist.

I carry a glass to the kitchen
Admiring the hill of stoneware,
Silver and wooden spoons.
I caress Brillo in my fingers
Scrub each piece
And hand them to you to dry.

We hear the scrape of chairs pushed
From the table, the fumbling
For coats in the hall.
I wipe my hands when
You lock the door,
Help fold your grandmother's tablecloth.

# Maryfrances Wagner

Maryfrances Cusumano Wagner was born and raised in Kansas City, Missouri, her two sets of grandparents having immigrated from Italy. She is the author of four books of poetry, and her poems, many on the theme of family, have appeared in several publications. She has taught writing workshops all over the state and currently chairs the English department of Raytown High School where she teaches writing classes and was the recipient of an Excellence in Teaching award. With her husband Greg Field, she sponsored the Simpson House Writing Series and co-edited *New Letters Review of Books;* she and her husband received the Writers Place Award for contributions to the arts in teaching, writing, and editing.

# Ragazza

A good Italian woman
will cover her dust-free house
with crocheted doilies,
bear dark-eyed sons,
know what to do
with artichokes and chick peas.
Her floors will shine.
She will serve tender brucaluni
in her perfect sauce,
make her own cannoli shells,
bake biscottas for every wedding.
Supper will be hot at six o'clock.
She will always wear dresses.
She will not balance the checkbook.
He can doze behind the paper
when she washes dishes.
Because she will never leave him,
he will forgive her bulging thighs.
Because he will never leave her,
she won't notice unfamiliar stains.

Italian men always know *ragazze*
who work the fields in Bivona.
For airfare one will come.
In time she will learn English.
In time they may learn to love.

# The Winemaker

Father collects red earth
in the cracked canals
of his paddle fingers.

At dinner the oars,
flat and splintered,
grip his wineglass.

He tells us hard work
fulfills a man,

lifts his wine to the light,
smiles, "Pure. One glass a day.

Good for the blood.
Elderberries for color."

Inhaling the fragrance, he
rubs his fingertips with his thumb

trying to find the right word there,
trying to construct wisdom
on his forefinger.

I notice a sliver of tape
butterflying an open channel.

"Pure. No sugar added."

# Acknowledgments

Grateful acknowledgment is made for permission to reprint:

Carol Bonomo Albright, "Definitions of Womanhood: Class, Acculturation, and Feminism": copyright 1984 by Carol Bonomo Ahearn.

Helen Barolini, Introduction, in an earlier form, and "Turtle Out of Calabria," from *Chiaroscuro: Essays of Identity*, copyright © 1999 by Helen Barolini. Published by the University of Wisconsin Press, and reprinted by permission.

Anna Bart, "Giovanni 1854–1940," "Ravioli," "Preserving," "c. 1896": copyright 1983 by Bernadetta D'Arcangelo Gorski.

Marion Benasutti, selection from *No Steady Job for Papa*: copyright 1966 by Marion Benasutti. Reprinted by permission of The Vanguard Press, Inc.

Jacquelyn Bonomo, "The Flashlight," "The Ninth Life," "Hens," "Patience in the Endless Rain": copyright 1984 by Jacquelyn Bonomo. "Patience in the Endless Rain" is reprinted from *The Massachusetts Review*, Summer 1981, by permission of The Massachusetts Review, Inc.

Dorothy Bryant, selection from *Miss Giardino*: copyright 1978 by Dorothy Bryant. Published by Ata Books, Berkeley, Calif.

Phyllis Capello, "Camping Out," "at my breast," "getting my jazz down": copyright 1982 by Phyllis Capello. Reprinted from *The Wind in Our Sails*, published by Midnight Sun, New York.

Octavia Capuzzi Waldo Locke, "The Rocks": copyright 1973 by Octavia Capuzzi. Reprinted by permission of *New Orleans Review*, Loyola University, New Orleans.

Rose Carmellino, selections from a novel: copyright 1983 by Rose Carmellino.

Diana Cavallo, selections from *A Bridge of Leaves:* copyright 1961 by Diana Cavallo. Published by Atheneum, New York. Guernica Editions, 1997.

Fran Claro, "South Brooklyn, 1947": copyright 1976 by UNICO National. Reprinted by permission of UNICO National, Bloomfield, N.J., publisher of *A New Day*, where this first appeared.

Maria Iannacome Coles, "Gray Waters and Geraniums": copyright 1980 by Maria Iannacome Coles. First appeared in *Calyx*, vol. 5, no. 1 (June 1980). "Millinocket, Maine," copyright 1983 by Maria Iannacome Coles.

Lorraine DeGennaro, "Table Manners of an Only Child": copyright 1983 by Lorraine DeGennaro.

Tina De Rosa, selection from Paper Fish, reprinted by permission of the author and the Feminist Press at the City University of New York. Copyright © 1980 by Antoinette De Rosa. Republished, with an afterword by Edvige Giunta, in 1996 by the Feminist Press.

Louise DeSalvo, selection from "A Portrait of the *Puttana* as a Middle-Aged Woolf Scholar," appearing in *Between Women: Biographers, Novelists, Critics, Teachers and Artists Write about Their Work on Women*, edited by Carol Ascher, Louise DeSalvo, and Sara Ruddick: copyright 1984 by Carol Ascher, Louise DeSalvo, and Sara Ruddick. Reprinted by permission of Beacon Press.

Diane di Prima, "April Fool Birthday Poem for Grandpa," "Marriage," "Backyard," "To My Father," "Minnesota Morning Ode," "Prayer to the Mothers," "Letter to Jeanne," "Lullaby," from *Selected Poems: 1956–1975:* copyright 1975 by Diane di Prima. Published by North Atlantic Books, Plainfield, Vt.

Grace DiSanto, "In Defense of Plath, Berryman, Sexton," "Last Supper," "The Eye Is Single," from *The Eye Is Single:* copyright 1981 by Grace DiSanto. Published by Briarpatch Press, Davidson, N.C.

Ree Dragonette, *This Is the Way We Wash Our Hands:* copyright 1977 by Ree Dragonette. Published by Calliope Publications, New York. Reprinted by permission of Juanita Corsiglia, daughter of Ree Dragonette.

Marie Hall Ets, selection from *Rosa: The Life of an Italian Immigrant:* copyright 1970 by University of Minnesota. Reprinted by permission of University of Wisconsin Press, 1999.

Jean Feraca, "Vision in the Grove," "Scirocco," "Memorare," from *South from Rome: Il Mezzogiorno:* copyright 1976 by Jean Feraca. Published by Larkspur Press, Monterey, Ky. Reprinted by permission of Gary Zeitz, publisher.

Rina Ferrarelli, "Fictions," "A Georgia O'Keeffe Bloom," "On the Outer Banks": copyright 1981, 1983 by Rina Ferrarelli. "On the Outer Banks" appeared in the Summer 1981 issue of *Dark Horse;* "A Georgia O'Keeffe Bloom" appeared in a slightly different version in the Summer 1983 issue of *Poets On: Celebrations.*

Kathy Freeperson, "Italian Bread": copyright 1976 by Kathy Freeperson.

Sandra Gilbert, "Mafioso," "The Thoreau Pencil," "The Grandmother Dream," "Doing Laundry," from *In the Fourth World: Poems:* copyright 1978 by Sandra Gilbert. Published by University of Alabama Press. "The Summer Kitchen" copyright 1983 by Sandra Gilbert.

Maria Maziotti Gillan, "Public School No. 18: Paterson, New Jersey": copyright 1983 Maria Mazziotti Gillan; "Petals of Silence," from *Flowers from the Tree of Night:* copyright 1981 by Maria Gillan. Published by Chantry Press, Midland Park, N.J.

Daniela Gioseffi, Sonnet 1 from "American Sonnets to My Father" and "Bicentennial Anti-Poem for Italian-American Women," reprinted by permission of Daniela Gioseffi, copyright © 2000, first published in *Eggs in the Lake,* Boa Editions, Ltd., copyright © 1979 and reprinted in *Word Wounds & Water Flowers,* Via, Folios/Bordighera at Purdue University: West Lafayette, Ind., copyright © 1995.

Mary Gordon, "Zi'Marietta": copyright 1976 by UNICO National. Reprinted by permission of UNICO National, Bloomfield, N.J., publisher of *A New Day,* where this first appeared.

Rose Grieco, "The Sunday Papa Missed Mass": copyright 1955 by *Commonweal* magazine. Reprinted by permission from June 3, 1955, issue of *Commonweal.*

Barbara Grizzuti Harrison, "Godfather II," from *Off Center* (New York, The Dial Press, 1980). Copyright © 1980 by Barbara Grizzuti Harrison. Reprinted by permission of Georges Borchardt, Inc., on behalf of the author.

Lynette Iezzoni, "Window Seat": copyright 1983 by Lynette Iezzoni.

Jennifer Lagier, "second class citizen": copyright 1983 by Jennifer Lagier.

Michele Linfante, *Pizza:* copyright 1980 by West Coast Plays, Berkeley, Calif.

Severina Magni, "Poetry": copyright 1955 by Severina Magni. "Poetry," from *Anthology of Italian and Italo-American Poetry,* edited by Rodolfo Pucelli, has been reprinted courtesy of Branden Press, Inc., 21 Station Street, Brookline Village, Mass. 02147.

Karen Malpede, Introduction to, and Scene 2 of, *A Monster Has Stolen the Sun:* copyright 1981 by Karen Malpede.

Nancy Maniscalco, selection from *Lesser Sins:* copyright 1979 by Nancy Maniscalco. Published by Avon Books.

Gigi Marino, "Angelina": copyright 1983 by Gigi Marino.

Elizabeth Marraffino-Rees, "Blues After 35¢ Beers in St. Louis," "Night After Night": copyright 1983 by Elizabeth Marraffino. Published in June 1980 issue of *Waterways* and reprinted with permission.

Mary K. Mazotti, "La Ciramella": copyright 1983 by Mary K. Mazotti.

Linda Monacelli-Johnson, "Home Movies," copyright © 1999 by Linda Monacelli-Johnson. Reprinted from *Campanile,* published by Drummer Press, Columbia, South Carolina. "Morning Walks," copyright © 1996 by Linda Monacelli-Johnson. First published in *Voices of Cleveland,* Cleveland State University Peotry Center, Cleveland, Ohio. Reprinted from *Campanile,* published by Drummer Press, Columbia, South Carolina.

Anna Monardo, "Roman Ruins": copyright 1982 by Anna Monardo. First published in September 1982 issue of *Redbook* magazine.

Pacé Nicolino, "Goodbyes and Hellos": copyright 1982 by the Poetry Society of Vermont. Published in *Second Harvest: An Anthology of Poems by Members of the Poetry Society of Vermont;* "Dandelions" copyright 1982 by Pacé Nicolino.

Kathryn Nocerino, "El Sueño," "Maria Domonica," "Empty Factory, N.J.," from *Head with Hat:* copyright 1983 by Kathryn Nocerino. Published by New Rivers Press, St. Paul. Minn.

Anne Paolucci, "Party Overlooking the Narrows," "Acuto," "Back in the Old Country," "To My Fat Friends," from *Poems:* copyright 1977 by Anne Paolucci. Published by Griffon House Publications, Bergenfield, N.J.

Antonia Pola, selection from *Who Can Buy the Stars?:* copyright 1957 by Antonietta Pomilla. Published by Vantage Pres, N.Y.

Elaine Romaine, "fan letter," "you were always irish, god," "Song and Dance Lady": cpyright 1983 by Elaine Romaine. Published in *Gravida* and reprinted by permission.

Julia Savarese, selection from *The Weak and the Strong:* copyright 1952 by Julia Savarese. Published by Putnam. Reprinted by permission of William Morris Agency, Inc., on behalf of the author.

Leslie Scalapino, "In Sequence," from *Considering How Exaggerated Music Is,* copyright 1982 by Leslie Scalapino. Published by North Point Press, San Francisco, and reprinted by permission.

Sister Blandina Segale, selection from *At the End of the Santa Fe Trail,* copyright 1948 by Bruce Publishing Co. Used by permission of Glencoe Publishing Co.

Tia G. Talamini, "I Learn Three New Words": copyright 1983 by Tia G. Talamini.

Gioia Timpanelli, selection from "Italian Traveling": copyright 1983 by Gioia Timpanelli.

Mari Tomasi, from the New England Press edition (1988) of *Like Lesser Gods* by Mari Tomasi. Reprinted by permission of the New England Press, Shelburne, Vermont.

Rita Valentino, "o walt": copyright 1982 by Rita Valentino. Reprinted from *The Wind in Our Sails,* published by Midnight Sun, New York. "The funeral parlor's in brooklyn," copyright 1983 by Rita Valentino.

Alma R. Vanek, "Zio": copyright 1978 by Alma Vanek. First published in *True to Life Stories,* volume 1, Diana Press, Oakland, Calif.

Janine Veto, "Naturally, Mother": copyright 1979 by *Earth's Daughters* and first published in *Earth's Daughters,* October 1979. "Body Wisdom": copyright 1983 Janine Veto. Reprinted by permission of the author.

Theresa Vinciguerra, "This Small Universe," "Rope," "Aftertaste": copyright 1980, 1981, 1982 by Theresa Vinciguerra.

Maryfrances Cusumano Wagner, "The Winemaker," "Ragazza": copyright 1983 by Maryfrances Wagner. First published in *Blue Unicorn,* Kensington, Calif.

Frances Winwar, selection from *Poor Splendid Wings:* copyright 1933 by Frances Winwar Grebanier. Published by Little, Brown, Boston. Reprinted by permission of Jerry Warwin.

# Index

395